GOING BY THE BOOK

THE PROBLEM OF REGULATORY

UNREASONABLENESS

A TWENTIETH CENTURY FUND REPORT

———————————— • ————————————

EUGENE BARDACH & ROBERT A. KAGAN

TEMPLE UNIVERSITY PRESS   PHILADELPHIA

Temple University Press, Philadelphia 19122

Copyright © 1982 by the Twentieth Century Fund, Inc.

Published 1982

Printed in U.S.A.

Library of Congress Cataloging in Publication Data
Bardach, Eugene.
Going by the Book.
"A Twentieth century fund report."
Includes index.
1. Administrative law—United States. 2. Independent
regulatory commissions—United States. 3. Industrial
laws and legislation—United States. I. Kagan, Robert A.
II. Title.
KF5402.B35   342.73'0664   81-16606
ISBN 0-87722-251-7   347.302664   AACR2
ISBN 0-87722-252-5 (pbk.)

To Nancy and to Betsy

CONTENTS

•

FOREWORD

———————————————— • ————————————————

The long record of government regulation of business as a means of protecting the public is one of advances and retreats. A rise in abuses of one sort or another usually leads to demands for rules and regulations to curb or eliminate them. But once the rules are set down and enforced, a reaction typically sets in. This pattern was especially marked during the last decade, when regulation of everything from nursing homes to the environment was very much in vogue. Inevitably, affected business firms complained about the increased costs and deterrents to initiative that regulation has wrought. With the advent of the Reagan administration and its promise to revitalize a flagging and inflation-prone economy (attributed at least in part to regulation), the inevitable reaction of deregulation has set in.

This study by Eugene Bardach and Robert A. Kagan of the University of California at Berkeley was approved by the Trustees of the Twentieth Century Fund in 1977, a time when the proregulation movement was at its height. Politicians and policymakers were beguiled by the notion that establishing clear rules to protect against abuses and dangers, along with measures for their enforcement, was a fair and simple solution for many of the environmental and social ills that resulted, frequently unintentionally, from the operations of American industry.

It was the view of the authors that the architects of increased regulation failed to realize the unintended consequences—in terms of increased costs and complexity, frequently harmful to productivity—of their best laid plans. As Bardach and Kagan saw it, a good deal of regulation was self-defeating, and they wanted to demonstrate their belief that efforts to assure the safety and health of American workers and consumers were not necessarily helped by more and more rules (and penalties) that sometimes discouraged rather than encouraged responsible behavior.

Impressed by them and their thesis, the Fund agreed to support their project.

Over the ensuing years, the authors have carefully investigated a number of different industrial areas subject to regulation and found ample evidence that policymakers, prodded by politicians and public interest groups, have indulged in overregulation that has generated unreasonable and inflexible behavior on the part of the official inspectorate, which, in turn, has bred resentment and resistance among businessmen. The result has undermined many regulatory objectives and created the contempt for regulatory authority that is so evident in the current attitude of dismantling regulation.

Yet Bardach and Kagan argue that in a world that continues to advance technologically and scientifically the pattern of regulatory and deregulatory extremes must be broken. They see a need for strong and effective protective measures. They recommend working within the current system to make it more responsive and reasonable, with inspectors having the discretion to fulfill the spirit rather than the letter of the law. They also suggest that methods of indirect regulation—liability law, mandatory disclosure, and taxes to discourage certain behavior—can be used to supplement and strengthen direct regulation.

We believe that Bardach and Kagan have produced a persuasive and thorough study of a troubling problem. They ran counter to the prevailing wisdom of increased regulation in making their original proposal, and they remain counter to the new demands for regulation in their own policy prescription. Their study should make for stimulating and informed debate, and we are grateful to them.

M. J. Rossant
Director
The Twentieth Century Fund
August 1981

PREFACE

———————————— • ————————————

In a well-ordered society, people would be willing and able to take responsibility for protecting themselves against the annoyances, the petty injustices, and the perils of everyday life. They would not allow themselves to be cheated by door-to-door salesmen, injured by faulty home appliances, or tyrannized by bosses and supervisors. They would also take responsibility for protecting family members, particularly the very young and the very old, not only from these everyday hazards but from the special dangers that beset the inexperienced and the physically weak. Measures would be taken to scare off schoolyard bullies or to fend off neighborhood vandals. In a well-ordered society, furthermore, people would take at least some responsibility for protecting individuals with whom their associations were more indirect and indeterminate. Householders would refrain from abandoning old refrigerators in vacant lots, lest children lock themselves inside; managers of firms that manufactured dangerous drugs or chemicals would see to it that their products were packaged and disposed of safely and with adequate warning labels; and businessmen would discourage their colleagues or subordinates from pursuing racist policies in promoting and hiring personnel.

In a complex society that is not well ordered—or at least not perfectly ordered—by such natural, spontaneous, and informal means, government is wont to step in with rules, regulations, and laws, defining and assigning specific bits of social responsibility. Since not everyone immediately fulfills his legally assigned obligations, the government also deploys inspectors and investigators to detect violations and penalize the violators. To facilitate that process, regulated entities are required to keep prescribed records and file periodic reports or applications for permits. Even then, new hazards are discovered that have escaped the previously established regulatory nets—disease-causing particles in the air of factories, toxic wastes in the soil under housing projects, boarded-up fire doors in the crime-plagued welfare hotels of the inner city, further indignities in nursing homes. And the response of a humane and democratic society is the further elaboration of laws and regulations, inspections and prosecutions, reports and permits, all designed to eradicate these manifestations of disorder and indifference, to repair the gaps in the social fabric with government-prescribed and -enforced standards of responsible behavior.

Through this process, we have experienced in this country during the past fifteen years a wave of government programs known (mainly to their critics) as "the new social regulation" and which we call "protective regulation." This book is about the implementation of this general class of programs, and particularly about their tendency to expand excessively their coverage and their stringency.

In late 1975, when we began work on some specific studies that led to this book, public opinion did not hold that Americans were greatly overregulated and desperately in need of relief. In fact, we ourselves did not see the problems of overregulation as being nearly so interesting or so socially significant as the problems of underregulation. Rather, we noted that relative to the vast number of people and sites potentially subject to most protective regulatory programs there were apparently too few regulators on the public payroll charged with doing the job. We also wondered whether regulators had sufficient sanctions at their disposal to deter the irresponsible, or whether the protections and delays of due process of law made such sanctions ineffective. That any substantial amount of protective regulation was effected at all was, in this light, astonishing. We set out, indeed, to figure out how such accomplishments came to pass, and to find ways to extend and deepen the effective reach of regulation. Both public opinion and our own concerns have shifted during the intervening years (although we would like to believe it was our own early researches and reflections rather than the latest vogue that led us to change our emphasis from the problems of underregulation to the problems of overregulation).

Yet as we observe the course of the Republican regulatory counter-revolution in mid-1981 and are greatly pleased at its general direction and strength, we are also frequently troubled by the possibility that in many respects it will go too far, hack away too much. We are concerned, for example, that the problems presented by toxic substances and hazardous wastes will be too little remembered and appreciated. Reasonable controls and intelligently managed inspectorates may become casualties in the retreat from excessively costly air and water quality standards that have rightly given "environmentalism" a bad name in some quarters. In addition, while many of the problems of overregulation arise from treating all regulated entities as though they were greedy malefactors, at least *some* regulated entities really *do* fit these strong negative stereotypes. While the drive to loosen up on regulation will remove certain burdens from the vast number of parties where they fall inappropriately, there is no question that the drive will result in more evil and stupidity sneaking through than presently do. Up to a point, this higher price will probably be worth paying. But it is always necessary both to watch that the price does not rise too high, and to conjure with ways to obtain the benefits of less regulation without paying a higher price than is necessary.

Our book does not deal with all the problems of overregulation but only with that subset we call regulatory "unreasonableness." Part I of the book discusses the causes and the manifestations of regulatory unreasonableness. Chapter 1 defines the concept and describes the underlying and continuing social and political pressures for protective regulation. Chapter 2 reviews the historical development of relatively centralized and highly programmed regulatory institutions that inhibit regulatory flexibility and lead, quite directly, to regulatory unreasonableness. Chapter 3 analyzes the fundamental disjunction between legalistic regulation and the diversity of the world to be regulated, and the conflicts between the "official" perspective of the regulators and the "civilian" perspective of the regulated that exacerbate tendencies toward unreasonableness. Chapter 4 is devoted to the potentially perverse and unanticipated effects of excessively stringent regulation, namely, that regulated parties will become less cooperative, less attuned to solving the real problems that lead to the social harms regulation wants to avoid.

We were concerned, of course, not only with diagnosing problems but with finding possible remedies as well. What might be done to make regulation more reasonable and more constructive? Our fieldwork did uncover some instances of how unusually good field enforcement officials managed to operate sensitively, judiciously, and constructively. Drawing on these discoveries, Part II of the book discusses the possibility of a more flexible style of regulatory enforcement. Our ideal of "the good inspector" is presented in Chapter 5. In Chapter 6 we explore some of the ways in which thoughtful and creative agency managers might introduce more flexibility into the enforcement function. But in Chapter 7 we assess the political and bureaucratic obstacles to the ideal of flexible regulation. As we put it there, the ratchet wheel of regulatory controls can become tighter but cannot easily be loosened. While there are many reasons for this, we emphasize the political vulnerability of regulatory officials (and legislators, too) to the appearance of laxity, corruption, "softness," and "co-optation." Alas, the same democratic virtues that enshrine "accountability" in our public philosophy also conspire to make regulatory officials slavish devotees of "going by the book."

In Chapters 8, 9, and 10—Part III of the book—we explore some strategic alternatives to direct "command-and-control" regulation that might circumvent some of the strictures imposed by the law and morality on strict accountability. We cover certain forms of "self-regulation," a greater reliance on the liability law, the levying of taxes and charges on conduct we wish to discourage, and the mandatory disclosure of various sorts of information that might better allow consumers, workers, and citizens to act as private "regulators" on their own behalf. Our conclusion is that, while these forms of "indirect regulation" are in some respects more likely to be reasonable than direct regulation, they *too* pose risks of unreasonableness. Moreover, indirect regulation cannot effectively substitute for direct regulation for many social problems.

Given such imperfect tools to choose from, in the final chapter we discuss how a policy planner might review his or her options at the design stage of launching a new regulatory program. We also discuss some institutional procedures for "regulatory oversight," that is, restraining the potential excesses of regulatory agencies. Finally, we speculate about the possible long-run cultural effects of a regime of regulatory unreasonableness: a legal and political system that seeks to make everyone *accountable* for everything—as the logic of the regulatory state would ultimately have it—might paradoxically make us less willing to act as *responsible* citizens and human beings.

APPROACH AND METHOD

As political scientists we have naturally been inclined to emphasize the political, bureaucratic, and legal processes that produce and sustain regulatory unreasonableness. But we have also used the conceptual lenses of another discipline, economics, to identify important normative and analytical issues in regulatory policy. To put the matter differently, economics has helped us ask the questions, while political science has helped us search for answers.

The powerful contribution of economics to the study of regulation is in its raising the question of why one should ever expect government protective regulation to be beneficial at all. It suggests, in fact, that in most cases a combination of the marketplace and the liability law makes regulation unnecessary at best and very disruptive of economic welfare at worst. A great deal of economic analysis in recent years—especially from the "Chicago School"—has been devoted to challenging the underlying rationale of many protective regulatory programs. (The main exception here is environmental regulation, where there is almost no dissent from the view that government intervention is required.) Our own view, however, is that protective regulatory programs virtually always address a genuine social problem that is imperfectly dealt with by the marketplace and the liability law, but that (1) in some cases the problem is not as significant as many people believe and (2) imperfections in the way government implements regulatory programs can sometimes offset the social benefits that might be derived from regulating in a more nearly "ideal" way. Unfortunately, economists have generally not thought much about how to *improve* protective regulation—as opposed to simply abolishing it. And political scientists, preoccupied by the "capture theory" formulated in an earlier and quite different generation of regulatory programs, have thought almost exclusively about the problem of making regulation more effective and almost not at all about the problem of making it more reasonable.*

Much as we have tried to blend the intellectual perspectives of economics and political science at the conceptual level, at the level of data collection and interpretation we have relied solely on the methods of the "softer" social sciences like sociology, anthropology, and political science. This approach was dictated principally by our overall research objective, which was to lay the groundwork for framing hypotheses rather than to test hypotheses or theories already worked out.

We began thinking of regulators and regulated as predator and prey. We wondered how the regulated attempt to evade the regulators, how the regulators adapt to tactics of evasion, and what environmental conditions favor successful adaptations by the regulators. But the prey/predator metaphor, we came to see, does not always work. The interaction

---

*This is not to say that the problems of effectiveness, especially vis-à-vis the most recalcitrant regulated enterprises, are not real and significant in protective regulation; indeed, it is partly because so many others are concerned with increasing effectiveness that we have felt justified in concentrating on regulatory unreasonableness in this study.

may be more like two species that achieve a more harmonious pattern of mutual adaptation. There might be evolutionary patterns in some regulatory environments, from conflict toward cooperation. Alternatively, the evolution might be in the reverse direction. If so, the relevant inquiries become: what environments and adaptations induce different patterns of interaction, and with what results for the effectiveness and reasonableness of regulation?

A program that clearly follows from this ecological metaphor is to study both species in a variety of environments, rather than to mount a few detailed case studies of specific policy areas. Another strategy is to focus on the dimensions of, or adaptations to, the underlying process of mutual challenge and response. The method for studying such adaptations would be essentially to examine cases of stressful interaction between regulatory officials and representatives of regulated enterprises. We gathered data by means of lengthy, open-ended interviews with inspectors and higher enforcement officials in agencies that specialize in a single industry or technology, such as the Motor Carrier Safety Unit of the California Highway Patrol, and in agencies that inspect many kinds of firms, such as the Occupational Safety and Health Administration. We spoke with officials in agencies that enforce regulations covering well-understood technologies, such as California's milk and dairy inspection agency and municipal building code inspectors in Oakland, California, and we looked into regulatory processes involving poorly understood technologies, such as the nursing home licensing section of the California Department of Health. We examined agencies that enforce rules that are generally costly and unprofitable for industry to comply with, such as the San Francisco Bay Area Air Pollution Control District, and agencies whose regulations generally reinforce the safety and quality concerns of the regulated enterprises themselves, such as the Food and Drug Administration's Bureau of Biologics (manufacture of blood plasma products and intravenous solutions) and the Food and Drug Division of the California Department of Health (manufacture of food products). In several instances, we or our research assistants accompanied inspectors on their daily rounds.

In addition, to better understand the actual effects of regulatory enforcement, we interviewed executives and technical specialists in enterprises regulated by each of the above agencies. We concentrated on a limited number of firms in specific industries, trying to get some variation by size of firm. With respect to air pollution regulation, for example, we spoke to executives and environmental engineers in four small steel foundries, three large petroleum refineries, and two aluminum manufacturing companies, one large and one medium sized. With respect to workplace safety and health regulation, we interviewed officials responsible for safety in the above foundries and aluminum firms, plus safety engineers in two automobile assembly plants, and labor union safety officers for five of those enterprises. This enabled us to compare how managers in the same regulated enterprise reacted to inspectors from different regulatory agencies. We also discussed the experience of dealing with inspectors with officials in at least two dairy products companies, six nursing homes, three canneries, three trucking firms or trucking departments, two blood banks, and one manufacturer of intravenous products, as well as representatives of private inspectorates that deal with regulated firms, such as insurance company safety inspectors, the head of inspection for Underwriters Laboratory, and an inspector for the American Association of Blood Banks.

Finally, we conducted a two-day workshop at the Graduate School of Public Policy at the University of California at Berkeley during which we recorded round-table discussions among enforcement officials from most of the above-mentioned agencies, plus a few others, along with representatives of regulated enterprises.

The sample of agencies and regulated enterprises is not "representative" in a scientific sense. But it does constitute a sufficient range, we believe, to illuminate the main patterns of enforcement and response, and the main kinds of problems experienced by inspectors and by regulated enterprises in their mutual interaction.

One element of our approach has been to accumulate a variety of stories about more typical encounters between regulators and regulated. Thus our strategy was not to seek out only the horror story—tales of irresponsible and deceptive enterprises or tales of arrogant and arbitrary regulators—but also to compel our interviewees to put those stories in perspective. For example, we asked managers of regulated enterprises, and in some cases labor union officials, to describe *all* their encounters with regulatory officials in recent years, including those they regarded as reasonable and constructive. We asked the managers to describe, in technical detail, the most important recent changes in their systems, say, for controlling air pollution or improving worker safety, and to explain whether those changes came about as a result of interactions with regulatory officials (or stemmed from other sources). We also asked managers to assess what deterioration, if any, they thought would occur if the inspectors were never to come again, if the regulations were repealed.

A second element of our approach has been to try to understand the more vexatious aspects of regulatory encounters as the by-products of regulators' efforts to do a good job with respect to their mission of preventing or rectifying social harms. Regulators do not relish the experience of being—or at any rate, seeming to be—unreasonable. Our initial forays into the field made this point very clear. By and large, their conduct is dictated by circumstances beyond their control, the legal and bureaucratic and political conditions that define what it means for them to be "doing a good job." We have argued that the most important conditions under which unreasonableness occurs are these: regulatory programming is centralized and detailed to prevent regulatory agencies from being "captured" by the regulated industry; regulatory rules are overinclusive, covering situations for which they are inappropriate; the fear of criticism for alleged "backing down" and "getting soft" prevents regulators from revising the formal rules to correct this problem; and the fear of criticism for alleged laxity or corruption prevents field-enforcement officials from not enforcing rule-based requirements that are inappropriate to particular situations (and may even be acknowledged as such). Our understanding of how these conditions have shaped regulators' conceptions of, and abilities to perform, their jobs grew in large measure from aggressive questioning of enforcement officials and managers of regulated enterprises and hence from their considerable analytical capacities. For example, we repeatedly asked both kinds of officials how, ideally, they would conduct the regulatory process if put in complete charge, and then asked what political, legal, or organizational factors currently prevent such reforms from occurring. We asked why certain ostensibly unreasonable regulatory actions had been taken, and what pressures they thought had forced enforcement officials into such a posture.

We have also, of course, relied on the more sedentary forms of scholarly research, such as mining recent studies of specific regulatory agencies and programs, clipping newspapers and magazines, and reading statutes and administrative regulations. We have not conducted systematic surveys of all agencies or a perfectly representative sample of inspectors and regulated firms; we present no frequency distribution of instances of unreasonableness. Our approach has been appropriate, in short, to our purposes of the exploration and the development of a richer and deeper theoretical understanding. It remains for further research to address in a more systematic way the many intriguing empirical questions that emerge from our present effort.

ACKNOWLEDGMENTS

——————————————— ● ———————————————

Many individuals and institutions supported us throughout our work. Our debt to them is enormous; and so, of course, is our gratitude. The Twentieth Century Fund furnished a generous budget, considerable moral support, and much useful criticism. In the very earliest stage of the research a summer grant from the Ford Foundation provided much-needed seed money. The Center for the Study of Law and Society and the Graduate School of Public Policy, both of the University of California at Berkeley, provided office space and various forms of logistical support.

John Scholz, now an assistant professor of political science at the State University of New York at Stony Brook, was our Research Associate for two years. John was an invaluable associate. He deserves co-authorship credit for some of the material in several chapters, such as aspects of the history of protective regulation in Chapters 1 and 2, the analysis of the causes of noncompliance in Chapter 3, and the depiction of the various roles of the "good inspector" in Chapter 6. Assisting us very ably in our fieldwork and library research were: Jerome Bayer (nursing homes), Ken Bloch (fire safety regulation), Ross Cheit (building codes), Donald Downs (air pollution and truck safety), Donna Leff (milk and dairy regulation), Michael McCann (a variety of tasks), Larry Ruth (OSHA), and Peter Siegelman (blood plasma and biologics regulation and consumer protection). During the summer after she completed her doctoral work and before she assumed a teaching post at Lewis and Clark College, Mari Malvey worked on a study of California nursing home regulation for us. Shortly thereafter, Mari and her son Nicky were killed in an auto crash. Like all of her many friends and professional colleagues, we have mourned her loss deeply.

We have received valuable advice, criticism, and moral support from numerous professional colleagues who read all or part of the manuscript or who discussed it with us: Henry Brady, Lee Friedman, Victor P.

Goldberg, Steven Kelman, Martin A. Levin, Frank Levy, Jerry Mashaw, John Mendeloff, Robert Nelson, Dail Phillips, John Quigley, Allan Sindler, Christopher Stone, Stephen Sugarman, David Vogel, and Aaron Wildavsky. We have attempted to satisfy their objections and to approach their always too-high expectations. We hope they will forgive our lapses. In any case, only we, and not they, bear the responsibility for any errors of fact or interpretation.

Dozens of students, too numerous to name individually, read portions of the manuscript during the course of many a graduate seminar we have taught, and we have profited greatly from their reactions and comments.

Masha Sinnreich of the Twentieth Century Fund reviewed our work on an ongoing basis and consistently made many helpful suggestions. Brenda Price, also at the Fund, edited the manuscript with tact and intelligence.

Perhaps most importantly, we wish to acknowledge the kind assistance of our many interviewees and informants. Their names will not be mentioned here or in the text, for we hoped that a pledge of confidentiality on our part would encourage frankness on theirs. Many of those we interviewed gave generously of their time and insight. We think especially of the enforcement officials who spoke so frankly at our workshop, the inspectors who took us or our assistants on their rounds, the corporate officials who arranged for or conducted us on detailed tours of their factories, the labor union safety officers who spent long hours discussing their frustrations and their successes. The interest and concern expressed by these people are, for us, the most memorable legacy of our research.

Finally, we thank our wives and daughters—Nancy, Elizabeth, Rebecca, and Naomi Bardach, and Betsy and Elsie Kagan—for their inexhaustible support, love, tolerance, and good humor through our interminable discussions of inspectors and our endless hours walled off in our studies, lost in the world of regulation.

PART ONE

THE PROBLEM OF
REGULATORY UNREASONABLENESS

CHAPTER ONE

THE GROWTH OF PROTECTIVE REGULATION

———————————— • ————————————

The rule of law was invented to restrain the willfulness of kings and nobles. In modern republican states, it is invoked by citizens to restrain all manner of public institutions and practices that threaten their sense of security and justice. But the restraints of the rule of law are willful in their own way. They command certain procedures, and they dictate that all statutes and regulations be applied uniformly, consistently, and fairly. The realm of human activity to which these rules are applied, however, is diverse and complex. It is not always possible to successfully connect the procedural and substantive requirements of law to the variety of experience. Yet government must govern, and if it cannot do so by forging perfect connections to the society it governs, then it will make do with imperfect connections.

An important consequence of this essential mismatch between government and society is that there are bound to be points of friction, which have multiplied in recent years, especially through the proliferation of protective regulatory laws enacted since the mid-1960s. The impulse behind this growth has been to protect citizens from a broad range of social harms, perhaps too long neglected, including occupational injuries and diseases, environmental pollution, product-related injuries, highway accidents, discrimination in employment and education, and consumer fraud. The basic techniques of these regulatory programs have been the legislation of rules of law specifying protective measures to be instituted by regulated enterprises and the enforcement of those rules by government inspectors and investigators, who are instructed to act in accordance with the terms of the regulations, not on the basis of their own potentially arbitrary judgment. But uniform regulations, even those that are justifiable in the general run of cases, inevitably appear to be unreasonable in many particular cases. Consider, for example, the experience of Al

Schaefer,* the director of worker safety for a major aluminum manufacturing company, with the Occupational Safety and Health Administration (OSHA).[1]

By all accounts, including those of a labor union safety officer, a regional OSHA official and a plant-level safety engineer with experience in other firms, Schaefer's company seems to have a positive attitude toward worker safety and an aggressive safety program. Still, the corporation's numerous plants have been visited by OSHA inspectors a total of 30 to 50 times a year; the company received an average of 225 citations each year and paid a total of $25,000 in fines over the last seven years. But, argues Schaefer, OSHA inspections have made little positive contribution to safety in his company. "The major problem with OSHA," he says, "is that they mandate safety standards even where they are not the highest priority risk in a particular plant." He gave an example involving an OSHA regulation that called for "alternative means of egress" from public gathering places, such as restaurants. An OSHA inspector applied this rule to the lunchrooms in an aluminum smelting plant. The heart of the smelter is composed of long rows of furnaces (or "pots") in which molten aluminum is formed from alumina (refined bauxite). Crucibles of molten aluminum are transported along these rows by motorized vehicles. Small, airconditioned lunchrooms are adjacent to the "potline" but separated from it by a cinder-block wall; the doors to the lunchroom do not open directly into the potline, but open off side corridors. The lunchrooms had no rear exits.

OSHA said rear exits were required. The only justification OSHA could offer (other than the text of the regulation) was that if the molten aluminum spilled and went into the side corridors and a fire started, workers in the lunchroom would be trapped.

"Now that citation does not represent a rational assessment of risk," Schaefer says. "Of course, it *could* happen. Almost anything *could* happen. Never mind that it's more likely that an earthquake could happen. Never mind that in the 15 years the plant has been operating nothing like that happened, or even any incidents that suggest it might happen."

---

*The names of many individuals interviewed have been changed, and the names of the organizations for which they work are not given.

Besides, he points out, because the lunchrooms are of cinder-block construction, the only thing that could burn is the wooden door. To cut through the other side and install a door, he says, would cost $6,000 per lunchroom, times 10 lunchrooms. "This is a total misapplication of resources. I could use that money for real risk reduction in plenty of other places."

To Schaefer, OSHA appeared unreasonable. But was OSHA unreasonable? Although we did not investigate the details of this or several similar instances described by Schaefer, we did interview many regulatory officials from a variety of agencies, including OSHA, and a rebuttal to Schaefer might have sounded like this:

Either directly or through state agencies that enforce the OSHA regulations for us, we regulate worker safety and health in almost five million workplaces. They are extremely varied. If we had rules that were exactly suited to each hazard and each situation in every one of those workplaces, the inspector's manual would have to be transported in a truck. So we have to simplify and standardize, and obviously some cases of overinclusive rules and regulations are going to result. Remember, Al Schaefer or people like him can always file for a variance because the law does give us latitude to waive compliance in cases where equivalent protection is provided by other means.

True, we don't let the inspector at the field level have the discretion to waive compliance. But that is because he would then be susceptible to manipulation, bribery, and perhaps intimidation. Besides, not all 3,000 occupational safety and health inspectors are sufficiently trained or clever or morally upright to be entrusted with discretionary power. It may be somewhat inconvenient for Al Schaefer and others in his position to seek waivers through the proper channels, and in some cases they just might choose to comply with regulatory rules rather than do it, but remember that workers' lives and well-being are at issue. If the system has to make errors, which of course it does, it is better to err on the side of safety. We at OSHA think that, our statutory mandate indicates that Congress thinks that, and public opinion polls suggest that the public overwhelmingly thinks so too.

Who, then, was unreasonable?

A famous old story has a litigant coming before a rabbi and pleading his case with great passion. When he is done, the rabbi pronounces, "You are right!" Thereupon the second litigant hastens to tell his side of the story with even greater passion, and when he is done, the rabbi also pronounces, "You are right!" Dismayed, a bystander who has heard the entire proceeding leaps forward to observe that the two litigants' stories had been utterly incompatible and that it could not logically be the case that both were right. To which the rabbi responds, "You too are right!"

Al Schaefer has what we term a "civilian" perspective on his experience with regulation, and our hypothetical spokesman for OSHA is invoking what we call an "official" perspective. Both perspectives are right. Even the best efforts at regulation, which might produce, on the whole, quite laudable results, are bound to produce many unreasonable and even deplorable results. The official perspective, emphasizing the positive results, is legitimate and defensible, but so too is the civilian perspective, which is tinged with anger and resentment at regulatory departures from common sense. The fact that regulatory unreasonableness is unintended and incidental to the accomplishment of a larger purpose does not make it less unreasonable to the individuals who endure it. The objective of this book is to explore the character, the sources, and the consequences of regulatory unreasonableness.

THE SEVERAL DIMENSIONS OF
REGULATORY UNREASONABLENESS

Basically, "unreasonableness" involves economic inefficiency. A regulatory requirement is unreasonable if compliance would not yield the intended benefits, as when installing a government-mandated safety device would not really improve worker safety because of the operating conditions in a particular factory. Further, a regulatory requirement is unreasonable if compliance would entail costs that clearly exceed the resulting social benefits. For example, mandatory installation of a "second-generation" water pollution treatment system might be unreasonable, even if it were to improve water quality incrementally over the level provided by existing equipment, if that improvement were to be achieved only at extraordinary expense. Finally, unreasonableness means cost-ineffectiveness; for example, regulations requiring the retrofitting of buses and subways to accommodate wheelchair-bound citizens would be unreasonable if a special door-to-door jitney or taxi service could be provided at a fraction of the cost.

The focus of this book is on the social dimension of unreasonableness: the *experience* of being subjected to inefficient regulatory requirements. The distinction is made, therefore, between "rule-level unreasonableness," which has to do with aggregate economic inefficiency, and "site-level unreasonableness," which has to do with particular encounters between enforcers and the regulated. To be sure, the latter is a logical corollary of the former. Nevertheless, site-level unreasonableness is a distinguishable phenomenon. Even regulatory rules that in the aggregate produce social benefits that exceed compliance costs can lead to countless instances of site-level unreasonableness. Moreover, there is a difference in social impact. Site-level unreasonableness exists not as a cost-benefit ratio or some such abstraction, but as a mosaic of personal, and often very troubling, experiences. Site-level unreasonableness explains much of the present political and social discontent with protective regulation. Admittedly, a great many people are disturbed by the high aggregate economic costs of protective regulation, costs that are estimated in the billions of dollars a year.[2] But the present discontent with protective regulation, as expressed in most complaints about it, has almost nothing to do with aggregate costs and almost everything to do with particular costs and aggravations imposed by particular enforcement officials on particular institutions and businesses.

Everyone who has ever been subjected to regulation, whether at the hands of a welfare eligibility evaluator, an affirmative action compliance specialist, or a county sanitation officer, has a stock of horror stories about particular regulatory encounters. These stories enter into the stream of conversation and ultimately into the cultural consciousness that defines and measures the evils of regulation. Horror stories may not represent the modal pattern of regulatory agency activity, and may in fact mask good that is achieved, but they do reflect a genuine truth about the inevitability and vexatiousness of regulatory unreasonableness.

THE ORIGINS OF PROTECTIVE REGULATION

Of course, regulatory unreasonableness would not exist at all if there were no protective regulation in the first place. To understand the phenomenon of regulatory unreasonableness, we must also understand where the regulators and their regulatory programs come from. For example, protective regulation, it should be clearly understood, is by no means a recent invention. Regulation has long been employed in America to prevent misleading or dangerous commercial practices. In the colonial era, a Massachusetts law required each town to appoint a "gager or packer" to see to it that "the best be not left out" in sealed packages of beef and pork; it provided that "if such goods so packed shall be put to sale without the gager's mark, the seller shall forfeit the goods . . . the one halfe to the Informer and the other halfe to the countrey."[3] In the early nineteenth century, New York had an "inspector general of provisions" with authority to confiscate unwholesome food.[4] Resentment of inspectors is not new either. In 1846, delegates to the New York Constitutional Convention voted to rescind laws regulating many products and forbade the reestablishment of inspection offices, expressing dissatisfaction with the multitude of officials and their perquisites.[5]

The first explosion of modern regulatory inspection programs, however, came in the late nineteenth and early twentieth centuries in response to the new hazards generated by industrial technologies and to new scientific discoveries about the relationship between unsanitary conditions and disease. Most famous were the federal pure Food and Drug Act and the Meat Inspection Act, both passed in 1906. They led to close government inspection of meat processing plants for poor sanitation and sampling of food products for signs of adulteration. Workplace safety and health were other targets. By the end of the nineteenth century, many states, following the English model, had passed laws requiring factories and workshops "to be kept in a cleanly state and free from effluvia" and "so ventilated as to render harmless, so far as practicable, all the gases, vapors, dust or other impurities generated."[6] Regulatory officials were empowered to inspect factories for violations and, in some cases, to order factory owners to install protective devices. Iowa enacted a coal mine inspection law in 1880, authorizing inspectors to check ventilation and safety conditions.[7]

A surge of federal legislation at the turn of the century set safety standards for railroads and provided for inspection as a means of enforcement. The Locomotive Inspection Act (1911), for example, required railroads to establish a routine self-inspection system for boilers and locomotive parts, using testing procedures and personnel certified and supervised by Interstate Commerce Commission (ICC) inspectors.[8] Urbanization and new technologies led to government inspection of potentially explosive containers of heating oil and of electrical wiring.[9] New York's first tenement housing law, enacted in 1867, required apartment buildings to have air shafts, fire escapes, proper chimneys, and adequate waste disposal facilities. By the early twentieth century, detailed municipal housing codes, requiring a check by a government inspector before buildings were approved for occupancy, were quite common.[10]

In some industries, established firms sought government coercive and inspection powers in order to discipline (or drive out) competitors whose unsafe practices or products weakened consumer confidence and jeopardized the growth of the industry. Some major manufacturers and distributors supported the pure Food and Drug Act.[11] The California State Dairy Bureau, described as "the virtual representative of the California Dairy Association," was authorized in 1895 to inspect sanitary conditions in dairies and to order improvements; by 1917, it had 20 inspectors.[12] The state veterinarian and county livestock inspectors were authorized to inspect horses and cattle and to quarantine or destroy diseased animals.[13]*

These and other regulatory programs designed to prevent accidents and disease should be seen in perspective: society's *first* line of defense against dangerous products and processes usually has been the economic market and the incentives it creates. The prospect of gaining customers and the fear of losing them, after all, motivate most enterprises to build a certain level of safety and reliability into their products or services. Consumers often act as their own inspectors. They feel the tomatoes and sniff the cottage cheese. They warn their friends about products that turned out to be unsafe or about tradesmen who performed poorly. They hire experts to check out buildings before they buy. To win the confidence of consumers and retain their loyalty, many enterprises guarantee their products and hire their own cadre of inspectors. Manufacturers insert slips marked "Inspected by No. —" in the pockets of a new garment or the boxes containing new appliances.

Consumer demand has led to professions and organizations that specialize in assuring reliability. Large retailers, such as Sears Roebuck and J. C. Penney, have departments that check the safety of products they sell.[14] Teams of quality control engineers and their staffs oversee assem-

---

*By 1907, with the aid of federal inspectors from the U.S. Department of Agriculture, cattle tick and deadly anthrax had been wiped out in California—a regulatory success story.

bly lines in canneries and automobile factories. Architects and engineers are hired to establish principles of sound construction and to supervise builders. Casualty insurance companies have played a major role in developing standards of fireproofing in construction and insisting on the installation of sprinkler systems. Because workplace accidents disable experienced employees and stop production, which hurt profits, industry has a long history of hiring safety engineers to promote workplace safety.* This is not to say that the market and its economic incentives always provide an "adequate" level of safety or social responsibility. Business enterprises consider the costs of protective equipment as well as the costs of accidents. Many cut corners and take their chances. Hence regulatory programs and inspectors can be viewed as *supplemental* control devices, bolstering or filling gaps in a more pervasive market-based system of private pressures.

Another major source of private inspection systems is liability law— private lawsuits for damages, primarily based on common-law standards of negligence and fraud, but sometimes on statutory standards, as in the case of workers' compensation statutes. In theory, the prospect of damage awards will motivate enterprises to invest in safety precautions and "honesty" in order to minimize their liability and to avoid the bad publicity associated with losing lawsuits, but this idea does not work perfectly. Lawsuits are slow, expensive, and chancy; the full deterrent potential of the liability system is thus muted. Still, they pose a threat that cannot be entirely ignored by providers of goods and services and give rise to extensive private control systems. Thousands of insurance company "loss control representatives" inspect insured enterprises and press them to make liability-avoidance efforts. With the cooperation of industry, the Underwriters Laboratory sets safety standards for hundreds of wire and cable products, electrical motors, and household appliances and deploys a corps of inspectors to ensure compliance with the standards.

The creation of new protective regulatory programs, therefore, might be thought of as selective political judgments that the market and liability laws were inadequate to encourage socially responsible behavior. The immediate trigger often was a highly publicized disaster or a powerfully written expose, such as Upton Sinclair's *The Jungle*, a novel that por-

---

*When the California Industrial Accident Commission sought a director of safety inspection in 1914, it referred to the considerable number of competent mechanical engineers working on safety in industry and hired the safety director of the 7,000-employee Pennsylvania Steel Company. Report of the Industrial Accident Commission, 1914, pp. 26–27.

trayed filthy conditions in Chicago's meatpacking houses. These revelations played on the emerging value system in America noted by Lord Bryce in the 1880s: "The sight of a preventable evil [becomes] painful, and is felt as a reproach."[15] Control strategies that relied essentially on the self-interest of producers were seen to have certain weaknesses. For products and services whose true characteristics might be hidden or otherwise inaccessible to inspection by consumers or workers (e.g., household electrical wiring or chemical solvents), producer self-interest would not be checked by the self-interest of those parties that ordinarily could and would police the marketplace. Furthermore, in an era of rapid technological development, with scientific knowledge leaping ahead of common knowledge and management skills, there would always be food processors unaware of the latest theories of disease causation and small manufacturers who would be skeptical of newly developed safety gear. In these cases, the machinery of the law not only had to threaten but also had to discover points of ignorance and offer instruction. Sometimes the threat of death was so emotionally compelling (as in the case of falling elevators) or of economic losses so massive (as in the case of epidemics that destroyed entire herds of cattle) that positive, *collective* steps to prevent the disaster, rather than reliance on the economic self-interest and managerial abilities of businessmen, seemed the only tolerable course of action. The public, it was thought, must have its own eyes and ears, an early warning system, and a corps of protectors free from the flaws of greed, miscalculation, or ignorance that made the market and private liability laws less than perfect deterrents.

In the 1960s and 1970s, a quantum leap seems to have been taken in legislators' eagerness to provide this kind of extra protection. The new wave of protective regulation was especially forceful at the federal level. Old programs were stepped up. New safety standards and expanded inspection operations were established for meat and poultry processing plants and for food and drug manufacturing processes. Strengthened enforcement agencies took over existing federal inspection programs.* The federal government took on a vastly expanded regulatory role,

---

*For example, railroad safety enforcement was transferred from the ICC to a new Federal Railroad Administration; the inspection of blood plasma centers and intravenous products manufacturing plants was transferred from the Public Health Service to an enlarged Bureau of Biologics in the Food and Drug Administration; licensing and safety regulation of nuclear plants was transferred from the Atomic Energy Commission to the new Nuclear Regulatory Commission.

including enforcement responsibility, in the field of worker safety and environmental protection pursuant to the Coal Mine Health and Safety Act (1969), the Occupational Safety and Health Act (1970), the Clean Air Act amendments (1970), the Water Pollution Control Act (1972), and the Surface Mining Control and Reclamation Act (1977), to name only some of the most prominent of the new measures. Although not necessarily entailing inspection, enforcement duties were given to federal officials by many new consumer protection and product safety statutes, such as the Consumer Product Safety Act. Federal enforcement of anti-discrimination standards grew enormously pursuant to the Civil Rights Act (1964), forbidding race and sex discrimination in employment, and related laws. Federal "inspection" of local school programs took the form of auditors ensuring compliance with federal guidelines that accompanied financial support for special programs to aid disadvantaged and handicapped students. Similarly, expanded federal aid to hospitals and nursing home patients led to inspections by federal officials to ensure compliance with quality-of-care regulations. Federal grants to local housing agencies encouraged and financed regulatory programs to enforce higher maintenance standards for slum housing.

The reasons for this regulatory upsurge were complex, and we can only comment speculatively on them. One factor was the increasing *knowledge of risks*. The discovery of the carcinogenic properties of commonly used chemicals that entered the food chain or that pervaded the air, along with the scientific arguments that even low levels of exposure were harmful, was analogous to the discovery that bacteria caused disease, a discovery that stimulated much protective regulation in the late nineteenth century. There was also much speculation that the *objective levels of risk* were increasing. During the 1950s and 1960s, the cumulative expansion of industrial production, the consumption of fossil fuels, the use of pesticides, and the sprawl of urban America increased exposure to environmental pollution. In the 1960s, instances of lakes dying, fish disappearing from rivers, and chemicals poisoning the environment began to be reported with disturbing frequency. Auto-related accidents and injuries appeared to increase during the early 1960s, and workplace-related accidents and injuries increased almost throughout the decade.

Wholly aside from objective changes in risk, cultural changes in the past two decades have increased our *intolerance of risk*, resulting in greater expectations of security from physical hazards, illness, environmental degradation, and even from being cheated in the marketplace.[16]

The possibility of "excess deaths" resulting from an industrial process or from hazards that traditionally were assumed to be "part of the job" was no longer socially acceptable. A growing counterculture, environmental and consumer-protection organizations, and public interest advocacy groups stressed the undesirable side effects of technological change and the allocation of goods and risks via markets. A ready market existed for such books as Rachel Carson's *The Silent Spring* and Ralph Nader's *Unsafe at Any Speed*. Television documentaries provided an even broader platform for environmentalists and consumer advocates. Oil spills and "Earth Day" demonstrations became part of the evening news.

Part of the reason for these higher standards perhaps lay in the economic and technological optimism bred by rising affluence. During the sustained growth and prosperity of the 1960s, there was a heady notion that basic economic problems had virtually been solved and that redistribution and "quality of life" were the prime social issues. A key assumption of the environmental and consumer movement was that business was financially and technologically capable of preventing the harms in question and that all that stood in the way was an insufficiently restrained profit motive. The costs of cleaning up the air, redesigning workplaces and products, and filing reports and compliance plans with the government were not regarded as especially onerous or problematic.

The reformist activism of the civil rights and anti-Vietnam war movements, which heightened awareness of and impatience with any instance of inequality, injustice, or harm caused by "the system," also played a role in the push for higher standards. Social problems became moral issues. If the poor were often cheated or confined to badly maintained housing, it was the result of "exploitation." Insensitive care for nursing home patients (whose rising numbers were due largely to more generous Medicare and Medicaid programs) was characterized as "a national disgrace" by Gray Panthers' leaflets. As in the civil rights movement, a vocabulary of "rights" was employed. Social harms were characterized as violations of moral rights, automatically to be converted into protectable legal rights. Citizens have a right to breathe clean air, it was said, just as they have a right to equal and nondiscriminatory treatment. Workers claimed a right to a safe workplace, consumers a right to the safest automobiles that can be made, hospital patients and students a right to see their charts and files. Many such specific "bills of rights" were written into law. To view social problems in terms of legal rights, moreover, implies the forceful and complete eradication of the causes because each act of pollution and each practice that creates a risk of violating a right then becomes an unqualified "wrong" requiring tougher regulation and enforcement.

Similarly, this emphasis on rights encouraged the shifting of responsibility for preventing harms from the individual to society and especially to business. Employers were responsible for redesigning workplaces and machines to make them safe even for workers who neglected to wear respirators or use safety devices. If drivers were too irresponsible to use seat belts, auto manufacturers should be compelled to make cars inoperable if belts were not hooked up or to develop and install automatic protective devices such as air bags—even if consumers did not demand them. If consumers—especially the poor and less-educated—made ill-advised purchases because of superficial product appeal or ignorance of good nutrition, advertisers should be made responsible not only for not practicing deception but also for education. The details of such socially responsible conduct, however, could not be left to business to define and follow; the very existence of the problems testified to business irresponsibility. The definition and enforcement of standards of responsibility had to be a government function.

In a media-oriented political system, these concerns were readily picked up by senators looking for issues with wide popular support and by the young lawyers on their staffs. For a legislator, sponsoring consumer, environmental, and worker protection statutes and antidiscrimination legislation were ways of being on the side of the angels without having to vote for higher taxes.[17] Regulatory measures added relatively little to the federal budget because the expense of providing the added protection was imposed primarily on the private sector. Until the late 1970s, sponsoring regulatory legislation was politically advantageous.

PROTECTIVE REGULATION—
PROSPECTS FOR CONTINUED GROWTH

In the last three or four years, the regulatory momentum has slowed, at least at the federal level, and indeed, it has been subjected to a powerful counterattack. In 1979 and 1980, inflation and interest rates exceeded 10 percent, and unemployment levels hovered at around 7 or 8 percent. "Too much government spending" and "too much government regulation" were often held to be the responsible villains. Officials of the Chrysler Corporation blamed government regulation for contributing to its financial distress and huge layoffs (and some academic economists agreed).[18] Congress was hard at work on legislation that would block recent Federal Trade Commission (FTC) initiatives and curtail OSHA's inspection powers, as well as on general procedural reform bills that would force regulatory agencies to attend to the economic consequences of new regulations. The administrator of the Environmental Protection Agency (EPA) repeatedly announced his agency's commitment to reasonableness.[19] Ronald Reagan campaigned successfully for the presidency on a platform that, among other things, called for much less government intervention generally and much less regulation specifically. Many other Republican candidates—and Democrats—did the same. Hardly a voice was raised during the 1980 campaign to defend the federal record on regulation. Upon taking office, President Reagan immediately announced the suspension of scores of regulations proposed (but not formally promulgated) by the outgoing administration.

Does this political counterattack signify that the movement toward more protective regulation has ended or that the problem of regulatory unreasonableness will become a historical relic? Probably not. The regulatory momentum may be slowed, but it will not stop. In 1979, when Congress was earnestly debating antiregulation measures, a compilation of "Major Regulatory Initiatives During 1979" recorded no less than 20 significant new federal measures that increased the stringency of various protective regulation programs.[20] And the striking thing about this array of new rules is that, on balance, they seem to address significant hazards or social problems (e.g., the use of carcinogens in consumer products, the licensing and design of nuclear power plants, the sale of "junk food" in schools, the control of hazardous wastes). Indeed, considering the publicity given these hazards, some rules seem late in coming. The lesson is that, notwithstanding justifiable concern about inflation, productivity, and foreign competition, an almost endless series of comparable regulations could be enacted in the future, as long as technological changes and humanitarian impulses continue to pervade the political process. Even in 1979, amid antiregulation publicity, a majority of the public approved of protective regulation policies in particular, and were willing to pay higher product prices, even at the same time that it voiced suspicion of "big government" in general.[21]

THE ROLE OF SPECIAL INTERESTS

Perhaps more important than the diffuse popular support for regulation are the various special interests that pressure politicians to provide more regulation. The most obvious special interests are the citizens who are able to identify themselves as likely recipients of more protection from new regulatory programs but who also believe that they will be able to escape the costs of furnishing it. The Oil, Chemical, and Atomic Workers Union, for example, whose members are exposed to higher health risks than the great majority of the work force, was a prime mover in the political struggle for the Occupational Safety and Health Act. Getting the government to mandate particular protective devices, from the union's point of view, is preferable to seeking such changes at the bargaining table, where the "price" might be smaller wages and fringe benefit increases.

Special beneficiary interests of this readily self-identifying sort are not too common in the politics of protective regulation, however. Ordinarily, the presumptive beneficiaries are thought to be numerous and undifferentiated, for example, consumers of (safer) therapeutic drugs or passengers in (safer) automobiles or inhalers of (more healthful) air. From the limited evidence available, however, it appears that the political as well as the economic demands for more protection against environmental, health, and safety risks are somewhat greater among the better educated and more prosperous.[22] This fact, if it is indeed a fact, would help to explain the growth of protective regulation in two ways. First, the demand for protective regulation increases simply as a function of the growth in the proportion of the population that is better educated and more affluent. Second, this constituency tends to have somewhat disproportionate political influence. The relatively affluent and well educated participate more in politics than do other citizens, and they can provide more money and a greater sense of efficacy and organizational skill. They provide financial support, staff, and legal assistance for consumer protection, environmental, and other public interest groups that monitor existing regulatory programs and that lobby or litigate for tougher rules.

The leading edge of this constituency is a particular subgroup, whom Irving Kristol and others have called the "new class." Although much has been written about this phenomenon, there is still great ambiguity about what this "class" is and even about whether or not it exists. Kristol's account lacks precision, but its basic thrust is clear.

> This "new class" consists of a goodly proportion of those college-educated people whose skills and vocations proliferate in a "post-industrial society" . . . scientists, teachers and educational administrators, journalists and others in the communications industries, psychologists, social workers, those lawyers and doctors who make their careers in the expanding public sector, city planners, the staffs of the larger foundations, the upper levels of the government bureaucracy, and so on.[23]

Many members of this group, according to Kristol, are the intellectual descendants of an intelligentsia in Western society that has long been hostile to the institutions and culture of capitalism. Protective regulation, the argument goes, is a weapon in the emerging conflict over status and political power between the old business class and the new antibusiness and progovernment class.[24]

Explanations of American politics that rely heavily on the idea of "class" have never been very satisfactory. And many government officials and professionals in the new groups Kristol catalogs—not to mention economists and graduates of schools of business administration who are found in government in increasing numbers—have little antibusiness and antimarket animus and are cautious in endorsing more government regulation. But that is not an argument against the existence and importance of a recently emergent class of well-educated people, employed in the public and nonprofit sectors, who subordinate "economic" to "humanitarian" values and almost automatically think of direct and stringent governmental regulation as the appropriate way to control social harms. These "new-class" values are frequently encountered when speaking to regulatory officials and public interest advocates. It is reflected in the remark of a senior staff member of a Senate environmental committee who, when told by industry representatives that certain planned emission regulations would make it economically infeasible to build any new aluminum smelters in the United States, responded in all seriousness, "Then maybe there shouldn't *be* any more aluminum smelters in this country."[25] It is reflected in the moralistic response of Joan Claybrook, director of the National Highway Traffic Safety Administration, when certain NHTSA standards were criticized as adding somewhat more safety than most consumers would be willing to pay for: "Producers who know how to make a product safer have an obligation to do so," and, she noted, her critic "passes over the fact that sanctity of life has the highest value in our society."[26] The extent and depth of this sensibility could be debated without reaching a firm conclusion, but it is probable that adherents of these views will continue to be quite well represented in regulatory and legislative bodies and staffs, in the news media, and in the public interest law firms and interest groups that advocate new regulatory solutions.

Antibusiness social groups are often joined in pushing for more protective regulation by distinctly "probusiness" groups and, in fact, by businesses. Regulation usually affects competitors unevenly, imposing relatively higher costs on some than on others and creating advantages for low-compliance-cost firms.[27] It also creates markets for suppliers of whatever is needed to comply with the regulations. The businesses and labor unions that stand to gain such advantages, along with politicians in whose districts those favored businesses are located, often push for tougher rules. For example:

> An engineer in a firm that manufactures intravenous solutions told us that firms (including his own) in that highly regulated industry invest in research to develop increasingly sophisticated sterilization equipment and sanitation techniques with higher margins of safety. Then they try to get those higher standards incorporated in FDA regulations; their competitors then will have to license the new techniques from the innovator or perhaps suffer a decline in market share until they develop an equivalent device.*
>
> A Small Business Administration study records the lament of a small manufacturer of recreational boats whose products were characterized in the trade as of very high quality. The federal government had sought to require installation of "fireproof" electrical systems. According to the study, "He indicated that the committee formed by the Coast Guard to . . . draft standards . . . was made up, in large part, of technical people from the electrical equipment industry . . . obviously interested in the inclusion of electrical com-

---

*One result is that entry costs for potential new producers are virtually prohibitive, and ostensibly simple products, such as 5 percent sugar solutions (in distilled water), carry list prices of more than $10 a bottle.

ponents. . . . The standard developed called for junction boxes, large size conductors, extensive grounding and shielding . . . amounting [in the owner's view] to a 'ridiculous' extreme."[28]

Furthermore, *disadvantaged* businesses will counterattack, pushing for even more "equalizing" regulation: under the 1970 Clean Air Act, EPA regulations establishing maximum levels of sulfur dioxide emissions provided an advantage to producers of western low sulfur coal (which utilities could burn without expensive scrubbers) compared to producers of eastern high sulfur coal. In response, eastern coal producers and the United Mine Workers Union teamed up with environmentalists to obtain amendments in the 1977 Clean Air Act that required the best "emission reduction" technology in all power plants, a provision that, as Peter Navarro describes it, forced "the use of scrubbers on *all* coal, *regardless of its sulphur content.*" This provision largely eliminated the cost advantage of using western coal and vastly increased the cost of achieving sulfate reductions in the air.[29]

Regulators, too, create a demand for increased protective regulation. Their motives are always complex, of course, and the importance of their desires to promote "the public interest" when they propose new and farther reaching regulations cannot be denied. But an expanded domain of regulatory responsibilities also implies, in many cases, greater prestige and satisfaction for those who seek careers in that domain. It used to be said that regulatory officials did their work in government with an eye to the prospects for subsequent employment in the industry they regulated. Whatever truth this proposition had or, indeed, has (notwithstanding the current statutory prohibitions on working for the regulated industry for one year after leaving one's regulatory duties), it is now true that government itself is a field of rich career opportunities for aggressive regulatory officials.[30] There is nothing necessarily undesirable about such career paths or about the ambition that leads one to traverse them successfully. Such ambitions, however, do become a fertile source of ideas for new regulations and enforcement practices.

THE LOGIC OF REGULATORY EXPANSION

The natural tendency to follow things to their logical conclusion may be as powerful an engine of regulatory expansion as the activities of interest groups. When legislatures establish ambitious regulatory goals or rights to protection, even aggressive regulators armed with specific rules and strong sanctions will not achieve them. The rules will have loopholes, and even perfect compliance will fail to contain some elusive dangers. To regulators assigned to realize the statutory goals, therefore, and to citizen advocates who seek to vindicate statutory rights, it seems entirely logical to devise new rules in order to plug the loopholes and to bring newly discovered dangers into the ambit of the regulations. And to policymakers who have endorsed the original goals and rights, it seems a departure from logic to oppose such new rules.

The logic of meeting original goals, with its progression toward more costly, detailed, and intrusive forms of regulation, is manifested clearly in pollution control regulation. A California regional air pollution control official told us:

> We are given an air space to control, but we have little control over all the many causes of pollution. We have a little control over industry. The standards and responsibilities are given to us, and we have no choice but to continue tightening and extending our requirements until those goals are met.

Thus in recent years, after forcing industry to adopt many of the best current control technologies for major new point sources, state and regional agencies in California have promulgated new regulations concerning emissions from petroleum tankers and gasoline delivery trucks during loading and unloading operations, concerning fugitive emissions from valves and pipe joints in refineries and from gaps at the edges of the floating tops on gas storage tanks, and concerning the maintenance of pollution control equipment. Similarly, when it became apparent that ambitious air quality standards could not be met in many regions by controlling industry and new cars, the EPA moved to impose on localities land-use plans designed to channel industry and traffic away from high-pollution areas; it also tried to impose "transportation control plans" to reduce vehicle-miles driven and to require states to enact mandatory inspection plans for all motor vehicle operators.*

The logic of expansion applies to other regulatory spheres as well. The California State Energy Conservation and Resource Development Com-

---

*The EPA was required by the Clean Air Act to impose some of these general requirements, but it retained some discretion over the program design.

mission specified maximum sizes for massage shower heads on the grounds that these devices, if not controlled, encourage people to take longer showers, using more water and more energy to heat the water. Noting that consumers can be deceived even if advertisers comply with its rules prohibiting unsubstantiated verbal claims, the FTC began work on regulations that would ban misleading pictures in advertisements or television commercials. Once the principles of nondiscriminatory treatment and affirmative action were established for blacks, it seemed logical to extend similar rights to members of other groups that had been discriminated against (even if not so pervasively) and to draw upon the whole armamentarium of enforcement procedures developed to fight racial discrimination, such as affirmative action plans, requirements that hiring and promotion criteria be written and "validated," class action suits, and threats to withhold federal funds and contracts. Thus through court order or legislation, affirmative action or antidiscrimination rules have been extended progressively to Mexican-Americans, Puerto Ricans, American Indians, Spanish-surnamed persons, Asian-Americans, women, physically and mentally handicapped persons, aliens, illegitimate children, and workers over the age of 40. Mandatory bilingual education (including requirements for annual plans, tests, and progress reports) for non-English-speaking students was expanded to include "limited English-speaking students" (those whose primary language at home is not English) and, by some court decisions, to require instruction in "black English" for ghetto black children.[31]

Deductive logic also suggests—and makes it very difficult to resist—the elaboration of regulations establishing new enforcement techniques and related compliance obligations. Since there are always some regulated enterprises that evade control by devious means, virtually all regulatory officials call for stronger enforcement powers, such as regulations requiring more complete record keeping and reporting by regulated enterprises, more checks on the veracity of those records, more permits or tests before new products or processes can be introduced. There is also the logic of available leverage, which holds that since the public interest requires compliance with duly promulgated regulations, all available techniques of ensuring compliance should be employed, including whatever leverage can be exerted by other governmental units. Thus, to ensure that manufacturers do not provide the EPA with inflated estimates of compliance costs, the Securities and Exchange Commission (SEC) is urged to enact rules requiring firms to make full disclosure to investors of present and projected expenditures on environmental controls, thereby adding SEC enforcement officials and all their sanctions to the environmental control effort.[32]* The federal government's financial leverage over contractors and grant-in-aid recipients has made it a source of additional regulations in various enforcement efforts. To retain eligibility, federal contractors must comply with union wage scales, implement affirmative action plans, grant subcontracts to minority-owned construction firms, and, for a while, respect President Carter's "voluntary" wage-price guidelines. Universities that receive federal grants or contracts or that enroll students receiving federal assistance must comply with affirmative action requirements in the hiring of faculty and in the provision of athletic facilities, observe procedures to protect human subjects in research projects, and undertake extensive renovations to accommodate the physically handicapped, all under pain of losing federal subventions.[33] Regardless of the justification for these additional sanctions and enforcement techniques, the second enforcement body such as the SEC, the federal Office of Contract Compliance Programs, or the Medicare administration, must develop its own specific guidelines, supplementing those of the "primary" or "direct" enforcement agency (such as the Equal Employment Opportunity Commission and its state equivalents, or state nursing home agencies).

THE OCCASIONS FOR REGULATORY EXPANSION

The growth of regulation is not merely a product of the steady and relentless forces of logic and political and economic interests. Regulatory victories, as well as initiatives, are products of intermittent events or "occasions" that fire the political imagination and overwhelm the normal defenses of antiregulatory interests. Most prominent are physical catastrophes; scandals that expose presumptive laxity, corruption, or incompetency in the regulatory agency; dramatic scientific discoveries; flareups of racial or intercommunal violence; and changes in administration, at least when Democrats take over from Republicans. For example, although Jimmy Carter campaigned in 1976 on a platform calling for a more efficient and a more streamlined government without "red tape," he also promised to advance consumer and environmental protection.

---

*The assumption, of course, is that firms will not want to give investors inflated estimates of compliance costs, suggesting diminished future profits.

Among his appointments to high regulatory posts were a number of proregulation advocates, including former associates of Ralph Nader, under whose aegis the reach of regulation indeed increased.

Catastrophes are probably the most important catalysts of new regulation. In some cases, these events break stalemates: the Food, Drug, and Cosmetic Act (1938), requiring premarket testing of new prescription drugs, languished in Congress until revelations that over 100 people had died from ingesting sulfanilamide—a preparation that sought to make promising sulfa drugs available in liquid form but used an untested solvent that turned out to be toxic.[34] In other cases, catastrophes furnish an opportunity for a political entrepreneur to set new forces in motion. At a workshop on regulatory law enforcement, an official in a state fire marshal's office acknowledged that his agency has sometimes intentionally waited until after a particularly dramatic fire to petition the state legislature to enact new fire code requirements or to grant the agency more funds and greater powers. In still other cases, catastrophes are the occasion for a look at problems already long overdue for evaluation. The explosion of California's Sylmar Tunnel in 1971, killing 17 construction workers, led to a highly publicized legislative investigation of the Division of Industrial Safety, revealing that inspectors had failed to close down the site despite having found violations of safety regulations; most of the agency's top officials resigned, and the legislature mandated automatic enforcement actions. In any case, such dramatic and often emotion-laden events create a more receptive climate for increased regulation and weaken the defenses, however worthy or unworthy they might be, of those who would oppose increased regulation. If an existing regulatory agency is already on the job, the catastrophic event may signify presumptive incompetence or laxity on the agency's part, and the agency too becomes a force for expansion in order to demonstrate its commitment to its assigned mission.

Newspapers and television news strengthen the link between catastrophe and regulation, partly because prominent coverage of regulatory issues tends to focus so heavily on accidents[35] and to imply that they may be the product of lax regulation. In the aftermath of a catastrophe, long discourses from the representatives of the regulated enterprise about the costs or the difficulties of compliance, the nonrepresentative character of the event, or the redundancy of proposed new restrictions are not treated as "news." "It takes two breaths to explain a trade-off," one observer has noted, and "television allows only one."[36] The newspapers, too, are more likely to emphasize the demand for stricter requirements and to echo the assertion that "cost cannot be a factor in safety."[37] Television reports and documentaries often undercut the arguments of regulated enterprises by giving the last word (and more time) to "experts" advocating stricter regulatory controls[38] or to emotionally distraught statements by grieving relatives of accident victims.

The public investigation following a catastrophe usually reflects the media treatment of regulatory problems, in part because such investigations themselves are, to a certain extent, media events. Before the headlines describing the accident have faded, congressmen or state legislators call for a probe of the "responsible" regulatory agency and sometimes for a cleaning of the regulatory house.* The ensuing legislative hearings typically involve a search for the point of regulatory "softness" as well as the underlying technical or managerial problem in the industry in question. Some weeks after a DC-10 airplane crashed in Chicago in May 1979, killing 250 passengers and crew, Federal Aviation Administration (FAA) officials testified before a congressional investigative committee. At the time, their leading theory of the cause was that the pylon attaching the engine to the plane's wing had been damaged in the course of the airline's maintenance procedures, which differed from those recommended by McDonnell-Douglas, the manufacturer. Congressmen, and the newspapers reporting the story, focused critically on the airline's alteration of maintenance procedures without informing the FAA (even though McDonnell-Douglas representatives were notified and had observed the change without any objection). FAA regulations require that the agency be notified of "major" changes in maintenance procedures, but the airline had not defined this change as "major." A congressman asked the FAA administrator, "Then the *airlines* determine whether it is major or minor?" Predictably, the FAA administrator responded, "Our system did not pick it up. I want to assure you that we will cure that difficulty."[39] And indeed, it appears that a large number of new reporting, monitoring, and prior approval regulations did stem from this colloquy.[40]

Contemporary legislatures, especially in periods when regulation has come under suspicion, may not react as impetuously as the nineteenth century Massachusetts legislature that heard about a train falling into a draw and immediately passed a law requiring all trains to make a full stop

---

*After the Three Mile Island nuclear power plant accident, a presidential commission called for the transfer of safety inspection from the NRC to a new single-headed executive agency. The president responded, inter alia, by demoting the chairman of the commission.

before entering onto any drawbridge.[41] Yet it is hard to imagine law-makers completely resisting demands for corrective legislation or failing to call upon the agency to issue new regulations when they hear that infants have sickened from a carelessly made formula, that railroad cars have ruptured and spewed toxic chemicals over a town, or that fatal fires have broken out in supposedly fireproof systems. Such accidents or revelations are frequent and will continue to occur in a technologically complex society, despite strict regulatory regimes. As a result, there will continue to be scores of occasions each year that "demand" new regulation.

THE SIGNIFICANCE OF REGULATORY UNREASONABLENESS

Both the "public interest" and numerous private interests create a demand for protective regulation; the logic of "filling in gaps" and using all available leverage creates still more; and the underlying strengths of proregulation constituencies or the momentary weaknesses of antiregulation constituencies occasionally translate into concrete victories. But if regulation per se increases, does this necessarily imply that *unreasonable* regulation also increases? More precisely, does it imply that *site-level* unreasonableness also increases?

We believe it does. First, virtually all regulations, even such a sensible one as requiring eating places to have two exits because of the risk of fire, are inevitably overinclusive, imposing additional costs to provide few benefits in some proportion of the many sites to which those regulations apply. Second, the experience of the past decade provides little basis for expecting regulatory officials to systematically revise or "bend" the regulations, thereby alleviating much site-level unreasonableness; the institutional forces and constraints that shape regulatory conduct operate as powerful deterrents to the needed flexibility. Site-level unreasonableness arises from an inescapable tension between the virtues of equal treatment and accountability required of government officials and the opposite virtues of diversity and spontaneity that are the essence of our social and economic life.

But even if site-level unreasonableness is a common phenomenon, now or in the future, is it a truly important social problem? Or should it be regarded merely as a necessary cost that society must pay for progress in dealing with more fundamental problems, such as environmental degradation, workplace and product-related deaths and injuries, and the various injustices that occur in an unregulated marketplace? Does the annoyance stimulated by specific incidents of overregulation have any more social significance than the complaints of spoiled children who face strict discipline for the first time? Again, we believe it does.

First, as suggested earlier, much of the political backlash against regulation arises from the cumulation of individual experiences of site-level unreasonableness. Emotional reactions to regulatory unreasonableness undermine the implementation of necessary and reasonable rules, as well as block or delay the enactment of needed new requirements. Second, the cumulation of instances of site-level unreasonableness entails considerable social and economic costs that are borne by society. The scope and amount of these costs are reflected in the many scholarly studies that show aggregate costs of complying with particular protective regulations to exceed aggregate benefits.

Consider first some of the very large cost figures that turn up in these studies. The U.S. Council on Environmental Quality, for example, estimated that regulation-imposed costs in 1978 for water and air pollution control totaled $26.8 billion.[42] Direct compliance costs for meeting OSHA standards were about $3 billion in 1978. Federal safety and pollution control regulations contributed a cost increment of $500 to an average 1976 automobile; this figure multiplied by the 6.7 million cars sold in 1975 comes to $3.35 billion.[43] In some industries, such as iron and steel foundries, compliance with pollution control and OSHA regulations accounted for more than 30 percent of all capital investment in the mid-1970s.[44] Some costs, moreover—such as losses in productive efficiency; the diversion of capital that would otherwise have been allocated to productivity-enhancing investments; and the diversion of managers' and engineers' time into planning, negotiating, and monitoring regulatory compliance measures—do not always show up in studies of direct compliance costs, although such indirect costs can be quite substantial. For example, the Department of Labor's "Inflationary Impact Statement" on its proposed coke oven emission standards estimated that, as a result of mandated changes in work practices, coke production per worker might decline by as much as 29 percent.[45] A Commerce Department study indicated that compliance with environmental, health, and safety regulations would cost U.S. copper producers $3.5 billion between 1978 and 1987 (including $1.69 billion just to operate and maintain antipollution equipment), resulting in slightly lower production, fewer jobs, increased copper imports, and a substantial increase in price.[46]

Proregulation forces have responded with determined efforts to tally the economic benefits of regulation and to rebut the implication of unreasonableness produced by a focus on costs alone. In addition, some critics of the cost-benefit approach argue that industry estimates of compliance costs are inflated—which has in fact been true of some cost projections before a regulation was promulgated[47] and probably has been true of certain retrospective cost estimates, partly because the appropriate methodology is far from simple and far from settled.[48] Other critics correctly point out that cost-benefit analyses often fail to take distributional considerations into account; even if a regulation produces excess costs in the aggregate, it might be justified if it alleviates harms concentrated in a discrete disadvantaged group (such as cotton-mill workers, physically handicapped students, or poor and uneducated consumers) and if the costs are spread across a reasonably well-off majority. In addition, some critics denounce on moral grounds the very concept of weighing human lives "saved" by regulation against the associated economic costs or losses in productivity.[49]

Despite these technical and normative difficulties, and despite the failings of particular studies, serious attention should be paid to the costs and consequences of regulation. The *idea* of cost-benefit analysis is inescapably correct. To make automobiles completely safe obviously would make them too energy-inefficient, too slow, and too expensive. It would entail equally cumbersome, expensive, and essentially intolerable restrictions to eliminate all environmental contamination, all industrial accidents, all risks of mistreating nursing home patients. Money spent on prevention is not available for education, welfare, housing, recreation, or investment in productivity-enhancing plants and equipment. Thus, since a totally risk-free society is not feasible, some lines must be drawn at lower levels of protection. One need not accept the idea of quantifying every cost or benefit, or abandon concern for human life and equality, to accept the idea that regulations are reasonable only if the results are worth more than the social benefits that would have accrued if the same resources had been invested elsewhere. And certainly, it is important to ask whether a given social goal could be achieved in a less costly manner than proposed by a particular set of regulations.

By those standards, studies of many regulatory schemes, even when read with skepticism, suggest strongly that "the unreasonableness problem" is real and economically significant. Studies of the Occupational Safety and Health Act and its administration indicate that, despite major increases in expenditures for enforcement and safety devices, the program has had either no positive effect or a very small one on workplace accident rates.[50] By 1985, water pollution control regulations will cost about $18-19 billion per year (including annual operating costs plus depreciation and interest on capital), but the best "point estimate" (as opposed to a range) of benefits is only $12.3 billion.[51] Regulations compelling U.S. auto manufacturers to reduce exhaust emissions very rapidly caused them, in effect, to adopt catalytic converters, a comparatively inefficient technology that creates substantial maintenance problems and increases fuel consumption.[52] On several occasions, President Ford's Council on Wage and Price Stability and President Carter's Regulatory Analysis Review Group have pointed out that major proposed regulations—such as strip-mining controls and OSHA rules requiring employers to completely eliminate harmful chemical emissions—would entail massive costs with only slight incremental benefits as compared with far less costly alternatives (such as requiring employers to provide workers with personal protective equipment).[53]

These showings of economic inefficiency in the aggregate necessarily imply the prevalence of unreasonableness in specific situations, and the larger the problem reflected in the aggregate statistics, the stronger the presumption that large numbers of particular sites are contributing to the aggregate measure.

In addition to the economic costs of regulatory unreasonableness, there are other, less tangible, costs. An instance of regulatory unreasonableness can also be experienced as an instance of government-imposed injustice. Each injustice weakens the belief that we live under a system of fair and rational laws. For each "victim" of regulatory unreasonableness—including local politicians, public servants, health care professionals, and educators, as well as businessmen and corporate engineers—the experience of regulatory injustice is exasperating, infuriating, or, even worse, demoralizing.[54] The burden of unreasonable regulation falls most directly on such people, whose daily duties involve them deeply in taking responsibility for the welfare of others. It is this "trusteeship stratum" in the society whose prerogatives have been curtailed and whose discretion has been limited by the protective regulation movement. If regulation helps them do their jobs in ways that make sense to them, they might well support it. Indeed, there are many expressions of just such enthusiasm. If, on the other hand, regulation, as applied at the site-level, treats this "trusteeship stratum" as unreasonable and unjust and unresponsive, the result can be alienation from government and all its works. Furthermore, if the tension between the government stewards of the values cherished by protective regulation and the private trustees of these same values persists long enough, another result can be the erosion of self-confidence and morale on the part of the private trusteeship stratum itself.

Whether this will in fact occur depends, no doubt, on the long-run balance of power between the public and the private sectors. Admittedly, all these possibilities are merely speculative. Protective regulation in its contemporary form is still too new to predict with much confidence its likely long-run effects. Yet it is mainly because we need to catch a glimpse of the more distant future of public and private morals that we embark on an exploration of the institutional processes that led to the present regulatory unreasonableness.

CHAPTER TWO

TOWARD TOUGHNESS: THE

CHANGING LEGAL STRUCTURE

OF ENFORCEMENT

•

*A man goes to buy a mule from a farmer. The farmer says that with
a little tender loving care the mule will work like hell. In a few days,
the man comes back and says he's nice to the mule, but he won't do
a damn thing. The farmer hitches the mule to a plow and whacks
him on the head with a two-by-four. The mule pulls the plow.
"What about the tender loving care?" the buyer asks. "That's important," the farmer says, "but first you've got to get his attention."*
—Story told by OSHA inspectors

A regulatory inspector is a law enforcement official. When he tells the
stern-visaged guard at the factory security gate that he wants to inspect
the firm's maintenance records for air pollution control equipment, the
inspector draws courage (or even a self-righteous officiousness) from the
fact that he is empowered by law to do so. When he walks through a
refinery, a nursing home, or a cannery and encounters a profusion of
potentially hazardous procedures and machines, the inspector looks to
his book of regulations for general guidance and for specific safety
criteria. In conversation with the managers of the regulated enterprise,
the information an inspector can confidently demand, the excuses he feels
authorized to recognize, the sanctions he can credibly threaten to invoke
are closely related to the specific provisions of "the regs."

Of course, there is room for varying interpretations of the rules in some
cases. Different inspectors may see different things and evaluate the
relative seriousness of a particular offense in different ways. But a major

preoccupation of most enforcement agencies is to reduce the variations by developing common interpretations of the rules and a unified philosophy of enforcement. To regulatory officials, therefore, the law matters. They constantly refer to specific provisions in the statutes they administer, the legal powers the statutes grant, and the goals those statutes seek.

In a workshop that we convened in 1978, many enforcement officials referred to a shift in the nature of the laws they administered. Statutes and court decisions in the last decade, they said, enhanced their legal powers. At the same time, however, they lost discretion; now they must conduct inspections more with an eye toward what is legally proper. Much to the amusement of industry representatives at the workshop, the regulators complained of being closely regulated, of being compelled to "go by the book."

The purpose of these changes has been to make regulatory enforcement tougher—more aggressive, more uniform, and more of a deterrent to undesirable conduct on the part of regulated enterprises.* But by constraining regulatory discretion, these legal changes also lay the premises for the problem of site-level unreasonableness.

THE TRADITIONAL LEGAL STRUCTURE OF ENFORCEMENT

In most law enforcement, the government investigator responds to a complaint about a past event—a burglary, a fraud, a discriminatory firing. He tries to resolve conflicting versions of what happened, gather evidence, or find a suspect who has disappeared. Enforcement of protective regulation by inspectors is different. Inspectors sometimes respond to complaints, but they usually come on their own initiative to enterprises that have not been accused of any wrongdoing. They search for *ongoing* violations, things that might go wrong in the future, and they check that

---

*The changes in the legal structure of regulatory enforcement that we will describe have not been universal. There are literally hundreds of inspectorates, each concerned with a distinct array of processes and legal powers. Generalizations do not fall easily into place: legislatures enact regulatory programs one at a time and partially in response to specific political demands and technical enforcement problems. Some older agencies have remained largely immune to change, and all newer agencies are not created alike, so that it is easy to find examples that go against the trend toward the tougher enforcement that we describe. In addition, changes in the legal structure of regulatory agencies do not wholly determine how enforcement officials actually behave; they are only indicative.

certain precautions are being taken. Unlike policemen, who ordinarily patrol public places, inspectors regularly enter private buildings, pore over corporate records, and take product samples. To use the terminology of the Fourth Amendment, inspectors are regularly engaged in searches and seizures, often without "probable cause."[1] In addition, inspectors in some agencies are granted summary powers to impose severe restrictions. Beginning in the nineteenth century, inspectors who discovered serious regulatory violations (or what they believed to be serious violations) could stop loaded ships from leaving port; order locomotives out of service; prevent occupancy of buildings; and quarantine or destroy diseased livestock, fruit trees, or food products. Today, inspectors can order a plane or pilot to stay on the ground, ban rail shipment of hazardous chemicals over poorly maintained sections of track, or "yellow tag" a dangerous machine on the spot, enjoining further operation.

These extensive powers of intrusion and control raise the possibility of misuse. A trigger-happy inspector could embargo food that is not in fact adulterated, generating adverse publicity about the firm in question. An overzealous enforcement officer might issue orders much broader than necessary, disrupting useful economic activity.[2] A malicious inspector, annoyed at not being treated with the deference he feels he deserves, can deliberately harass an enterprise operating within the law. A venal inspector could steal trade secrets, extort bribes, engage in blackmail, or favor one firm while imposing heavier regulatory burdens on its competitors.

Under the theory of the state that has reigned since the founding of the republic, the possibility of government abuse of coercive and intrusive powers must be checked. The inspectors themselves must be subjected to law. The enforcement process, in consequence, traditionally has been pervaded by a complex of legal rules and principles, which in turn have influenced actual enforcement practices.

The most salient legal rules are those that constrain coercive enforcement against allegedly serious violators—attempts by the agency to compel them to take certain remedial measures or to punish them for noncompliance. The basic legal model is the criminal justice system and its familiar principles of due process—the presumption of innocence, punishment only for proven and specific violations, separation of prosecutorial and adjudicatory powers, and adversarial hearings. Most agencies, accordingly, have been granted no formal remedial or sanctioning powers themselves, except for certain emergency situations. Inspectors can issue citations for violations of the law, but if the enterprise refuses to comply, the traditionally structured agency cannot levy fines or order the establishment to shut down; its only legal recourse is court action or the threat of such action. The agency petitions a *judge* to impose the penalty prescribed by law, be it an injunction, a fine, or a suspended license, and to "win," an agency must meet demanding standards of proof and legal certainty required by the judiciary. In other words, before an enterprise must accede to a regulatory order or penalty, it has a right to insist on a formal hearing before a judge—an official who is separate from the regulatory agency and therefore likely to be more committed to standards of formal legality and due process for the accused than to the particular agency's mission.

The legality of the agency's case, moreover, typically is examined a number of times before the case actually is presented in court. An agency seeking to punish a recalcitrant violator must persuade the public prosecutor assigned to do its trial work—the county district attorney, the state attorney general, or the U.S. attorney—to act. To convince the prosecutor that it has a valid legal case, the agency must have documented evidence of a violation of an applicable statute or regulation and a witness (usually an inspector) whose testimony will withstand cross-examination. This insistence on a case that will stand up in court usually extends back into the standard operating procedures of the agency. Inspection often is organizationally separated from prosecution. Even if an inspector is convinced that a violation exists and an enforcement action is necessary, *he* cannot initiate prosecution. He must first convince his superior or the district chief of enforcement, who must then turn the matter over to the agency's legal staff, who then determines whether or not the case is legally sound before forwarding it to the public prosecutor.

In certain emergency situations, as noted earlier, some statutes give regulatory officials authority to impose immediate penalties or orders on their own, without going to court and even without a prior administrative hearing. But what if the inspector mistakenly embargoes food that is not in fact adulterated or issues a "shut-down" order much broader than seems reasonably necessary? The regulated enterprise can refuse to abide by the order and raise the defense when prosecuted in court for that refusal—but it is a rare enterprise that has the confidence to do so. Or the enterprise may later bring a civil action for damages against the inspector or the agency, although chances of recovery are very slim because of the judicial doctrines of sovereign and official immunity.[3] Therefore, most agencies, pursuant to statutory requirements or their own regulations, provide internal safeguards. The front-line inspector must receive authorization from at least one tier of superiors before taking summary action.[4] Often the regulated enterprise is given notice of the agency's intention to take immediate action and the opportunity to call and confer with agency officials. Thus even in an alleged emergency, the agency, in keeping with due process—and to maintain the confidence of the legislature, which grants (and retracts) enforcement powers*—generally provides its own internal checks and balances.

This array of due process mechanisms in both normal and emergency enforcement makes its weight felt at the front-line level—an inspector knows that his request for enforcement action will pass through legal reviews inside the agency, even before action is taken, and *might* involve review by a hearing officer or court. Few inspectors and enforcement officials take this possibility of review lightly; most treat legal rejection as embarrassing, a mark of their lack of professionalism.

THE DILEMMA OF RULES AND DISCRETION

While regulatory legal structures traditionally have been strongly committed to the procedural rules and multiple reviews of the due process ideal, they reflect a certain ambivalence about how closely enforcement practices should be "programmed" by substantive rules. From a legalistic perspective, all regulatory requirements and penalties should be prescribed in detail; all regulations and penalties should be applied uniformly. The contrasting view values official discretion. No system of detailed regulations, it would be argued, can adequately capture the diversity of experience; fixed rules and noncompliance penalties will sometimes be too lax, sometimes too strict. Thus enforcement officials must be given broadly worded grants of discretion that will allow them to order regulated enterprises to do whatever seems necessary and prudent under the particular circumstances, as well as discretion to relax the rules and tailor their enforcement procedures to the situation. From the legal viewpoint, however, such discretion invites chaos: without specific rules,

---

*At our 1978 workshop on regulatory enforcement, a nursing home regulator, referring to emergency powers, stated, "You've got to have some cool heads. All it takes is one bad move and you can lose that law."

regularly enforced, the deterrent effect of the law will erode, resulting in unpredictability, unequal treatment, a high risk of corruption, and ultimately serious harm to unprotected citizens; the rule of law, whatever its defects, is preferable to the discretionary rule of imperfect officials.

The dilemma of rule versus discretion is an ancient one, of course, pervading many areas of law and administration. In the area of regulation, lawmakers and agencies have tried to cope with the dilemma in different ways. Legislatures often have qualified strict-sounding statutory standards by adding such terms as "to the extent feasible,"[5] or they have proscribed activities or substances "presenting an unreasonable risk of injury."[6] The open-ended character of words like "feasible" and "unreasonable" permits enforcement officials a degree of flexibility.

However, regulatory programs involving continuous enforcement of health- and safety-oriented laws through field inspections are subject to especially strong pressures to substitute precisely worded technical regulations for "flexible" statutory terms. Builders and manufacturers want construction, sanitation, and product safety requirements to be carefully specified in advance so that they can be incorporated into blueprints. Precise rules, the businesses hope, will limit their exposure to unpredictable and expensive post hoc changes demanded by zealous individual inspectors. Specific rules, uniformly enforced, also provide businessmen some assurance that they will be regulated no more stringently than their competitors. Advocates of stringent regulation, too, demand more specific regulations. Precise rules close off "loopholes," facilitate the advocate's ability to expose underenforcement by the agency, and make it easier for workers and consumers to assert their rights to protection.

For enforcement officials, rules that specify standards in objective, numerical terms facilitate proof of violations. It is easier to gather evidence and convince a judge that a nursing home has failed to maintain a specified numerical staff-patient ratio, for example, than it is to show that it has failed to provide "adequate staffing to maintain a decent standard of care." For the same reason, precise regulations make enforcement faster and more efficient: decisions can be made mechanically, more inspections can be performed each week, and the inspectorate can be staffed by relatively low-paid operatives rather than by highly trained engineers. Moreover, because direct supervision of a far-flung field inspectorate is inherently difficult, the more specific the rules and the more strictly inspectors are "programmed" to stick to the rules, the better the agency's chances of preventing piecemeal erosion of official policy by inspectors who are too easily influenced by the arguments of regulated enterprises. Rules also bolster the agency's reputation for fairness. Making decisions in accordance with specific rules, enforcement officials say, helps rebut charges that the agency is biased and helps repel attempts by politicians to reverse enforcement decisions on behalf of irate businessmen-constituents.

Inspectors themselves often call for more specific regulations. When a quality control or safety engineer in a factory contends that a deviation from standard procedure "really isn't dangerous" under the circumstances, it is hard for the inspector to assess the true level of risk. It is comforting to have an authoritative rule, a determination by someone "higher up" in the system, to resolve the question. Finally, from the inspector's point of view, specific rules give an air of neutrality and legitimacy to his actions. When a housing inspector knows there is a housing code provision that specifically requires landlords to keep all windows in working order (even if the tenant broke them), he can tell a landlord to repair a window and say, "This is not just *my* say-so. Moreover, I'm not just picking on *you*. It's the *law*." In this respect, inspectors *want* to be programmed.

Consequently, many inspection-type agencies do attempt to give ever greater precision to their regulations, continually elaborating and re-specifying them to plug newly discovered loopholes and to adapt them to new production processes and emerging risks. The San Francisco Bay Area Air Pollution Control District's basic substantive regulations, three pages long scarcely more than a decade ago, now extend over 87 single-spaced pages. The Motor Carrier Safety regulations issued by the U.S. Department of Transportation, setting forth operating and maintenance (not design) standards for trucks, maximum hours of service for drivers, rules for transporting hazardous materials, and so on, fill a handbook of over 400 pages. U.S. Department of Agriculture (USDA) regulations specify the kinds of facilities, machines, and sanitation procedures that meatpackers must use, including such details as the composition of the salt solutions used to dress carcasses; a single section in the "Manual of Meat Inspection," governing routine postmortem inspection of beef carcasses, contains 15 single-spaced pages of instructions for the inspector.

But the drive for such detailed rules, of course, raises the specter of excessive rigidity. Concerning the meat-inspection regulations, Peter Schuck observes: "It is a commonplace in the industry, denied only by official USDA spokesmen, that if all meat-inspection regulations were enforced to the letter, no meat processor in America would be open for business."[7] The needed flexibility, in such agencies, traditionally is attained by not enforcing the rules literally. In the USDA, says Schuck:

> The inspector is not expected to enforce strictly every rule, *but rather to decide which rules are worth enforcing at all.* In this process, USDA offers no official guidance, for it feels obliged, like all public agencies, to maintain the myth that all rules are rigidly enforced. Unofficially, the inspector is admonished by his USDA superiors to "use common sense," to do his job in a "reasonable" way.[8]

Many legal institutions, like the USDA, cope with the rule/discretion dilemma through a combination of specific official rules and unofficial selective enforcement. In the criminal process, for example, police officers are allowed, tacitly if not officially, to overlook some violations of the law and to let the offenders go with a warning. Federal prosecuting attorneys often do not prosecute violators brought to them by the FBI or administrative agencies, even when they have a strong legal case.[9] Judges regularly suspend sentences and grant probation to proven lawbreakers. In sum, the criminal law on the books may be relatively clear and legally specific, but as a society, we willingly enable legal decisionmakers to suspend the rules (in the direction of leniency), to rely on warnings and informal adjustments, to distinguish between serious and nonserious violations, to consider extenuating circumstances, to use the rehabilitative potential of giving a second chance, and to strike a more discerning balance between social control and liberty than lawmakers, far removed from the particular case and the local culture, could envisage in advance.

A similar practice of prosecutorial discretion has characterized the traditional regulatory inspection program. Despite a structure of legal rules that seem to cast the inspector as a rule-applying bureaucrat, and despite the uniformity and control that might come from tightly programming inspectors to go by the book in every case, enforcement officials often have been allowed a good deal of leeway—to withhold prosecution even when they detect violations, to settle for partial rather than literal compliance, and to act more like a "persuader" or educator than a rule-bound bureaucrat. In some agencies, rather than issue a citation, inspectors simply call the violation to the attention of the regulated enterprise, provided it does not entail an imminent hazard. In other agencies, inspectors issue a citation that effectively is only a warning—that is, no further action is taken unless the inspector returns to the site and finds that remedial measures have not been instituted. Inspectors in some agencies negotiate informal, on-the-spot agreements about corrective action and the time period for completion, taking into account the costs and mechanical difficulties involved; only if the regulated enterprise breaks its agreement without good reason are formal charges made or "penalty actions" initiated. Indeed, many regulatory statutes implicitly authorize discretionary withholding of prosecution for first violations by stipulating that penalties are required only for "willful" or "knowing" violations.

Regulatory officials have justified their reluctance to prosecute all violations by asserting that most regulated enterprises in fact "do the right thing" once an inspector points out violations of the law. The California Industrial Accident Commission, charged with enforcing worker safety laws, stated in 1914:

> The attitude of the Safety Department toward employers and employees is not one of compulsion, but of cooperation. It is expected that compulsion will have to be resorted to in rare cases only. The letters on file show that the keenest interest is evinced by manufacturers who express in highest terms their appreciation of the practical suggestions offered by [our] safety engineers.[10]

More recently, enforcement officials of the Motor Carrier Safety Unit of the California State Highway Patrol, in charge of enforcing truck safety and maintenance regulations, told us that they regard it as a failure when an inspector recommends formal prosecution of a trucking company; effective enforcement officials, they believe, should be able to win "voluntary compliance."

In keeping with this attitude, many agencies, even after an inspector or his supervisor loses patience and urges prosecution, inform the violator of the agency's intentions and call him in for an informal hearing; a top enforcement official or the agency's legal counsel presents the agency's case and attempts to extract a compliance agreement in return for suspending steps toward prosecution. Paul Downing and James Kimball, reviewing enforcement practices by certain state antipollution agencies, noted a decided preference for "telephone calls, site visits, warning letters, and conferences at the agency offices" over court action, and a willingness to forgive past violations if compliance is achieved or "in the offing."[11]

In the few cases that resist settlement or are so serious that enforcement officials seek formal legal sanctions, the district attorney or U.S. attorney provides another discretionary screen. The prosecutor's office typically is dealing with a crowded docket of "real crimes"—rapes, burglaries, bank robberies, tax frauds. Agency officials, accordingly, must convince the public prosecutor not only that they have a strong legal case but also that the violation is sufficiently serious to warrant criminal prosecution and a portion of his scarce legal resources. Prosecutors do refuse to handle regulatory matters they regard as trivial. And they too are often quite happy to drop formal prosecution in return for a consent agreement.[12] Finally, even after prosecution is initiated, judges often urge the parties to settle out of court rather than go to trial; even after conviction is obtained, judges often impose probationary arrangements rather than the full legally prescribed penalties.[13]

THE TRADITIONAL LEGAL STRUCTURE AND REGULATORY INEFFECTIVENESS

Prosecutorial discretion allows the inspector (and the prosecutor and the judge) to distinguish between serious and nonserious violations, between the basically well-intentioned regulated enterprise that can be brought into line with a warning and the recalcitrant firm that clearly deserves punishment. At the same time, the constraints of legal rules and due process impose a check on regulatory overreaching: the regulated enterprise can, if it is genuinely outraged, insist on formal hearings and proof, or it can insist that the inspector's "suggested" remedial action go no further than is authorized by the facts and by a specific legal rule. But the legal rules, used in this way, constitute only maximum limits on what enforcement officials may demand; they do not establish fixed minima for what inspectors *must* demand (and hence for what citizens may expect in the way of uniform protective measures). Moreover, the multiple reviews made possible by due process protections impede the prompt application of the sanctions established by law. In a variety of ways, therefore, the traditional legal structure of enforcement may well diminish achievement of regulatory goals.

An inspector's discretion, for example, easily can lead to underenforcement. When he "writes up" a violation, an inspector's work is carefully reviewed by superiors; he may have to go back to the site to gather additional, more formal evidence; he may incur the anger and hostility of personnel in the regulated enterprise who berate him for being unreasonable.[14] Thus it is certainly *easier* for field inspectors to overlook violations or to rely on informal prodding than to initiate formal prosecution, even when prosecution is clearly warranted. In addition, when inspectors have discretion to overlook unimportant violations or to determine what is a reasonable time for remedial action, experts in regulated enterprises have an opportunity to do a "snow job" on the gullible inspector.

Even if the inspector is not deceived and seeks to impose legal sanctions on a violator, the multiple reviews and adversarial processes associated with the due process tradition provide the recalcitrant enterprise repeated opportunities to delay the day of judgment. A California Department of Health nursing home regulator told us, "I have never seen a license revocation legal proceeding go for less than 14 months if they fight it." An official of the California State Fire Marshal's office noted that "a legal contest" arising from an effort to prosecute fire code violators "takes from 9 months to a year. And once it goes to litigation, we can't issue further recommendations or reinspect." An air pollution enforcement official in a southern state acknowledged that his agency was averse to formal enforcement actions because of the complicated—and slow—legal requirements.

Nowadays you need to make repeated inspections and complete documentation to show that this condition is persisting over time and your sampling is entirely fair. You've got to give the company notice so they can take their own measurements at the same time as ours. Then the inspector, once he's put together his enforcement package, has got to take it to the Commission to request a complaint. Then you've got to set a hearing, giving the company a chance to respond, and that will generally take at least a month. Then, if the company fails to respond or the Commission decides to go ahead with enforcement, it's got to issue an order. There are the problems of formulating a precise and legally enforceable compliance order. Then, if there is still noncompliance, we've got to take the case to the state attorney general, and he's not always cooperative.

And if the case goes to court, additional problems and delays usually are encountered.

Aside from the delays resulting from legal formalities, multiple stages of review can gradually weaken the impulse to impose formal penalties. Decisionmakers farther removed from the front line may have the advantage (in terms of formal legal values) of detachment and objectivity, but they are less familiar with the details of the particular inspector-enterprise relationship, and less able to sense the urgency of the problem and to see through insincere or weak excuses. An air pollution inspector, driving near a refinery he frequently inspected, complained about lack of support from the lawyers at headquarters and their tendency not to trust his assessments and intuition when he recommends prosecution. "They figure the inspector is a dummy. . . . But I don't care how tall the headquarters building is over there. They can't see over here!" Officials in many agencies complain that public prosecutors and judges fail to treat violations and violators as seriously as the enforcers believe necessary.[15]

Due process protections, moreover, sometimes mean that a regulated enterprise will be found legally innocent, when in fact it has acted irresponsibly. What was intuitively overwhelming proof to the inspector on the scene in the factory may appear to be unsupported speculation when the inspector is cross-examined on the witness stand. According to Keith Hawkins, British water pollution inspectors find the formal courtroom process an "alarming . . . ceremony, in which the available knowledge about [an act of] pollution . . . is submerged beneath the weight of procedural controls" and in which defense lawyers "can tear you to pieces."[16]

In addition, judicial discretion in sentencing traditionally led to light regulatory penalties. Dr. Harold Wiley, the great force behind the pure Food and Drug Law, complained 20 years after its enactment:

> Last week a penniless thief was sentenced by one of the judges in Washington to ten years in the penitentiary for stealing twenty dollars. Those convicted under the food law often get by with a fine of five dollars.[17]

Such results can be labeled a corrupt sell-out to powerful business interests, but they usually represent a consistent application of general principles of penal law, one of which calls for a rough proportionality between the penalty and the relative seriousness of the offense. Seriousness generally is assessed in terms of the degree of harm caused by the offense; the criminal law, looking at results, punishes speeding less severely than vehicular homicide. Many regulatory rules, like those against speeding, are preventive; violations often involve failure to take some precaution that only *might* lead to harm. If no harm has actually resulted, the violation of a sanitation regulation in an otherwise respectable food-processing plant often does not seem very serious.

Another aspect of seriousness, and hence of proportionality, is culpability, which entails knowledge of wrongdoing, combined with some degree of malice, selfishness, or irresponsibility. Courts are thus notoriously hesitant to assign criminal responsibility to individual corporate employees: underlings directly knowledgeable about harmful activities often lack authority and responsibility, while high officials often lack specific knowledge.[18] Moreover, regulatory offenses often are not clearly wrong, as are theft and assault. Unlike the burglar or the narcotics dealer, the regulatory offender often is a legitimate, socially useful enterprise whose officers believe sincerely, and sometimes justifiably, that their behavior was not really very bad.

Another basic penal principle is social utility, that is, that legal sanctions should provide a net social benefit. Thus the idea of rehabilitation, despite its frequent failure, pervades the penal process because it seems more efficient than incarceration. From this perspective, pushing a substandard nursing home to improve often is wiser than closing it down for having violated quality-of-care regulations. Just as courts prefer restitution to incarceration in many criminal cases,[19] judges may prefer to extract an agreement from a factory to spend money on a sprinkler system rather than impose a "nonproductive" fine for violations of the fire code.

Because formal prosecution is characterized by delays and appeals, losses on technical legal grounds, and judicially "watered down" penalties, inspectors and higher enforcement officials tend to avoid the formal route even when it seems justified. When faced with a recalcitrant landlord, some housing code inspectors bargain for prompt repairs of certain violations in return for dropping citations against others.[20] The compromise does provide some protection for the tenants, and more quickly and surely than court action.

More importantly, the agency may deliberately avoid bringing controversial charges or seeking innovative remedies when there is a good chance that the defendant will mount a strong legal defense; contested cases impose an enormous burden on the agency's understaffed legal section. It may seem more efficient for enforcement officials to concentrate on routine cases that are unlikely to be contested; although they contribute relatively little toward the achievement of regulatory goals, such routine cases guarantee the inspector and his agency a quick disposition and a numerically impressive enforcement record.[21] This also means, however, that the most hardened and experienced violators, those that are ready to engage in protracted legal battles, are the regulated enterprises most likely to escape, or at least to delay, the burdens of compliance.

Finally, the practice of backing away from legal conflict can sometimes become a habit so that the inspectorate loses all thirst for aggressive enforcement, even when it is badly needed, and loses enforcement know-how. Testimony by inspectors in the pre-OSHA California Division of Industrial Safety indicated that formal legal sanctions—such as criminal prosecutions or orders shutting down jobs presenting imminent hazards—had been resorted to so infrequently that many inspectors were ignorant of the precise nature and applicability of the sanctions available. Others claimed that their superiors had berated them for taking formal action.[22]

The traditional structure of inspection and enforcement is not necessarily a *major* source of ineffectiveness, and a tendency to bargain for compliance and cooperation may generally be wise policy, whatever its susceptibility to abuse or failure in particular areas. Railroads[23] and processed foods[24] have become safer, even though the ICC and the FDA infrequently resorted to formal prosecution of safety rule violators. In other fields, such as housing code and environmental law enforcement, some studies show that inspectors usually can obtain compliance merely by threatening prosecution or penalties, even if they have no intention of following through.[25] They succeed because most businessmen and corporate engineers are not quite certain what the agency can or will do and because the threat of prosecution seems more fearsome and potent than it really is. Nevertheless, in the late 1960s, social reformers—or any concerned citizen or newspaper reporter—could readily point to serious injuries, injustices, and social harms that were not being prevented in fields already subject to regulation. There were numerous exposés of specific instances of lax enforcement: factories that violated state air or water pollution standards with seeming impunity, carcinogenic pesticides left on the market by the USDA and the FDA,[26] fatal coal mine explosions not prevented by government inspectors,[27] dangerous substances and occupational diseases ignored by state regulators and compensation systems,[28] inhumane nursing homes that local licensing authorities allowed to stay in operation.[29]

Partly for these reasons, the demand for more effective and comprehensive government regulation grew in the 1960s. These demands often took the form of an attack on the traditional enforcement style and the legal structure of regulatory agencies. Overall, the reformers called for a shift from the discretionary inspector-as-consultant style to the more aggressive prosecution-and-deterrence model of regulation. The inspectors and the agencies themselves were to be held to stricter account by outside critics.

CAPTURE AND ITS CURE

Reformers believed that enforcement had to be tougher and that the regulators had to be more closely regulated because business enterprises were fundamentally amoral profit-seekers, unwilling to abide by the law unless the prospect of legal punishment was swift, sure, and severe,[30] and because regulatory agencies invariably were (or soon became) weak-willed, lethargic "captives" of the industries they regulated. The "capture theory," a tenet of academic political science,[31] was popularized in the late 1960s and early 1970s by a steady stream of exposés of federal agencies by Ralph Nader's "Raiders."[32] Regulatory officials were pictured as industry-oriented, as reluctant to jeopardize their postgovernment careers by being too tough, or as gradually co-opted by informal contact with representatives of regulated firms. In a passage reflecting the attitude of these books toward business as well as toward informal methods of enforcement, the author of Nader's study of food and drug regulation wrote:

> It became the practice of the FDA . . . to hold hundreds of meetings each year with representatives of industry to discuss . . . cooperative methods . . . to ensure that the provisions of the law were not violated. . . . If the Justice Department held regular meetings with the Mafia suggesting that it knew of gambling . . . which if not stopped would lead to a raid of the premises, it would be following a procedure not unlike that used by the FDA to convince the food industry to obey the law.[33]

By 1970, the capture theory was the conventional wisdom, repeated by Supreme Court judges and by intellectuals of the right.[34] As for inspectors, everyone "knew" they could be "bought." Finally, many reformers and even congressional staff members believed that "American industry . . . could easily absorb all the costs imposed by [tougher] regulation out of its profit structure without significantly affecting the economy."[35]

From this perspective, the reform agenda was clear: (1) install new regulators, preferably at the federal level (where proregulation public interest groups could concentrate their efforts), rather than at the even more discredited state or local level; (2) write more comprehensive and explicit regulations, without gaps and "balancing" language that would permit legalistic defenses; (3) curtail administrative discretion and leniency by more specific and stringent rules and by advocacy-group participation in rulemaking and enforcement; and (4) enhance deterrence by increasing the severity, speed, and consistency of sanctions.

This reform agenda was not adopted in toto; the legal structure of some existing agencies remained untouched, and new legislation often reflected compromises between the proponents and the opponents of tougher legislation. But to a considerable degree, the outpouring of regulatory legislation in the late 1960s and 1970s did reflect these enforcement goals. Congressmen showed themselves to be sensitive to the capture theory and to criticism in the media for enacting regulatory legislation with ostensibly weak enforcement provisions.[36] Perhaps it is significant, too, that many major regulatory measures were enacted by a Democrat-controlled Congress that was deeply mistrustful of the Republican president, Richard Nixon, who was in a position to appoint the top regulatory officials. Hence, there was added reason to curtail regulatory discretion and to enhance legal controls over enforcement. The same political alignment prevailed in California during Ronald Reagan's tenure as governor. In any case, legislative willingness to change the traditional legal structure of regulatory enforcement can be readily outlined by referring to the major enactments of the 1960s and 1970s.

THE FEDERALIZATION OF REGULATION

In the late 1960s and early 1970s, Congress created the Environmental Protection Agency, the National Highway Traffic Safety Administration, the Consumer Product Safety Commission, OSHA, the Mining Enforcement and Safety Administration, and the Equal Employment Opportunity Commission. Moreover, the jurisdiction and enforcement powers of established federal agencies were expanded.* Although the newly created federal regulatory authority occasionally superseded state and local regulation, it more often supplemented and strengthened it. Sometimes the federal legislation established minimum protective standards for the entire country but permitted states to establish more stringent standards. Enforcement of some federal legislation was delegated to (or forced upon) state agencies under federal guidelines, federal agency oversight, and, in some cases, federal funding, which could be withheld for inadequate enforcement. For example, under the Occupational Safety and Health Act, states could either leave enforcement to federal inspectors or maintain their own programs, provided their regulations and enforcement procedures were "at least as effective" as OSHA regulations and practices. The 1970 amendments to the Clean Air Act required states to prepare detailed State Implementation Plans for meeting federally set ambient air standards for various pollutants.

In some instances, regulatory functions were transferred from one federal agency to another to remove enforcement responsibilities from a group of officials that had long been committed to an education-and-cooperation regulatory style. In 1972, for example, federal regulation of blood and plasma products was extended to intrastate blood banks and plasma collection centers, and enforcement shifted from the National Institutes of Health to the new Bureau of Biologics in the FDA. That change, the head of the bureau wrote, "was more than a simple change in the organization chart. . . . [It] conveyed [enforcement] from a research-oriented organization, NIH, to the FDA, which was historically concerned with the compliance aspects of regulation."[37]

MAKING STATUTES MORE STRINGENT

To reformers who were mistrustful of the regulators' integrity, traditional statutory terms, such as "reasonable" and "feasible," allowed for too much compromise. Reformers sought legislation that would articulate citizens' rights to protection in unambiguous terms, enabling citizen

---

*For example, the FTC's jurisdiction was expanded from interstate commerce to intrastate transactions "affecting commerce," and hence to local deceptive or unfair sales practices.

groups to take vacillating regulatory officials to court and compel them to achieve specific levels of safety or environmental protection. Most major environmental and protective legislation of the late 1960s and early 1970s followed this reform pattern. Statutes mandated ambitious levels of protection, set fixed deadlines for achieving them, and empowered citizen groups to take slow-moving agencies to court. And although most statutes indicated that economic costs and difficulties in achieving compliance could play some role in the formulation and enforcement of regulations, the weight accorded such considerations was diminished and carefully restricted.

Regulatory discretion in balancing competing values, for example, was more hedged in by explicit statutory provisions. Congress was not so apt to say, in effect, "Here's the problem. Do something about it!" The text of the 1970 Clean Air Act amendments, together with the extensive 1977 amendments, covers 135 pages. Primary ambient air quality standards, the law said, should be set at levels "requisite to protect the public health" with "an adequate margin of safety," rather clearly excluding concerns about the economic costs of compliance or cost-benefit analysis in establishing those standards.[38] EPA administrators could consider economic costs in designating "best available control technologies" for new factories,[39] but other provisions of the law forbade them to grant variances, because of economic costs or even technological infeasibility, from stringent enforcement plans designed to roll back pollution from existing sources.[40]

The weight to be given economic considerations was also restricted by the statutory practice of stating basic regulatory goals in absolute, unqualified terms. The goal of the 1972 Water Pollution Control Act amendments was to eliminate *all* effluents by 1985; under the Clean Air Act carbon monoxide and hydrocarbon emissions from new cars were to be reduced 90 percent from 1970 levels by 1975. The Occupational Safety and Health Act articulated the employer's obligation to provide, and the worker's right to have, a job "free of known hazards" (although this is probably an impossibility for many jobs).[41] The federal strip-mine legislation of 1977 prohibited *all* stream siltation and required the restoration of mined land to its "original contours," rejecting language calling for restoration "to the maximum extent feasible."

Buried in those statutes is language that gives the agency some flexibility in rulemaking, or that allows individual businesses to apply for exceptions or extensions on grounds of technological difficulties. But the congressional intent to achieve stringent controls was expressed so clearly that regulators often have been reluctant to give economic considerations substantial weight in rulemaking or in requests for variances. For example, the Occupational Safety and Health Act's emphasis on complete freedom from hazards is qualified by the concept of "maximum feasible protection." This provision, OSHA concluded, permitted it to consider whether proposed safety rules were beyond the economic (as well as the technological) capacity of employers. But OSHA had to fight lawsuits brought by labor unions that challenged that interpretation, and the agency has insisted that it is not legally obligated to balance cost against safety in rulemaking or to conduct cost-benefit analyses of proposed standards. Thus it has required employers to install expensive engineering controls to achieve the lowest detectible level of emissions shown to be hazardous in high concentrations, despite arguments that standards set at slightly less stringent levels (or the use of personal protective equipment) would probably provide adequate protection at much lower costs.[42]

Statutes also restricted regulatory discretion in dealing with scientific controversy over possible hazards, compelling agency rulemakers to forbid products and practices that create a recognized *possibility* of harm, rather than making their own judgment about the *probability* of harm or the tolerable level of risk. For example, many public health professionals contend that it is impossible to establish with certainty "threshold values" (concentrations below which exposure is not carcinogenic) for substances shown to cause cancer in animals or humans exposed to high concentrations. Others reject the "no safe threshold" theory, arguing that carcinogens vary widely in degree of potency, that potency may drop off dramatically at lower exposures, and that extrapolations from animal studies to low-dose exposures to humans are quite problematic.[43] Faced with this controversy, legislators (and regulators) sometimes—although not always—have acted on the no-threshold theory, forbidding any human exposure to the substance, despite the practical difficulties and high costs of moving from a standard calling for carefully controlled low exposures to one calling for zero exposure. The most famous example is the Delaney Amendment to the Food, Drug and Cosmetic Act, which absolutely forbids the sale of food products or additives shown to be even a very weak cause of cancerous tumors in laboratory tests of animals.[44] The FDA, moreover, is not permitted to weigh the risk of cancer against the social benefits the product might provide or against the economic costs the ban might entail. Regulatory officials, in fact, often are grateful for the opportunity to escape responsibility for the intellectually difficult and politically touchy task of making such trade-off decisions. Donald Kennedy, commissioner of the FDA in 1977, stated, "Our law says to protect the public health, not the industry. Fortunately, our statute does not allow us to weigh adverse health conditions against dollars."[45]

On the other hand, when regulators *have* been willing to consider the costs of enforcing an absolute prohibition or a rigid standard, other agencies, proregulation advocacy groups, or courts can invoke the statutory language as a barrier to any exceptions:

- The 1973 Endangered Species Act, read literally, protected all species: not only the furry mammals and attractive birds that probably were foremost in the legislators' minds, but also obscure and unloved lizards and spiders. The Supreme Court reluctantly concluded that the statute required the courts to order a stop to the construction of the huge and costly Tellico River dam because opening the dam would destroy the habitat of the snail darter, a rare (but now famous) fish.[46]

- The San Francisco Bay Area Air Pollution Control District promulgated an "upset/breakdown" regulation in 1970, which allowed enforcement officials to excuse violations when excessive emissions resulted from mechanical failure or periodic maintenance of control equipment, or from temporary "upsets" in production processes. The firm had to report the situation immediately (or 24 hours in advance for scheduled maintenance of pollution equipment), and the exemption from penalties would only be granted if "the frequency or duration of upset conditions, breakdowns, or scheduled maintenance is . . . reasonable under all of the circumstances." The district was forced to repeal this exemption under federal pressure in 1978—the EPA claimed that the district had no legal authority under the Clean Air Act to grant such exemptions. District inspectors have since been directed to cite any violation of emission limitations regardless of cause.

SHIFTING THE BURDEN OF PROOF

In addition to stringent rules that enforcement agencies cannot easily water down, many new regulatory statutes attempted to bolster the enforcement process directly by making it easier to prove violations. One technique was to require regulated enterprises to maintain more detailed records of compliance-related activities and to make those records available to enforcement personnel. The enterprise, in effect, must constantly be able to demonstrate that it is in compliance. Enforcement leverage is further enhanced by making inadequate record keeping a separate, punishable—and easy to prove—violation. Trucking companies, for example, must keep detailed logs recording daily hours of service for each truck and each driver so that Department of Transportation inspectors can check on compliance with maximum-hours rules designed to prevent accidents. Operators of chemical plants and refineries in the San Francisco Bay area must install continuous monitoring devices for all sources of sulfur dioxide emissions, calibrate and test the monitors regularly as prescribed by agency regulations, and make the monitoring records available to inspectors on demand. The companies also must report to the agency within 96 hours pollution violations recorded by the monitors. Several statutes require firms to report incidents that merely suggest possible violations or danger to the public.[47] Thus the Toxic Substances Control Act states that corporate personnel who obtain information indicating that a substance "presents a substantial risk of injury" to human health or the environment must immediately inform the EPA. Failure to do so is itself a serious violation.[48]

In situations where enforcement agencies find it especially difficult to prove violations, regulated enterprises have been required to prove their innocence. A clear example involves not safety regulation but antidiscrimination law. It is difficult for agencies to prove that any individual who was not hired or promoted was in fact rejected because of sex or race, as opposed to merit. Certain affirmative action regulations, therefore, refer to "underrepresentation" or "underutilization" of women or minorities in the employer's work force, a much easier fact for the agency to establish. If underutilization is found, the employer then has the burden of proving that its criteria for hiring and promotion are not discriminatory.[49] Construction contractors on federally- and on many state-funded projects who do not meet affirmative action guidelines for percentage of minority workers (and few of them do, in view of union practices), or who do not award subcontracts to minority-owned firms, must provide federal inspectors with detailed records showing "good faith efforts" to recruit or subcontract to minorities.[50]

The ultimate method for shifting the burden of proof is to require the regulated enterprise to seek agency approval before undertaking an activity, such as marketing a product or operating an industrial process.

In such prior clearance schemes, the enterprise must prove to agency officials that its methods are lawful and technically adequate. Compared with a post hoc inspection system, the recalcitrant enterprise's chances of evasion are diminished, and it gains no advantage from legal delay. The agency's refusal to grant a permit is a potent sanction. Prior approval laws have existed for many years for building code enforcement, for new prescription drugs, and for builders of new aircraft models. In the 1960s and 1970s, however, such requirements proliferated. In effect, agency clearance was required, for example, for companies that sought to market new pesticides, potentially harmful chemicals,[51] and (to assure compliance with antipollution regulations) cars and gasoline additives.[52] Meatpackers and drug manufacturers who wished to build plants were required to file detailed blueprints and to get clearance from the Department of Agriculture and the FDA, respectively, concerning compliance with detailed regulations governing the sanitary nature of facilities. Operators of both new and existing major sources of air and water pollution were required to obtain operating permits from state and federal agencies, conditional on a satisfactory plan to install legally required control equipment.

The burden of proof associated with prior clearance procedures is often quite substantial. In the San Francisco Bay area, for example, to obtain a permit for a new or expanded industrial process that will emit over 250 pounds of pollutants per year, the applicant must submit an extensive "Air Quality Impact Analysis" as well as detailed control plans. Enforcement officials point out, moreover, that the sanction of suspending a permit for violating specific pledges in the permit application is much easier to uphold in court than the postviolation fines or injunctions sought in traditional abatement actions.

INCREASING REMEDIAL AND SANCTIONING POWERS

Another striking characteristic of the regulatory legislation of the past decade is a major increase, by historical standards, in the severity of maximum penalties and in the range of legally available remedial orders.

Many new statutory penalties reflected the theory that only mammoth fines could deter violations by mammoth corporations. For example, the 1970 Clean Air Act and the 1969 Federal Mine Safety Act authorized the imposition of criminal fines against violators of $25,000 *per day* (thus reducing the incentive to delay the day of judgment), and $50,000 per day for repeat offenders. The 1977 Clean Air Act amendments and the 1976 Toxic Substances Control Act also authorized "civil penalties" of up to $25,000 per day; these differ from criminal fines primarily in that the agency does not have to prove guilt beyond a reasonable doubt, prove that the violation was intentional or "knowing," or jump other hurdles of criminal procedure. The proof standard in civil actions is usually "a preponderance of the evidence." The financial sanctions, however, are just as high, and judges may be more willing to impose them.

Following the lead of the 1938 pure Food and Drug Law amendments, many statutes in the 1960s and 1970s stated that criminal penalties could be imposed on individual officers for corporate regulatory violations.[53] Moreover, some of these statutes have been construed by the courts to impose criminal sanctions against high officials who had no direct knowledge, criminal intent, or involvement in the violation, but who were "responsible" and "should have known."[54] The 1977 Clean Air Act explicitly extends criminal liability to "any responsible corporate officer."

Regulatory agencies increasingly were granted the power to impose sanctions directly, without having to go to court and convince a judge that the penalty is warranted. OSHA, for example, was authorized to impose civil penalties on violators immediately, as were some state agencies, such as California's air pollution control districts and its agency that inspects nursing homes. Under the 1977 amendments to the Clean Air Act, the EPA was empowered to assess civil penalties equal to the financial "benefit" gained by not making the required abatement or by dragging out court proceedings. In these agencies, prosecution is assigned to an expanded legal staff, enabling the agency to avoid the delay (and the additional discretionary screen) of presenting enforcement cases through the public prosecutor. Most agency-assessed civil penalties, such as those imposed by OSHA, are not large, but they are swift and according to our interviews, are troubling even to very large corporations.

In addition, summary remedies—orders prior to any hearing—have been made available to enforcement officials in a broader range of situations and sometimes with looser definitions of "imminent hazard" than the older social regulation. The 1977 Clean Air Act, for example, empowers the administrator of the EPA to order an immediate shutdown of polluting operations in periods of dangerously deteriorating air quality. EPA officials also can order automobile manufacturers to close down their assembly plants and to recall cars to redesign and correct pollution control gear that is not meeting regulatory standards.[55] Federal mine inspectors are authorized by the 1969 Mine Safety Act to order immediate closure of mines not only when they think that miners are in imminent danger but also when prior abatement orders have not been complied with because of "unwarrantable failure." Perhaps the most drastic remedial power provided by the new regulation is the authority to order "recalls" of entire product lines. The National Highway Traffic Safety Administration regularly orders the recall of (or induces the company to recall) tens of thousands of automobiles for replacement of parts that may be causing problems. The expense is usually equivalent to a much larger fine than a court would ever impose, and the publicity attending such recalls often has an adverse effect on sales that far exceeds the direct recall costs.[56] The Consumer Product Safety Commission has similar powers to recall hazardous toys. EPA can order manufacturers to recall industrial machinery that violates noise control regulations.[57] The Department of Agriculture can suspend sales of pesticides and fungicides, without prior hearing.[58]

As the federal government's purchasing and spending activities have penetrated more sectors of the economy and state and local government, another regulatory sanction has been created: the threat to bar violators of federal regulations from future contracts or to cut off existing grants. This sanction has been authorized, for example, for violations of federal antidiscrimination employment guidelines, federal criteria for local school programs funded by Congress (bilingual education, education for the handicapped, "special education") and federal regulations governing local water and waste treatment projects. The EPA recently cut off $301.5 million in aid to Colorado for highway construction and sewage-treatment plants because the state failed to establish a federally mandated inspection program for controlling automobile pollution.[59] Although cut-offs are rarely used, they are threatening enough to get substantial results. Inspection of hospitals by Medicare officials to check compliance with quality-of-care regulations—which is a condition for continued Medicare payments—has had a greater effect on substandard hospitals, according to some observers, than years of local regulation and threats of license revocation.[60]

REDUCING DISCRETION IN SANCTIONING AND ENFORCEMENT

More stringent rules, more record keeping by regulated firms, and more potent statutory sanctions might not add up to tougher regulation if inspectors and higher regulatory officials retained discretion to overlook or to decline to penalize violations. A major priority of regulatory reform, therefore, was to "program" the dispersed regulators more tightly, inducing them to adhere to the regulations that proregulation forces managed to get promulgated in Washington or state capitals.

One strategy for reducing discretion was to break up (or to restore balance to) informal relationships between regulators and regulated. In pursuit of this goal at the rulemaking level, many statutes and judicial decisions expanded citizen-group rights to participate in the regulatory policymaking process; stipulated that agency decisions must be made in public session, after open public hearings; held that agency rulemaking decisions must be based on a publicly disclosed evidentiary record; and made agency rules appealable to the courts by almost any "aggrieved citizen."[61] As noted before, proregulation groups were empowered to sue agencies in court for failure to promulgate regulations in accordance with statutory deadlines or substantive statutory standards.

The parallel strategy was to make the *enforcement process* more visible, accountable, and subject to monitoring and influence by private advocacy groups and individual complainants. Here, too, one method was the lawsuit. Public interest law firms were authorized to seek judicial orders requiring agencies to enforce the law more literally or aggressively, and some statutes provided that successful public interest litigants could have their counsel fees paid by the government. In several instances, most prominently in the civil rights field, courts responded to suits by beneficiary groups alleging "systemic enforcement inadequacies" by ordering an agency to respond to complaints more rapidly, to adopt certain enforcement priorities, and, in one case, to petition the Office of Management and Budget for more enforcement funds.[62] The precedents also seem applicable to health and safety regulations: a Denver public interest law firm sued the Department of Health, Education and Welfare, demanding a cut-off of Medicare funds or better enforcement of quality-of-care regulations for nursing homes; the federal district court ordered a thorough survey of enforcement inadequacies. A few courts have indicated inspection agencies might be liable for damages to persons injured as a result of negligent or weak enforcement; the leading precedents involve fire marshals' offices that failed to detect fire code violations or force repairs on buildings that subsequently caught fire.[63] These precedents hardly eliminate the tradition of prosecutorial discretion and the doctrine of official immunity, but they represent steps in that direction, and they are well known to many enforcement officials, who regard them as significant messages to guard against charges of lax enforcement.

There are other techniques to make enforcement officials more responsive to complainants. The Freedom of Information Act expands the access of citizens, including investigative reporters, to agency inspection records. Agencies are explicitly commanded by some statutes to conduct an inspection within a specified number of days after receiving a citizen complaint and to report the results to the complainant. To encourage complaints, agencies are forbidden to reveal the complainant's name, and in many regulatory schemes, discrimination by the enterprise against complainants is a punishable offense. California's nursing home law also provides that any attempt to expel or deny privileges to a complainant or one on whose behalf a complaint is filed within 120 days of the complaint raises "a rebuttable presumption that such action was taken . . . in retaliation for the filing of the complaint." The Occupational Safety and Health Act contains similar provisions to protect worker-complainants. Employment discrimination laws, the Consumer Product Safety Act, and the Occupational Safety and Health Act authorize citizen lawsuits against the violator (and against the agency, too, in OSHA's case) if the agency fails to act against an alleged violator within a given period of time. To exert pressures against undue concessions in plea bargaining, a California statute requires the nursing home regulatory agency, if it modifies or dismisses a citation or proposed penalty in an informal conference, to "state with particularity in writing . . . the reasons for such action," and immediately to send a copy to any complainant. Citations involving serious violations must be posted in the view of patients and visitors. OSHA and the federal mine safety laws specifically empower employees to accompany inspectors on their tour of the workplace.[64] Complaints are encouraged by such judicial rulings as the California Supreme Court decision allowing tenants to withhold rent when housing inspectors have found serious housing code violations on the premises.[65]

Another important outside pressure on state agencies is federal review of their enforcement practices. Federal OSHA periodically reinspects establishments inspected by state occupational safety and health agencies. Federal health officials check dairy companies primarily inspected by state agencies. Federal Medicare inspectors resurvey nursing homes covered by state inspectors. The same occurs in truck safety regulation, meat processing, and blood banks. Reinspection is usually designed to encourage stricter enforcement and more complete reporting of violations by state enforcement officials.

Some legislation explicitly attempts to preclude inspectorial discretion, at least in the sense of overlooking minor violations or deciding to deal with violations merely by oral advice or warnings. One of the most extreme versions, perhaps, is OSHA, where inspectors are required to cite every violation of safety regulations they see and to assign a statutory fine for all "serious" violations.[66] But the federal mine safety law prescribes the same approach, and some other agencies are close behind. FDA inspectors are told to report every violation of the immensely detailed "good manufacturing practice" regulations that they see in food and drug manufacturing firms. California nursing home and air pollution inspectors must cite all violations, and fines or "penalty actions" are prescribed for most of them. The Federal Water Pollution Control Act not only requires companies to report any discharge of oil into navigable waters but also mandates the automatic imposition of a "civil fine" on the reporting company (although the fine for not reporting would be higher).*

Many statutes now forbid inspectors to give any advance notice of inspections, thus curtailing their discretion to build a less suspicious and intrusive relationship with certain regulated enterprises.[67] Discretion at the supervisor's level also came under review in some instances. The California legislature stipulated that, if an occupational safety inspector recommended criminal action and his supervisor disagreed, the decision to forgo prosecution first must be reviewed by top agency enforcement officials.[68] Finally, discretion in the selection of inspection sites has sometimes been limited by statutes that prescribe specific priorities and frequencies for certain regulated enterprises. Thus the Federal Mine Health and Safety Act mandates four inspections per year for all underground mines and one each week for 200 mines with poor safety histories.

---

*In June 1980, the Supreme Court rejected an oil driller's contention that the reporting plus fine requirement violated the Fifth Amendment's protection against self-incrimination. The court reasoned that the Fifth Amendment applies to criminal liability and that the fine in question is a civil, not a criminal, penalty. *U.S. v. Ward*, 65 L.Ed. 2d 742 (1980).

CONCLUSION

These legal changes have not characterized all regulatory programs. They represent a trend, not an invariant transformation. Many "traditional" enforcement programs remain, especially at the state and local levels.[69] Even in the more "legalistic" programs, not every statutory standard is expressed in absolute terms. Applications for pollution discharge and building permits inevitably entail a good deal of negotiation. Statutory deadlines can be and have been bent when agencies or industry have had difficulty meeting them. Inspectorial and prosecutorial discretion is difficult to eliminate, no matter what the rules say. Determined enterprises can still delay compliance through legal challenges. The penalties authorized by law are still subject to administrative and judicial moderation in many instances. Courts have been reluctant to issue injunctions that would actually close down factories that are violating stringent pollution regulations because a shutdown creates unemployment. Moreover, as the 1980s began in an atmosphere of energy crisis, unprecedented inflation, and economic limitations, there were strong indications that the trend we have discussed may have peaked. Statutes and presidential orders required agencies to take economic and other costs of compliance into account in the rulemaking process and to recognize more scope for private autonomy and responsibility.

Nevertheless, these statutory changes constitute a real and important trend. Strict legal provisions and rights to protection are difficult to remove, and enforcement styles, once structured by law, are slow to change. In the most significant regulatory areas, the law has been deliberately structured to prevent capture, to program inspectors to apply regulations strictly, to pressure enforcement officials to apply formal penalties to violations, and to adopt a more legalistic and deterrence-oriented stance vis-à-vis regulated enterprises. Not surprisingly, the power of enforcement officials in these regulatory programs has indeed increased, but so has the incidence of unreasonableness and unresponsiveness.

CHAPTER THREE

UNREASONABLENESS

———————————— • ————————————

Centralized, detailed, and programmed regulation can be a powerful social instrument, but it is not a subtle one. By requiring all enterprises to take a prescribed set of protective measures, it assumes a certain uniformity in problems to be controlled. The world to be regulated, however, is diverse, changeable, and ambiguous. The causes of harmful events are not entirely predictable; risks arise in different degrees; and solutions are not always ready-made.

Regulators are well aware of many mismatches between uniform rules and diverse circumstances, if only because they are quickly apprised of them, and they often try to improve the match. But friction persists, especially when enforcement officials are denied discretion to adjust the rules or to overlook deviations. The results are unreasonableness (the imposition of uniform regulatory requirements in situations where they do not make sense) and unresponsiveness (the failure to consider arguments by regulated enterprises that exceptions should be made).

THE VARIABILITY OF REGULATED ENTERPRISES

Regulation by programmed application of uniform protective standards obviously runs a risk of underestimating the diversity of the ways in which things can go wrong. Consider the consumer-product safety "problem," for example, as described by Lawrence Bacow:

> Millions of products are marketed annually in the United States by thousands of different producers. The risk associated with each product varies with its design; the quality of the materials and the workmanship; the directions provided to the users; the user's skill,

judgment and caution; the age of the product; whether the product is being used for its intended purpose; the way the product has been maintained; and the extent to which the product is used with other products.[1]

A similar complex of possible causes of injury underlies most problems addressed by protective regulations. Thus any regulation based on a single-pronged notion of how injuries occur, and hence relying on a single "solution"—such as mandatory safety features on sunlamps, lawnmowers, or bicycles—may be appropriate for some products and users, but may be needlessly cumbersome, costly, and ineffective for others.

Even when the cause of social harms seems much simpler, as in the case of air pollution produced by relatively few sources using a designated industrial process, rulemakers can easily underestimate the variability of ostensibly similar technologies. For example, there are only 16 major copper smelters in the United States. But according to a detailed study of occupational health in that industry, devising abatement equipment for in-plant arsenic and sulfur dioxide emissions has proved surprisingly difficult. Some smelters use old reverberatory furnaces, some use electric models, some modern flash ovens; some use "Pierce-Smith converters," some use very different "Hoboken converters," and some use both; some plants use anode furnaces for further purification, while others do not. Each of these variations yields different concentrations of emissions and engineering problems in collecting and "cleaning" gases and fumes, and presents widely divergent costs of control. A single government-prescribed control technology, such as acid plants or sulfur dioxide liquefiers—machinery that can cost millions of dollars —has worked well in some plants but has proved utterly ineffective in others. Variations in raw materials complicate the picture further. In a Michigan smelter that uses copper ores containing very little sulfur and arsenic, for instance, mandatory use of the best available control technology would be totally unnecessary.[2]

Such technological variations, however, are a relatively well-understood obstacle to the formulation of standards that will "make sense" in most instances. A more fundamental and perhaps less recognized difficulty is the varying degree to which regulated enterprises are motivated and have the capacity to comply with protective regulations. Many regulatory reforms seem to reflect the belief that most regulated enterprises, in their pursuit of profit, are uniformly indifferent if not hostile to regulatory goals; hence, they can be expected to evade regulatory requirements unless rules are absolutely clear and legal penalties are immediate and strong. Popular notions of business behavior, too, reflect this image. Motion pictures and television programs commonly picture corporate executives as greedy villains, insensitive to human values and environmental concerns, ruthlessly suppressing evidence of dangerous radiation or getting rid of a lone decent manager or worker.[3]

Many regulatory violations are indeed the product of calculating and amoral business behavior. The files of consumer fraud divisions in prosecutors' offices bulge with examples.[4] Any regulatory official can easily tell several horror stories that are an important part of each inspectorate's folklore. A Minnesota firm was indicted for repackaging contaminated dry milk and selling it to bakery supply firms. Cattle raisers continued to use a potentially carcinogenic growth stimulant (DES) for months after an FDA ban.[5] Consumer fraud investigators acknowledge, nevertheless, that many complaints do not involve deliberate deceptions that reflect official company policy.[6] Most dairy firms comply almost fanatically with purity regulations, and 90 percent of feedlot operators complied with the DES ban, notwithstanding its high costs and cattlemen's belief that there was insufficient evidence of harmful effects to warrant the FDA's action. In view of the huge daily volume of potentially dangerous activities, disasters stemming directly from willful disregard of clearly applicable regulations, however serious, are relatively rare. Experienced regulators acknowledge that if most regulated enterprises were inclined to comply only when the threat of inspection and punishment was imminent, then the entire regulatory program would quickly collapse.

In many areas of protective regulation, voluntary compliance is prevalent because economic pressures and the threat of private lawsuits compel enterprises to institute safety measures that parallel the content of government regulations. Most food manufacturers, for example, comply with the core of FDA "good manufacturing practice" regulations because a single outbreak of food poisoning traced to one of their products can devastate their market position.[7] Compliance with truck safety regulations helps corporate shipping managers combat the tendency of maintenance men, dispatchers, and drivers to cut corners. Managers of companies that make chemicals, automobile components, intravenous solutions, and oil drilling rigs, to name just a few products, are well aware of recent multimillion dollar damage awards for personal injury or concentrated environmental damage;[8] compliance with applicable regulations may limit liability, mitigate damages, or prevent costly accidents entirely.

With respect to worker safety and health, market-based financial incentives are not quite so congruent with regulatory goals, and the threat of large damage judgments is limited by workers' compensation law. Still, workers' compensation insurance premiums add at least 10 percent to labor costs for dangerous jobs, and the annual increase in compensation costs that follows a bad safety record far exceeds the average fines levied by OSHA. High accident rates, moreover, produce even larger indirect costs—down-time, retraining expenses, high labor dissatisfaction and turnover. Of course, these incentives may not produce adequate investment in safety measures for all risks, such as chemical emissions, whose ill-effects are not obvious or other hazards that require very expensive abatement systems.[9] But for many risks, good economic reasons other than the threat of an OSHA fine encourage compliance with most safety rules.

Even when compliance with regulations would increase an enterprise's costs without providing any obvious benefits to the firm itself, enlightened self-interest might still dictate compliance. Although investing in air pollution abatement equipment, for example, diverts large sums from productivity-enhancing investment, many firms comply once antipollution regulations are on the books, without regard to the frequency of inspections or the amount of fines for violations. They sense that the long-run gains of retaining a reputation as a law-abiding corporate citizen may outweigh the short-run gains from regulatory noncompliance.[10] A reputation for environmental irresponsibility can mean closer scrutiny from regulatory inspectors,[11] a cold shoulder from legislators who want to avoid the appearance of cooperating with corporate lawbreakers, and a harder time working with other regulatory agencies, permit granters, zoning boards, and governmental contract offices. Bankers and institutional investors may regard such firms as poorly managed and prone to trouble.[12] In extreme cases, the company may be publicly attacked by environmental and consumer groups, and sales may be hurt. These effects do not invariably ensue, of course, but they *might,* and that suggests to risk-averse corporate managers a conservative, trouble-avoiding policy.

There are intraorganizational pressures for compliance too. Large corporations now have staffs of professionals concerned with regulatory matters—academically trained industrial hygienists, environmental engineers, toxicologists, safety experts, biologists, lawyers, occupational physicians, and specialists in administering affirmative action programs. These specialists are by no means uninterested in their corporation's balance sheet, but they also have some loyalty to the standards of their profession. "I'm a licensed engineer. I'm not going to risk my license by lying to an agency," a corporate environmental engineer told us. Some of them have worked for regulatory agencies. On their desks, one sees the latest issue of the *Federal Register* and books, newsletters, and technical manuals related to regulatory compliance. Their job is to keep their company out of legal and political trouble, and in many corporations, compliance or some approximation thereof, not outright evasion, is the predominant strategy for keeping out of trouble.

To be sure, neither market pressure, the desire for a good public image, nor the "voice" of safety and environmental engineers and lawyers inside corporations is entirely sufficient to produce regulatory compliance. Without the threat of legal sanction, these forces might lose much of their influence, at least with respect to some social problems. Even with the threat of enforcement, some firms try to evade regulations that they feel are unreasonable, and others evade regulations simply because they think they can get away with it. It is important, nevertheless, to recognize that in still other regulated firms there are powerful cultural and market-based forces that encourage compliance.

The differences among firms in disposition to comply, moreover, are reflected in the systems of worker protection, quality control, and pollution prevention that they install. Some are excellent, far exceeding the minimum standards provided by regulation, and some fall far short. While the same firm may have satisfactory protections against certain hazards, it may have poor protections against others for which economic, liability, and "public image" incentives are weaker.

In addition to (but probably correlated with) variations in motivation, regulated enterprises differ in their capacity both to comply with regulatory requirements and to forestall social harms. A factory with younger workers and high employee turnover will have a harder time preventing accidents and ensuring compliance with quality control rules than will a factory with an experienced, stable work force. A firm with greater financial depth, full-time environmental engineers, and an industrial hygienist usually is better able than is a small, financially hard-pressed firm to keep up with applicable regulations, monitor compliance, and invest in the latest control technologies. Newer, more highly automated plants are far easier to keep safe and clean than are older ones.

Differences in capacity to comply are especially significant because compliance usually is not a matter of a one-time expenditure (such as the installation of fire doors and additional sprinklers to meet the fire code) but a matter of ongoing supervision and management. As Steven Kelman points out in his study of workplace safety and health, even if an employer is willing to comply with regulations:

> Compliance is often no once-and-for-all matter, but requires constant vigilance. . . . Closed [chemical-control] systems must be checked for leaks. Respiration filters must be replaced frequently. . . . Slippery or cluttered floors may be cleaned today and relapse tomorrow. Flammable solvent-soaked rags may be placed in the proper containers today, and tomorrow will be left out as a worker lights a cigarette nearby.[13]

The same can be said about maintenance of air and water pollution control equipment. Baghouses, scrubbers, and other devices are complicated pieces of machinery requiring constant attention; they compete with production machinery for scarce maintenance time.* Moreover, it is not any easy task for busy executives to keep up with all the regulations and to correctly apply them to a particular operation. For example, OSHA regulations stipulate maximum worker exposure to different chemical emissions in terms of average parts per million in the air of the workplace over an eight-hour period; to stay in compliance, a firm must conduct careful air sampling readings, controlling for cross drafts and recirculation and worker movements, while repeatedly recalibrating and cleaning the sampling equipment itself.

Not surprisingly, therefore, a great many regulatory violations arise not from deliberate policies of evasion but from instances of ignorance, incompetence, or inadequate supervision. Poorly trained or simply indifferent workers fail to close a valve or heed a warning buzzer or dispose of wastes according to instructions. (The infamous accident at the Three

---

*An environmental engineer employed by a large metal fabrication company told us he noticed that a fan in a pollution-control "baghouse" was vibrating. Fearing a breakdown and a violation of pollution regulations, he went to the chief of plant maintenance. The maintenance man, his desk full of urgent work orders for repairs on a variety of production machines, responded, "Here's a wrench. You fix it."

Mile Island nuclear power plant in Pennsylvania in 1979 is a highly publicized example. Maintenance technicians had failed to close a valve in the cooling system, and control room operators misinterpreted gauges and warning systems.[14]) Managers of subunits, told simultaneously to "cut costs" and to "obey all regulations," take calculated (or miscalculated) risks and circumvent established safety routines to handle sudden crises. They sometimes suppress information about defects or provide false information to a regulatory agency about pollution levels in order to "look good" to their superiors or to accomplish certain short-term goals for their particular departments.[15] Regulated enterprises vary in their organizational and managerial capacities to prevent these kinds of violations. While it may be possible to induce some improvements by fearsome law enforcement, it is not clear that high levels of managerial excellence or supervisory vigilance can be produced by detailed regulatory prescriptions.

What proportion of regulated enterprises is likely to comply with regulations, and what proportion is deliberately evasive? What proportion has a well-developed managerial capacity to anticipate and control risks, and what proportion does not? The answers depend on a multitude of variables, such as the perceived probability and severity of legal sanctions associated with a particular regulation, the extent that compliance costs can be passed on to customers, the average size of firms in the industry, and the degree to which the regulations are consonant with liability law, market pressures, and the long-run economic interests of the enterprises. What does seem clear, however, is that the regulated enterprises in any program will be distributed along a spectrum of dispositions ranging from most to least compliant—from "good apples" to "bad apples."

The good apples are firms or other enterprises that essentially are guided by some conception of long-term self-interest. They are concerned about their reputations in the marketplace, maintaining smooth labor relations, preventing lawsuits, and avoiding the stigma of being labeled a socially irresponsible lawbreaker. They would not necessarily act in a socially responsible manner if there were *no* realistic threat of regulatory enforcement, but they are predisposed to comply once regulations are on the books and being enforced. They are also concerned about costs and are not always willing to subordinate short-run cost considerations to long-term and less tangible considerations. They undertake a good deal of balancing and compromising. They may resist regulatory requirements that they believe are clearly unjustifiable. They may also have a low "capacity" for compliance and hence commit violations through employee or supervisory negligence. The best apples will have the strongest internal control systems to prevent mistakes. But reasonably good apples exist too. They are less efficient in anticipating and preventing problems, but they willingly undertake compliance efforts when a violation or weakness is pointed out, by inspectors or their own personnel, rather than cold-bloodedly weighing the cost of compliance against the cost of a possible fine.

The worst apples are guided only by short-term and narrowly financial considerations. Some avoid compliance because their owners or managers are selfish and asocial, others are in desperate financial straits and therefore cannot afford to take the longer and broader view. They resist regulatory requirements wholly on the basis of the cost or inconvenience of compliance, rather than on the basis of any serious argument about its unreasonableness. They will break promises to comply when the enforcement official gives them a second chance and readily resort to litigation as a mechanism for delaying compliance. They will not willingly invest in maintaining those protective or abatement devices they are ultimately compelled to install.

The distribution of good and bad apples with respect to any particular regulatory standard obviously has implications for appropriate enforcement strategy. For analytic purposes, assume that the bad apples make up about 20 percent of the average population of regulated enterprises in most regulatory programs. The other 80 percent would be arrayed over a spectrum of borderline to moderate to really good apples. This distribution almost surely overestimates the proportion of bad apples in most regulatory programs, but it does square roughly with what commentators have said and with much regulatory practice. A study of housing code enforcement in New York City found that 65 percent of recorded violations were attributed to 12 percent of all multiple-dwelling buildings.[16] "Enforcement officials have long recognized," wrote two FDA officials years ago, "that at least 95 percent of compliance comes voluntarily and that this is the major source of consumer protection."[17] Reflecting on his experience as Office of Price Administration administrator during World War II, Chester Bowles said that 20 percent of the regulated population would automatically comply with any regulation simply because it is the law of the land, 5 percent would attempt to evade it, and the remaining 75 percent would go along with it as long as they thought the 5 percent would be caught and punished.[18] In practice, even OSHA relies to a great extent on the presumption that businesses, once apprised of their legal obligations, will abide by the law. After issuing a citation, they conduct very few follow-up inspections; the letter accompanying the citation tells the employer that he must send a letter to the area director describing the steps taken to abate the cited violations, and OSHA, by and large, relies on such "abatement letters."[19] The 80/20 break also reflects the general picture painted for us by numerous people both in the regulated industries and in the regulatory agencies, who said or implied, "Ten percent of the firms cause 90 percent of the problems." This 80/20 distribution is only an assumption. There is no point in trying to be too precise about the numbers, even if an accurate survey could be conducted. The distribution undoubtedly would vary from one regulatory domain to another and, within the same regulatory domain, from region to region and even among different manufacturing plants in the same corporation. Finally, assuming a 90/10, 70/30, or 60/40 break would not appreciably change our argument, which is that (1) good and bad apples are intermixed in the regulated population; (2) the absolute and relative proportion of good apples is large, almost certainly constituting a sizable majority within the total population with respect to most regulatory domains; (3) the absolute number of bad apples is also large; and (4) while uniform, specific regulatory prescriptions and ready recourse to coercion may be necessary to induce bad apples to act in a socially responsible manner, the same degree of uniformity, specificity, and coercion applied to good apples is likely to produce a considerable amount of unreasonableness.

THE OVERINCLUSIVENESS OF LEGAL RULES

Legislators and regulatory rulemakers do not intend to be insensitive to the technological variability in the processes they seek to control or to the differences in motivation and capacity among regulated enterprises. But insensitivity inevitably occurs because of inherent constraints on the rulemaking process, especially when the rulemakers are compelled by political pressures to adopt a strategy of control by uniform, detailed, and stringent rules.

Consider how the demand for many new protective measures arises in the first place. Legislators are apprised of some pattern of misconduct, a series of particularly frightening accidents, or an exposé of the toxic effects of an imperfectly controlled substance. These harmful effects typically are traced to the actions of firms that have somehow evaded the law, which in turn is attributed to insufficient specificity or stringency of the law. The legislators, however, are not concerned with punishing those bad apples by passing ex post facto penal laws, but with shaping or reshaping the future. They are petitioned to prevent "that kind of thing" from happening again by reforming the system that created it. They thus transform individual acts of malfeasance into social problems requiring society-wide solutions.[20] Statutes and regulations are cast in general terms, applicable to entire classes of individuals, organizations, or phenomena. Regulation thus comes to "cover" the good firms as well as the bad, minor risks as well as major ones, well-working parts of the system along with those that have broken down.

Quality-of-care regulations for nursing homes, for instance, cover every facility from "the most awful speculative fleabag" to "the most excellent philanthropic home," in Bruce Vladeck's words. Detailed regulations designed to prevent the worst operators from cutting corners also apply to the good home. They direct government inspectors "to cite a first-rate nursing director for being behind on keeping patient charts the same as they cite incompetent nursing directors who could not maintain a decent chart if they tried."[21] Similarly, Jeremy Rabkin has written of the Office for Civil Rights in HEW, "It was one thing to charge particular Texas school districts . . . with discrimination ('on the basis of national origin') because they had left otherwise capable Chicano children to vegetate in classes for the mentally retarded simply because of their difficulties with the English language." But it was quite another thing for HEW to attack the "underlying problem" by requiring all school districts in the nation to take affirmative steps to remedy language deficiencies of "national origin minority group students" by undertaking elaborate surveys and "educational diagnoses" of all students from non-English–speaking homes, to provide instruction in their native language with "culturally suitable" materials, and to examine and abandon any tests or assignment practices that might put children on a lower track because of deficiencies in English rather than lower intelligence.[22]

One reason for this expansionary, across-the-board thrust of regulatory rules is the national commitment to equal treatment before the laws, impartiality, and objectivity. A legislature or regulatory body that prescribed one set of rules for first-rate directors of nursing and another for bad apples, however defined, would be attacked for drafting vague standards that could be used in a discriminatory manner. To impose affirmative bilingual instruction requirements on the offending Texas schools and not on other school districts (even those with no hint of a bad record) would be politically unacceptable, as would requiring expensive precautionary and reporting rules for one infant-formula factory that negligently left out a vital ingredient during a production change, while leaving its competitors exempt from those extra costs.

Social harms usually spring from a variety of causes, and this complexity is another source of overinclusive regulations. Regulatory rulemakers usually sense that the world to be regulated is indeed diverse, but it is not easy to know precisely what factors are most important in producing or preventing the harm in question. Yet rulemakers must choose, usually before all the relevant complexities can be specified; hence, they must adopt, implicitly or explicitly, some causal theory about what variables are most important. Suppose the rulemakers learn that a serious accident was caused by company A's failure to do X. They theorize that the same thing may happen in other companies (especially if they are viewed as "amoral calculators") unless a regulation is written and enforced compelling all companies to do X *and* to take precautions Y and Z that will make sure they do X, *and* to keep records showing that X, Y, and Z are performed regularly. As the director of regulatory compliance in a drug manufacturing plant told us, "If the FDA finds anything wrong in any plant, they write a regulation [applicable to all plants] to prevent it from happening again, usually by requiring more checks and records." The problem is that procedure X might not be nearly so important in factories B and C, whose production and quality control techniques are somewhat different from company A's, and where safeguards Y and Z might be close to irrelevant. The larger and more varied the population and processes subject to regulation, of course, the greater the risks of such overinclusiveness. The movement toward federal regulation thus intensifies the problem. As former Secretary of Labor John Dunlop observed, "A rule that is fair and workable in New York may be excessively severe or unnecessary in Utah. . . . Uniform national rules may assure equity, but they do not reflect the reality of the workplace."[23]

In theory, rulemakers could cope with variety and avoid simplistic causal theories by holding longer hearings, listening to a wider range of affected enterprises, or commissioning more studies. In practice, however, detailed analysis is often precluded by political pressures. Ecological catastrophes and threats to human health engender strong emotions, and rulemakers are urged to act promptly. When there are disclosures about possible dangers posed by chemical additives or contaminants in food, a Senate report observed, "Delay and indecision [by the FDA] intensify fear and concern," consumer activists and the news media continue to publicize possible ill-effects, producers urge the agency to reassure the public, and "members of Congress, reacting to a legitimate concern of their constituents, demand a prompt resolution."[24] Yet the scientific evidence on risk and its variation under different circumstances is rarely clear. A former FDA general counsel acknowledges, "We often regulate more out of fear of the unknown than out of respect and appreciation of the known."[25]

Sometimes, it should be added, the propensity to ignore the complexity of regulatory problems is deliberate. To gather the momentum to push regulatory legislation through Congress, political scientist James Q. Wilson has pointed out, proponents attempt to create an atmosphere of crisis. They exaggerate the extent of the problem and understate the difficulties or the costs of the proposed regulatory solution.[26] Michael Levin, a former U.S. Department of Labor attorney, noted that the hearings on the bill creating OSHA were dominated by frightening recitations of statistics on disabling injuries and occupational disease, but that "Congress never looked at the causes of workplace injuries or asked whether direct regulation was likely to work. Nor did it consider compliance costs, assuming that these could easily be paid by business or passed on to consumers."[27] And there is always the temptation for politicians, even when presented with cost-benefit analyses of different regulatory alternatives and studies showing the complexity of the problem, to choose the "toughest" option for symbolic reasons alone.[28]

Openly political pressures and motivations are moderated at the agency level, but not eliminated. Pressures for prompt decisions are intensified by statutes compelling agencies to issue standards within certain deadlines, sometimes resulting in inadequate investigation. To prevent undue influence by regulated enterprises, the agency rulemaking process has been forced to operate less through informed consultation and negotiation with affected interests and more through open (sometimes televised) public hearings, where the search for facts and solutions is often distorted by dramatic and moralistic posturing for the record.[29] And most fundamentally, the information-gathering and -processing costs for determining all relevant variations are simply overwhelming. Consequently, rulemakers inevitably seek simplifying ways to order complex phenomena and to build these simplifications into their regulations.

Simplifications also are inevitable because bad outcomes can arise through negligent actions that are fleeting and hidden from view or that leave no detectible or easily measurable evidence. Ironically, it is this very elusiveness of bad actions or outcomes that gives rise to protective regulation in the first place: if the harmful attributes of a product or a work situation were easier to detect, consumers or workers would be able to protect themselves. If harmful food products always sprouted a distinctive fluorescent mold that could be detected by consumers while the product was on the supermarket shelf, there would be no need for factory inspections by state and federal pure food agencies. If workers knew exactly what risks they were exposed to in a given job, and what the best methods were for protecting against them, employers would be obliged to invest more in prevention. But even regulators cannot solve such information problems completely. The nursing home inspector is no better able than a prospective patient to stick a measuring instrument in the air and assess the degree of tender loving care present in the facility, and even if the inspector's experience and intuition told him that patients often were mistreated, that would scarcely be legally sufficient to justify the imposition of a fine or a mandatory remedy if the management disputes his view. Hence, social regulation usually must establish legally enforceable—and therefore simple and easily measurable—requirements that are *proxies* for the outcome or quality we really care about. Rules are written to require installation of certain equipment, say, or the adoption of certain specific procedures that are believed to have a causal connection to the desired outcome. To ensure the wholesomeness of beef products, for example, the Wholesome Meat Act of 1967 and its supporting regulations specify in great detail the kinds of machinery, flooring materials, and procedures to be used in slaughtering cattle and processing beef. The FDA regulations concerning intravenous and blood plasma products specify, inter alia, technical requirements for water systems, air filters, sterilization cycles, and record keeping in regulated manufacturing plants.

By focusing on these imperfect correlates of "safe products," regulations often require protective measures whose absence is not necessarily bad in a particular setting. The failure of an intravenous fluid manufacturer to keep required "laminar air flow equipment"—and here we quote from FDA regulations —"in operation for at least 15 minutes before beginning filling operations" *might* lead to product contamination, depending on, among other things, the capabilities of the enterprise's quality control system as a whole. The absence of a government-approved written affirmative action plan *might* lead to discriminatory hiring in some department of an organization, but such requirements are overinclusive with respect to organizations that have strong norms against discrimination.

The imperfect correlation between proxy requirements and actual hazards is reflected in the recurrent complaints by regulated businessmen that compliance with a regulatory rule in their particular operation has only a negligible effect on real hazards or environmental conditions. Some academic studies have confirmed these complaints; for example, even industry's perfect and continuous compliance with OSHA safety regulations—many of which require specific guards, railings, warning signs, and other possible barriers to accidents—probably would reduce injury rates by only 15 to 25 percent.[30] In countless individual instances, therefore, the requirement that employers install a particular device contributes very little to the level of safety in the plant, especially if the firm has a strong training program.

LEGALISTIC ENFORCEMENT

Unreasonableness would not flow automatically from overinclusive, centrally formulated legal rules were those rules not enforced in a literal manner. If regulatory rulemakers in Washington or the state capital cannot draft rules that are sufficiently sensitive to the diversity of the regulated world, widely dispersed enforcement officials might step in to mediate between general rules and particular situations, to tailor the regulatory requirements more closely to the individual case. Inspectors meet representatives of regulated enterprises face-to-face; they look directly at particular production processes, the risks they create, and the existing techniques for controlling them; and they make intuitive judgments about the motivations and capabilities of the enterprises they deal with, mentally rating them on the hierarchy of good to bad apples. Vladeck observes, "An experienced nursing home . . . surveyor can tell within a half hour whether any given facility is very poor, very good, or somewhere in between. In a day and a half, [she] can tell with some precision . . . ."[31] Workplace safety inspectors, too, claim to be able to tell in a short time whether a factory has a meaningful safety program. If inspectors were free to bend or adapt overinclusive regulatory rules to situations in which they were inappropriate or only marginally important, site-level unreasonableness would be curtailed.

Undoubtedly, such instances of flexibility at the enforcement level do occur. But such adaptations are distinctly inimical to the spirit of the new-style protective regulation, which is worried about "capture" and prescribes an explicitly legalistic enforcement style. To prevent the erosion of protections established by the rules, regulations must be strictly and literally enforced, violations must be met with legal penalties (not extensions of time), and the inspectors themselves must be closely monitored for signs of laxity. If in the past inspectors often had functioned as "consultants,"attempting to advance regulatory goals by persuasion and advice, the new inspector would conduct himself as a "cop," quick to apply legal sanctions against deviations from the law— but less able and willing to adapt the law to the situation.

How broadly or how deeply this set of prescriptions has reached into inspectorial practice is difficult to determine, but it is easy to point out prominent examples of its effect—and, incidently, hard to find examples of a contrary transformation, that is, toward making cops into consultants. California's pre-OSHA Division of Industrial Safety had an enforcement style based on warnings and advice to employers. It was staffed by engineers who were organized to conduct inspections according to their professional specialties (e.g., electrical, construction). They rarely turned to prosecution or used their summary powers to close hazardous operations on the spot. But under the OSHA regime, a citation must be issued for all violations, and fines must be imposed. The OSHA Field Operations Manual actually instructs an inspector to issue a citation even if the employer corrects the violation before his eyes. Even though this probably does not often happen, there is little doubt, based on interviews with inspectors and factory managers in California, that Cal-OSHA, as it is now known, is a radically transformed organization. Violations of the detailed regulations—even those that businessmen argue are trivial or that they quickly abate—are regularly cited, and fines are assessed according to a fixed, statutory schedule. Heavier fines are assessed automatically for repeat violations, including failure to abate a violation within the deadline set by the agency. Special remedial orders are issued with some regularity.*

---

*Still, the agency is criticized regularly for not bringing many criminal prosecutions (as opposed to civil penalty actions) against violators. See Henry Weinstein, "Laxity in Prosecuting Job Health Violations Is Assaulted," *Los Angeles Times*, August 8, 1980, p. 1.

Armed with more stringent rules and more frequently employed sanctions, Cal-OSHA inspectors seem to have adopted a "tougher" definition of their role. One Cal-OSHA official whose career spanned both eras asserted: "An inspector has got to be an industrial policeman. . . . They are law enforcement officers . . . . If they don't like being cops, then they have no place in this line." Another said: "We tried in the old days to help violators find solutions, but at this point, federal law now requires us to be very legalistic. . . . We now refer to our surveys as 'cases.' "

A similar philosophy, apparently, has emerged in the FDA, whose inspectors, one senior enforcement official noted, are no longer expected to use judgment but to be walking "cameras" that detect violations, "the eyes and ears of the agency." A young regional FDA enforcement official told us:

> We're a law enforcement agency, not a service agency like USDA [United States Department of Agriculture]. If we go into a factory and see someone picking his nose while he is handling shrimp, we don't say, "Gee, you ought to buy gloves for that guy." We say, "You have violated Section whatever of the Act."

Inspectors for the San Francisco Bay Area Air Pollution Control District—a body criticized in the early 1970s for weak enforcement efforts—now adopt a similar posture.

The propensity to define the job in terms of single-minded enforcement of the rules (rather than "helping violators find a solution") is reinforced by the various review mechanisms established by law (such as federal reinspection) and the tendency of legislative oversight committees (usually dominated by the same legislators who sponsored the "get tough" legislation) to evaluate agencies in terms of their enforcement record. Once the agency is evaluated in those terms, the individual inspector's performance is likely to be measured by his personal enforcement record. Top enforcement officials usually deny that they evaluate inspectors in terms of how many citations they issue, but they admit that they check. "We have a printout for each inspector," said an official of the California Division of Food and Drugs. "We can look and see if he embargoes or not." In a survey of OSHA area office directors, seven out of ten said that they used printouts, including numbers of violations cited, to evaluate inspector performance.[32] Even if supervisors do not use a low citation record as an absolute measure of performance, inspectors are "on the safe side" if they produce a "normal" level of citations or enforcement actions. An air pollution inspector (a former police officer) assigned to watch for emissions at a large petroleum refinery that was generally regarded in the agency as very cooperative told us that he was personally inclined to overlook minor violations but that he tried to make sure he issued about 30 citations a year to avoid suspicion.

Evaluation in enforcement terms bureaucratizes the actual inspection process. In many agencies, inspectors are now supplied with detailed reporting forms and checklists, which provide the basis for statistical analysis of citations by supervisors and for spot checks by federal inspectors who reinspect the same establishments. Nursing home inspectors in California, for example, undertake surveys armed with a checklist of over 100 items, dictated for the most part by Medicare regulations. In filling them in, they must have been cognizant, at least for the several years that the practice was in effect, that a cadre of federal inspectors "validated" state surveys by reinspecting 10 percent of homes for Medicare violations.[33] An FDA enforcement official told us there had been an increased emphasis on detailed checklists and reporting forms in his agency as well. The changes are apparent to regulated enterprises. A research chemist, in charge of regulatory affairs for a manufacturer of drugs and biologics, felt that with the increasingly enforcement-oriented posture of the FDA in recent years, "Inspectors have become clerks. They're more interested in checking our record-keeping than looking at our actual production processes." He added that they were also increasingly literal in their reading and application of the regulations.

Close adherence to the rules and extensive documentation are also compelled by the formal enforcement process itself. An increased propensity to cite and prosecute violations means the inspector is more likely to find himself appearing in court (or, in agencies with the power to impose fines, before the agency's hearing board). Legalistic prosecution begets legalistic defenses. The inspector, in turn, must always be prepared to withstand cross-examination, which means that his inspections and reports must rest more on documented evidence of rule violations than on intuitive and qualitative judgments. "Every case now must be developed with an eye to a lawsuit," a top FDA field-enforcement official told us. A nursing home enforcement official noted:

> You can't decide that some facilities will get cursory inspections because they do a good job and you won't have to take them to court. In a nursing home, one can go from very good to very bad

in two weeks . . . . You have to document *everything*. If you don't
have it on paper, it didn't happen.

Cal-OSHA, faced with a higher rate of contested cases, set up special
inspector training courses on how to prepare cases for court and present
evidence. Enforcement officials from several agencies told us that, with
the increasing possibility of court cases, inspectors now carry cameras to
record violations.

More litigation also means that inspectors' reports must become more
narrowly legalistic, tied to the language of the rules, purged of qualitative
judgments about particular enterprises. A top California enforcement
official dealing with nursing home regulation explained:

> The [inspectors] used to write long reports on the *care* given insti-
> tutionalized people. But the attorneys criticized them for failing to
> "build a record"—not telling them what [the homes] have failed to
> do, not documenting each infraction.
>
> We have stopped having inspectors write narrative reports. If an
> inspector writes down "This guy is crazy" [and the report is dis-
> closed in court] the inspector is "prejudiced." We make them stick
> to questions of fact only.

Increased expectations of a strict enforcement policy seem to have
made regulatory officials in many agencies uncomfortable about admitting that they have discretion and about using the discretion they do have.
Inspectors often deny they use discretion as if they fear it will be equated
with laxity or corruption. Only if the question is asked in a different
way—"Do you have to use judgment in deciding to cite?"—is an affirmative answer forthcoming. We regularly questioned enforcement officials
about "plea bargaining"—dropping citations for minor violations in return for prompt remedial action on more serious ones. In several agencies, we were repeatedly told that this was no longer permitted, certainly
not at the field inspector level, and we received confirmation, by and
large, from regulated enterprises.

The bureaucratization and legalism we have described have not been
so pronounced in some older or local agencies. Even in the agencies
"programmed" to stick to the rules, enforcement officials use their own
judgment, for the most part, to determine which establishments to inspect most often and whether to seek criminal penalties against violators.

And an inspector's judgment is always at work in fitting a rule to the details of what he sees, in deciding, for example, whether a dirty rail on a conveyer in a meatpacking plant poses a risk of "remote product contamination" or "direct product contamination," the latter requiring a tougher response. But discretion for inspectors to overlook obvious or clear rule violations, to grant extended time for abatement, to "forget" citations after they are written up, seems, by all accounts, to have been restricted.

Some of the discretion that formerly was exercised at the inspector's level is now exercised only by top enforcement officials in charge of formal applications for variances or by agency lawyers in settlement conferences that occur after formal charges have already been filed. But even these reconsiderations can be characterized as legalistic. Higher level Cal-OSHA officials, for example, have informal conferences with employers who complain about citations. But they do not drop citations, they say, except on purely legal grounds (e.g., if the inspector was mistaken about the facts or the law). The only compromise permitted in the conference, they say, relates to the time required for corrective measures—a decision they have statutory discretion to make.

Statutes usually provide procedures for "variances" from regulations in individual cases, presumably as a substitute for discretion (at the inspector level) or bargaining (at the supervisory level). The statutory criteria for variances, however, often are detailed and stringent. Variance applications and decisions, accordingly, are much more formal than field-level negotiations. The regulated enterprise must support its case with legal briefs and technical evidence. Many enterprises complain that, in view of the time and expense involved, variance procedures are a poor substitute for more flexible field-level enforcement.[34] Finally, because variance cases are "on the record," in granting them the agency risks being taken to court for what proregulation groups may see as undue leniency.[35]

The statutory emphasis on citizen complaints also reinforces pressures on the inspector to stick to the rules. Disgruntled complainants can call superiors or political representatives and, invoking legal rights created by the regulations, criticize inspectors who fail to cite violations, calling *them* lawbreakers. Several corporate safety directors we interviewed said that OSHA inspectors called to a plant by a complaint often feel compelled to find *something* to cite, even if the original item complained about was not

a violation, so "it won't look like they're in bed with the company."
Uniformity of application, consistency, becomes a mode of staying out of
trouble. A regional enforcement official of the Office for Civil Rights,
responsible for enforcing laws preventing discrimination against handicapped students, was asked if enforcement ever varied because of different conditions or budgetary problems in different school districts. "There
better not be," he answered. "If I find out about it, those EOSs [equal
opportunity specialists] will hear from me. We're here to enforce the
laws."[36]

THE "OFFICIAL PERSPECTIVE"
VS. THE "CIVILIAN PERSPECTIVE"

If enforcement officials are evaluated in terms of how consistently they
apply the rules and penalize the violators, they are not likely to respond
to complaints from regulated enterprises that remedial steps are unduly
costly or unnecessary in a particular case or that a fine is unfair where
substantial good faith efforts toward compliance have been undertaken.
Such complaints, in fact, may drive the inspector further toward unresponsiveness. When the regulated businessman berates him for being
unreasonable, the inspector caught up in a bureaucratic system and
trained in law enforcement rather than persuasion finds it convenient to
answer, "Sorry, sir, but I'm just telling you what the regulation says. If
you don't like it, write to your congressman."

From what we have called "the official perspective," of course, the
inspector's response, if not eloquent, is essentially correct. From that
viewpoint, primary responsibility for defining and controlling socially
irresponsible behavior must rest in the government, with its commitment
to discovering and protecting the public interest, not rest in a multitude of
private entities concerned primarily with their narrower self-interest. If
the regulations are arguably improper, it is far better for them to be
changed by legislators or top regulatory officials, with the benefit of
expert advice and an overview of the entire range of regulatory problems,
than by an undisciplined corps of far-flung inspectors, susceptible to the
bluffs and blandishments as well as the justifiable complaints of regulated
enterprises. Despite the inappropriateness of regulatory requirements
for some situations, centrally programmed, tough enforcement, even if it

degenerates at times into mindless legalism, will on balance be more effective and more economical than a more sophisticated and subtle but corruptible approach.

In its own way, the official perspective is also sensitive to the diversity and ambiguity of the world. But the true and reasonable, it asserts, are hard to find. The inspector works in a world of conflicting claims and uncertainty about risks and costs of compliance in determining what is dangerous and how to deal with violations; he should hold fast to the carefully considered, publicly debated, officially promulgated regulations; he should make adjustments only on the basis of scientifically gathered or otherwise substantiated evidence, not on basis of undocumented cost estimates or intuitive risk-assessments in the field.

Those subject to regulation, however, have a rather different perspective on defining and controlling hazards. Whereas officials are concerned with the whole range of possible harms and the misbehavior of the worst of the bad apples, the manager of the regulated enterprise is concerned only with the risks actually generated by his particular operation. Whereas regulatory officials tend to focus on one particular set of protective values, managers of regulated enterprises are sensitive to the ways in which time, money, and energy directed toward compliance with regulatory rules will impinge on other important values and obligations, including the multitude of human commitments made in the course of the effort to keep an enterprise going. For the official, the legitimacy of regulatory specifications rests on their status as the law of the land, while the manager of an enterprise judges legal rules in terms of whether the specific problems they point to in his operation are serious or as imminent as other problems the enterprise faces. Inspectors are compelled to treat as "real" only that which is made relevant by the regulations and is formally proved. The regulated businessman typically has a broader sense of relevance, and because he is sensitive to the costs and delays of formal proof, he is accustomed to making decisions based on informal discussion and "approximate" evidence or "guesstimates."

To be sure, not all regulatory encounters match a stereotypically legalistic and unresponsive regulator against a stereotypically pragmatic and cooperatively disposed businessman. Tough—even legalistic—regulation is, after all, very appropriate to a good many situations. While bad apples may not make up the majority or even a very large minority of regulated enterprises, they are numerous enough to figure largely in the accumulated experience of enforcement officials and, because of the

special risks they pose, to absorb a disproportionate share of their energies. In addition, relatively firm pressure applied to reasonably good
apples may be necessary to *keep* them that way. Finally, in a certain
proportion of cases, regulatory officials do indeed back away from inappropriate toughness and perhaps even deliberately ignore the norms
that forbid discretionary underenforcement. Legalistic unresponsiveness
to complaints of unreasonableness, therefore, do not characterize all
regulatory encounters, although there is reason to believe they are common indeed. Talking to almost any businessman or engineer about concrete experiences with inspectors will produce half-a-dozen recent examples. And even if these clashes between the official and the civilian
perspectives occur in only 25 percent of specific regulatory citations or
orders (or 20 or 15 percent, although 30 or 35 percent is just as possible),
the absolute number of such cases still would be very high.

The clash in perspectives occurs most clearly in respect to official
versus civilian attitudes toward violations, the likelihood of harm, the
choice of abatement measures, and the need for documentation. In
illustrating these clashes, we will draw heavily on examples from OSHA
enforcement actions against private businesses that we had reason to
think were, if not good apples, at least not bad apples, since these
illustrate the problem in the most dramatic form. But they highlight
tendencies that emerge under any legalistic enforcement program
whether directed against organizations in the private or in the public or
nonprofit sectors.

VIOLATIONS VS. PROBLEMS

Perhaps the most common complaint about inspectors from legalistic
agencies is that "they are of little help." The emphasis on help underscores the tendency of businessmen to think of regulation as an ongoing
process of encountering problems and searching for cost-effective solutions, not a very different approach from the way they think of production. Accustomed to trying to achieve their goals in the face of the
competing concerns of other departments and workers, managers expect
the problem solving to proceed through negotiation and compromise,
according to a "morality of cooperation," rather than by legal fiat.[37] Thus
managers criticize inspectors who walk through the plant looking only for
"violations" of the rules rather than pointing out "real problems." The

inspector is viewed as irresponsible when he issues a citation or abatement order and walks away with no apparent appreciation of or concern with the problems involved in "coming into compliance."

The inspector's concentration on violations rather than problem solving is a natural consequence, of course, of institutionalized pressures. Discovering problems and helping to solve them would require the inspector to adopt the civilian perspective (at least temporarily), to discuss the operation being inspected with its operators, and to learn more about the technical and financial aspects of alternative control methods. From the official perspective, however, all such discussion is not only legally irrelevant but also a dangerous invitation to erroneous judgment by, or co-optation of, the inspector.

The emphasis on violations, formal prosecutions, and penalties under deterrence-oriented enforcement strategies seems to induce inspectors to think of their jobs in terms of winning cases. To managers of regulated enterprises, however, with their inclination to view violations as problems to be solved, inspectors who take an adversarial, us-versus-them stance are particularly annoying. For example:

> The safety director for a large multiplant manufacturing firm described an OSHA citation issued at a plant that manufactures culverts. The culvert is extruded continuously, he explained, and automatically sawed off in lengths. Every few seconds, the cut pieces roll off the line sideways to a collection point. "We had a small sign posted near that point, warning people to watch out for the rolling pieces." The OSHA inspector wrote up a citation for not having a larger sign. A company official later called up the inspector's supervisor and asked what standard had been violated. The inspector, it turned out, had used a standard that requires certain large warning signs of specified dimensions for machinery that periodically and automatically goes on and off. The company official argued that the culvert process was not the kind of machine the standard was written for. The standard, he argued, was designed to protect operators or maintenance people who work on machines that can suddenly start up without their knowing it, whereas "This is a *continuous* process." Moreover, he argued, the process in question had been in operation for years and there had been no injuries and no "incidents" (the safety engineers' term for "close calls"). The OSHA supervisor listened to this, conferred

with the inspector, and responded, "I told him what you said. But he thinks we have a winner here." And again, after some more argument from the company official, the supervisor said, "We still think we've got a good case." The safety director, annoyed by the tenor of that response, exclaimed, "What kind of thinking is that? We've got a winner! We've got a *good case!*"

The legalistic ethos also induces inspectors to treat business corporations as monolithic legal entities, with a single will and an internally consistent attitude toward social and legal responsibilities. To corporate managers, on the other hand, the corporation is a loose conglomeration of separate departments and managers, each with distinct problems, some very responsible and some less so. The difference in perspectives shows up in the handling of repeat violations. For example:

Automobile assembly plants are plagued by oil spills that create slip-and-fall hazards. Spills are impossible to prevent completely, and the companies assign maintenance crews to clean them up. The effectiveness of that program depends on how busy or diligent maintenance is because management understandably is reluctant to staff maintenance (which has other responsibilities) at a level sufficient to clean up peak-level oil spills immediately. In a plant we visited, management claimed most spills get cleaned up within an hour "if maintenance is working." The company recently appealed an OSHA repeat citation (which carries a much heavier fine) for an oil spill because it had actually occurred in a different area (although in a similar process) from a spill for which it received an earlier citation. Company officials saw them as two separate "mistakes," the responsibilities of separate foremen. To the OSHA official, it was all the same company.[38]

The citation for the oil spill also reflected the difference in time perspective between inspectors and business managers. An OSHA inspector sees a situation at one point in time. When he sees an oil spill, he literally takes a snapshot. If the spill is hazardous, it does not matter to the law whether it has been there for five minutes or five hours, whether spills are cleaned up on the average within forty-five minutes or eight hours. While inspectors focus on individual instances of illegal conduct, managers focus on programs, rates of bad events, and average response time.

Because inspectors in legalistic programs are often indifferent to those concerns, management sees them as unreasonable, as missing the important criteria for gauging the responsibility of the regulated enterprise. "If you live here a period of time," said the plant's chief safety engineer, "you can see if we have a housekeeping program or not."

PROBABILITIES VS. POSSIBILITIES OF HARM

Regulatory statutes and programs are designed to eliminate or reduce risk of harm, on the premise that there was "too much" risk under preexisting laws and practices. Enforcement officials are trained to perceive that kind of risk. They regularly encounter and are reminded of the worst cases, the accidents that in fact occurred. Thus they develop a specialized vision, more sensitive to possible risks and deceptions than the average person's. An employment interview or test seen by an employer as a method of ascertaining merit or motivation is viewed by an Equal Employment Opportunity Commission investigator as a possible source of bias or discrimination. The typical consumer sees an open bin of raisins or granola in a supermarket as an enjoyable self-service opportunity, but the state public health inspector sees it as a medium for spreading bacteria and disease.

If inspectors tend to go through a factory or store actively looking for certain possibly risky situations, businessmen, like the rest of us, get through the day by living with risk. Operating in a world of limited resources and conflicting demands, managers specialize in juggling and ranking a large number of different risks. Trying to meet a critical rush order, they may be simultaneously delaying machine maintenance (thus risking a breakdown), using an untested substitute raw material (because the regular supplier had to delay shipment), and sampling fewer units than the new quality control man tells him is optimal because "the old way has worked out fine so far." His response, when told something entails certain risks, is likely to be "How much risk?" He deals in probabilities. Therefore, a regulatory rule, order, or citation that requires a business manager to expend resources to prevent harms that are merely "possible"—without considering what it will cost, both financially and in terms of jeopardizing other goals or values—strikes him as unreasonable.

Of course, the way the plant manager balances or weighs risks is not necessarily in the public interest. It may well be that managers tend to underestimate certain risks, especially if, as is often the case, the company—not the manager—will pay for any mistake, and if it is not the health or safety of the manager that is jeopardized by any miscalculation. Hence, a regulatory program and periodic visits from an inspector may be needed to compel a higher level of attention and sacrifice to reduce certain kinds of risks. But that does not diminish the validity of the business manager's expectation that, once risks are pointed out, the regulatory response should be keyed to their relative seriousness. For example:

Dr. Philip Thuringer is a research chemist who now is director of regulatory affairs for a large corporation (which we shall call Maxwell Laboratories) that makes pharmaceuticals, blood plasma products, and other biologics used in the health industry. Maxwell, he says, had been purchasing plasma from an independent "plasmapherisis" center.[39] The center was suddenly closed down by the FDA for regulatory violations and its product embargoed. However, apparently by accident, 1,000 units of plasma were shipped to Maxwell after the formal date of the embargo. Maxwell, when informed, put the plasma under quarantine by labeling it as required by regulations. Nevertheless, the quarantined plasma accidentally was taken from its storage place by Maxwell employees who misunderstood the label (which is not at all clear). It was mixed with 2,000 other units and processed. The original plasma center had been closed down for "overbleeding" its "donors" (i.e., taking too much blood at one time or taking blood too often). Overbleeding does affect the donor's health, but has no adverse effect on the quality of the plasma produced. Hence, the 3,000 units Maxwell made incorporating the 1,000 quarantined units were not contaminated or unsafe in any way. Nevertheless, the FDA took the position that all the embargoed plasma and the 3,000 units produced by Maxwell could not be sold for human use. Moreover, Thuringer told us, Maxwell was faced with a fine for violating the quarantine order, even though the FDA conceded that no one was or would be endangered by the use of the products involved. Even Thuringer, who, like the other Maxwell officials we interviewed, seemed willing (quite uncritically) to spend "whatever is necessary" to enhance safety, criticized this enforcement stance as characteristic of the FDA's "increasingly bureaucratic attitude" of rule for rule's sake and wasteful both from a health and from an economic point of view.

The FDA view in this case, apparently, was "the law must be obeyed"; to "allow them to get away with it" *could* lead to a general laxity or disregard for the rules. In view of the massive lawsuits and horrendous adverse publicity that could result from the sale of a dangerously contaminated product, however, firms like Maxwell would seem to have every incentive to prevent any meaningful decline in quality assurance standards.[40] From the standpoint of probable risks, rather than possible ones, the embargo and fine seem unreasonable.

Another reason for the FDA's position in such cases is that it is much easier to focus on possible risks than to ascertain the true probability of harm presented by a violation or by the product itself. Hinich and Staelin report that in inspecting a food-processing plant, FDA inspectors, rather than sampling and testing the finished product, usually "look for evidence of insects in the processing area, uncapped jars of poisonous cleaning agents . . . indications that employees wash their hands after using the lavatory," and so on. (Under FDA regulations, a product is legally "adulterated" if it is made in a plant that fails to comply with such sanitation-oriented regulations.) Manufacturers complain, of course, that violations of individual sanitation regulations do not necessarily mean the product is actually dangerous, especially if subsequent steps in processing (such as heating or cooking) or other quality control procedures would remove or deactivate bacterial contamination. But the FDA, according to Hinich and Staelin, "feels it is more efficient . . . to look at the process than to try to find a few bad items among the total output" by sampling and testing.[41]

THEORY VS. EXPERIENCE

Regulated businessmen are mistrustful of theory. An official of the California Trucking Association told us, "A regulation based on good operational practices rather than [untried regulatory] theory makes a lot of difference. We abide by those laws with respect, even if we don't like them." But the official mode of interpreting reality, dependent as it is on simplification and standardization, inevitably tends to put a lot more weight on theory. Experience is too diverse, too hard to assess, too slow to accumulate, and too likely to risk apparently "preventable" catastrophes for it to stand as the principal guide to rulemaking.

Unfortunately, regulatory rule writers often rely on theory undisciplined by reference even to readily assessable experience as the basis for their work. In many agencies, the managerial climate does not support systematic exploration of the views of field-level enforcement officials and legitimates a "purist" approach to regulation writing by "specialists" cloistered in their headquarters offices. An inspector in a rather legalistic state agency responsible for licensing community care facilities for the mentally ill told us that in her six years on the job neither she nor any of her coworkers were ever consulted by headquarters about appropriate content of agency regulations or procedures. Facility operators were also ignored, by and large, except for occasional pro forma consultations with representatives of the operators' associations. Thus the theory of the causes of and the cures for poor care embodied in the regulations remained largely impervious to experience.

In recent years, the potential clash between the "official" (theoretically oriented) and the civilian (experience-oriented) approaches to problem solving has been exacerbated by a trend toward setting "technology-forcing" regulatory standards that attempt to direct experience, rather than reflect it. Some of these rules set a target date in the future when ambitious performance standards will gain the force of the law. It is then up to the regulated entities to devise their own means of compliance. Thus an OSHA regulation specified that no more than 1 part per million (ppm) of vinyl chloride fumes should be emitted into the air of workplaces, even though the existing standard and the associated technology allowed for 50 ppm. Another approach is for regulators to identify an innovative "best available technology" and make it mandatory for all enterprises in an industry, as the EPA has done for certain air and water pollution control devices.

The powerful rationale behind technology forcing states that the required technological advances simply would not occur without a government-contrived incentive. But this approach may result in the regulators aiming too high. Regulators, after all, are free to be idealists and work from a theoretical blueprint. But the regulated entities must bear the costs and suffer the frustrations of developing an effective technology within a fixed time or of adapting supposedly ideal abatement devices to subtle differences in production conditions or processes. This would not be an insuperable obstacle if the technology-forcing standards were administered flexibly, with due regard for the difficulties encountered and the lessons of experience. This flexibility, however, is not encouraged by the legalistic enforcement ethos or by the associated mistrust of excuses for noncompliance, as reflected in comments such as: "If they have the technology to make these complicated castings, they surely can get the dust out of the air; they don't want to spend the money," or "Consolidated Widget is using a vacuum dust-reduction system, why can't you?" Sometimes the regulated enterprise's problems are dismissed as the product of inexcusable delay or misdirected priorities—"The law has been on the books for two years now. If they had started when they were supposed to, they wouldn't be having these difficulties now. They just hoped they could get away with it as long as they could." From the official perspective, if legal pressure is consistently applied, the regulated enterprise can be forced to come up with the solution—which is attainable in theory.

Businesses, however, are reluctant to adopt new technologies. They are inclined to do so incrementally, starting with pilot projects or with only part of their operation—again, so as to rely more on experience than on theory.[42] Technologically superseded machines and processes are not immediately junked, but gradually phased out. When new devices are installed, it is expected that a period of "debugging" will probably be necessary and that the machine that works well in one plant may not automatically work in another. In contrast to regulatory assumptions about the ready availability of control technology, a Small Business Administration survey of scores of regulated firms noted that "pollution control equipment is often available only in certain modular sizes. Even for standard equipment, such as SO_2 scrubbers, lead times for delivery are currently running about 12 months." And "custom-tailored devices," of course, take much longer to engineer and obtain.[43] When regulatory officials treat these concerns as unjustified stalls or simply as legally irrelevant, the result is the perception of regulatory unresponsiveness. These cases illustrate this clash in perspectives:

- A corporate industrial hygienist reports OSHA inspections that found violations of noise standards at two of the company's can manufacturing plants. The company had been supplying industrial "earmuffs" to workers on those machines, but OSHA rules require employers to "engineer out" the noise problem, if at all possible, rather than rely on "personal protective equipment." The OSHA act also provides that repeat violations, or failure to abate after a first violation, must be penalized by higher monetary fines. The company did not disagree with the engineering out requirement, said the hygienist, "but we wanted to adopt similar controls in all our can plants. We started working on some lines in some plants, on an experimental basis, to see what works best. The Houston OSHA office recognized our good faith efforts and didn't cite us for *continuing* violations in our plant in that region. But the Jacksonville, Florida, regional director wouldn't do that. He said, 'I don't care if line three is closed down [for noise-reduction repairs]. There are *still* violations on lines one and two, and they're running.' "

- A copper smelter in a southern state was cited for excess SO$_2$ emissions, not removed effectively by its existing filtration system. The state pollution control agency called upon the company to install a certain type of scrubber system. The company's environmental engineer complained, "We argued that a scrubber was impractical. I called TVA [which has extensive pollution control systems]. They were anti-scrubber because of enormous maintenance and breakdown problems. But the agency people said it *could* be done. They felt *they knew better than us!*"

- Carl Kekonnen, a company industrial hygienist at a large aluminum manufacturing plant, reports that an OSHA inspector cited the company for not providing protective clothing, such as asbestos suits, to workers exposed to splash hazards and burns from molten metal. Company officials pointed out that, in aluminum "potlines," protective suits hold in the worker's body heat, greatly increasing risks of heat exhaustion (the most salient health problem in the smelter), as compared with the more remote risk of splash burns. The citation was issued anyway. Kekonnen complained further that, "The OSHA man made his recommendation without ever looking at our burn experience in our files, which show the results of our burn prevention program."

In some of these instances, the agency ultimately relented after the company appealed the citation. But in each case, enforcement officials rigidly insisted on penalizing failure to abate a violation "according to the regs," not because they had rigid personalities, but because of an enforcement philosophy that compels inspectors to adhere to the official view of what is feasible.

One of the most serious consequences of such unresponsiveness is that rigid enforcement of technology-forcing regulations can produce immensely costly mistakes. In the early 1970s, the EPA substantially tightened existing regulations to control sulfur dioxide emissions, requiring capture of as much as 90 percent of the gas—a level far beyond the capacity of first-generation SO_2 abatement equipment and admittedly more stringent than many scientific and public health officials' recommendations. (The standards were designed to ensure a "margin of safety," an EPA official was quoted as saying, in the event scientists revise their recommendations.) The regulations stipulated a five-year deadline for compliance. In a 1978 survey, many copper company officials complained that "companies weren't given enough time to develop effective and cost-efficient technology to meet the regulations." Inspiration Copper spent $62.5 million "trying to work out the kinks" in the equipment. It fell into debt—at least partly for this reason—and was taken over by a South African holding company. A vice-president of Phelps Dodge, a major copper company, said his company, too, "rushed to build a system that did not work."[44]

In the case of the National Highway Traffic Safety Administration's requirement of a new computerized braking system for large trucks, the results of technology forcing were not only expensive but also counterproductive. The federal Court of Appeals for the Ninth Circuit finally suspended the regulation, noting that the rule, designed to reduce stopping distance, would actually lead to greater highway dangers because of the tendency of the new systems to malfunction. NHTSA had insisted on a deadline for truck manufacturers to meet stringent braking standards after concluding that further delays would be less productive than forcing manufacturers to work out the bugs. Although individual components required to meet the new standard—strong front axles, new kinds of brake linings, and minicomputers to control wheel lock and skid—had worked reasonably well on test models, mass production of the components for the considerable variety of trucks led to grave problems—relay valve failures, warning signal failures, jackknifing, wheel lockup, and lateral instability. Subsequent surveys by manufacturers indicated that between 49 and 60 percent of the antilock mechanisms were nonfunctional, partly because drivers and fleet managers had disconnected them.[45]

Technology forcing does not always fail. Perhaps an equal number of success stories could be uncovered. OSHA's 1 ppm standard for vinyl chloride emissions led to a major processing innovation by B. F. Goodrich that reduced emissions much more than earlier methods, was much less expensive than projected, and enabled the manufacturer to recover vinyl chloride for further use. Other companies developed automated methods for cleaning PVC reactors, eliminating a significant cause of worker exposure.[46] Moreover, there are surely many instances in which regulators did adjust technology-forcing rules in light of experience or postponed deadlines or accepted reasonable substitutes for prescribed technologies. The point, therefore, is not that technology forcing is wrong or that rigid enforcement always occurs but that the official perspective all too easily leads enforcement officials to underestimate practical difficulties and to insist on the theoretically possible without regard for the lessons of experience.

DOCUMENTATION VS. PAPERWORK

"Which is worse," we asked a nursing home administrator, "having surveyors [inspectors] come around or completing regulatory paperwork?" "The paperwork," she said, "because it is there all the time, twenty-four hours a day, three hundred sixty-five days a year."

Most documentation—the term that regulators prefer to paperwork—requires enterprises to maintain an ongoing record of activities or events that intermittently present inspectors cannot hope to observe reliably. Nurses must record various steps in the treatment of nursing home patients; trucking firms must keep records showing performance of preventive maintenance; intravenous fluid manufacturers must record the details of sterilization cycles for each production batch; personnel departments must document the criteria and factual basis for hiring and promotion decisions; a wide variety of firms must send to agencies periodic certificates, with supporting evidence, stating that they are in compliance with relevant regulations or including plans that detail how they will ensure compliance in the future. Gaps in such records presumably warn enforcement officials about possible violations of substantive rules or possible hazards.

Because such violations or hazards are hard to detect, however, the alternative to mandatory documentation is not necessarily fewer regulatory requirements but more intensive surveillance by means of on-site inspectors. This would certainly be a good deal more expensive than monitoring a paper record, and one may doubt that the regulated parties would prefer it. The official perspective appreciates this point much better than the civilian perspective. But the civilian perspective appreciates another point, which is harder for the official perspective to grasp: the burdens of on-site inspection fall mainly on the regulatory agency, but the burdens of documentation fall mainly on the regulated parties. It is the latter who must keep the records, submit the periodic reports, and collect the data with which to fill out the forms.

The paperwork burden is ample; the Commission on Federal Paperwork estimated that the cost of completing mandated federal paperwork (including tax and census forms) was $25-32 billion per year.[47] A *Newsweek* article in mid-1978 referred to 4,400 forms required by 87 federal regulatory agencies and consuming 143 million man-hours a year of executive and clerical time.[48] The chairman of a large pharmaceutical firm complained that the firm spent "more man-hours filling out government forms or reports than we do on research for cancer and heart disease combined," which translated into $5 million a year.[49]

Documentation, by its very nature, is a declaration of innocence, and most of it is received by officials who ignore it almost entirely. The situation can hardly be otherwise. If regulatory officials knew in advance who was "guilty" of violations or presumptive violations that required further evaluation, they would not need the documentation that was intended to tell them where to look. And if they could rely on the "guilty" to report accurately their compliance-related activities, they would not need to require so much supporting data to check on reliability and accuracy of the records and reports. From a law-enforcement standpoint, the possibility of deception requires that all assertions by regulated enterprises be adequately certified and proved. Documentation is required, therefore, of good and bad apples alike. Yet the civilians who are innocent know that they are innocent even if the officials do not know it. And the officials know that documentation of innocence is not worth looking at; hence, they know that most of the documentation flowing into the agency pursuant to its requirements is a waste of their time and can safely be ignored.

There is not much that can be done to escape this dilemma—a point that officials are in a better position to appreciate than are civilians. Yet the inevitability of at least some amount of excessive paperwork does not make its burdens lighter or less demoralizing. The problem is especially severe for professionals, whose discretionary powers over others make them frequent targets of regulation through documentation requirements. An elementary school teacher—and doctoral candidate in education—has prepared this stunning account of the demoralizing paperwork burden:

> In a typical day an elementary teacher deals with sign-in sheets, lunch counts, hall passes, absence slips, rollbooks, attendance cards, class count forms, parent communications, textbook and materials requests, lesson plans, student evaluations, documentation, [and] paperwork relating directly to teaching students. Additionally, different levels of the bureaucracy frequently request distribution and collection of questionnaires, ethnic surveys, free lunch applications, permission slips, walking trip permits, emergency cards, class schedules, federal forms for Impact Aid, home language surveys, audio-visual surveys, needs assignments, nine-week objectives, yearly objectives, report cards, requests for special services, testing materials, program descriptions, time cards, field trip requests, and several profile cards for each student. . . . (All this at a time when teachers are also being told there is not enough paper for lessons and art projects.)
>
> Much of the paperwork is related to monitoring, evaluating, regulating and verifying the teacher's behavior. . . . It results from mandates at the federal, state, district and school levels. . . . Those teachers who do attempt to criticize the paper overload find that they cannot get to the source of it. It becomes simpler to do it pro forma than to try to comprehend it. Teachers learn that their documentations are usually passed up the line without being read. Even when they are read, administrators have no time to verify the accuracy of the statements. Morale is lowered and paperwork becomes a meaningless exercise.[50]

Ironically, failure by regulated individuals or enterprises to comply fully with paperwork requirements tends to produce demands for even more documentation because, from the standpoint of law-enforcement officials, a gap in the reporting record, an unsubstantiated "certification" of compliance, is a sign of possible failure to comply with underlying substantive norms, and enforcement officials must be prepared to have a fully documented case if necessary. Any opposition by managers to requests for more information—which are often experienced as unjustified slurs on the honesty of their earlier submissions, can be interpreted by enforcement officials as "withholding evidence."

IS REGULATORY UNREASONABLENESS INEVITABLE?

Regulation implies standardization, for without standardization we cannot hope to honor the values of due process and equal treatment before the law. But the standardization that is necessary to make officialdom effective and accountable is ill-suited to the diversity, complexity, and fluidity of the real world. Hence, regulation in some sense cannot help but be somewhat unreasonable.

However, unreasonableness comes in degrees, and *tough* regulation is more often unreasonable than most. This occurs because stringent regulation is designed to cope with the bad apples and the unusually hard cases, which constitute only a minority of all the problems in the domain of regulatory supervision. The majority of firms, being good apples and not-so-hard cases, are subjected to unreasonable regulation. And the larger the majority relative to the whole of the regulated population, the greater the scope of regulatory unreasonableness.

This is not quite the end of the matter, however. While there are powerful political, legal, and bureaucratic reasons for regulators to treat all regulated entities more or less "alike"—the equalitarian idea being what it is in our culture—under certain conditions it may be possible to justify *dissimilar* regulatory treatment. In dissimilar treatment rationally conceived and applied lies at least one hope for more reasonable regulation. While it is difficult to introduce much rationally planned differentiation into the set of regulatory rules, something more can be done at the enforcement level. But before turning to the topic of the prospects of flexible enforcement, from which greater reasonableness might emerge (chapters 5 and 6), a second theme concerning the drawbacks of legalistic rules and inflexible enforcement, namely, that they are often not very effective at achieving their stated objectives, will be explored.

CHAPTER FOUR

THE PERVERSE EFFECTS

OF LEGALISM

•

The move toward more aggressive and more legalistic enforcement undoubtedly has made regulation more effective in at least some important respects. Inspectors armed with severe sanctions and instructed to act like policemen are not likely to be ignored. As a California workplace safety enforcement official put it, "Before OSHA, most firms almost always tried to do a better job after we surveyed them. Now, with the threat of legal action, they feel compelled to do a better job."* Aggressive and controversial regulation has drawn greater attention to regulatory concerns and has increased consciousness of the possible hazards in modern technology and chemistry.

The beneficial effects of legalistic regulation, however, should not blind us to the fact that the unreasonableness and unresponsiveness associated with those regulations can keep the full potential of regulation from ever being realized. From the sum of contributions to regulatory effectiveness brought about by threat we must subtract the unnecessary costs and lost opportunities for progress that can result from legalistic narrowmindedness, from its tendency to destroy cooperation, and from its stimulation of legal and political resistance.

SOME POSITIVE EFFECTS OF TOUGH REGULATION

Tougher enforcement of protective regulations has brought some tangible results.[1] For example:

*In a survey of OSHA inspectors in the mid-1970s, 74 percent agreed with the statement that most employers "seem to be afraid of you." Steven Kelman, "Regulatory Job Safety and Health: A Comparison of the U.S. Occupational Health and Safety Administration and the Swedish Worker Protection Board" (Ph.D. diss., Harvard University, 1978), p. 591.

- Strict legalistic enforcement of nursing home regulations in California improved the overall quality of physical facilities (e.g., installation of sprinkler systems, better kitchen equipment), partly by driving financially marginal nursing homes out of business—or into takeovers by corporations that operate several homes and enjoy economies of scale.[2]
- Strict enforcement of Food and Drug Administration regulations requiring use of a new test for hepatitis in blood samples apparently contributed to the rapid spread of this technique to reduce the incidence of serum hepatitis from blood transfusions.
- A detailed study of copper smelters found that by insisting on rigid quantitative limits on airborne emissions, installation of engineering controls (rather than respirators), and fixed timetables and by imposing regular penalties for violations (a fine of $45,000 was levied on one Anaconda smelter), OSHA had made much more progress in reducing health hazards than had nonlegalistic state occupational safety agencies.[3] (The authors found that significant hazards still remained in many smelters, however.)
- Neither air nor water pollution control made major strides until the strict deadlines, permit systems, and enforcement strategies of the Clean Air Act of 1970 and until the Federal Water Pollution Control Act of 1972 transformed cooperation-oriented state agencies into enforcement-minded ones. By 1977, according to the Council on Environmental Quality, over 90 percent of the major water pollution sources in the nation had installed the "best practicable technology." By the end of the 1970s, national ambient air quality standards had not been achieved, but the curves for most major kinds of air pollution, after rising throughout the 1960s and early 1970s had leveled off, and there were absolute declines in levels of sulfur dioxide, carbon monoxide, and particulate emissions.[4]
- Legalistic enforcement of the tough 1969 Federal Coal Mine Health and Safety Act sharply reduced fatalities in coal mining, even after controlling for changes in mining technology. (Safety practices have also increased deep mining costs sharply and reduced output per miner by 30 percent, according to some studies.)[5]
- By threatening to decertify the California state mental hospitals eligible to receive federal Medicaid and Medicare funds (on

grounds of substandard quality), the tough-minded chief of the state health department licensing section stimulated more investments in those facilities in a shorter time than anyone can remember.

- In the early 1970s, polychlorinated biphenyls (PCBs), toxic chemicals used in large volume in a variety of industrial processes, were discovered in potentially dangerous concentrations in poultry, milk, fish, and other food products. As a result of aggressive regulation by the EPA and the FDA, the government announced in 1979 that traceable amounts of PCBs in food, although probably impossible to eliminate entirely for some time to come, had dropped very considerably and were virtually absent in poultry and dairy products.[6]

A tougher enforcement strategy seems also to have brought about significant changes in corporate management. Faced with more enforcement actions and higher sanctions, larger firms have scrambled to hire full-time experts to keep up with the regulations and to devise programs to "keep the company out of trouble." Television stations and advertising agencies have hired more in-house lawyers to scrutinize advertising copy in hopes of avoiding Federal Trade Commission charges that the ads contain misleading or unsubstantiated claims.[7] Corporations compete to hire well-trained affirmative action officers, safety engineers, toxicologists, and industrial hygienists; salaries of such specialists have soared in recent years.[8] After the Supreme Court decision in the *U.S. v. Park* case, affirming criminal penalties for corporate managers who fail to "follow up" on compliance problems, the president of a major drug manufacturing firm set up a special "regulatory compliance unit" in each plant to double-check the quality assurance department, which was already supposed to monitor the production department. When an aluminum company started for the first time to make light-weight forgings for automobile and truck manufacturers, company lawyers advised production managers to establish a much more expensive "zero defects" quality control program because of the potential financial impact of recall orders from the National Highway Traffic Safety Administration for defective motor vehicles.

Only after OSHA, and the threat of harassment by innumerable inspections triggered by employee complaints, did General Motors agree, after negotiations with the United Automobile Workers Union, to pay for, train, and equip full-time union safety representatives in all large plants.[9] Both parties assert this program has improved conditions.[10] The vice-president of a major workmen's compensation insurance company told us that in the mid-1970s almost 25 percent of his staff of safety inspectors, trained to do OSHA-type inspections, was hired away each year, predominantly by industry. He attributed this to the increased concern for safety that OSHA helped to bring about. A plant-level safety engineer for an automobile manufacturing company said that OSHA's existence and tough reputation had galvanized corporate headquarters in Detroit to undertake systematic surveys of noise, ventilation, and emission levels in all plants. This resulted in accelerated redesign of several tools and new machine enclosures to meet published noise standards; only 15 jobs in the 3,000-employee plant now require employees to wear ear-protection equipment, he told us with some pride. In two metal companies, corporate-level safety directors told us they circulate bulletins to plant-level safety personnel reporting on recent OSHA citations and fines at other plants in the industry; a plant safety engineer said he often calls such blurbs to the attention of production managers at the regular 8 A.M. staff meeting.

As regulatory officials have become more aggressive, compliance specialists in regulated enterprises have moved to higher levels in the corporations, gained greater authority to intervene in corporate decision-making, and acquired more opportunities to influence the attitudes of line managers and boards of directors.[11] A government study of major chemical companies, noting remarkable growth in central and plant-level staffs of experts in industrial medicine, toxicology, occupational health, and air and water pollution, observed that "in almost every company, mechanisms are now in place to help insure that these control staffs have the opportunity to comment on any significant new facility investment and new product line."[12] President Carter's Interagency Task Force on Workplace Safety and Health, in a report that is exceedingly critical of legalistic enforcement, nevertheless noted that since OSHA, "workers are more informed and concerned about job safety and health issues. Safety engineers and managers, once relegated to obscure roles in many plants and industries, now play more prominent parts."[13] The impact of those changes can be conveyed to some extent by an account by Vernon Post, chief industrial hygienist for a large aluminum company:

Before OSHA, Post told us, he was the corporation's sole occupational health specialist and it was difficult to get anything done about potentially hazardous chemical emissions in the workplace. Plant managers, when told of a problem, would sometimes be incredulous. ("What do you mean? We've been doing it this way for years, and we've never had any problems.") Sometimes, they would simply be unresponsive: "I'd give them a report and show them the medical data. They'd be very polite and say that they would get on to it. Then I'd go back to corporate headquarters, and when I hadn't heard from them, I'd call. They would say that they had instituted an engineering study [which Post clearly interpreted as a stall] or they'd say they had forgotten because they had some production crisis or another." It seems that Post's only power was that of persuasion. It was risky to alienate production people by going over their heads because he might want their cooperation in the future.

Post added that before OSHA he rarely could get his way by strictly economic arguments, for example, that controlling fumes would eventually save the company money. "Diseases of the lung, cancers, and the like take a long time to manifest themselves, so you're always talking about something that *might* happen some time in the future to a plant manager who is judged on profitability *now* and might not even be *in* that job in a couple of years. And even if you could say for certain that one man a year would die, what would that mean in present dollars? If you total up the [workers' compensation] benefits, it would cost you $100,000 to kill a man. [The company is self-insured.] That isn't much compared to the costs of totally redesigning a factory or eliminating a process."

Post says things have changed since OSHA, however. The company now has 13 industrial hygienists, supported by some plant-level medical staffs, representing an expenditure of $1 million annually. Most important, he says, there has been a change of attitudes toward occupational health problems. Managers are less likely to dismiss the *reality* of long-run hazards. When faced with an OSHA inspection, "They want help." The prestige of the company's industrial hygienists rises accordingly, and Post has been able to get industrial hygienists assigned to individual plants on a permanent basis. He thinks that when plant managers who have worked with industrial hygienists move up to higher management positions they have a positive attitude toward the company's occupational health program.

Another executive in the same corporate headquarters told us:

"OSHA *made* Vern Post's career." Post now reviews all plans for capital spending on production facilities and major changes in raw materials used in order to be able to raise warnings about potential employee health problems. His research and recommendations on maximum exposure levels, appropriate protective equipment, and procedures for monitoring exposed workers are translated into authoritative company policy manuals and directives.

Corporate compliance specialists now explicitly refer to the threat of tougher enforcement to support their requests for expensive abatement equipment. Quality control specialists, we were informed, often quote—and sometimes deliberately misquote—FDA regulations to convince production managers that certain lots should not be shipped. The rise of personal criminal liability for corporate executives also helps (or forces) corporate compliance specialists to "box management in." The specialist does his corporate job poorly if he fails to alert management to *every* potential legal problem; the manager, in turn, loses the capacity to argue that he was unaware of the problem. Carl Kekonnen, a corporate industrial hygienist, told us plant managers now have to worry about and invest in controls on in-plant health hazards, even though the effects might not turn up for years, because:

> If it is a known hazard, and the industrial hygienist *tells* him about it, and then he doesn't act on that information . . . and *then* the inspection agency comes in and identifies the hazard and finds out about the manager's dragging his heels, that would look very bad for him. It's too great a risk for him to take.

The same prospect of being "caught" by an inspector in a knowing lie or procrastination works to keep the in-house specialists honest:

> At the plant where Kekonnen works, the collective-bargaining agreement provides for a full-time union safety officer, elected by the union membership, salary paid by the company. The union safety officer, Anthony Marais, believes he gets honest information on experiments or tests run by Kekonnen, partly because "It's very risky for Kekonnen to give me bad information because he never knows if I'm going to call in OSHA to check his measurements."

Perhaps the most important positive effects of the newer-style, tougher regulation, these examples suggest, are indirect. The benefits flow less from concrete directives by government enforcement officials, than from a broad range of anticipatory actions taken by regulated enterprises because of the generalized threat of tough enforcement. But legalistic enforcement also does entail a large number of direct, factory-floor-level orders based on specific rule violations, and in this regard, its effects are not entirely beneficent. In their face-to-face encounters with regulated businessmen, inspectors programmed to go by the book often appear infuriatingly unresponsive to claims that citations or orders are unreasonable under the circumstances. The resulting tensions are not just unfortunate by-products or costs of effective regulation. In the many situations amenable to nonlegalistic enforcement, the tensions induced by regulatory unreasonableness have a negative impact on regulatory effectiveness.*

PERSONAL ATTITUDES VS. FORMAL RULES

A nursing home inspector, when asked to state the single most important variable in making a nursing home into a decent place, replied without hesitation, "The charge nurse. If she is competent and *cares* about her job, the place will be all right; otherwise forget it." Another knowledgeable observer of the industry said, in answer to the same question, that the attitudes of the nursing home administrator were all-important. The significance of favorable attitudes in producing higher quality nursing home care, more worker safety, or more reliable products lies in part in the positive causal force of attitudes per se and in part in the fact that attitudes are not governed by formal rules. Attitudes work in ways that rules cannot. First, because rules are enforceable only if the enforcers can measure compliance, "soft" variables—such as the degree of warmth and

---

*The specimens of self-undermining regulatory behavior that we will adduce come largely from OSHA and its state agency counterparts. For various reasons, OSHA may be a somewhat extreme case, but it has the value of putting into sharp relief the essential characteristics of the sort of counterproductive behavior that stems from legalistic enforcement. On the other hand, even if the frequency with which this sort of behavior actually turns up in regard to worker safety and health regulation is higher than in other areas—say, food processing or nursing homes—it is certainly common in those and other fields of regulation that have adopted legalistic enforcement strategies.

sympathy nursing home aides should give to residents—cannot realistically be the subject of rules no matter how important they may be in reality. Second, by their nature, formal rules are enforceable only if they specify *minimum conditions* of performance or quality or whatever. They cannot be designed to bring about higher levels of *aspiration* or continuous improvement or concern about quality.[14] Pietro Nivola, in his study of the housing inspection agency in Boston, noted:

> While the law was fairly explicit as to the "facilities," "services," and "structural elements" constituting standard housing, it did not say much about *how well* the required code repairs were to be executed. For instance, plumbing facilities had to exist, and be in working order, but nothing was stated as to their physical appearance. . . . A bathtub, so chipped and cracked—not to say ugly—as to make bathing uncomfortable and cleaning arduous, could still meet code standards if it provided and held hot and cold water.[15]

Third, formal rules usually cannot be detailed enough to cover all the diverse hazards that emerge from technological changes and the accompanying patterns of human interaction. Finally, even when rules can in principle cover all the relevant situations, compliance is problematic unless there is an underlying attitude of willing cooperation. Not one-time orders to comply, but continuous managerial vigilance, imagination, and leadership are needed to keep a diverse body of middle managers and workers in compliance with the rules. Without these managerial attitudes, rule violations due to delay and footdragging and error are ineradicable under all but the most draconian of conceivable enforcement systems.

The limited reach of regulation by legal rules and the corresponding importance of attitudes are reflected in the comments of the chief of loss control operations in a major workers' compensation insurance company. OSHA inspections, he observed, are rule oriented, "aimed at the mechanical aspects, the physical aspects" of the factory. But with that approach, he said, "you can't control what goes on five minutes after you go out the door."[16] In contrast, insurance inspectors, while they do look for physical violations, focus primarily on the attitude of management. "If management shows little concern for safety, they're a bad risk. So we do more on the human side than we do on the mechanical or physical side." As John Mendeloff observed in his detailed study of OSHA,

"Most workplace injuries are not caused by violations of standards, and even fewer are caused by violations that inspectors can detect."[17] Similarly, while a Department of Transportation study indicated that many vehicles on the highway have poorly maintained brakes and worn tires, it also indicated that rigorous enforcement of truck safety regulations could cut accidents by only a small fraction. Recent studies show that 87 to 95 percent of road accidents involving truck fleets are due to nonmechanical causes. Thus while insurance company inspections cover compliance with Department of Transportation maintenance regulations, their major emphasis in loss control programs is on management and supervisory systems: "We cover hiring of drivers, their training, and disciplinary programs as well as maintenance."*

Consider, too, the limits of rule enforcement as a means of forestalling even major disasters. The major cause of the DC-10 crash in May 1979 that killed 275 people was a series of minor, step-by-step alterations in maintenance practices (and training courses for maintenance personnel), which could hardly be detected by FAA inspectors enforcing rules concerning the frequency—not the quality—of maintenance.[18] After a huge scaffold fell from a 100-foot cooling tower being constructed in West Virginia, killing 50 workmen, a reporter, standing at the site, informed the national television audience that no OSHA inspector had been at the tower for three months—as if that would have made a difference. In such a case, it is hard to imagine that an OSHA inspector, armed with regulations on ordinary construction safety techniques, could have applied them meaningfully to the unique and extraordinarily complicated scaffolding problem involved. At best, the OSHA inspector could have discussed with construction officials the complex set of cement pouring and testing techniques and safety procedures that they had devised and used without incident on 19 other towers and could have checked into the control system the company had set up to make sure those procedures were being followed. Similarly, investigators of the causes of mishaps in nuclear power plants concluded that "the principal deficiencies . . . are management problems . . . problems [that] cannot be solved by the addition of a few pipes and valves—or, for that matter, by a resident federal inspector.[19]

---

*Mechanical maintenance and human error, of course, are not unrelated. An experienced enforcement official with California's Motor Carrier Safety Unit emphasized that "a vehicle that has good brakes can cover for a guy who dozes off for a second, and a comfortable, smooth-running vehicle leads to less fatigue in the first place."

Clearly, progress toward responsible conduct requires, above all, the active cooperation of regulated enterprises—only their personnel are there all the time and sensitive to crucial variations in the quality of safety procedures. Like the police officer who can sense signs of trouble on his beat, company personnel, familiar with the hundreds of unique details of their operations, are far more capable of detecting most kinds of problems than are intermittently present inspectors. Only the management systems of regulated enterprises can provide the supervision and leadership needed to sustain responsible attitudes and to maintain existing protective routines. Government coercion, or the threat of it, often is relevant. Specific regulations may be needed to provide guidance, and sometimes, when they embody a technologically proven "solution" for a uniform, recurrent, closed-ended problem, strict enforcement is appropriate. Some threat of enforcement, too, almost always is necessary; the inspector does have to come. But legalistic enforcement strategies that are indifferent to the insights and attitudes of key personnel in regulated enterprises destroy rather than build cooperation and thereby undercut the potential effectiveness of the regulatory program.

DIVERSION OF EFFORT

Legalistic enforcement has been accompanied by a bureaucratization of the inspection process itself. Inspectors are expected to detect, document, and prosecute violations, rather than engage in an open-ended search for "problems." They tend to look only for the set of hazards or record-keeping lapses listed in the manual of regulations. To the extent those rule-defined risks are not the most serious, however, the inspector's attention is diverted to trivial matters, and he may fail to see (or to take responsibility for) important sources of harm that inevitably escape the rules. His rule-bound myopia afflicts the regulated enterprises as well, for their managers are induced to avoid penalties by curing rule violations, rather than by devoting time and money to more serious problems.

Nursing home inspectors, for example, come to facilities armed with lengthy, detailed checklists. They devote a great deal of inspection time to checking compliance with record-keeping requirements, such as careful completion and updating of patients' charts. Bruce Vladeck, an advocate of more effective nursing home regulation, points out:

No complaint is more frequently voiced by nursing home staff, nor more worthy of sympathy, than that the backbreaking load of regulation-induced paperwork can only detract from the quality of care. But patients' charts and other records are tangible and observable; they give an inspector something to look at.[20]

Similar emphasis on the tangible but trivial violation recurs in other fields. Safety directors we interviewed (labor union safety officials as well) invariably complained of the irrelevance of most OSHA citations and could point to very few significant safety measures that had been instituted in direct response to rule violations detected by inspectors. OSHA's own reports for the 1971-76 period showed that less than 2 percent of violations cited were classified as "serious."[21] Thus a task force appointed by President Carter charged that OSHA "has diluted the impact of inspectors" by citing "all violations, regardless of whether they cause injuries,"[22] and a study of the chemical industry indicated that OSHA inspectors, by focusing on simple, visible, and avoidable hazards, failed to uncover serious problems known to company personnel.[23] We observed the problem in two wire cable plants.

Wire cable is made on tubular stranders: each strand of wire is drawn off one of a series of reels or "bobbins" affixed to a rapidly spinning wheel. If a 500-pound bobbin comes loose, it can be hurled by centrifugal force through the plant. It would kill anyone it struck. Although such events are rare, and there are no such deaths or injuries recorded, in each of the two companies visited, a strander once "threw a bobbin." In each case, it went upward rather than laterally, and no one was hurt. In Company A, the safety director seized on this event to get a $1 million appropriation to design and install huge protective cages. In Company B, the safety director determined that the breakaway was caused by an overfilled bobbin, which allowed wire to slip off and get hooked around the bearing. Procedures to prevent a recurrence of that defect (by limiting bobbin weight) were implemented, but the idea of building much stronger enclosures was rejected by the safety director's superiors as too expensive in relation to the risk. When OSHA undertook a wall-to-wall survey of Company B's plant, the inspector did not even question the adequacy of provisions to prevent bobbins from flying off the stranders. Rather, he required the company to put complex electrical guard rails around the machines to prevent workers from inadvertently walking too close to them and being struck by whirling, but firmly affixed, bobbins. Company B installed this system on several stranders, at a cost of over $20,000. But the safety director didn't think *that* was a worthwhile investment. In all the years the stranders had been used, there had never been an injury caused by workers getting too close to the moving machines—probably, he thought, because it was such an obvious hazard.

In this case, an inspector's focus on routine "rule-book" violations (such as the absence of guardrails) apparently diverted him (and other OSHA inspectors who have been through the same plant) from probing the experience of corporate safety officials and identifying the more significant hazard.*

In addition, when inspectors miss the forest by looking only for certain kinds of defective trees, it may have a negative effect on the activities of compliance specialists in the regulated enterprise. A workplace safety engineer in a large manufacturing plant, speaking of OSHA inspections, complained:

> They make me spend a great deal of time and money on unimportant things. I work 60 to 65 hours a week on injury prevention. If I spend 30 developing defensive positions on unimportant things OSHA wants, I'm not doing my job well.

And perhaps just as important, such diversion leads managers and compliance specialists to denigrate the inspectors, to characterize them as ignorant and legalistic nitpickers, and to resist rather than cooperate with them.

INCURRING RESENTMENT

Resentment and hostility from those who are regulated are direct effects of legalism and its attendant unreasonableness. Some businessmen we interviewed complained far less about the costs of complying with un-

---

*Why didn't the Company B safety director call the problem to the attention of the OSHA inspector, and thereby get *his* assistance in arguing for stronger enclosures? One reason may be that he was convinced by his company's decision that it wasn't worth it. But another is that OSHA's legalistic stance has made most companies regard OSHA as an adversary that will use any admission to impose fines and unreasonable abatement measures, and hence, it has become unacceptable to "tell OSHA too much." See pp. 109–111 below.

reasonable orders than about the arbitrariness of agency actions. Businessmen who think of themselves as trying to do a decent job are not likely to cooperate with an agency that in effect disregards their judgment and good-faith efforts or that even denies (by its actions) that they are to be trusted at all. For example:

Bill Jones is the plant manager of a California steel foundry, a factory employing about 200 workers. Like most foundries, it is an especially dangerous place to work. It is noisy and dusty. Hot metal is transported from furnaces and poured into molds. Castings are machined on high-speed grinding wheels.[24]

Jones has accepted safety ideas from workers' compensation insurance company loss control agents (such as conducting regular hearing tests). He hired a consultant to help systematize a safety control system, giving supervisors and work groups "tickets" for unsafe practices and accidents. He leads a committee that meets weekly to analyze the causes of all accidents and to consider preventive action. The inducement to institute these practices, he said, was an increase in accidents a few years ago stemming from more "new hires" and higher compensation costs. "We pay $500,000 a year in workmen's comp," he said, "a rate of $15.95 per $100 [in wages]."

Jones says he would welcome assistance from OSHA on safety problems. "If an OSHA inspector came up to me and said, 'Hey, Jones, you ought to do so and so,' and he knew what he was talking about, they could come around as often as they want. But not if all they want is to write citations." That last sentence reflected Jones' opinion that, in general, the OSHA inspectors who have come to his plant offered no constructive advice and "seemed to be interested only in finding something to fine." On one occasion an inspector pointed out some violations that Jones—and apparently even OSHA—did not regard as significant in terms of hazards, for example, the absence of an exit sign or some inadequate railings. Jones quickly had them fixed. But he was outraged to later receive a citation letter from OSHA imposing fines for the violations "without the inspector even taking the time to come back to see if we eliminated the violations."* The fines, however, amounted to

---

*The regulations, of course, call for imposition of the fines *regardless* of whether the employer had fixed the violations. (Failure to abate calls for a second, *higher,* fine.) Employer good faith is taken into account, according to a formalized statutory discount, only in fixing the amount of the penalty.

less than $100, and Jones admitted that the correction costs were minor. "But I don't like injustice, no matter how small it is."

The fines, to Jones, were an injustice not merely because they were disproportionate to the offense but also because they symbolized official blindness to his efforts and motives. OSHA's first-instance-citation-and-penalty policy assumes that employers will make little effort to improve workplace safety and health conditions if they know they can avoid penalties by attempting improvements after the inspector's infrequent appearances. While that may be a plausible assumption for many employers and many kinds of violations, it did not hold for Jones, who was conducting a safety program *better* than that prescribed in the rules. Thus legalism, blinding the official to the true situation, arouses a sense of injustice because it deals with a person as if he were worse than he actually is. It "convicts" the innocent, which can be felt as an outrage even when the penalty is small.

Moreover, the agency's conduct seems unjust because it violates the basic norm of reciprocity that is essential to all cooperative relationships. Jones justifiably felt that he had made an extra effort by quickly repairing the violations OSHA pointed out. The efforts were "extra," in his view, because they were substantively almost meaningless in the context of the real safety problems at that foundry. Yet the agency, routinely penalizing the violations, responded to his gesture of cooperation with a gesture of indifference.

OSHA's policy of unannounced inspections is resented for similar reasons. Unannounced inspections, of course, may be essential in dealing with noncompliant firms, but they offend the many factory managers and safety engineers who feel they have nothing to hide and resent having to drop what they are doing whenever the inspector knocks and then perform escort duty through the plant.* Consider the psychological dynamics here. If you have made special efforts to do what you think is good and right, and the law treats you as if you were likely to act very badly, it is hard to accept that law as proper unless you admit you have not done enough—which would be contrary to your self-image as having been virtuous. The more likely response to that dissonance, of course, is to

---

*The executive *must* escort the inspector to provide information the inspector asks for, to correct any misleading impressions, and to ensure the outsider's safety. (In the course of our interviews, safety directors were always pushing us out of the way of speeding forklifts and warning us where not to step.)

denigrate the law, the enforcement agency, and the political process that produces it. A vicious circle is thereby created. When regulatory systems seem to act unreasonably, businessmen react defensively. Enforcement officials, when challenged, respond with enhanced mistrust and legalism.[25] Businessmen become still more resentful and retaliate with various forms of noncooperation and resistance.

MINIMAL COMPLIANCE

Resentful of fines imposed when they felt they acted responsibly, some business managers respond by taking the position that they will act no more responsibly than the agency's rules require. We encountered several examples of this phenomenon of minimal compliance, even on the part of firms that seemed to be relatively good apples. For example:

The director of industrial relations in a large manufacturing plant acknowledged that because of OSHA's *existence,* "On some things we maybe move faster. We maybe read the book [of OSHA regulations] more carefully." But like many industry safety specialists, he insisted that OSHA *inspections* rarely have produced a constructive change in the plant.* More to the point, he argued that inspections are sometimes positively unconstructive. "OSHA makes us do X, so we think 'Why should we do Y?'"

Asked for an example, he said, "We had some concerns about the ventilation in our vehicle shop, some complaints from workers. We did some tests and it seemed to be OK, that is, within OSHA standards. But we decided to put in an exhaust system anyway, just to eliminate the complaints. The cost of it would be about $20,000, and management went for it. But the men weren't satisfied with our plan, which called for big wall openings. They wanted ceiling fans. Our engineers came and said in that place the fans wouldn't add anything. But the men weren't satisfied. Three times they

---

*We asked this executive, as we asked others, to list the five most important worker safety improvements in his plant in the preceding few years. They included a system whereby workers could issue "safety tickets" requiring immediate repairs of defective machines or guards, managerial safety ratings of foremen, and substitution of motorized equipment for manual tasks. None had entailed violations of OSHA rules or stemmed from an OSHA inspector's observations.

called OSHA and OSHA came. He measured, and said there was no violation. So management decided not to do the ventilation system at all."

Stories like this suggest that management's retreat to a "no more than the regs require" position is sometimes adopted more from an annoyed reaction to repeated regulatory intrusions than from straightforward financial calculation. A labor union safety official, too, drew a sharp contrast between safety measures brought about by private pressure and the minimal compliance that stems from OSHA's emphasis on the letter of regulations.

For the last seven years, Anthony Marais has been full-time safety officer of a United Steel Workers local that represents 3,000 workers in a large aluminum manufacturing plant. His salary is paid by the company. The collective-bargaining agreement also provides for monthly on-the-record meetings between a union safety committee and the company safety staff and sets forth an elaborate procedure by which employees can file safety grievances and even close down jobs they believe are unsafe. That way, he says, "I get 70 percent of what I want . . . I get most important things done." Marais prefers not to call OSHA because "they can hurt us more than they help." One worker, for example, had read that there were dangers in exposure to mercury vapors escaping from mercury lights. The worker called in OSHA. The inspector took measurements and found no violation. (This was not the kind of situation that resulted in emissions, he explained.) "Now," says Marais, "if I want to get the company to, say, increase the distance the man is from the lights, even if it's only because they bother him, the company takes the position that OSHA says the lights are OK. If the guy had come to me, I might have been able to do something."

Bureaucratic and rule-minded enforcement also can lead to a minimalist attitude on the part of enforcement officials themselves, leaving them unresponsive to more serious—but not technically illegal—situations or opportunities for effective action. Again, an experience of Anthony Marais, the union safety steward, is revealing.

Marais is especially frustrated by OSHA's refusal (or inability) to act in the absence of explicit regulations. For example, he says, heat in the aluminum potlines presents a worrisome health problem. "Five or six ambulances a day, in hot times of the year, go into the potlines to pull people out with heat exhaustion." We asked whether he had complained to OSHA about this. "No. I don't think there is any OSHA regulation on exposure to heat. If there's nothing in black and white, I can't expect them to act on it."

In addition, numerous ladders in the plant are 60 feet high. In accordance with consensus standards adopted by OSHA, there are landings every 20 feet. Marais thought they were still dangerous and should have barrel backs. The company said that it was in compliance with OSHA standards. One day a painter employed by an outside contractor fell 60 feet to his death. Marais made several suggestions for cost-effective improvements, but the company still argued that the risk was remote and the changes not compelled by OSHA. Marais called OSHA: since there was no violation, all the compliance officer would do was to send Marais some forms with which to request a change in the regulations. But he sent the wrong form because, he later admitted, he could not find the appropriate one. Marais raised the issue with another OSHA official he met at a safety seminar, but he, too, was not very responsive. Marais was disgusted that they didn't take any initiative. "When someone tells you about a problem, you ought to be able to pick up the ball and run with it."

CUTTING OFF COOPERATION

Since regulated enterprises themselves usually have major advantages over governmental inspection systems in detecting sources of harm, the government needs their cooperation in problem identification and problem solving in order to do its job effectively and reasonably. Effective regulation requires regulated enterprises to tell enforcement officials about suspected hazards, past failings, and constraints on abatement efforts. However, a regulated enterprise will not voluntarily disclose its problems to an agency unless it feels confident that information about its weaknesses and mistakes and experiments will not become the basis of prosecution, adverse publicity, or competitive disadvantage. Legalistic regulation, on the other hand, reflects an abiding mistrust of "secret" communications by regulated enterprises; confidentiality is seen as an invitation to undue influence or corruption. To keep the agency honest, interactions with regulated firms must be on record, so far as possible, and be subject to disclosure and public review.

As might have been expected, the legal assault on informal communication and confidentiality has inhibited the voluntary exchange of information and industry-agency cooperation. For example, a top FDA official told us that in his opinion the Freedom of Information Act amendments have severely harmed the agency's enforcement efforts. Under the act, inspection reports in agency files are public records, and they commonly are obtained by manufacturers seeking information about their competitors' failings or capabilities. Not surprisingly, therefore, manufacturers try to block the flow of information to inspectors and agency files. A plant manager we interviewed, for example, refused to tell an FDA inspector how many lots of a product were made at the plant that year because "we didn't want our competitors to find out," and the inspector's supervisor refused to guarantee confidentiality. "Before FOI," he added, "we would have told him." The legal jousting over rights to information or confidentiality that often follows such incidents produces only additional suspicion on the agency's part that the company is trying to hide something, and further reduction of cooperation in investigation of problems.[26]

If fear of disclosure of information to a regulated firm's competitors inhibits cooperation with an agency, that resistance is redoubled when the firm fears that the agency will use even the slightest adverse information to impose formal penalties or to formulate stringent orders. For example:

> Nursing homes, in order to receive their Medicare reimbursement income, must comply with a detailed set of record-keeping and reporting regulations. The requirements are so complex that many homes hire outside "record consultants" to advise them about compliance; typically, the consultant gives the facility detailed reports on deficiencies in their present system, how records should be kept in the future, and the like.
>
> In California, with its legalistic enforcement system, state inspectors issue first-instance citations for violations of record-keeping rules. Moreover, according to one nursing home administrator, "The surveyor comes in and requests the *consulting report* and then

writes citations for violations indicated in the consulting report. . . .
Now facilities are conducting record consultations *verbally*. They
put only bland written reports in the files that say that the place is
doing a terrific job and doesn't need to improve on anything, but in
reality the verbal report might mention a couple dozen areas which
need improvement."

Thus legalistic enforcement, instead of facilitating the work of potential
allies like record consultants, discourages and dilutes their positive contributions.

Even more disturbing is the implication that trade associations have
been reluctant to undertake safety research in some instances for fear the
government would seize upon the findings and establish "unreasonable"
requirements.

After a reel of wire broke loose and was hurled off an aluminum
cable stranding machine in 1974, Al Schaefer, chief corporate
safety official, discussed the idea of building protective devices on
stranders with safety engineers from other firms at the Safety Committee of the Aluminum Association. They resolved to ask the
association to fund a research project to determine the extent and
causes of the problem and methods of controlling it. The proposal
was thoroughly defeated, however. Most companies, especially the
smaller ones, Schaefer said, were afraid that once the study was
undertaken, the problem would be made public and OSHA would
"take the data out of context" and force the firms into precipitous
action such as the immediate retrofitting of all stranders with specified guards or enclosures. Their attitude about OSHA, said
Schaefer, was "Give them an inch and they'll push you a mile."

Moreover, once an agency acquires a reputation for unreasonableness,
cooperative relationships may be difficult to restore even if the agency
wants to adopt a more "reasonable" posture. Regulated enterprises,
once burned, become more reluctant to let down their defenses or turn
over any information not clearly required by law. They never can tell,
enterprise officials feel, whether the agency might misinterpret information or use it to impose unreasonable restrictions, even if the current
inspector appears to be "more reasonable" than the previous one.

RESISTANCE

Legalistic regulation can turn a regulated enterprise's disposition to comply with the law into a positive disposition to resist. We encountered a striking illustration of this reaction when we compared interviews conducted with a chief environmental control officer and the chief worker safety officer in the same corporation.

> The environmental officer described an elaborate multimillion-dollar, second-generation air pollution control system his company had designed and installed to meet EPA regulations, plus a continuous monitoring system for each of the baghouses used to catch particulate matter. Because the monitoring system was not strictly required, we asked why the company installed it, rather than leaving the detection of violations to the regulatory agency. He responded, a bit incredulous that we asked the question, "Well, because it's company policy to comply with the law."
>
> A very different attitude was expressed by a corporate safety engineer down the hall. He acknowledged that he sometimes has attempted to persuade plant managers who receive OSHA citations that they should not comply. "Suppose I get a call from a plant, and a safety engineer there wants my advice on putting in a set of railings in response to an OSHA citation. I ask him 'Is it important from a safety standpoint?' He says 'No, but we're out of compliance!' I say, 'How much would it cost?' '$12,000.' 'Is it dangerous?' The engineer says, 'Hell, no. Nobody ever goes up there.' I ask him, 'If it was *your* plant, would you voluntarily put it in, if OSHA wasn't asking for it?' He says, 'Hell, no!' 'Then let's fight it,' I tell him."
>
> In fact, he recently persuaded engineers not to try to "engineer out" a noise violation on a boiler, as required by OSHA, because, despite the projected $60,000 expenditure, "noise levels for the whole operation would *still* not be down to 90 decibels. There were too many other noise sources. The men would still have to wear protective devices and we'd still have to monitor them for hearing loss." "What will happen?" we asked. "We'll appeal to the administrative law judge. We'll appeal to the courts. We might win. Some administrative law judges consider economic feasibility, and some judges do, but some don't. In any case, we delay." And de-

lay enables the company to make abatement expenditures at what it considers a reasonable rate.

In this corporation, at least, OSHA has dissipated a potentially invaluable asset—the generalized commitment, apparent in the environmental engineer's response, "to comply with the law."[27]

One result of resistance to compliance is more litigation. Experienced enforcement officials in Cal-OSHA told us that since a more legalistic enforcement policy was instituted—especially citations and fines for the first-instance rule violations—there has been an enormous increase in the number of appeals. The phenomenon is nationwide. Kelman reports that when the Occupational Safety and Health Review Commission was first formed its staff estimated that its caseload of appeals from OSHA citations would be about 100 or 200 cases a *year*; in fact, it had received 300 or 400 appeals a *month*.[28] Similarly, the number of administrative appeals and court cases increased dramatically in the California Department of Health and the Bay Area Air Pollution Control District after those agencies were granted the power to assess fines and were impelled toward a more legalistic enforcement policy in the 1970s.

For good apple firms, resistance may be interpreted as a policy directed at what the firms view as a *pattern* of regulatory unreasonableness. Such a policy elevates resentment to a consistent and calculated tactic. The basic idea is that each encounter with the agency might set a *precedent,* leading to costly regulatory demands in future encounters. If the agency is believed to be unreasonable in general, therefore, the firm may resist even if the agency is not necessarily thought to be unreasonable in a particular case. Adverse precedents, moreover, branch out in many directions. Automobile manufacturers do not like to accede to requests by NHTSA for recalls, because such concessions make them more vulnerable to private damage suits.[29] Nursing homes do not like to admit to alleged violations of state agency standards lest their admissions prejudice further negotiations over Medicaid reimbursement contracts. Corporate relations with OSHA are very much complicated by their potential effects on the much more important and continuing negotiating agenda with organized labor. An automobile company resisted an OSHA order to supply safety shoes to some workers in one plant because compliance might have set a precedent supporting recurrent UAW demands for free safety shoes for all workers in all plants.

Inevitably, the idea of a "precedent" is ambiguous. Neither side can know for sure whether or not the resolution in any single disputed case will set a precedent. Just as the agency must often judge whether the firm is demonstrating a pattern of recalcitrance that might have been discouraged if the agency had taken a tough line initially, so a firm must often judge how well it can work with an agency in the long run. Such a judgment, of course, may be based on the agency's reputation in the industry, not necessarily on the "typical" or "representative" conduct of the agency. OSHA inspectors and their supervisors, for example, may be perfectly reasonable in 70 or even 80 percent of their disputes, but a business firm may premise its strategic decision of resistance to OSHA on the 20 to 30 percent of cases in which it has experienced, heard of, or anticipated official unreasonableness. In absolute terms, these disputed cases might be very significant, involving large sums of money and managerial effort. If a firm thought it could avoid losing these cases by adopting a strategy of thoroughgoing resistance in *all* encounters with OSHA, it would no doubt feel legitimate in doing so. And in fact, such a decision may be as logical as the agency decision to tailor its enforcement strategy to deal with the 20 percent of bad apple firms, even at the expense of imposing unreasonable regulation on the other 80 percent. Moreover, if the firm adopts a posture of legalistic resistance or minimalist compliance in 80 percent of the cases, in order to protect its ability to be staunch in the 20 percent involving unreasonable regulatory citations, agency officials understandably might classify the firm as a bad apple and adopt an even more suspicious and legalistic enforcement style. This reciprocal sensitivity to the qualitatively important minority proportion of bad conduct in "the other guy" explains the paradox of social regulation: regulated enterprises and regulatory agencies each think of themselves as virtuous and reasonable and of the other side as bad and unreasonable, and each judgment is strongly rooted in actual experience.

When an individual firm appeals a justified citation or order as part of a strategy of resisting regulatory unreasonableness, regulatory effectiveness suffers; but perhaps even more important, legalistic enforcement can spawn an organized *culture of resistance* among regulated firms, a culture that facilitates the sharing of knowledge about the methods of legal resistance and counterattack. The agency responds in kind, and a full-fledged set of adversarial relations develops, tying up both regulators and regulated firms in a kind of legal gamesmanship. For example, a political scientist interviewing regulators and nursing home administrators in California, where there was a pronounced turn toward aggressive enforcement often characterized by legalism on the part of the agency, commented on "the *vindictiveness* that both sides—the Department of Health and the industry—attribute to each other. It leads to constant . . . calculations where each side is saying, 'If you do this, then they will respond by doing that.' "[30]

OSHA, too, has stimulated a culture of resistance that promotes legal and political contests and at times borders on the hysterical in exaggerating OSHA's bad points. A 1977 story in *Foundry Management and Technology,* a trade magazine ordinarily devoted to technical production problems, was entitled "What To Do When OSHA Knocks" and discussed the possible unconstitutionality of warrantless inspections. The foundry industry, in fact, raised that issue in the courts, as did a small Idaho manufacturer who ultimately obtained a U.S. Supreme Court ruling that a judicial warrant could be demanded before acceding to an OSHA inspection.[31] Some commentators did not think that the decision would be too important, both because the Court's decision suggested that warrants ordinarily could be obtained easily and because they thought most employers would not insist on warrants, partly to avoid antagonizing OSHA. But a recent article by Robert Moran, former chairman of the Occupational Safety and Health Review Commission (during the Nixon administration), printed in the foundry industry's trade magazine, advised managers always to insist that inspectors get search warrants, to say as little as possible to inspectors, to resist the temptation to point out the strengths of their safety program, and to respond to inspectors' questions about processes or machines "with a polite but firm 'no comment.' " He criticized the U.S. Chamber of Commerce's advice to small businessmen not to insist on warrants and to adopt a cooperative stance. Moran also advised companies to appeal all citations, not just those they object to strongly, in order to gain more time to search for cost-effective abatement measures and "to settle a case by giving up on some items in exchange for dismissal by OSHA of others. Those who leave certain things uncontested are needlessly giving up this possibility."[32] In the appeals process, employers are advised to bombard OSHA with interrogatories and subpoenas for inspection reports and to raise all defenses authorized by law, including challenges to the specificity of the citations and the vagueness of the regulation. In fact, some analyses suggest that in 1978 and 1979 almost 40 percent of OSHA inspections resulted in contested citations (a substantial increase from prior years), and a union official has claimed that 90 percent of citations issued against the oil and chemical industry are contested.[33] Both figures are probably exaggerated, but the claim itself is indicative of the degeneration of relationships with OSHA.

Resistance sometimes moves beyond ideology to political organization as well. The regulated sector can always appeal to legislators and other elected officials to abolish or at least to contain the powers of an unpopular agency. The repeated political attacks on OSHA have been the most prominent example. There have been an inordinate number of oversight hearings on OSHA, often focusing not so much on the aggregate costs of compliance as on the way OSHA regulations are enforced. Each year, OSHA and its supporters are forced to fight bills that would either strip the agency of its jurisdiction over small businesses or rescind its powers to issue first-instance citations.[34]

Mushrooming resentment against regulation by one agency can spill over into political counteroffensives against regulation in general. The California iron and steel foundry industry, composed of relatively small firms, had never been politically organized. In recent years, however, annoyance at OSHA stimulated concern about the mounting volume of all kinds of laws and regulations affecting the industry; member firms agreed to a threefold increase in Foundry Association dues in order to hire a full-time lobbyist. At the national level, new business organizations to study regulatory issues and to engage in lobbying have grown in recent years,[35] along with business-funded "public interest law firms" that challenge regulatory decisions or procedures in the courts. In the case of the FTC, resentment stimulated by a few arguably unreasonable prosecutions[36] and controversial proposed regulations—particularly the FTC's proposals to control the content of (or ban outright) television advertising aimed at children—led to congressional proposals that would reverse entirely justifiable prosecutions and trade rules and deprive the FTC of potentially useful rulemaking and jurisdictional powers.[37]

It is wrong to assume that all opposition is the product of legalistic enforcement alone or even of unreasonable—as opposed to merely costly—substantive regulations. But the rhetoric that accompanies such counterattacks is pervaded by references to regulatory style, suggesting that legalism and unresponsiveness have been significant factors.

THE COSTS OF LEGAL CONTESTATION

If law is the medium of legalistic enforcement, it can also be the medium of legalistic contestation, and as the adversaries exhaust their energies in legal battles the basic goals of the regulatory process remain unattended. They are either displaced by the idea of winning or are simply forgotten because resources needed to achieve them are dissipated in the legal struggle. When citations and orders meet with legal resistance and the agency must resort to prosecution, the traditions of due process, formal legal proof, and strict construction of penal rules inevitably help the guilty to escape. The regulated enterprise geared up to defend itself against legalistic unreasonableness will also find loopholes to escape some entirely legitimate citations. In response, the regulatory agency must become even more legalistic.

Regulations, for example, are redrafted to close all possible loopholes and defenses, not to make them more intelligent guides to action. A Cal-OSHA regulation writer, referring to the high rate of contested cases under the agency's first-instance citation and fine system, lamented that in drafting rules, "We are under a practical compulsion to choose legalism [over common sense and comprehensibility] because we have to win our appeals." But making regulations defense-proof also makes them more cumbersome and increases the likelihood that they will cover trivial or remote risks.

Similarly, when legal contestation becomes common, inspectors must be more cautious in applying regulations. Under the pre-OSHA regime, according to a California enforcement official, "We interpreted the regs according to the intent of the standards writers. But now we must go by the wording, or else the appeals board will overturn us." The inspection process takes on a defensive cast, designed to avoid "losses" in court. The California Department of Health instructed nursing home inspectors not to insert qualitative judgments in their survey reports—although comments on the personality of key administrators and nurses, for example, are often critical to building up a history and evaluation of a nursing home, its inclination to cooperate, and its capacity for improvement. Such judgments were to be removed because they could be used as evidence of undue subjectivity or bias on the part of the inspector *if* a court case ensued. Instead, the emphasis is on careful and exhaustive documentation of physical facts.

Concentration on documentation of violations, however, emphasizes the adversarial and legal character of the inspector-business relationship and further diminishes the possibility of cooperation. Businessmen perceive inspectors as interested only in writing down violations, which further erodes an inspector's reputation and authority. "OSHA generally has low-quality inspectors who don't *teach* anything," a steel foundry president complained. An FDA enforcement official noted that, even when so requested by regulatory enterprises, inspectors are *instructed* to withhold any advice on how to comply with labeling regulations, thereby foreclosing regulated firms from basing a defense on the claim that the defendant had been misled by the inspector. In order not to lose a proportionately tiny number of court cases, therefore, the FDA passes up opportunities to elicit cooperation and prevent harm. This stance may reflect the tendency for lawyers to become the most important enforcement officials in legalistic agencies involved in a great deal of litigation, and their tendency to stress the winning of legal battles.

The initiation of formal legal action further staunches the flow of information from firm to agency and limits the possibility of cooperation. The chief environmental engineer at an aluminum plant told us that he effectively forestalled an EPA enforcement action, even though the company had exceeded a legal deadline, by continuously telling agency engineers, in person and in writing, "exactly what we were doing, where we were in the process, what we thought would work and when." By contrast, in another plant owned by the same company, he told us, a posture of mutual hostility developed between company officials and the pollution control agency over an almost identical abatement problem. The agency sued the company for noncompliance, "and now the technical people, the engineers, in the company and in the agency, can't even communicate with each other, by order of the lawyers on both sides."

One of the most serious costs of legal contestation is curtailment of actual field inspections. Several experienced Cal-OSHA enforcement officials observed that the dramatic increase in legal contestation that began with the first-instance citation and fine policy has the effect of pulling inspectors out of the factory and pushing them into administrative hearings or into the OSHA office, preparing to go to the courthouse. One skilled safety engineer complained that he spent much of his time designing training programs to teach field inspectors to fill out reports so as to improve success-on-appeal rates rather than teaching them to identify or control hazards. And because inspectors must now spend much more time documenting their reports, they make far fewer inspections—by the estimate of some staff members, fewer than half as many per week as in the pre-OSHA period.

As litigation increases, moreover, the legal resources of the agency are taxed. The chief enforcement officer of the Bay Area Air Pollution Control District referred to any increase of litigation with apprehension—"We can only handle one big case at a time"—fearing that any further increase or, worse yet, a concerted strategy by regulated enterprises to bring appeals, would overwhelm the agency's legal staff. In consequence, inspectors in that agency are pushed even more strongly to stick to the book and the rules of evidence, and their inspection reports are carefully reviewed by agency lawyers before any recommended "penalty action" is taken. For a busy agency, as noted earlier, the prospect of tying up scarce legal resources in "heavy" cases creates temptations to "back off" when determined legal resistance is encountered and hence to concentrate, ironically, on the more compliant regulated enterprises. Robert Moran, now a private attorney representing employers in OSHA matters, asserted that in a dozen recent instances where employers followed his advice to insist on a warrant and to refuse access not specifically authorized by the warrant (including the inspector's request to attach measuring devices to employees), "not one of those companies received an OSHA citation."[38] When a large copper company successfully contested citations for excess worker exposure to lead emissions on the grounds of technical sampling or documentation errors by the inspector, the agency did not resample and reprosecute.[39] The agency seemingly did not want to tangle with the company again on a complex contested issue.

In conclusion, while legalism and other expressions of regulatory toughness may sometimes be appropriate—indeed, unavoidable—for dealing with the minority of bad apples, they may be self-defeating in dealing with the majority of good apples. Although the scope of the problem is unknown, it is likely that in a very large number of cases regulatory toughness in its legalistic manifestation creates resentment and resistance, undermines attitudes and information-sharing practices that could otherwise be cooperative and constructive, and diverts energies of both sides into pointless and dispiriting legal routines and conflicts.

PART TWO

FLEXIBLE ENFORCEMENT
AND ITS LIMITS

CHAPTER FIVE

THE GOOD INSPECTOR

•

Regulatory agencies need powerful tools of legal coercion because there *are* bad apples, eager to exploit vague rules and the cumbersome mechanisms of due process. Moreover, the threat of effective enforcement also is needed to keep good apples good. Thus the legal reforms of the 1960s and 1970s, designed to increase the regularity of detection and punishment, can be viewed as a natural evolution of regulatory enforcement, "selected" by a political environment that sought more security from social harms. But the tools of coercive enforcement easily can be used for legalistic, indiscriminate, and unresponsive enforcement. The newly evolved, tougher breed of inspector too often seems to take unreasonably costly bites from good apples along with justifiable bites from bad apples, thus provoking resistance and ending needed cooperation. If the political environment sought to select the fittest enforcement strategy, therefore, it might favor the evolution of a still more sophisticated type of enforcement official, one who would retain strong, modern enforcement tools but would use them more flexibly and selectively, what we would call the "good inspector."

As we have seen, legalistic enforcement cannot encompass in formal, enforceable rules the sheer diversity of the causes of harm that arise in a large, technologically dynamic economy. The inspector who walks through a factory and faithfully enforces each regulation may not detect or do anything about more serious sources of risk that happen to lie outside the rulebook; at the same time, he alienates the regulated enterprise and encourages noncooperative attitudes. In light of these developments, one might expect regulatory agencies to evolve enforcement strategies designed to persuade the regulated enterprise to do *more* than is strictly required by law. An agency's goal would not be merely to secure compliance with rules per se, but to mobilize available resources to solve particular social problems in the most efficient and least disruptive way. Its mission would be to affect the consciousness, organization, or culture of the regulated enterprise in order to make it sensitive to serious sources of harm. Enforcement officials would use their powers to induce management to invest in the training of middle- and lower-level personnel so that *they* would devise appropriate preventive measures and implement them alertly.

Agency personnel, in attempting to adapt more closely to their environment, might take on another and perhaps more difficult task— making regulation more reasonable. They would allow inspectors to permit enterprises, in the appropriate circumstances, to do *less* than the law requires. Regulations would not be enforced in situations where they do not make sense. And if, for whatever reasons, inspectors were denied discretion to suspend rule enforcement themselves, the good inspector would draw upon his experience in the field and inform top regulatory policymakers about overinclusive or ineffective rules. In the same vein, agency officials would attempt to educate legislators and elected chief executives about the causes of and correctives for unreasonable overregulation that originated in statutes and in broadly conceived policies.

But the good inspector still would be tough when toughness was required. His effort to seek cooperation would not blind him to the possibility that personnel in the regulated enterprise may seek to evade even reasonable regulatory requirements, provide him with misleading information, or exaggerate the costs or technical difficulties of compliance. Thus the inspector would attempt to distinguish violations due to narrowly profit-motivated calculations from those that stemmed from mistakes, poor management, or legitimate disagreement with the rules, and he would be willing and able to use coercive enforcement techniques when necessary.

All this is, of course, somewhat utopian. Not every regulatory official can be a perfect judge of what is or is not reasonable or an expert in eliciting cooperation. Yet the ideal of "the good inspector" serves as a model toward which enforcement might evolve and, as the examples to be presented will suggest, one that is not entirely unattainable.

THE "GOOD COP" AND THE "GOOD INSPECTOR"

If regulatory inspectors in many agencies intentionally have been transformed into "cops," a further step in their development is suggested by the literature on urban police officers. Being a good cop in fact is far more complex than the commitment to unswerving law enforcement implicit in the use of the term "cop" by some regulatory reformers. A description of good cops thus might provide a useful analogy, at least in some respects, for a good inspector.

The overriding goal of policing the city, most people probably would agree, is not to enforce all of the scores of criminal laws as they stand in the penal code, but to reduce serious crime, particularly crimes of threat and violence. One way of achieving that goal, of course, is to step up coercive enforcement against any and all transgressions of the law and even against activities, such as gatherings of juveniles or domestic quarrels, that may *tend* to lead to serious crime. But most police departments are not so unremittingly legalistic. Observed or identified lawbreakers often are let go with a lecture and a warning.[1] Most people tolerate and even approve of such selective nonenforcement because they recognize that there are other values at stake.

One of these values is a preference for private dispute resolution or "problem solving" because informal settlements are more sensitive than the law to the character and needs of the particular individual involved.[2] A second, somewhat related value, is the idea of rehabilitation, which calls for the withholding of punishment in favor of admonition, stern chastisement, or an informal grant of probation. To arrest some offenders, it is commonly believed, would do more harm than good. And a third is the recognition that law violations are not all equally serious or reprehensible; for example, speeding a sick person to the hospital is different from drag racing.

The police traditionally take these values into account both for practical reasons and to further good community relations. The idea that good community relations is an essential element of effective law enforcement is commonly accepted in much scholarly and professional thinking about the crime problem. It reflects a recognition that, however diligent (or feared) a police force is, it will never be able to make more than a marginal contribution to the reduction of crime in a free society, in which the main burdens of social control fall on informal systems—the family, the neighborhood, the schools, the workplace.[3] Moreover, even the marginal contribution that the police can indeed make depends on community cooperation. Citizens must be willing to inform the police of serious law violations, provide evidence, and support or even protect the policeman when he tries to make an arrest.

The good policeman, as delineated in an insightful study by William K. Muir, Jr., learns how to develop these community resources to gain information and support through the use of a mixture of force and service, threats and appeals to reason, toughness and teaching.[4] At times, he suspends enforcement of the law and grants curbside probation to encourage reform or private dispute resolution. But he also resorts to the threat or actuality of coercion when necessary to protect the weak and to retain citizens' respect.

Some policemen, of course, are too quick to use physical force and legal powers of arrest whenever applicable. For such "enforcers," as Muir describes them, all law violators or suspected rebels must be dealt with swiftly and harshly before they do more evil. The difficulty with this indiscriminately tough and unsympathetic approach is that it often leads to brutality and resentment and attempted retaliation. But it is also possible to go too far in the direction of nonenforcement. The extreme version is the cop who avoids trouble, who does not work hard, or who may take money to overlook a violation. Another, less blatant style of nonenforcement, attributed to cops Muir calls "reciprocators," is practiced by the officer who is dedicated and hard working but is uncomfortable using coercion. He is sympathetic to the law violator and the pressures that brought him to that condition. He often seeks to educate the offender, to talk him into future compliance rather than arresting him. But his sympathy sometimes distracts him; he is taken advantage of by the unscrupulous and the irrationally violent offender.

The "professional cop," in Muir's typology, shares with the reciprocator a "tragic sense" of life—a recognition that law is not the sole measure of morality, that values often are in conflict, that causation and blame are not simple matters. But he combines that perspective with passion—a desire to do justice and to protect potential victims, and hence a willingness to use coercion and strict enforcement of the law in those cases where the offender deserves it or when cooperation cannot be elicited by forebearance.[5]

Richard McCleary's detailed study of parole officers[6] also provides a useful analogy; the relationship between a regulatory inspector and an errant regulated enterprise is similar in some respects to the parole officer-parolee relationship. "POs" are expected to enforce a dense web of regulations designed to control and keep tabs on parolees; violations carry the penalty of return to prison. But to the dedicated parole officer, the ultimate goal of parole programs, rehabilitation of the former lawbreaker, requires a more fundamental effort to win and retain the respect and cooperation of the parolee, which often entails helping the client through minor scrapes, guarding his confidences, and not enforcing certain regulations. This effort involves risks. "As far as DC [Department of Corrections] officials are concerned," McCleary writes, "a 'good' PO is one who among other things does not embarrass the DC." Hence the PO is expected to file detailed records of all his clients' activities, and not to "take chances" with a client whose subsequent criminal behavior might create adverse publicity for the department. The legalistic PO—like Muir's enforcers—takes no chances. Others, akin to Muir's reciprocators, do not enforce regulations strictly but eventually are shown to have been too gullible or too soft.

The best parole officers, however, are capable of being strict when necessary but also have the knowledge and skill to take calculated risks with parolees on some occasions, and to be right when they do so. They learn to be selective, to keep a sense of proportion, to maintain a reputation for being tough-minded for the most part, so that their work is not scrutinized too closely for signs of undue softness and their pleas of leniency carry weight.

The good inspector, as described by experienced regulatory enforcement officials, is remarkably similar to both the ideal police officer and the most effective type of parole officer. Such an inspector, supervisors say, must have sufficient scientific knowledge and understanding of the law to enable his citations to stand up in court. He must be able to take accurate measurements, document violations, and interpret the regulations intelligently. But beyond that legal-technical minimum, certain personality traits and communications skills are especially important.

The good inspector, enforcement officials say, has the capacity to empathize with those subject to the law and to understand their concerns, problems, and motivations. "Knowledge is important," said a truck safety inspector, "but ability to get along with people is just as important." Enforcement officials are nearly always unhappy with the overly zealous inspector—one who regards regulated enterprises with excessive mistrust and self-righteousness. Because this attitude often causes resentment and resistance on the part of regulated firms, the excessively arrogant or legalistic inspector often causes trouble for his agency.*

---

*For example, after an overly suspicious air pollution inspector barged into an oil refinery without permission, the company henceforth was exceedingly defensive and uncooperative with other inspectors from the same agency.

The good inspector, on the other hand, has the knack of gaining compliance without stimulating legal contestation. In agencies not imbued with a legalistic ethos, persuasiveness becomes the supreme virtue. An occupational safety and health inspector in Sweden told Steven Kelman, "Anytime [I'm] forced to use orders or prohibitions to achieve compliance with the regulations . . . it implies I've failed. I'm supposed to try to persuade; if I come in with a hammer, it makes the employer negative."[7] A supervisor of inspectors in the California State Fire Marshal's Office said, "Going to court is an admission that you've failed." In the Consumer Protection Division of the Massachusetts Attorney General's Office, "The investigator who . . . manages to extract large refunds and manages to do so in a friendly, congenial manner without apparently brandishing his authority is considered to be a very good investigator."[8]

A friendly, congenial manner, however, is only one aspect of being effective and persuasive. One critical ingredient is the capacity to be reasonable, to distinguish serious from nonserious violations, and to invest effort in the former. This capacity seems closely related to technical competence—an ability to provide technically persuasive explanations for regulatory requirements and to understand how the regulations affect production or managerial functions. Lack of technical competence is a likely corollary of legalistic enforcement. Without reasonably developed knowledge of the degree of risk raised by a particular practice or process, an inspector cannot judge with any confidence whether a violation is serious or whether "giving more time" to comply is too risky. Without a sense of the technical and economic problems of compliance, the inspector cannot evaluate the businessman's excuses or complaints with any confidence. According to FDA and air pollution control agency supervisors, poorly educated or inexperienced inspectors have no self-confidence when confronting company engineers because they cannot tell whether they are "being snowed" or presented with valid arguments. Their most likely response, the supervisors agreed, is not to give in but to try to gain some control over the situation by retreating to the rule book, insisting on literal adherence to the regulations. A blood bank administrator noted such a retreat to legalism when federal blood bank inspection was transferred from the Bureau of Biologics in the National Institutes of Health to the FDA:

The [Bureau] inspectors were all old hands in blood banking. They really knew the ropes. When inspection changed to the FDA, a lot of new people were added. A lot of them had experience in the pharmaceutical or food industries, but knew very little about blood. They seemed to have a more policing, nit-picking attitude.

The president's Interagency Task Force on Workplace Safety and Health observed that a major reason of OSHA inspectors' ineffectiveness and legalism was that they "know too little about the industries and operations they are inspecting"; hence, they lack the confidence to evaluate actual levels of risk or safety, and "citing a long list of violations may be the field inspector's only way of showing he or she has done a good job."[9] A study of 58 enforcement officials in 43 municipal regulatory agencies found that officials who had less training were more befuddled by the complexity of the entities they regulated, more legalistic, and more inclined to "hide behind the code" than more highly trained professional officials; the latter were more likely to espouse a substantive law enforcement style, being attentive to ultimate purposes and conflicting values.[10]

When allowed, experienced inspectors seem quite ready to make judgments about the relative seriousness of violations and the relative culpability of violators. To housing code inspectors in Boston, closely observed in action by Pietro Nivola, "Legal notices were not gratuities to be doled out whenever violations were alleged. If an inspector's day-to-day work proved nothing else, it was that some cases appeared more deserving, engaging, or workable than others."[11] Their sense of justice and the fair assignment of responsibility came into play. The inspector tended to "differentiate between two classes of violations: those he could impute to the misdeeds or negligence of the proprietors, and those attributable to slovenly or destructive residents."[12]

Similarly, Keith Hawkins observed that British water pollution inspectors attempt to figure out *why* specific violations have occurred—deliberate evasion, or negligence on the part of company personnel responsible for preventing pollution, or production cycles that almost unavoidably cause periodic excess effluents for a short time; the more irresponsible the firm is, in their view, the more closely they scrutinize its operations and the more readily they resort to legal action.[13]

Because such judgments are sometimes difficult, the good inspector must have not only technical competence but also the tough-mindedness to probe the businessman's explanations and excuses in a polite but critical manner. He must be willing and able to exercise authority. Experienced enforcement officials we interviewed often referred to inspectors who simply could not come down hard when regulated businesses were unjustifiably stalling them. This problem recurs, according to some enforcement officials, because the field attracts idealists, young people who want to do good but who are not prepared to deal with conflict. Technical training is "only one of many necessary qualities," a nursing home regulator said. "For instance, you need presence. You have to look and act like you know what you're doing. Schools of social work train practitioners, not inspectors."

A corollary of the ability to be tough when need be is the ability to be patient and persistent in the face of resistance, to sort through heated charges of unreasonableness for those that are valid, while calmly rejecting those that are not. A nursing home regulator said:

> We want people that can accept a stressful situation. . . . It is important that they be able to deal with the situation by being creative and by not becoming upset. When push comes to shove, the inspector has to be able to handle abuse—take charges of harassment.

The good inspector, in short, tries to keep disagreements with business from degenerating into a hopelessly adversarial relationship.

RECIPROCITY

An enforcement official's ability to win cooperation is rooted in the relationship of reciprocity or exchange that he manages to establish. The effective parole officer described by McCleary kept quiet about a minor rule violation; the parolee, in return, was more forthcoming and cooperative. In Muir's account, a police officer dispersing a group of disruptive teenagers treated them with respect, not contempt; his unexpected gift of nonlegalistic treatment helped obtain their cooperation in keeping the peace. Reciprocity also underlies efforts by some regulatory officials to elicit cooperation—that is, to elicit strong managerial efforts by the regulated enterprises to ensure compliance and responsible behavior.

It is easiest to visualize the elements of such a reciprocal relationship at the level of face-to-face encounters between inspectors and regulated businessmen. The inspector has three major things he can trade for greater efforts toward responsible social behavior. First, at a bare minimum, he can give the regulated businessman a fair hearing; he can treat him with respect and take his arguments and problems seriously. When he must insist on strict compliance, he gives reasons. In other words, he exhibits *responsiveness*. Second, the inspector can selectively negate, modify, or delay the enforcement of regulations when their literal application to a particular violation would be unreasonable or of secondary importance. In short, he can give *forebearance*. Third, he can provide *information* to the regulated enterprise that reduces the difficulty or cost of compliance, or at least makes the required compliance measures seem understandable and justifiable. The same elements of exchange—responsiveness, forebearance, and information—can also be offered on a more systematic basis by higher enforcement officials or explicitly embodied in the regulations themselves.

The inspector's ability to initiate an exchange relationship derives in large measure from his power of threat and coercion. He gains a hearing by virtue of his power to cause trouble for the regulated enterprise—by issuing citations, threatening legal penalties, and creating the risk of adverse publicity. "We get to see the manager right away now," said a Cal-OSHA enforcement official who had also served as an inspector in pre-OSHA "no sanction" days. In this sense, the increased sanctioning power and specificity of rules that have accompanied the legalization of regulation *increase* the inspector's ability to elicit cooperation, provided that he uses those powers to that end.

Those sanctioning powers, however, must be used judiciously. Indeed, the inspector's ability to obtain information and evidence that would support the use of legal sanctions depends, at least in part, on the implied promise that the information supplied will be interpreted fairly and that those legal powers will not be employed indiscriminately and unreasonably. A federal official in charge of enforcing quality-of-care regulations in nursing homes observed, "Unless you have some way of eliciting information, you don't know whether your rules fit the situation or not." A reputation for reasonableness brings the enforcement official more complete access and better information. More information increases his legal power. And more legal power gives him more to trade for cooperation.

RESPONSIVENESS: THE INSPECTOR AS POLITICIAN

One premise of the concept of responsiveness[14] is the old assumption that power can be abused: the government might be wrong; the regulations might be overinclusive; governmental officials entrusted with a single altruistic mission might be unduly self-righteous or narrow-minded. The concept of responsiveness also rests on the premise that regulated enterprises by and large are involved in providing valued goods and services to the community, that their managers have at least some concern about the same social problems that preoccupy the regulators, and that those managers typically have a good deal more knowledge than the regulators about how those problems might be solved most efficiently. What is reasonable for the government to demand in a particular case involves many pieces of information about risk, cost, market factors, and human relations unique to the particular enterprise. The reasonable regulatory order, therefore, often might be better determined through a dialogue between inspector and regulated firm than by governmental fiat or unilateral judgments by enforcement officials. From this standpoint, it seems desirable to treat regulated enterprises and their managers not only as objects of regulation but also as participants *in* regulation, as thoughtful citizens entitled to some say about the implementation of public policy— especially as it affects their particular enterprise.

If regulated entities are citizens whose participation is valued, the individual inspector, in some sense, can serve as a politician who represents them (among other constituents) in their interactions with the government. Like a democratic politician, the inspector can be a messenger through whom the government is educated by those it seeks to govern, a receptor of information about unanticipated costs of the laws as written and of information about how the regulations could be modified. That does not mean, of course, that the regulatory official should be the unthinking mouthpiece of the enterprises he regulates. The politician must mediate between conflicting elements in his constituency and in the polity as a whole. The inspector-as-politician represents those to be protected by the regulatory program as well as the regulated enterprise and indeed ought ordinarily to give the former element in his constituency the heavier weighting.

Resistance to regulatory requirements is sometimes based on misunderstanding of their purpose and necessity.[15] Sometimes the popular understanding of regulations exaggerates the stringency of actual legal obligations or neglects exceptions built into the rules that counter ostensible unreasonableness. Sometimes regulated businessmen fail to recognize the pervasiveness or seriousness of the problems the regulations were enacted to solve. Like a good politician, the inspector can attempt to elicit compliance in such cases by providing substantive reasons for particular regulatory requirements or by giving his constituent some understanding of collective problems that may extend beyond the individual constituent's perspective. Hawkins observed that British water pollution inspectors, in their encounters with operating officials in enterprises that create pollution,

> will sometimes explain the various uses to which the water containing the effluent will be put downstream . . . or sometimes they will impose a moral burden on the polluter by describing the treatment which the water has already received upstream to render it suitable for his own use . . . saying, "How would you like it if you had this sort of discharge coming into your intake?"[16]

The inspector of factories in Great Britain wrote with respect to occupational safety rules: "Better compliance most of the time can be secured in most premises if one persuades the occupier of the need for compliance as a matter of good practice, rather than to avoid conflict with the law."[17]

Like most good politicians, good inspectors are also good salesmen. A supervisor in the Wages and Hours Law Enforcement Office described by Peter Blau said, "We are selling something here, just like a business is selling shoes. The agent doesn't only sell himself and the government, but he also sells a very special form of democracy," by which he meant the theory of industrial fairness underlying the law.[18] Susan Silbey, who studied the way investigators in a consumer fraud prosecutor's office interacted with businessmen, pointed out that they seemed to be "selling the eminent justice of protection against fraud, deception and misrepresentation."[19] The appropriate analogy is not the high-pressure foot-in-the-door retail salesman, but the more low key industrial salesman, who first elicits information about the buyer's specific needs and production problems and then *teaches* the purchasing agent or engineering department how his product will in fact advance the buyer's interests. To establish his authority as a teacher, however, the inspector must first communicate to the regulated businessman that he is aware of the complexity of the world, that he is open minded rather than single-mindedly legalistic. Some enforcement officials do so by indicating that they are aware of differences among firms with respect to social responsibility and that there may be two sides to any question. Thus the consumer fraud investigators Silbey observed made a "very great effort to counter [in their discussions with businessmen] the predominant public opinion that the consumer is always right and that the businessman is out to scalp you when he can."[20] The inspector must often point out to good apple firms that the regulatory program or the law in question is socially necessary because many other firms do not act as well as they do. Thus, Silbey points out, the antifraud investigators constantly remind the businessmen about the big cases the office has prosecuted in the past, as if to show the respondent "that there *are* bad guys out there, worse than they are, and that the Attorney General is trying to get them."[21] Such efforts toward consciousness raising, in fact, are perhaps the most important contribution regulatory agencies can make. An inspector who begins his site-visit with a discussion of the persistence of industrial accidents, or poor nursing care, or discrimination, and who asks the regulated enterprise what it is doing to reduce such problems (and how successful it is), might do much more good than an inspector who begins by leafing through his rule book and recording violations.

FOREBEARANCE

Forebearance entails: (1) overlooking violations that pose no serious risk under the circumstances; (2) not enforcing regulatory requirements that would be especially costly or disruptive in relation to the additional degree of protection they would provide; (3) granting reasonable time to come into compliance and accepting measures that would provide substantial if not literal compliance; and (4) making allowance for good faith efforts on the part of the regulated enterprise.

If the inspector explicitly communicates these acts of forebearance to managers of the regulated enterprises, he is actually giving them something—and at little cost to those the program is designed to protect. In a world dominated by legalism and mistrust, simply refraining from treating someone as if he were a criminal gives the inspector a reputation for reasonableness—something he can use in asking the regulated firm for significant and perhaps costly changes in procedures or facilities.

Many agencies make some formal efforts to distinguish serious from nonserious violations and willful from nonwillful ones. The Occupational Safety and Health Act mandates stiffer fines for serious and willful violations than for nonserious first-time violations and provides stipulated discounts from the fine for factors such as employer good faith. The FDA sends an "adverse findings letter" to food processors and drug

manufacturers for violations of "good manufacturing practice" regulations that supervisors judge to be nonserious, and stronger "regulatory
letters," requiring a response, for defects thought to raise great hazards
for consumers. California regulations for nursing homes distinguish between Class A and Class B violations; the former involve risks of more
serious harm to patients and carry heavier fines. The California legislature in late 1978 prohibited the assessment of a civil penalty against an
employer for a first-instance "nonserious" violation of an occupational
safety regulation unless the inspection results in citation of 10 or more
nonserious violations.[22]

Nevertheless, in those agencies, the inspector is obligated to cite each
violation, and the response to violations tends to be a unilateral, deductive one on the part of inspectors and supervisors: they look at the
predefined category the violation fits into and fix the fine accordingly. For
the strategy of forebearance to have its greatest effectiveness, however,
inspectorial responses should probably emerge from an interactive process, as in the practices of the Motor Carrier Safety Unit (MCSU) of the
California Highway Patrol.

> Inspectors have the legal power and obligation to order a truck
> "out of service" if it "would pose an imminent hazard." The in-
> spectors' operations manual, however, emphasizes that this sanc-
> tion is not to be used automatically for any set class of regulatory
> violations they notice, but should be used as a matter of "profes-
> sional judgment." Nor does a violation, or any set number of
> them, automatically result in a penalty action. Rather, the inspec-
> tor is instructed to consult with the terminal manager after the in-
> spection, to point out hazards and evaluate them jointly, and to
> obtain his written commitment to make repairs in some agreed-
> upon order. The inspectors, accordingly, are quite open about their
> priorities. "The main objective is to keep the roads safe," said one,
> "so if the fleet is good but the records are bad, then I might let it
> slide for a while." Discussing violations of safety regulations, an
> MCSU inspector told us, "I try to remain flexible. If he can't take
> care of [a certain violation] today—say his truck has got to go to
> Fresno—I'll say, 'O.K., as long as you do X, Y, and Z before you
> go,' and he promises to fix it after the run."

The strategy of not penalizing violations automatically does seem
to help in eliciting cooperation. Both trucking association and gov-

ernment enforcement officials observed that many truckers *encourage* MCSU inspectors to list problems on compliance reports because it alerts them to potentially dangerous problems. An enforcement official said, "Companies call up and ask us to come in and inspect them." Yet independent and knowledgeable observers, such as inspectors from companies that insure trucking firms, are strongly of the view that the MCSU's cooperative posture does not lead to undue softness or capture by the industry.*

Offering forebearance to elicit compliance is a common practice in some European inspection agencies as well. One occupational safety inspector in Sweden told Kelman that rather than write up a violation, "I would rather reason together with the employer and the safety steward, and come up with a solution everyone accepts."[23] Another said, "Sometimes we don't try to enforce every point. . . . We prefer to help employers and employees come to a common agreement, because then we've helped their feelings of dignity." Similarly, in order to elicit willing compliance, the British water pollution inspector, says Hawkins, "will recognize the inherent [technical] constraints the polluter may be under . . . and he will respect a previously good relationship. He will offer time . . . to come into compliance. And he will offer a less authoritarian response than called for in the law." The British inspectors explicitly tell regulated enterprises that the forebearance-compliance package is a preferable alternative to legalistic enforcement. One inspector said, "I explain to them . . . that they can do it in active cooperation with us . . . and we give them as much advice as possible, or . . . they can do it having been prosecuted . . . and with us watching them like a hawk forever afterwards."[24] The practice of not automatically penalizing violations, moreover, increases the enforcement staff's access to information. Hawkins notes that "field men are fond of pointing out that a manager of a pollution source who trusts his field man not to be punitive or unreasonable is willing to alert him on the first sign of trouble and will not seek to play problems down."

In some U.S. agencies, the concept of forebearance has been embodied in official policies that accept substantial compliance or even partial compliance—rather than insisting on literal compliance—with respect to smaller enterprises confronted with large expenditures for new

---

*An important factor in winning truckers' respect as well is the apparently high level of competence of MCSU inspectors.

and more stringent regulations. The Department of Agriculture, in enforcing the Wholesome Meat Act of 1967, which substantially upgraded standards for sanitation and plant facilities, issued special, more general standards for small meat-packing firms, a "step-by-step" guide to achieving a sufficient degree of compliance to satisfy the department, even though they would not be achieving the strict letter-of-the-law compliance required of larger firms. "The philosophy behind that approach is simply that it is better to keep these operators in business and to help them achieve a reasonable degree of compliance than to hit them with the book and thereby put them under."[25] A Small Business Administration study noted a similar philosophy in the air pollution section of EPA in dealing with small iron foundries and asphalt producers.[26]

Even without explicit legal authorization, some enforcement officials build good will and obtain added cooperation by quietly extending deadlines for especially costly abatement measures. The Food and Drug Division of the California Department of Health seems to follow this practice systematically. Its inspectors check food and drug manufacturers' compliance against immensely detailed "good manufacturing practice" regulations that are said to be more strict than federal standards.* Although inspectors are obligated to cite each deviation, the agency does not automatically initiate any penalty action, civil or criminal, or order an embargo. Rather, the inspectors' supervisors or regional office directors negotiate time limits and conditions for correcting each violation and then order a reinspection. The agency is willing to consider extenuating circumstances, such as the difficulty in getting a new part or the seasonal production deadlines for perishable fruits, if it concludes the hazards are tolerable and the company is acting in good faith. Where disputes (or violations) persist, the division usually holds an informal conference before initiating prosecution or a civil suit. No records are kept of these conferences. The firm usually sends a quality control engineer and a line manager; only occasionally does an attorney appear. Rarely, according to industry executives, does the agency relent on substantive requirements, but it often will grant more time and will accept temporary, less expensive solutions if the plant offers a convincing permanent corrective plan and has a reputation for reliability.

---

*To prevent contamination, the regulations prescribe physical facilities for manufacturing plants (e.g., screens on windows, floors with easily cleanable surfaces), the equipment and utensils that can be used, sanitation rules for personnel, how raw materials should be stored, and detailed procedures for testing, batch-coding, and record keeping (such as the "signing out" of batches from one process to another).

Justifiable extensions of time are sometimes given tacitly even in agencies that are bound by statute to enforce deadlines literally. Raymond Sturtz, an environmental engineer for an aluminum company, provided this example:

> Sturtz's company had decided to develop a novel dry-scrubber and recycling system for aluminum fluoride emissions rather than using the wet-scrubber demanded by EPA experts in Washington. This led to delays, however, and a phased step-by-step installation that clearly would prevent the company from meeting the statutory deadline. Still, Sturtz continually apprised EPA regional enforcement officials of the progress (and expenditures) his company was making. The statute did not allow the agency any discretion to extend the time. The agency's official stance, moreover, was that the abatement system should be installed all at once, rather than phased in gradually. EPA regional enforcement officials, therefore, could not and would not *approve* the abatement schedule submitted by the company. But they apparently recognized the reasonableness of the company's step-by-step development, testing, and installation plan, and that the company was operating in good faith. Agency officials, therefore, simply stalled. They sent letters pointing out the inadequacy of the plan "for the record." They did not come to the site, however, to document a possible enforcement action.*
>
> Sturtz said he recognized what they were doing and in return "tried to be as honest as I could. I need to build my credibility with those people. I want them to be honest with me. If something is going wrong, I want to know about it."

Thus the agency's reasonableness in not insisting on strict enforcement helped elicit a cooperative posture from the regulated enterprise.

One of the few areas of discretion OSHA enforcement officials have under the law concerns the establishment of compliance deadlines. Substantively, OSHA rules insist on "engineering out" health hazards, such as violations of noise standards, rather than abatement by use of personal protective equipment. Exceptions on the basis of economic feasibility are defined so stringently that formal variances are virtually impossible to

---

*This account was substantially verified by state air pollution control officials.

obtain. Many regional enforcement officials seem to deal with this rigidity, however, by granting long abatement times when high compliance costs are involved. For example, of 23 OSHA enforcement files involving noise violations—selected randomly in a study by John Mendeloff—the average abatement period granted by regional officials was two years, usually followed by further extensions.[27] One underlying value that can justify such extensions was expressed by a state air pollution control official. A manufacturing company in his district has a huge "coke calcining" oven that for some time had been in violation of the state's relatively new, and more stringent, standards on particulate emissions, even though the oven was equipped with a first-generation emission control device. The enforcement official recognized that there were technical problems involved and that no ready-made emission control device was available; the oven had to be redesigned. What was important to him was that the company had designed a new burner and had begun installation—a complex job involving building a whole new physical support structure: "As long as they're willing to spend money on the problem and they *are* spending money, they're showing a good-faith effort, and I don't think any penalty is appropriate."

Another justification for an extension is the recognition that it is usually much more expensive to retrofit existing equipment to control in-plant emissions or outside air pollution than to design those controls into new equipment. It is sensible, therefore, to coordinate abatement schedules with the regulated firm's amortization and equipment replacement schedules, at least when replacement is imminent and the risk to the public or workers is not great (as, for example, when workers can use personal protective equipment in the interim). The president's Interagency Task Force on Workplace Safety and Health urged OSHA, in enforcing its regulations, to require engineering controls only as new equipment comes on stream, provided adequate personal protective devices were available and old equipment would be rapidly replaced.[28]

One other area in which forebearance can often win an agency goodwill concerns reporting requirements. Presumably, the more information that flows to an agency, the more easily it can monitor compliance and build a data base for use in policy analysis. Carried along by this logic, however, the tendency of reporting systems to become oppressively costly and time consuming is by now almost legendary. The detailed records and reports are required of the good apples and the bad apples alike. They often generate more information than agency officials can hope to comb through. The Bay Area Air Pollution Control District, for example, recently repealed a regulation requiring manufacturing firms to report to the agency by telephone every breakdown in production or abatement equipment that might cause the firm to exceed legal emission levels. A district enforcement official estimated, however, that only 200 of the 10,000 or so reports received had involved significant pollution problems. Now, he said, the number of calls is greatly reduced, saving agency officials the labor of recording and responding to each call (as they had to under the repealed regulation). Yet the serious problems, he felt, were still being reported—reports were reduced, but not important information. This result, he acknowledged, was contrary to the expectation of agency enforcement staff, which had opposed the repeal (an industry-sponsored measure), fearing it would impair effectiveness.

BARGAINING: TRADING FOREBEARANCE
FOR MEANINGFUL COMPLIANCE

Enforcement officials, of course, often can justifiably demand an explicit price for withholding legalistic enforcement and penalties—a commitment by the regulated enterprise to undertake serious reforms. A familiar model is the criminal prosecutor who strikes some counts from an indictment and recommends a suspended sentence and probation in return for (1) a guilty plea with respect to the central offense and (2) a legal obligation to act in designated socially responsible ways during the probationary period. The threat behind the bargain is that a breach of the terms of probation by the defendant, a second offense, will result in a heavier penalty. The plea bargain saves everyone the costs and tensions of full-scale litigation and, when it results in probation, establishes at least some possibility of rehabilitation rather than exacerbating the defendant's resentment against the system.

Housing code inspectors commonly engage in this kind of bargaining:

> We observed New Haven housing code inspectors who would not cite the landlord for holes in plaster walls that obviously had been made by the tenants or their children (especially if the landlord had fixed earlier holes), or at least the inspector would imply that the landlord's delay in making the repair would not lead to prosecution. That forebearance, however, would be regarded as a credit

the inspector could draw on should a more serious violation occur in *any* of the landlord's properties in the future. If there were also serious violations present, inspectors would explicitly trade nonenforcement of minor violations for rapid, agreed-upon abatement measures for more serious problems, such as a broken-down heating or plumbing system.[29] In Boston, Nivola observed that withholding citations for minor violations could be used not only to trade for compliance measures but also to make the threat of prosecution more pointed and credible.[30]

A more far-reaching—and potentially more dangerous—practice is for the agency to exact, as a quid pro quo for nonenforcement, actions not specifically required by the regulations, such as changes in operating procedures that would help prevent serious violations in the future. By analogy, a judge sometimes attaches certain conditions to suspension of a sentence of incarceration—such as regular reporting of activities to a probation officer, or participation in a drug therapy or safe-driving program, or specified community service—even though such remedial actions are not the normal legal obligations of citizens. Most examples of this kind of bargaining in the regulatory process that we have heard of did not occur in on-site encounters between inspectors and regulated enterprises. More often, bargains were struck at the courthouse door, after prosecution had begun. Some statutes, however, explicitly try to establish an earlier forum for plea bargaining; before initiating prosecution or before issuing a recall order, the agency is instructed to provide the regulated enterprise with an opportunity for an informal hearing.*[31]

There seems to be a tendency for such lawyer-conducted hearings, however, to take on a legalistic cast—to focus on whether the agency has a good legal case rather than on whether enforcement should be suspended on policy grounds. Such a hearing does not provide the same flexibility and opportunity for building cooperation as plea bargaining conducted by front-line inspectors or investigators. Still, agency-level informal hearings do provide the opportunity for bargaining over what kind of *remedy* will be effective yet reasonable. Sometimes they can be quite creative, as when they focus on improving organizational capabili-

---

*In late 1980, OSHA for the first time granted its area directors explicit authority to hold informal conferences and to amend citations, abatement orders, and penalties in return for employer agreements to abate violations when "employers can present valid reasons for making adjustments." *National Law Journal*, December 1, 1980.

ties for future compliance, rather than on mandating specific facilities. The most far-reaching models for such bargains have been provided by the federal Securities and Exchange Commission. In return for dropping civil penalty actions, it has extracted "consent decrees" whereby defendants agreed to establish audit committees to monitor corporate procedures that had led to security law violations or to appoint a majority of "independent" directors to the corporate governing board.[32] Some other agencies have taken smaller steps in that direction.

- The California Health Department's Food and Drug Division dropped a civil penalty action against a small drug company with a history of violations of good manufacturing practice regulations in return for an agreement by the company to hire a recognized consultant and to implement the consultant's recommendations for a modern quality control system. An agency official said, "We haven't had any trouble with them since."
- One delinquent auto repair shop, threatened with legal action by the California Department of Consumer Affairs, agreed to hire a "consumer representative" to contact past customers to offer refunds for inadequate repairs. That agency also won an agreement from a chain of optical stores with a history of violations to cover the agency's costs for sending an inspector to the firm's twenty-six stores each month to ensure that personnel were being properly trained.

There *are* risks of abuse in this plea-bargaining process. Silbey's study of the Massachusetts Attorney General's Consumer Protection Office recounts a number of instances in which investigators threatened businesses with strict enforcement of entirely tangential regulations unless the firms gave refunds to dissatisfied customers, even when the agency had no evidence of violation of the consumer deception law in the transactions in question.[33] Many agencies, consequently, shy away from demanding any extra effort or compliance measures not specifically mandated by law, even in return for dropping or not initiating formal enforcement. That, they say, is harassment. In any case, the regulated enterprises might well complain to legislators that it is harassment, and in truth, it is difficult to distinguish the legitimate plea bargain from the illegitimate extortionate bargain, although we would think it is not impossible to articulate criteria for doing so.[34]

SUPPLYING INFORMATION: THE INSPECTOR AS CONSULTANT

Insofar as regulatory violations and hazards stem from employee inattentiveness, inadequate supervision, corporate misperception of risks, or ignorance of preventive measures—and according to enforcement officials in many fields, this is often the case—the regulatory agency may well have something to teach the regulated enterprise. Drawing on its cumulative experience with a variety of firms, it can provide information about risks and abatement techniques and ways of avoiding future violations. Backed by the implicit threat of enforcement, the agency, rather than compelling change by formal legal action, can "buy" it by providing information that will help the enterprise avoid expensive trouble in the future. Like a private business consultant, the inspector who finds a violation can attempt to analyze its causes, to diagnose weaknesses in the company's control system, and to point out cost-effective ways of preventing a recurrence.

The most obvious information an inspector can provide, of course, is about significant hazards that have escaped the attention of company officials. Quality control engineers in food and drug manufacturing firms, for example, repeatedly say they welcome inspectors who detect breakdowns in sanitation routines that might actually result in product contamination. The government inspector, in such cases, is serving as a free quality control consultant to the enterprise, preventing potentially catastrophic economic losses. A blood bank inspector told us that he draws upon innovations he sees in the most modern establishments to tell smaller, less-specialized hospitals how blood-warming machines, for example, can best be maintained, monitored, and repaired. Virtually every factory safety engineer we interviewed said that OSHA inspectors could play a potentially valuable role because, as one manager put it, however hard the company tried, "An outsider can notice something dangerous in your house that you just take for granted." This is especially true with respect to smaller firms that lack specialized safety or quality control personnel. But large corporations also occasionally report helpful contributions from inspectors who consciously adopt a more consultative stance.

Kenneth Wold, for example, is director of worker health and safety for an aluminum reduction plant in Kentucky. A state office called KOSHA has taken over enforcement of the Occupational Safety and Health Act. "The federal people who came in weren't very effective," Wold told us. "They didn't point out significant hazards and concentrated on unimportant things." But KOSHA inspectors who have visited the plant on an average of once a year "have been helpful in the closing conferences. . . ."

"They might see a bench grinder with a tool that's not well-adjusted. . . . The KOSHA man might find it at a time when our inspectors have missed it and the man and the foreman have become a bit lackadaisical."

In another instance, KOSHA industrial hygienists tested for emissions of "coal tar pitch volatiles." The measurements did not disclose a violation, but the inspectors nevertheless convinced company officials, in large part simply by focusing their attention on it, that it was a potentially serious problem. The company now requires workers in exposed operations to wear respirators, and it installed a $20,000 exhaust system.

The inspector may also be able to further his agency's mission by giving a regulated enterprise information that enables it to make reforms more cheaply, and with less disruption of routine, than its managers initially thought. An experienced air pollution inspector informed a steel foundry manager about a source of nonpolluting (nonoily) sand for foundry molding processes; with this information, the company, originally upset by the citation, willingly switched suppliers and abated the violation. Thus a regulatory requirement that the enterprise might think unreasonable on cost grounds can be made to seem more reasonable. Although businessmen claim that this kind of help is not usual, it sometimes does occur. The chief of the California Food and Drug Division, charged with enforcing regulations to prevent contamination, told us:

We realize that the more efficient a thing is . . . the more likely it is to be kept clean. Our inspectors talk about just that. . . . We go a little bit beyond what we probably should, what the law really says. We encourage the use of good materials, cleanable materials, to build things with, and good design. And we're not reluctant, some of our staff are very confident. If we look at some new piece of food machinery that comes along and we don't think the thing can be cleaned by the average cannery—they've just got too many closed sections on them—we say "Open it up. Put doors on them. What's wrong with putting a hinge here in this panel?"

Creating that kind of problem-solving dialogue with regulated firms, the same official emphasized, is a cost-effective means of enforcement.

There probably isn't a day that goes by that we don't spend several hours . . . dealing directly with industry trying to resolve mutually some type of problem, which probably negates the need for any inspections or anything else there. Now sometimes that may take only five minutes of time . . . it would be a hell of a lot cheaper than sending an inspector out there for maybe a day or two days, possibly going to court, the whole thing. . . . Enforcement is expensive. Very.

Agencies could enhance inspectors' ability to play this role if they consciously tried to serve as a data bank of abatement techniques, at least where problems are not standardized and hence where such information is not being supplied by the private market (such as pollution equipment suppliers or consulting firms). Ignorance of solutions, in fact, is surprisingly common. Although business enterprises may share information about the existence of safety or environmental problems, they are often reluctant to share information about solutions, for success in finding more cost-effective methods of complying with regulations has become an important way of gaining a competitive edge. Consequently, business managers often say they would welcome advice from regulatory officials about abatement methods. For example, maintenance of sophisticated air pollution control equipment, such as baghouses and scrubbers, is a major expense. Breakdowns are frequent. There is a constant search for ways of extending "bag life." Companies withhold that information from one another, but they must report breakdowns to agency officials, who perhaps could analyze and disseminate aggregate data. Environmental engineers we spoke to at petroleum refineries thought inspectors and agencies might be able to generate information about companies' successes and failures in dealing with difficult control problems, such as vapor recovery. "Sharing information would open up doors for them," one engineer added. Similarly, an exhaustive plant-by-plant study of occupational health problems in major copper smelters discovered considerable variation in measurement and protective engineering techniques to deal with known chemical hazards. The authors urged OSHA to establish "a widely accessible data bank" concerning health measurement and abatement technologies, rather than sending in inspectors with general checklists not geared to the specific problems of the industry.[35] In 1979, in fact, California founded a Toxic Substance Repository at the University of California to accumulate information about occupational hazards and provide technical information, including abatement methods, to manufacturers and unions.[36]

Diagnosis of the *causes* of violations is perhaps the most important kind of information an inspector can provide. To do so, the inspector's inquiry must go beyond the mere fact of a violation and extend into motivational areas. Does the violation stem, for example, from knowing and blatant disregard of standards, or from an unthinking failure to perceive certain risks or problems? Or is the violation a result of failure to supervise adherence to essentially responsible compliance programs that had in fact been prescribed by management? To plumb motivation and to analyze the human factors in the causal pattern may require a subtle probing of a manager's knowledge and priorities. For example:

> Wallace Stein, an inspector for the American Association of Blood Banks (a private organization), says, "It's hard to assess these 'intangibles.' " To assess the quality and diligence of a facility's quality control program, he looks at compliance with the association's standards and other tangible indicators (e.g., the training manuals they use, their procedure manuals, attendance by staff at seminars and conferences on blood banking, and recordkeeping). But the most important thing is "talking to them." After a while, he says, he's developed "almost a sixth sense about supervisors," and whether they are dedicated and effective.

To draw out and evaluate a manager's knowledge and priorities, however, an inspector usually must establish a nonthreatening atmosphere, an interpersonal relationship that seems premised on cooperative problem solving, so that the manager is not completely defensive. Such a relationship was established by an experienced Cal-OSHA inspector, in spite of his agency's legalistic reputation.

> Peter Stroud is a holdover from pre-OSHA days in the California worker safety and health agency. He is especially knowledgeable

about electrical hazards. He visited an automobile tire sales and service enterprise where an employee had been injured recently by getting his loose sleeve caught in a tire retreading machine. When Stroud first talked to the manager, he did not mention that he was investigating the injury, but presented himself as if he were merely conducting a routine inspection. "I try to be as innocuous as possible," he told us. "I like to slide in."

Stroud worked hard at creating a helping image. In presenting his OSHA identification, he pointed out that the manager should always ask to see it if someone came around and said he was an OSHA inspector. Reviewing the company's injury log, he told the manager, "Let me show you something. This column, the one that describes the nature of the injuries, is the important one. Look, you've had two repeat injuries of the same kind since March—foreign object entering the eye. That should tell you something: 'We've got a problem.' We're really here to help you prevent injuries, especially repeat injuries."

When Stroud toured the working area with the manager and an employee representative (he explicitly asked the manager to ask any "complainers" in the work force to come along), he kept up a steady stream of conversation with the manager in particular. He drew him into a discussion of precisely how the accident had occurred on the retreading machine, and discussed whether a worn guard, if it had been in repair, might have prevented it. The inspector pointed out to the manager each safety violation or problem he saw and discussed it with him.

He tested the manager's attitudes and knowledge by continually making low-key suggestions: "It appears you have a housekeeping problem [especially rubber shavings and dust, plus cluttered aisles]. Why don't you have your men work a bit as janitors, or hire a service?" "Well, we have a service for the store and the offices. . . ."

By the end of the visit, Stroud had formed a general impression of the manager's level of concern about occupational safety and health, and the adequacy of the company's program, differentiated by type of hazard. For example, Stroud saw one new employee replacing a tire without using the protective cage that had been supplied for each work station (mandated both by OSHA rules and company policy). Stroud was convinced that this was unusual, and partly attributable to a particularly intractable employee. ("Sure,

but I don't need it—it just slows me down," the employee told
Stroud. Stroud said, "You're not being paid for piece work, are
you? And you're certainly not being paid to get yourself killed.")

After leaving, Stroud commented about the manager: "I think
he'll try. He was really shocked when we saw that guy inflating
without using the cage." But other things, he sensed, were not very
high on the manager's agenda, and so, "on the smaller things like
housekeeping . . . he needs a little prodding, so we'll prod him."

By providing information—pointing out problems, telling about rules,
discussing solutions—and listening to the manager's responses, the inspector in this case was better able to gauge which enforcement strategy
would work best. He gained a feel for where there was a basis for
cooperation and where, on the other hand, strict prescription and fines
were necessary.*

One could imagine an inspector who would go even further in the
direction of diagnosis and thereby provide a more important type of
information. Stroud tested the manager's attitudes. But inspectors, at
least in theory, might go on to expose organizational weaknesses in the
regulated enterprise that contribute to irresponsible behavior. They
might diagnose faulty supervisory routines and managerial omissions.
The safety director of a large corporation sketched this scenario when we
asked him what he thought OSHA inspectors should do.

OSHA inspectors have the right to talk to employees. They'll go
up to a machine operator and ask if everything is OK. What they
really mean is, "Is there a violation I can write up?" If the man
points out a broken electrical cord or plug, the OSHA guy will just
write it up and put it on the list of citations.

What they should do is this: He should ask the employee, "How
long has it been that way? Did you tell your foreman about it?" He
should call over the foreman and ask why it was still that way.
Maybe the foreman will say, "I've told him three times . . . you're
supposed to go to Supply and get a new cord." Then why didn't
he? Maybe his job is set up so he can't. Maybe the inspector will

---

*Of course, because of OSHA's general policy, the agency later sent the company a citation
and fine for the protective cage violation, even though that was a problem Stroud thought
would be unlikely to be a problem in the future.

find out there's no procedure for checking cords, or that there is, but the employees don't know it well.

In legalistic enforcement, the inspector treats the regulated enterprise as a monolithic legal entity. But the inspector in the above scenario stimulates a much more fine-grained assignment of responsibility for preventing accidents. Individual managers clearly resent being found legally culpable for violations they did not cause or for risks *their* particular part of the operation did not create, and resentment, as we have seen, drives out cooperation. By the same token, if the true culprit is not tracked down, while corporate headquarters may pay the fines, the plant manager or foreman or employee who in fact caused the problem will not feel the pain; an inspector who contents himself with the fact of the fine alone will have lost an opportunity for reinforcing the consciousness of personal responsibility in the individuals who really need the prodding.

To undertake this diagnostic and catalytic role, an inspector would have to spend proportionately more time talking with managers and professionals in the regulated enterprise and interviewing operating employees, and would have to spend proportionately less time looking at physical facilities in search of violations. To play the diagnostic role, moreover, the inspector often must study the enterprises' records to try to locate *patterns* of accidents or defects, partly in order to target his own investigation and, more important, in order to focus managerial attention on serious problem areas in the particular enterprise. For example:

Frank McDonald is an inspector for the division of the California Department of Health responsible for enforcing safety regulations for blood and plasma centers. On site visits, he says he sharply questions employees performing transfusions about the procedures they routinely follow, and how they would deal with certain emergencies. If anyone fails his test, he informs the employee's supervisor and discusses methods of correcting the problem, such as better training or changes in supervisory procedures, but usually does not issue a citation. He says, "We're not here to put people out of business. The reason for inspection is to help them improve. You can't just kick 'em in the ass without telling them how to make things better. If you have to get tough, you do, but what we really want is for them to do a better job."

Similarly, McDonald says he reviews the detailed records that must be kept for each donor not so much to find violations—failure to make or countersign an entry—but as a clue to the center's operating style. For example, he looks to see if the information taken from donors (which is essential to guard against "overbleeding" and to maintain blood quality) is recorded neatly. "This may seem picky but it's not. If it's scribbled in that might be a sign that they're asking the questions very hastily or just going through the motions. Then I get suspicious, and I try to listen in on a few interviews."

The inspector-as-consultant can also alert company management to incompetent supervisors or gaps in internal control systems. One federal Railroad Administration inspector, checking Conrail records, noticed that there was no record of any managerial response to certain reports of rail defects filed by company track inspectors. He spelled out his findings in a citation and levied a fine against Conrail; the corporation suspended the responsible supervisor.[37] This kind of discovery seems to elicit a more cooperative attitude from the regulated enterprise.

The good inspector would also attempt to use his legal leverage to induce enterprises to study and improve their own procedures for preventing harm. An example is a special diagnosis-oriented inspection program under which FDA officials prod each food and drug manufacturer to analyze its own production processes to locate the most common sources of contamination and key indicators of potential breakdowns in quality control processes. Inspectors are then instructed to focus their investigations on these critical points, as opposed to routinely checking compliance with the FDA's almost endless list of "good manufacturing practice" regulations. In effect, this is a program for evaluating and improving the company's own quality control system and capacity for problem detection.[38]

THE GOOD INSPECTOR AND GOOD INSPECTION

Our portrait of the "good inspector" very nearly endows him with the wisdom of Solomon, the craftiness of Ulysses, and the fortitude of Winston Churchill. In the world of real regulatory agencies and real inspectors, the subjects are not idealized types but are real human beings.

Nevertheless, this portrait depicts a model to be emulated when possible. It shows certain enforcement practices that, if not entirely or consistently achievable, would be able to blend both effectiveness and reasonableness.

Moreover, our portrait of the good inspector illuminates the nature of the enforcement task. The good inspector is really anyone who can do good inspection. But good inspection does not depend merely on the personal characteristics and skills of the inspector, however important these may be. Good inspection can flourish only in an organizational and political environment that cultivates it, or at least permits it. It is the regulatory agency, and not merely the individual enforcement official, that must foster flexible enforcement and try to foster cooperation through consultation and tough bargaining. In the following chapter we discuss several of the critical tasks that agency managers must perform to make it possible for good inspectors to get on with their task of good inspection.

CHAPTER SIX

MANAGING THE REGULATORY

AGENCY

•

Flexible enforcement is an ideal to which a regulatory agency can only aspire. How close it actually comes to reaching that ideal depends on such diverse factors as the technical difficulties of monitoring performance by regulated enterprises and the political conditions tending to encourage— or to punish—flexible enforcement compared with, say, a strategy of consistent toughness. Achieving flexible enforcement also depends on the competency and the attitudes of an agency's top managers. But managers have many things to worry about; how, or indeed whether, to develop a flexible enforcement strategy is only one of them. Top regulatory officials are also preoccupied with acquiring an adequate budget, deterring (or reducing) laziness and corruption,[1] adopting new regulations, negotiating jurisdictional boundaries with other agencies, and maintaining workable relations with legislators and the news media. There are however, a number of tasks regulatory leaders can and sometimes do take on in order to encourage flexible enforcement.

MANAGING INSPECTORS

Discretion is the key to flexible enforcement. Yet to the bureaucrat and the apprehensive businessman alike, the word "discretion" immediately raises the specter of inconsistency, corruption, and bias. Rather than trust the judgment of an imperfect inspector, they say, they would prefer that inspectors go by the book.

Abuse of discretion is a real problem, but the assumption that discretion can be erased—at least without intolerable cost—is a myth. Rigidly following the rules leads to unreasonable and unjust results, in turn producing legal resistance, greater inducements to corruption, and, frequently, surreptitious returns to discretion by agency officials. As Kenneth Culp Davis, a leading legal scholar of administrative law, has long maintained, the issue is not whether discretion does or should exist—the answer in both cases is "yes"—but how it should be guided, checked, and reviewed.[2]

Granting legal decisionmakers discretion does not necessarily produce inconsistency and arbitrariness. An administrative agency can guide discretion by inculcating its officials with a common sense of organizational purpose, an overriding philosophy for reconciling an organization's primary mission with competing social values.[3] To motivate and control its far-flung rangers, the Forest Service, as described by Herbert Kaufman, relied on continuous retraining, circulation of documents stating and explaining agency policy, shifting personnel from the field to central offices and back again, and recurrent field visits by supervisors.[4] The importance of adopting similar guidance techniques in regulatory agencies is emphasized when we look at the problem from the inspector's point of view.

The ideal of flexible enforcement makes formidable demands on the individual inspector; it requires technical competence, toughness of mind, communications skills, and, above all, good judgment. Combining the qualities of toughness and conciliation takes not only the right training but also the right personality. Experienced enforcement officials assert that being an inspector is a stressful job.[5] Not everyone can live with the conflict involved in dealing with noncompliant firms. Nor can everyone live with the realization—essential to the idea of reasonableness in regulatory enforcement—that all hazards cannot be abated immediately and, consequently, that some harms will occur. "That's the thing you've got to get used to," said one top enforcement official in the Food and Drug Administration. "You've got to teach your inspectors to live with unsolvable problems. Being an inspector is a very difficult job." Steven Kelman found that Swedish workplace safety and health inspectors, who were expected to move back and forth between cooperative and coercive enforcement styles as the situation demanded, seemed to experience stress more severely then did their more consistently legalistic counterparts in OSHA.[6] Not surprisingly, therefore, many inspectors deal with stress by reverting to a less ambiguous definition of their role, just as some policemen deal with ambiguity by always acting as enforcers or as conflict-avoiding reciprocators. Many inspectors just quit, which creates a substantial turnover problem in some agencies.

These problems cannot be overcome entirely, especially given budgetary limitations and civil service laws that impair supervisors' discretion to hire the competent and fire the incompetent.[7] Yet it is reasonable to think that those problems might be controlled. Experienced enforcement officials have ideas on the subject, and many say that they are getting better inspectors now than they did 10 years ago.*

Recruitment. Many regulatory officials hope to improve enforcement by recruiting highly educated professionals to inspection staffs. As the law itself becomes more complex, supervisors want well-schooled inspectors who can master pages of very technical regulations. From this perspective, inspectors would have to hold degrees from public health schools, nursing schools, safety engineering and industrial hygiene programs, or environmental science and engineering programs. Despite budgetary resistance, and despite affirmative action goals that, in the eyes of many regulatory officials, have led in some cases to lower educational requirements, the trend has been toward recruitment of specially educated inspectors. For example, inspectors for the Food and Drug Division of California's Department of Health currently must have a master's degree in public health, biomedical engineering, or food technology. The young well-trained sanitarian hired by a county health department today knows much more than his older counterpart, trained on the job. Much of this knowledge is related to problem detection, such as the latest findings about newly recognized hazards and the latest techniques of testing for their presence. He probably is better equipped to rebut the contentions of corporate experts about the seriousness of violations and better equipped in some ways to educate the small businessman about them. He may be steeped in the latest textbook designs for abatement and prevention systems.

But the professionally educated inspector may also have weaknesses from the standpoint of flexible enforcement. Specialized education in detecting environmental perils is rarely balanced with education in eco-

---

*In some respects, the state of professionalism in social regulatory agencies is like that in police departments a generation or two ago. Police forces today are still not ideal, but a body of experience and thought does exist on problems of recruitment, training, and discipline. Police academies, some of them excellent, have become commonplace. And the problem of police discretion, by and large, has been dealt with by trying to guide it, rather than by requiring undeviating adherence to legal rules.

nomic analysis, problems of production and management, and the need for reasonableness. Graduates of public health schools are trained to detect hazardous levels of bacteria or carcinogens but sometimes are imbued with an ideology of protection that makes them hostile to arguments, based on economic costs or competing values, that some risks are socially tolerable.[8] Moreover, the ability to detect problems is not the same as the ability to work out balanced solutions or to elicit cooperation. It is no accident that the kind of inspectors whom managers in regulated firms complain of most (after the untrained inspector who knows nothing) are the "young hot-shots who act as if they and they alone are responsible for the health of the consumer."

While a professional education is often useful and sometimes even essential for inspectors, it might also be useful for their education to be balanced with some experience among the regulated. While that kind of experience might seem, at first blush, to lead to a co-opted and compliant inspectorate, it might also be a route to a more competent and a more effective one. For example, to get a job as a truck and school bus inspector in the California Highway Patrol, an applicant must have had five years' experience in truck safety maintenance; these inspectors are respected both by trucking company officials and by insurance company loss control specialists for their competence, high safety standards, and integrity. This should not be surprising. The role an inspector plays is much more likely to reflect the incentives and constraints of his present job than the loyalties and habits from previous jobs.[9] Indeed, one major cause of co-optation—the dependence of enforcement officials on regulated enterprises for critical information—can be offset by inspectors who have had experience in industry and are therefore better able to evaluate excuses. Moreover, the inspector with experience in industry should be able to play the consultant role more intelligently. Being able to understand and think through the regulated enterprise's problems, he is more likely to be able to elicit cooperation by astute bargaining, by providing useful ideas, and by selling the reasonableness of certain regulatory requirements. Keith Hawkins, in his study of water pollution control in England, observed a marked contrast between younger inspectors, typically fresh from a university education in the natural sciences, and older inspectors, many of whom had prior experience in industry. To the older inspectors, pollution control was less a matter of "the dispassionate application of scientifically-derived principles" and formal legal prosecution (as the younger inspectors seemed to believe), and "more the art of managing personal relationships." "Success on the job," head-quarters staff told Hawkins (and he seems to concur), is closely related to the older inspector's ability to take the civilian perspective. Success depends primarily on negotiating ability and interpersonal skills, on the capacity, as a supervisor put it, "to appreciate other peoples' points of view but to be able to swing them 'round to yours if necessary."[10]

Training. Where budgetary constraints make it difficult to recruit inspectors with relevant business experience,[11] it might be useful to explore industrial internships for new inspectors and for new supervisors; larger corporations especially might be willing to serve this function. Certainly there should be few obstacles to incorporating instruction in economic analysis and principles of production into inspector-training programs. Progressive police academies, by way of analogy, not only provide instruction in criminal law and enforcement skills but also try to teach young officers to understand the social world and attitudes of the population they patrol. Sergeants (the equivalent of supervisors in regulatory agencies) are brought back into the training academy for seminars in which they exchange experiences and discuss field-training techniques.[12] The best day-to-day field training for patrolmen involves regular discussions at lineups concerning the problems that individual officers experience in reconciling the need for coercion with the need for cooperation.[13] For inspectors, too, it would seem that techniques for transcending legalistic regulation would have to be *taught,* and the personal stress engendered by attempts to enforce the law flexibly would have to be confronted openly.

Continuing education, moreover, might help combat the inspector turnover problem in certain regulatory agencies. Although some of the turnover problem derives from higher salaries in industry, the lack of advancement opportunities, and the rigidities of civil service systems,* it appears that education can frequently provide a balancing set of rewards. The chief of loss control operations at a major insurance company says that in order to retain and motivate his inspectors (whose salaries are

---

*Agency officials complain that civil service rules make it difficult to provide adequate rewards for excellent inspectors. Some agencies, therefore, have established two or three *grades* of inspector to provide promotion opportunities. They cannot match the flexibility of private organizations, but the example of such organizations might be worth emulating. The loss control division of a major insurance company has five salary grades for its 400-person staff of inspectors and four grades for supervisors. Inspectors are hired on a one-year probation system. The highest grade inspector is paid more than a branch manager in order to keep good men out in the field.

comparable to government inspectors'), "we train, train, train." Frequent workshops and technical courses at cooperating schools, he indicated, increase not only inspectors' knowledge but also their spirit. More knowledge improves the loss consultant's self-confidence in confrontations with technicians in industry, while attendance reinforces the sense of participating in a larger, socially valuable function. A senior official of the California Food and Drug Division reported, "When we put together an inspection manual, we got the inspectors to do it. They really liked that." Food and Drug Division inspectors are encouraged to become specialists on some aspects of their work and to write about it or give classes for other inspectors. One inspector had written a manual on controlling hazards in bottle-refilling operations and another prepared one on inspecting particular kinds of machinery used in drug manufacturing plants.

Specialization. The inspector's effectiveness and capacity for reasonableness are enhanced if he can specialize in the risks posed by a particular technological process or a type of regulated enterprise. With expertise and experience, the inspector is better able to spot problems, see through unjustified excuses, and elicit cooperation by giving useful advice. For agencies that must police a broad array of industries and processes, specialization might require departures from the usual territorial arrangement. The FDA Bureau of Biologics inspectors, who oversee manufacturers of serums, plasma products, and intravenous solutions, operate as a specialized long-range strike force out of Washington, D.C.; they bring more expertise to biologics manufacturing plants than would the agency's regional inspectors, who move from one type of factory to another. The Robens Report on workplace safety inspection in England details a strategy of specialization within territories: workplaces were classified as technically simple, average, or complex; the inspectorate, too, was graded according to experience and training, and supervisors attempted to match individual inspectors with workplaces at their competence level.[14] Another way of producing some specialization is to intensify territoriality, each inspector concentrating on a specific group of firms in a geographical area, much as a policeman is assigned a beat. The San Francisco Bay Area Air Pollution Control District assigns an inspector almost full time to each of three major oil refineries in the area. "When I was first assigned to the Chevron refinery," one of these inspectors told us, "I was completely overwhelmed. Now I know it like my own yard." With such knowledge, the inspector could spot changes in company routines that might signal breakdowns in pollution control systems. Greater familiarity with specific companies helps Swedish inspectors adopt more of a problem-solving approach to worker safety hazards than their OSHA counterparts,[15] and it helps British water pollution inspectors distinguish environmentally serious upsurges in effluents from those that are ephemeral and nonhazardous.[16]

One deterrent to assigning inspectors to individual establishments is the fear of co-optation—the inspector might become too accepting of a firm's procedures or become too friendly with the personnel. Some supervisors, accordingly, insist on rotating inspectors; to support their theory, they note that the number of citations usually increases after a new inspector is assigned to a site. That proves little, however, unless the increase reflects *significant* uncorrected hazards. One can always find numerous violations in most large enterprises, including those that experienced enforcement officials acknowledge are "doing a good job." Hence the rise in citations might reflect only greater legalism or ignorance of mitigating circumstances. Such ignorance can also strain hitherto cooperative relationships. An environmental affairs engineer at a Bay Area oil refinery complained, "Every time we get a new inspector there is suspicion." Moreover, a study of housing code enforcement in New York City saw rotation as a source of low inspector morale:

> Although [inspectors] have opportunities to develop an understanding of housing conditions in local areas, they are given little or no incentive for such development. District rotation, intended to prevent graft but untested as to its effectiveness, reduces still further the relationship between inspectors and their neighborhoods.[17]

True, in some cases a new inspector might provide genuinely improved perception and renewed toughness. But on balance, the potential gains from specialization, in terms of both effectiveness and reasonableness, would probably be larger.

Controlling Discretion. Management tools other than frequent rotation, moreover, are available or might be devised to control corruption. Supervisors can monitor records of inspector activity, such as detailed reports concerning each inspection, the numbers of citations issued, and comparisons of citation rates across inspectors. But because quantitative comparisons can encourage legalistic citation of any and all violations,

agencies might stress more qualitative checks on inspectorial performance. Occasional team inspections allow supervisors and experienced
inspectors to view their colleagues in action. Team inspections also
facilitate more analytical approaches to enforcement; by comparing
notes, team members may be better able than the individual inspector to
go beyond the rule book and analyze the organizational dynamics,
strengths, and weaknesses of the inspected enterprise.[18]

Reinspection by other experienced inspectors is another common supervisory tool to prevent co-optation and corruption. Although it too can
lead to legalistic enforcement when done primarily to expose violations
overlooked by the primary inspector, the goal of flexible enforcement
could be served if agency management designed reinspections to detect
instances of unreasonableness as well as undue leniency and to reward
rather than chastise inspectors for being appropriately nonlegalistic.
Explicitly stating responsibility for reasonableness as well as aggressive-
ness in formal job descriptions and promotion criteria for inspectors
would help institutionalize a flexible approach to enforcement. An FDA
supervisor, for example, told us that his recommendations for responding
to a violation are reviewed by his superiors for excessive toughness as well
as undue leniency. He believed he had to be "right" at least 90 percent of
the time to receive a favorable evaluation.

A vital element in teaching controlled discretion is the establishment of
regular mechanisms for enforcement officials to discuss hard cases, both
among themselves and with superiors. Participant-observation studies
have shown that consultation among regulatory officials tends to produce
common understandings of how to interpret the rules.[19] Discussion of
particular cases is also a check on legalism: it brings out the facts and
values at stake, counteracting the bureaucratic tendency to see a case
wholly in terms of the application of rules.[20] In addition, through consultation an agency can build up an institutional memory concerning
noncompliant firms, cost-effective solutions, and other bits of information essential to making qualitative judgments about enforcement.

It seems important for supervisors and office chiefs to become involved
in such discussions. For lower level officials, the courage to make equitable exceptions to the letter of the law and the judgment to know when
such exceptions are advisable depend on the authoritative examples
provided by superiors.[21] A regional FDA enforcement official told us that
he appreciated the weekly meetings of all enforcement staff in his office,
in which inspectors and supervisors were told why any violations they

cited did not result in prosecution. After higher enforcement officials or agency attorneys in the Bay Area Air Pollution Control agency decide against filing a penalty action with respect to a violation—a decision usually made on legal grounds, but sometimes on reasonableness grounds—they send a memo to the citing inspector, indicating the citations they regard as unenforceable or not worth issuing in the first place. Detailed feedback to inspectors about higher level decisions, moreover, helps forestall a common form of inequality: unless higher officials' reasons for reinterpretations or variances are built into the citation process, some inspectors will continue to apply the rules literally, and less sophisticated firms will comply with regulatory orders that the experienced repeat offender knows can be relaxed by higher level officials.[22]

One could imagine even more immediate consultative mechanisms to guide and support field inspectors in discretionary decisions. When industrial salesmen are faced with a difficult discretionary decision (e.g., whether to quote a price less than "book" or promise accelerated delivery to win an order), they often telephone a sales or production manager to discuss whether the concession is necessary or justifiable. British water pollution inspectors have two-way radios in their cars, enabling superiors to redirect them to investigate reports of serious pollutants and enabling inspectors to check back with more experienced hands or to ask for technical information in the files. But for the most part, once regulatory inspectors leave agency headquarters, they might as well be in a trackless wilderness as far as communicating with their supervisors is concerned. When confronted with technical claims they cannot evaluate, inspectors' telephone calls to experts back at the agency might forestall the legalistic response they otherwise feel compelled to make—or it might enable them to ask more probing questions, suggest alternative abatement measures, or reject unjustifiable defenses.

COPING WITH RESOURCE CONSTRAINTS

Flexible enforcement requires resources that are in short supply in many regulatory agencies—time, knowledge, and money. Probing, consultative inspections may take more time than inspections guided by a checklist. Inspectors who are asked to make judgments and elicit cooperation must have more knowledge than inspectors told to go by the book. Longer inspections and more knowledgeable inspectors would require a larger, better trained staff, and that, of course, would take a larger budget—which often will not be available. A primary managerial requisite for flexible enforcement, therefore, is to use existing resources in a more selective manner and to avoid certain costs that tend to be associated with legalistic enforcement.

Table 1

Approximate Ratio of Inspectors to Sites to Be Inspected

Agency	Number of Inspectors	Number of Sites (approx.)	Ratio
OSHA and state affiliates	3,300	5,000,000*	1:1515
Cal-OSHA elevator unit	29	32,000† (elevators, hoists, etc.)	1:1103
San Francisco Bay Area Air Pollution Control District	40	10,500† (significant stationary sources)	1:263
		1,700† (establishments)	1:43
California Motor Safety Unit	14	3,560‡	1:254
Food and Drug Administration food processing and storage	1,000	77,000§	1:77
California milk and dairy	110	6,960†	1:63
Mine Safety and Health Administration	1,300	22,000 ‖	1:17
Nuclear Regulatory Commission	1,564	9,000 ‖	1:6

* Lawrence S. Bacow, *Bargaining for Job Safety and Health* (Cambridge: MIT Press, 1980), p. 13.
† Interview with agency official, 1980.
‡ Interview with agency official. Each inspector inspects about 2,000 vehicles per year.
§ Melvin J. Hinich and Richard Staelin, "Regulation of the U.S. Food Industry," in U.S., Congress, Senate, Committee on Government Affairs, *Study on Federal Regulation*, App. to vol. VI, *Framework for Regulation* (95th Cong., 2d sess., December 1978), p. 422.
‖ President's Interagency Task Force on Workplace Safety and Health, *Making Prevention Pay* (Washington, D.C., 1978), p. VI–8.

Most managers believe that their agencies are shorthanded, that their meager resources are spread thin across a veritable ocean of trouble spots. Indeed, as Table 1 shows, the number of inspectors divided by the number of establishments or entities to be inspected is usually a very small fraction (the number of inspector-hours available divided by the number of hours of operation of the inspected firms would produce an even smaller fraction). Observers often use such statistics to conclude that an average regulated enterprise need fear an inspection no more than once every year, or for some programs even less often. This observation, in turn, sometimes leads to the conclusion that understaffing is a chronic phenomenon explainable only by the fact that regulatory programs are not *meant* to be effective, that they are manifestations of symbolic politics. In this view, the political elite, in the face of obvious social harms, is periodically obliged to pass a tough-looking law, but once the problem is ostensibly being taken care of and has slipped from the front pages, the legislature quickly trims the agency budget or simply fails to increase it in tandem with the agency's ever-increasing formal enforcement responsibilities.[23]

Another possible interpretation, however, is that seemingly low budgets may actually be close to some optimum. As we argued in chapter 3, the preponderance of regulated enterprises usually are good apples; in these firms, the pressures of the market and the liability law roughly coincide with regulatory goals; citizen complainants and internal corporate compliance staffs use the threat of inspector's visits to push for adherence to regulations; and a relatively small number of well-publicized severe punishments for regulatory noncompliance act as a sufficient deterrent. Once this is recognized, continuous and equal surveillance of all firms by a very large band of inspectors could be reduced sharply, and the agency usually would have enough resources to concentrate on trouble spots. The president's Interagency Task Force on Workplace Safety and Health, for example, concluded:

> Only 335,000 fixed establishments have lost workday [injury] rates above the relevant industry average of 4.9 [per 100 work years]. Moreover, 211,000 of these . . . have less than 20 employees, and would be difficult to reach by any inspection strategy. . . . In other words . . . the relevant job safety problem is not how to cover 4–5 million establishments; it is confined to about 125,000 high-risk establishments which OSHA should address first, and which aver-

age out to . . . about 75 establishments per Federal and State OSHA inspector combined.[24]

There is not enough evidence for us to endorse for certain this view of the adequacy of funding for OSHA inspectors or the applicability of the same reasoning to other regulatory enforcement budgets. But constrained budgets do provide some opportunities for flexible enforcement, if only because they provide an incentive for agency managers to be efficient, to deploy their limited inspection staffs more selectively, and to extend their enforcement resources through informal enforcement techniques and cooperative strategies.

Informal Sanctions. The higher the legal penalty for evading the law, presumably, the less often the inspector actually has to show up. Seeking heavy legal penalties, however, is always costly for the agency, for the more that is at stake, the more the regulated enterprise and its lawyers insist on meticulous legal proof and take advantage of the innumerable opportunities for delay provided by due process protections. While these cases are not numerous, they consume a vastly disproportionate amount of an agency's resources, and the prospect of frequent litigation forces inspectors to be even more rule bound.

Some agencies, on the other hand, employ more informal kinds of sanctions that do not involve court action, for example, harassing recalcitrant firms by more frequent and intensified inspections or demands for documentation. To borrow Malcolm Feeley's characterization of lower criminal courts, "the process is the punishment."[25] In a study of enforcement of federal regulations concerning expenditures of federal funds for disadvantaged children in public education, Paul Hill found that the U.S. Office of Education's most effective sanctions against school districts that violate federal regulations are not the formal coercive ones, such as withdrawal of funds, which often entail appeals and lengthy legal proceedings, but informal ones, such as performing "unusually large numbers of program reviews" in noncomplying districts.[26] Referring to persistent violators, a British water pollution inspector told Hawkins, "I wear 'em down. I go back again and again so they don't want to see me any more . . . and they put right what's wrong because they're fed up with me hanging around."[27] John Mendeloff has suggested that more frequent OSHA inspections of enterprises with disproportionately high worker injury rates would amount to an "injury tax" that would provide meaningful incentives for improvement.[28]

Another informal sanction is deliberate generation of adverse publicity about regulated enterprises that commit serious violations. For food manufacturers, the mere threat by the FDA to call a press conference or to issue a press release warning the public about a dangerous product is usually enough to induce voluntary recalls and, more importantly, substantial compliance with good manufacturing practice regulations even before the inspector arrives. Hill's study of regulations concerning special education for disadvantaged children found that federal charges of noncompliance, published in local papers, deeply embarrass school superintendents and compliance officers on their staffs and provide a major incentive to institute appropriate programs.[29] Sometimes, adverse publicity can be beamed much more specifically to insurance companies, banks, valued customers, and suppliers that have leverage on the regulated enterprise in question and that do not want to be seen as having aided a noncompliant firm. According to Philip Schrag, former counsel for New York City's Consumer Protection Agency, the agency was enmeshed in drawn-out court proceedings against a recalcitrant burglar alarm company quite clearly guilty of fraudulent sales practices. The agency learned that the defendant, through its parent company, leased space to sell alarms in a major department store. Agency officials presented the store's attorneys with evidence of the defendant's fraudulent sales practices, and the store terminated its contract with the defendant.[30] An official of the California Motor Carrier Safety Unit told us, with perhaps a touch of exaggeration, "We get 15 calls a day from insurance companies about the safety ratings" that MCSU inspectors assign to truck fleets. A company that receives a low MCSU rating, therefore, risks paying a higher premium rate and receiving more pressure for corrective action from insurance company loss control representatives. For similar reasons, some nursing home regulators and fire marshals notify insurance companies when government inspection turns up particularly flagrant violations of fire and safety codes.

Disseminating adverse information about a firm is very risky, of course, for the agency may be wrong in some particulars, extenuating circumstances might be left out of the account, or the damage to a firm's reputation may outweigh the seriousness of the offense.[31] Nevertheless, it would seem that safeguards could be devised, such as the hierarchical bureaucratic and legal clearances the FDA now requires before initiating seizure of contaminated foodstuffs and issuing an accompanying press release.[32]

Efficient Deployment. No matter how intimidating an agency's armory of sanctions, the question always remains of where and how to deploy inspectorial resources. The principles generally thought to govern the deployment of inspectors are simple. First, inspectors should be concentrated where they can prevent the greatest harm to the greatest number. Second, inspectors should be mobilized to gain the most reliable information about the distribution of hazards in the population of regulated enterprises. Unfortunately, however, the principles conflict; deploying inspectors to gain information will necessarily divert them from places where they could in fact be preventing more harm. Time and energy are expended in checks on firms that probably are good apples that might be more profitably spent on known bad apples. Conversely, time and energy invested in ever-closer monitoring of known bad apples are diverted from discovering others and from prodding the moderately good firms where important gains could also be made. Exactly how the trade-off between the two principles should be made in specific cases cannot be formulated in the abstract.

Sometimes the search for the optimum in enforcement priorities is blocked by statutory dictates: all establishments of a certain kind, the law might say, shall be inspected once every so often (all underground coal mines, for example, must be inspected quarterly). Such statutory directives may reflect legislative responses to catastrophes or scandals that are imputed to insufficient frequency of inspection, or they may simply reflect notions of equal treatment or equal competitive burdens. Either way, they can be very inefficient, for they force inspectors both to go as often to firms with good records as those with bad ones and to conduct a full inspection in all cases when a more superficial sampling might be adequate for some. An experienced official of the California MCSU complained about the laws passed after a tragic school bus accident, mandating full weekly brake inspections for all school buses in the state. "Mandatory and unannounced inspections," the official argued, "are not really necessary, because most vehicles in a fleet are alike in terms of maintenance levels. If you do a few vehicles thoroughly, you usually have a good idea of the condition of the other vehicles." For truck inspections, on the other hand, where the statute is not so restrictive, the MCSU's frequency and intensity of reinspection is based on an "A," "B," or "C" rating assigned at the end of the previous inspection, based on the company's overall compliance record and the inspector's assessment of the quality of its maintenance program.

More important, perhaps, are the distortions of inspection priorities that stem from responding to complaints. On the one hand, complainants can be a valuable extension of the inspectorate's capacity for gathering information about actual or potential harms. Indeed, agencies sometimes launch special programs to train and mobilize this free reserve army of inspectors.* On the other hand, complainants—especially when they have received no special training—can tie up inspectors on legally unfounded or substantively trivial claims, or divert their energies toward enterprises with comparatively decent compliance records. Many complaints come from disgruntled employees, conniving competitors, or citizens who are simply mistaken about the law or the facts. If agencies were free to disregard such complaints, the diversion of effort might not be serious. But some statutes impose legal deadlines within which agencies must respond to all complaints, and there are political difficulties for an agency in disregarding complaints—or in responding when the agency gets around to them—as well as the nagging fear of ignoring the boy who cries "wolf" when the wolf is really there.

Even valid complaints may divert agency resources from higher priority activities. Leon Mayhew, for example, found that complaints of job-related racial discrimination in Massachusetts disproportionately involved those firms and industries that had made the *most* progress in hiring blacks, rather than those firms or industries that were most likely to have been following an exclusionary policy. Accordingly, the complaints tended to get the agency involved in disputes over allegedly discriminatory pay questions and job assignments, rather than the more serious discriminatory hiring and firing issues.[33] Bruce Vladeck, in his study of quality-of-care regulation of nursing homes, observes:

> Special teams of state surveyors whose function is to respond to complaints . . . have been established as a result of failure to respond to an inquiry . . . [or] in response to pressures from consumer groups. . . . But most of those involved in the survey process believe that the correlation between complaints and serious

---

*OSHA, for example, has contracted with the Labor Occupational Health Program at the University of California at Berkeley, among other organizations, to hold safety and health inspection workshops for union members.

deficiencies is tenuous and that, when manpower is scarce, responding to spontaneous complaints may not be the best way to employ it.[34]

(A nursing home regulator in California observed that, in his experience, complaints may reflect the relative touchiness of the complainants rather than the relative deficiencies of the management.) Similar reports come from officials in California's Food and Drug Division and from studies of OSHA, consumer protection, and housing code enforcement agencies.[35] Responding to unfounded or nonserious complaints, moreover, demoralizes both enforcement officials and officials in the regulated enterprise. A full-time labor union safety representative in a large factory said that he often tours the plant at break time to look for safety problems so that he can avoid getting bogged down with "piddling complaints" from workers and concentrate on things *he* thinks are most important. Moreover, he says, it hurts his credibility with company engineers when he is obliged to bring up minor problems raised by workers.

An important task for agency leadership, therefore, is to devise methods of screening citizen complaints before sending inspectors forth or to devise a division of labor that enables a cadre of skilled inspectors to concentrate on high priority inspections. A number of such efforts have been made.

Requiring Better Evidence from Complainants. For violations not observed by agency inspectors, the Bay Area Air Pollution Control District will not commit itself to action against an alleged polluter unless it receives complaints from five different individuals. In 1979, after its backlog of discrimination complaints had grown to 99,000, the Equal Employment Opportunity Commission, rather than continuing to investigate all complaints as given, began to require complainants first to provide some supporting evidence that failure to obtain the job or promotion in question was in fact a product of discrimination.

Responding by Letter or Telephone Call. The Interagency Task Force on Workplace Safety and Health recommended that OSHA should respond to employee complaints with a letter to the employer rather than an on-site inspection, except for complaints alleging imminent danger or serious hazards in mobile work sites.

The letter would instruct the employer to investigate the hazard complained of, to respond within 3 days, and to provide OSHA with written notice of remedial action taken within 30 days.[36] A telephone response in addition to if not in substitution for the letter method might be even better. The agency official would talk directly with the responsible company official, obtain a better sense of the nature of the problem and the company's attitude, and discuss the remedy. A follow-up telephone call to the *complainant* would help the agency test the company's good faith, decide whether an inspection is necessary, and deter acts of discrimination against such complainants by employers.[37] This approach in fact worked well in New York City's housing code enforcement program.[38]

Routing Complaints Through Intermediaries. Better Business Bureaus serve this filtering function, in part, for government consumer fraud agencies. The state of Connecticut estabished an ombudsman program whereby volunteer assistant ombudsmen, assigned to specific nursing homes, are instructed both to seek out and to screen complaints from patients and their relatives.[39]

Preemption of Complaints by Pro-active Inspection. When a California OSHA office was bombarded with repeated complaints from individual workers in a large automobile assembly plant and began to suspect this bombardment was a reflection of poor labor-management relations more than serious safety problems, it decided to undertake a comprehensive week-long, wall-to-wall inspection of the plant, apparently intending to use its findings to evaluate and perhaps parry subsequent individual complaints.

Special Inspectors for Complaints. A large municipal housing code enforcement unit uses less experienced inspectors to respond to tenant complaints about poor maintenance—matters that usually involve easily identifiable violations—while using more experienced inspectors for the more exhaustive and technically complex inspections conducted upon the sale of buildings.

Finally, agency leadership can lobby for more statutory discretion in responding to complaints according to their own priorities. Statutes that cast regulatory goals in the language of absolute consumers' or patients' rights and establish deadlines by which agencies must initiate enforcement actions give complainants and advocacy groups leverage over the agency and undermine the agency's capacity to negotiate with them about priorities. Instead, the law might explicitly provide agencies with discretion to suspend enforcement "in the public interest," just as criminal prosecutors, "in the interests of justice," are traditionally allowed discretion not to enforce an explicit law. Some antidiscrimination statutes provide that if an agency fails to act upon a complaint within a stated time, the complainant can bring a civil lawsuit against the enterprise in question; such statutes represent a useful compromise between agency officials' need to set their own priorities in responding to complaints and the rights of complainants to legal protection.

In some agencies, inspections are somewhat misdirected by mechanical reliance on quantitatively calibrated priority schemes. Sometimes the size of the regulated enterprise is used as a criterion, with large firms, as indicated by the number of employees or volume of output, being visited much more often. Certainly this makes a lot of sense at the beginning of an effort to enforce new standards. Once a compliance program is under way, however, especially in fields other than pollution regulation, more frequent inspections of larger firms may reflect considerations of convenience and politics rather than the rational allocation of inspectorial efforts. It is usually more acceptable politically to prosecute the big corporation than the small businessman, and it is easier to persuade judges to impose sanctions against large firms—"It's harder to prove intent on the part of the little guy," one inspector told us. Also, it will often be possible to find more violations per inspector-hour in one big plant than in a few scattered small ones, with travel time in between. But large corporations, more in the public eye and able to take advantage of scale economies in regulating their own activities internally, are much more likely to have in-house experts and programs to keep the company out of trouble with the law. The most flagrant and serious violations, therefore, are more likely to be found in smaller enterprises.*

---

*This is not to say, of course, that large firms should automatically be assigned to a lower priority than small ones. Experienced enforcement officials and compliance specialists in large corporations stress the point that big enterprises are not monoliths—they have good and bad divisions. Plant managers are subject to intense cost-cutting pressures; some remain strongly committed to compliance and some less so.

Similarly, resource misallocation occurs when inspection frequencies are mechanically keyed to the sheer numbers of violations found in an enterprise in the past, or to the number of complaints, or even to the number of accidents or pollution incidents. Such numerical rates often depend on factors beyond the scope of the regulations—such as the nature of the production technology, rates of employee turnover, or changes in production process—and hence are not always good indicators of the overall quality of the enterprise's preventive system. OSHA's area office in Idaho, for example, complained to the main office in Washington that the agency's elaborate High Hazard Inspection Planning Guide, directing inspections toward firms in industries with high lost workday injury rates, was too crude; the categories, it said, were too broad, "leading us to establishments which do not warrant inspections and preventing us from inspecting others that do." It might be useful, therefore, for agency managers to emulate the MCSU, which bases the frequency of inspection on *qualitative* assessments of individual enterprises' compliance efforts, or the New Haven housing code agency, which concentrated on buildings owned by those "large" landlords who had developed a reputation among inspectors for recalcitrance and poor maintenance.[40]

A final impediment to efficient deployment is the tendency to disregard the principle that what the agency can do must be assessed in the context of all the other things that are being done by other parties. In the language of economics, one should look at the agency's contribution "at the margin," that is, its "value added." From this point of view, it would make sense to inspect firms with bad performance histories only if the agency is able to do something about them. Another application of the "value added" axiom concerns OSHA's comparative advantage in preventing occupational diseases as compared with preventing accidents. Armed with the latest scientific findings, the agency knows a good deal more about detecting and controlling chemical emissions that may gradually cause disease than do many companies and most workers. Preventing accidents, however, is an older problem that companies have long been forced to address by worker compensation laws, and safety hazards are more obvious to workers; hence OSHA's ability to detect and abate dangers in a particular factory may be only slightly greater (if at all) than that of most managers and workers.[41] An argument could be made, therefore, that OSHA should allocate the majority of its inspections to occupational health problems, rather than continue its present practice of emphasizing safety.

The Use of Informants. Like a police officer, an inspector needs reliable allies and informants among the population he polices, and perhaps more so, for he is less often on the scene. With respect to every regulatory program, there are individuals inside the regulated enterprise who have knowledge or information-gathering capacity about regulatory problems in their firm that an inspector covering many firms could never hope to acquire. In his efforts to locate and diagnose the causes of regulatory problems or to assess the validity of management's claims that proposed solutions are too costly or unworkable, the information provided by in-house informants could be all-important to the inspector. The inspector also can act as catalyst, stimulating such allies to think hard about problems, priorities, and solutions. Allies, however, must be located and cultivated. Like the industrial salesman, the inspector in search of informants must personalize his relationships with a number of individuals in the company he deals with, ask about their concerns and their firm's problems, and provide trade gossip and useful information in return, gradually learning who is sympathetic to regulatory goals and who can be trusted.

The challenge for agency leaders is to encourage and support this type of ally-seeking behavior, something most legalistic agencies now do very little of. Inspectors' reports are dry legal documents, purged of any discussion of the personal characteristics of individual plant managers, engineers, or union representatives. Some personal information is exchanged informally among enforcement officials, of course, but it is often evanescent or unavailable, as inspectors rotate assignments or leave the agency. Inspectors are not made to feel that qualitative judgments and creation of personal relationships are among their major responsibilities.

By way of contrast, in British water pollution control agencies, as Hawkins has described them, "The supervisors will . . . expect the field man to know the personalities concerned."[42] In the Swedish occupational safety and health enforcement program, training manuals urge inspectors to talk about a variety of things with workers and employers, "in order to create good rapport."[43] In theory, the Occupational Safety and Health Act provides an opportunity for this type of contact. By giving worker representatives a right to accompany OSHA inspectors on walkarounds, it allows OSHA inspectors to talk with knowledgeable informants in the regulated enterprise and to stimulate labor-management dialogue concerning necessary and reasonable changes. In practice, though, because of OSHA's rule-and-citation enforcement style, that potential is probably not often realized.

In less legalistic American agencies, however, there have been some real steps in this direction. Inspectors from California's MCSU, a supervisor told us with approval, frequently make a point of having a cup of coffee with a group of drivers and mechanics to symbolize their solidarity and concern and to take time to bring out a picture of the company's overall truck maintenance practices, rather than to learn about specific violations.

Piggybacking. Another strategy for deploying a limited enforcement staff more efficiently is to contract out certain inspection duties to private inspectorates, such as licensed professionals, to "piggyback" on their ongoing work in other ways or to obtain legislation expanding their duties. Regulation of securities sales and corporate financial statements by the SEC provides a model. Corporations that sell securities to the public must have their financial statements audited and certified by private, independent accountants and report the results to the agency. Accountants in turn are subject to regulatory sanctions and private damage suits for covering up adverse financial information.[44] Lawyers, too, are drawn into this private inspection process. Since a corporation's accountants must disclose potential liabilities arising from law violations, they insist on letters from the corporation's law firm disclosing such liabilities, and the lawyers can be sanctioned for inadequate disclosure.[45] More recently, the SEC has extended this approach: corporations that replace their auditing firm, for example, must notify the commission and disclose any disagreements it had with that firm over disclosure matters during the past two years; the discharged accounting firm must review that report and confirm it to the SEC or report any discrepancies.[46]

Requiring inspections by professional private auditors conceivably could be extended to other regulatory arenas, for example, by laws compelling manufacturers to purchase periodic environmental, safety, and quality control audits by independent engineering or consulting firms and to submit certified reports of those audits to relevant government agencies. Scattered parallels can be found in some fields of social regulation:

- In California, inspections of cranes and hoists used in factories are conducted by licensed repair firms. Manufacturers must obtain periodic certifications from such firms that their cranes and hoists are in good working order, the chains in good shape, and that they are not being used for operations beyond their capacity. The inspecting firms, which sell replacement cranes, as well as repair services, have a strong incentive to check carefully. Cal-OSHA inspectors merely check whether or not cranes and hoists have up-to-date certifications.
- For high-rise buildings and other especially complex structures, many municipal building code enforcement agencies rely primarily on outside engineering or construction firms to do the inspection. The contractor must supply to the agency a certificate from a licensed specialist in, say, structural engineering, that the steelwork has been properly completed, before further work on the building can be done. The agency inspector may conduct a superficial visual check, but he is usually out of his depth; primary reliance is placed on the reputation of the certifying firm and on its legal liability for damages should the building fail due to defects in construction elements it had certified as adequate. The same strategy is used when a contractor wants to use a relatively new construction technique, such as a method of concrete pouring, that local building authorities are not familiar with and that the building code does not closely control.
- Under the federal Horse Protection Act, the Agriculture Department formally approves livestock markets, stockyards, and slaughtering establishments (to protect against spread of disease). Inspections are usually conducted by USDA-accredited veterinarians, primarily in private practice. Their accreditation can be suspended or revoked for failure to comply with the appropriate USDA inspection standards.[47]

It may also be possible to piggyback on the regulatory activities of trade or professional associations. The California Canners League, for example, seems to cooperate to a considerable extent with the Food and Drug Division in the state Department of Health, regularly giving advice to member firms about how to meet regulatory requirements. On occasion, it has passed on to the agency negative information about *nonmembers* of the league thought to be violating the regulations—and thereby gaining a competitive advantage.* A few firms have been expelled from the league for being flagrantly "not up to code." The Speed Equipment Manufacturers Association (SEMA), whose membership includes makers of aluminum wheels and other cast metal components for racing cars, denies members the right to use the SEMA seal of approval (apparently a valuable marketing device) unless those firms submit to a detailed quality control program (including periodic physical testing of samples by independent laboratories) prescribed and enforced by the association. The Department of Transportation, which approved SEMA's standards, in effect piggybacks on the association for the prescription and enforcement of safety rules. Similar possibilities may exist for agency officials willing to search them out and publicize their interest in such cooperative strategies.

Delegating the Details. If the main point of most protective regulation is to induce more social responsibility, where is the government's comparative advantage or distinctive competence for doing so, relative to nongovernmental parties involved in the same process? The answer is that government can authoritatively elevate certain goals to a higher priority than they might have had otherwise in private decisionmaking, and it can use tax money to mount a program that attempts to promote these goals through a mixture of threat, bargaining, and persuasion. But goals are not quite the same thing as the steps for reaching them. Although government often does, in fact, specify the particular steps in the form of detailed standards, there is no reason to think that it is unusually qualified to do so. Indeed, because of the variability from enterprise to enterprise of risks and appropriate controls and solutions, there are reasons to think that government is on the whole less qualified to do so. If the top agency policymakers and managers were willing and able in effect to delegate the responsibility for filling in certain regulatory details to parties—usually private—who were better equipped to make decisions about what is necessary in particular contexts, the result would be greater reasonableness and sometimes greater effectiveness as well.

*As the president of the California Canners League told us, "If the rest of us are bearing the cost of a particular regulation, such as fly screens on windows, and there's a company which isn't conforming and is getting away with it, then we ask, 'Why should he get off when it's costing us money?' We're generally happy to drop a hint or two to F&D that it had better take a look at so and so."

One way to delegate details is to specify performance (output) rather than design (input) standards. Revising the nation's building codes in accord with this principle is the dream of most reformers who are interested in spurring innovation in the construction industry and in bringing down costs. Why specify, as some codes do, that supporting wooden studs must be of a certain size and distance apart, rather than requiring only that the stud system must be able to bear a given load, however the architect or contractor may choose? Why specify wooden studs at all since an innovative plastic material might do the job? Unfortunately, because performance standards are often more controversial or harder to enforce than design standards, the historical tendency in many fields has been just the opposite of the reformers' dream. Regulations have specified in ever-greater detail mandatory physical characteristics for drug and food processing, meat-packing plants and equipment, and pollution control devices.

Nevertheless, there have been some recent moves toward delegating decisions about the details to regulated enterprises. Here is one highly publicized example.

The EPA recently announced a bubble concept for large industrial complexes, under which it would not strictly enforce "best available technology" or emission standards for each source, but would simply require the company to reduce overall emissions in an imaginary air bubble that covered the whole installation. Corporate engineers could then figure out which specific processes to change and abatement machinery to install, presumably finding the most cost-effective ways of reducing the total amount of pollution. The results could well be dramatic. A study by independent economists of controlling hydrocarbon emissions at 42 E. I. du Pont Company plants (based on cost estimates by company engineers) indicated that regulations requiring *each source* (a total of 548) to reduce emissions by 85 percent would cost the firm $105 million annually, whereas if *each plant* were placed under a bubble and allowed to select the optimum combination of sources and levels of control, the same overall reduction in pollution could be achieved at an annual expenditure of $42 million, and if *all 42 plants* were placed under a hypothetical bubble, the company could achieve similar reductions for $14 million a year.[48]

Actually EPA's bubble regulations apply a number of additional restrictions to this program,[49] but in principle it reflects the idea of delegating the detailed choices for meeting regulatory objectives.*

The stewardship program recommended by the president's Interagency Task Force on Workplace Safety and Health combines the principle of delegating details to private parties with the principle of flexible enforcement on the part of inspectorial personnel.

OSHA inspectors would be designated "stewards" for a limited number (100 to 200) of high-risk workplaces. Each inspector would negotiate a broadly worded, results-oriented "contract" with each of "his" firms, based on a company-devised plan under which company officials would locate the most serious hazards and implement programs to reduce injuries or health risks most efficiently. The inspector would monitor implementation and progress under the plan. Frequent telephone contact with company and union safety representatives might be substituted for most on-site inspections, and citations for all but serious rule violations would be suspended, except when progress was not being made. However, "participating establishments which do not cooperate fully, or are found to have misreported injuries, exposures or problems with scheduled abatements, would be subject to vigorous inspections and wilful citations and penalties, as well as criminal sanctions for false reporting."[50]

There are some precedents for such contractual arrangements. Cal-OSHA agreed with Bechtel Corporation, prime contractor for construction of a nuclear generating plant, to allow a union-management safety committee to plan and implement worker safety standards (including a worker training program) in lieu of regular government inspections and enforcement of regulations.[51]

TOP AGENCY OFFICIALS AS LEADERS

One does not ordinarily think of regulatory agency directors as leaders. We do not readily imagine them marshaling their troops and exhorting

---

*In addition, in late 1979 the EPA announced a policy allowing plant managers to present alternatives to detailed EPA equipment specifications, as long as overall Clean Air Act goals are met.

them to go forth and abate hazards. Yet inspiration is not all there is to leadership, and the higher echelons of social regulatory agencies do lead their agencies in dealing with at least four important constituencies: the population of regulated enterprises; the presumed beneficiaries of their agencies' activities and the spokesmen or advocates for these beneficiaries; employee groups or factions internal to the agency; and legislative oversight committees.

Educating Enterprises. Selling regulated enterprises on the need for the regulatory regime, the seriousness and immediacy of the social problems it is attacking, and the reasonableness of particular rules is perhaps the most valuable aspect of regulation. Recognizing this point, the top officials in many regulatory agencies devote a good deal of their time to making public appearances, especially before industry groups.

Once the enforcement apparatus is in place, in fact, there seems to be a positive hunger among regulated firms, or at least a great many of them, for detailed information about regulatory intentions and about cost-effective techniques for compliance. Trade association publications constantly circulate stories on these topics. The Mine Safety Appliance Corporation organized a symposium in June 1979 concerning respiratory protection equipment and programs, featuring speakers from industry, OSHA, and the federal Mine Safety and Health Administration (MSHA). By August, a detailed write-up of the symposium appeared in a monthly technical and management magazine serving the foundry industry. A union safety representative in an auto assembly plant told us how he identified a health problem—one that had eluded OSHA inspectors—after attending a conference on lead hazards. One of the best investments a regulatory agency can make may be fostering and feeding this appetite for information.

Agencies that regulate food manufacturing seem to operate on the premise that investment in industry education is a vital aspect of enforcement. After new regulations are formulated, the FDA disseminates supporting explanatory materials through trade associations and sends speakers to industry technical meetings. The Food and Drug Division of the California Department of Health invites not only quality control people but also company presidents and owners to workshops convened by the agency after it promulgates a new regulation. Selling these key figures on the seriousness of the underlying problem, in a top enforcement official's view, is the most important enforcement step the agency could take. Part of the selling job, of course, is to impress upon high company officials the agency's intent to punish noncooperation. At such workshops, for example, California Food and Drug officials sometimes underscore the personal liability of owners and managers for food and drug law violations; the executives' very presence at the meeting, the enforcement officials gleefully point out, deprives them of the defense of not having sufficient notice of the law's requirements.

But a critical part of the workshops is pure education and persuasion. Meetings with industries create a forum in which industry experts who would otherwise be deterred from talking to competitors exchange ideas on preventive techniques. For example, the diffusion of "foaming machines" in maintaining sanitation standards was accelerated in this way, according to the chief of the California Food and Drug Division.

> Some salesman came along to a few [food-processing] plants and said, "I've got a product here, foam. They've been using it on automobile engines. Maybe it'll disconnect [degrease] something for you." A few of these people start playing around with it. [At our workshop on sanitation] one guy said, "I tried it on gondolas that we brought in the peaches with, and I've never seen such clean gondolas." Another would say, "We've tried it on our cutting equipment and it works beautifully." Then they started . . . giving actual papers on how they had used these various things.

This example emphasizes that the pupils in agency-initiated education actions are not children; the education process, therefore, must be a two-way street. The regulatory agency must be open to education by the regulated enterprises. In this light, the agency's purpose in workshops and meetings would be not only to sell the regulations to the industry but also to gather information about possible unreasonableness in existing regulations.

Building Bargaining into Rulemaking. The goal of maintaining informal two-way communications channels also suggests it would be desirable for agencies to maintain a series of ongoing technical advisory committees, specialized by industry or product, at which regulated enterprises can suggest changes in existing rules and comment on proposed amendments. Such arrangements have often been criticized by consumer and environmental advocates, but there is no reason why consumer, labor, and environmental interests cannot be represented on such committees. In several industries we encountered, regulated businesses seemed more likely to accept the thrust of the regulations when a forum existed for regular consultation with agency officials about changes in the regulations. To mention just one example:

> Environmental engineers from regulated firms in California, however much they complained about costs of compliance, expressed much greater satisfaction with regulations formulated by the Bay Area Air Pollution Control District, which has an ongoing technical advisory committee with representation from business and environmentalists and public health experts, than with regulations of the state Air Resource Control Board, which abolished informal advisory committees. Among other reasons, the state board's regulations were constantly criticized for their *technical* deficiencies, for being based on inadequate or old data, or on inadequately tested theories and hence ill-adapted to the actual variety and complexity of production processes.

A major obstacle to the effective operation of advisory committees as vehicles for give and take, some observers contend, has been a trend toward formalism. To ensure accountability and avoid capture by the regulated industry, agency policymaking has been required by law to take place as much as possible in open session, with active participation by all affected interests, including consumer groups and environmental groups. All information and reasoning on which decisions are made must be on the record, hence reviewable by appellate courts. Some participants, however, have criticized this judicialization and its extension even to so-called informal rulemaking.[52] Judicialization, they point out, slows the development of new regulations and the modification of old ones to an excruciatingly slow pace. In public session, the adversary style dominates at the expense of fact finding, reason, and a sense of proportion and compromise. One side or the other—and perhaps even both—is more likely to emerge dissatisfied with the agency's ultimate decision and is ready to race to the nearest appellate court to challenge it either as a sell-out or as unreasonably stringent.

To decrease formalization, some knowledgeable observers have urged that forums to debate proposed rules should be established behind closed doors, but under the watchful eye and the prodding hand of a governmental official, similar to collective bargaining between management and labor conducted with the aid of a mediator. John Dunlop, a former secretary of labor, contends that this process would be more flexible in accommodating competing values and interests and in tailoring rules to the great variety of actual operating conditions.[53] Moreover, the process of negotiation itself might enhance the disposition toward subsequent compliance. Peter Schuck, a former consumer activist and deputy assistant secretary in the Department of Health, Education and Welfare, argues that:

> Good faith bargaining often unearths solutions lying between those extreme positions that would be asserted by the parties in litigation. Bargaining tends to expose the true intensities of the participants' preferences, while litigation tends to exaggerate those intensities. Bargaining stimulates the flow of information *between* parties . . . while litigation restricts inter-party communication. . . . For these reasons, bargaining can help participants to develop a better appreciation of the perspectives of their adversaries than litigation can, an appreciation that may reduce hostility, soften positions previously taken, . . . suggest solutions to generate support . . . for implementation.[54]

Steven Kelman's account of the development of occupational safety and health standards in Sweden support this argument. Standards are worked out primarily in meetings between industrial hygienists, safety engineers and other technical experts from major manufacturing groups and from labor organizations, meeting with government regulatory officials. Kelman notes that while the Swedish standards are substantively quite similar to those developed by OSHA, they arouse nowhere near the same level of political opposition and challenge before the courts.[55]

In this country, of course, industry trade associations or unions are not necessarily regarded as genuine representatives of smaller or maverick enterprises or worker groups. Public interest groups, too, are frequently split on an issue or are simply mistrustful of one another. Bargaining can become unwieldy (if all groups are included) or the solution can become unstable (if some feel unjustly excluded). Many administrative lawyers and legislators criticize any move toward back-room decisionmaking. Therefore, some combination of private bargaining and public rulemaking is indicated. This might entail a two-stage process. First, the agency would assemble representatively selected advisory groups to work out standards dealing with problems presented by agency staff members. These standards would become proposed rules, made subject to public discussion and comment, and then rejected, approved, or modified "on the record" by the responsible administrator. Peter Schuck cites a Consumer Product Safety Commission (CPSC) procedure that approximates such structured bargaining. The CPSC contracts with an outside organization (e.g., trade association or consumer group) to develop a product safety standard, which the CPSC then may adopt after public hearing. The outside organization must include representatives of consumer groups, small manufacturers, and retailers in the standards development process, and CPSC has sometimes subsidized such interests to help them participate. Schuck has noted, however, that the process would be more effective if agency officials played a strong role at the outset in framing the issues, suggesting alternative solutions, and providing relevant data.[56]

Bureaucratic and Legislative Constituencies. The toughest challenge for agency leaders might be in dealing with subordinates, who are theoretically followers but who in reality comprise semiautonomous bureaucratic constituencies with considerable leverage. When the EPA recently promulgated new noise standards for municipal garbage trucks, for example, some top agency officials had misgivings. They appeared to be too costly, in effect requiring the replacement of existing fleets of trucks. Moreover, the new standards also appeared unlikely to accomplish very much since a great deal of sleep-disturbing noise in garbage collection comes from the clanging of cans and the shouts of employees rather than from the compressor in the garbage truck compactor. However, the noise standards writers in the relevant office of EPA had been working on the standard for many years, and there was a sense that the agency owed them some recognition. In addition, the office had had a great deal of trouble promulgating other noise standards, and the bureaucrats in the office were unhappy that their office was losing status to the offices responsible for radiation and air quality protection, with whom the noise office was linked for budgetary purposes. Even though some top managers in EPA might have believed the garbage truck standards were ill-advised, they also felt that the noise regulators could not be denied some successes to keep up their morale.[57]

There are other kinds of problems in controlling subordinates as well. Serge Taylor has noted that environmentalists in the U.S. Forest Service and the Corps of Engineers have leaked inside information to outside environmental advocacy groups to facilitate legal pressures for more stringent environmental protection than their superiors seemed willing to accept.[58] Switching a corps of inspectors initially trained in legalistic enforcement to a policy of flexible enforcement raises similar problems. Morale can suffer if aggressive inspectors are not backed up because supervisors are now more inclined to compromise than to prosecute. The moralistic inspector, moreover, can make public statements designed to "expose" agency leaders for trying to get them to "ignore the law and go soft on powerful business interests."

The only antidote to these obstacles is leadership. Top agency officials can work to incorporate more research and analysis of the impact of regulations into their enforcement operations, just as they are being pressed to do at the rule-making level. They can stress the value of reasonableness as well as effectiveness in training and guiding and evaluating their inspectorate.

Whether or not agency leaders succeed in such efforts, however, also depends in part on their own imagination and energy in dealing with the political environment in which they operate. Ideally, agency leaders would take on the functions of a sort of permanent legislative committee staff, reviewing the consequences of the laws the agency is charged with enforcing; and top agency officials would be permanent lobbyists for desirable legislative amendments. Many agencies, in fact, do maintain a small staff of lobbyists. They seem, however, to regard their job almost exclusively as seeking expanded enforcement budgets, more stringent standards, legislation to plug loopholes, or additional information-gathering, prosecutorial, and sanctioning powers. These are all important activities, to be sure. But agency lobbyists rarely take responsibility for seeking amendments designed either to cure overinclusive legislative requirements or to relax unreasonably stringent standards. Most agencies' stance on these issues seems to be that "the regulated firms or their trade association can take care of that." Nevertheless, it would seem advantageous for agency leaders to take the lead in educating legislators and lobbying for statutory amendments that could enhance reasonableness.

For one thing, enforcement officials would carry a much lighter burden of persuasion than lobbyists employed by regulated enterprises. Regulators also would be in a much better position to elicit cooperation and to deploy inspectors efficiently if they assumed a leadership role in making the law more reasonable, rather than merely taking a neutral bureaucratic stance. The California agency that inspects nursing homes pushed a bill through the legislature allowing it to inspect licensed facilities a minimum of once a year, rather than twice a year as previously required, thus enabling it to concentrate more fully on known bad apples. Since a routine inspection involved five days of work by two surveyors, this was not an insignificant change.

Regulators also can do a better job of educating legislatures about the realities of the enforcement process. An FDA official complained that "legislators think that 100 percent compliance is possible, or for that matter desirable. . . . There's no perspective on what error rate is 'high.' " As Richard Elmore has indicated, when legislative oversight committees express concern about publicized instances of noncompliance, regulatory officials can respond by resisting legislative proposals for more elaborate laws and stricter enforcement; they can argue instead that the real problem is eliciting cooperation and building competence at the level of those who must actually do the job, and that legalistic enforcement might harm rather than help that effort.[59]

CHAPTER SEVEN

THE REGULATORY RATCHET

•

Protective regulation is a blunt instrument. When applied to a complex and subtle world, it is bound to make mistakes, that is, to be unreasonable. But everyone makes mistakes, and government should not be expected to be less fallible than the rest of us. The question is whether regulators are capable of correcting their mistakes. This would mean reducing aspirations when regulatory objectives turn out to be excessively costly, pruning rules whose prescribed remedies are often found to be inappropriate, and suspending enforcement in the many cases of site-level unreasonableness that emerge under even the best set of rules.

Unfortunately, regulatory programs were not designed to carry on trial-and-error learning. The political constituencies that created most of them in the 1960s and 1970s were largely unaware of and uninterested in the problems of potentially rigid and nonadaptive regulation. Indeed, as we pointed out in chapter 2, these are the very traits that were meant to ward off the evils of capture and co-optation. On the other hand, independently of whether or not they were actually designed to learn from their mistakes, regulatory institutions might nevertheless develop the capability to do so, and even if they did not themselves develop the capability, forces in their political environment might thrust improvements on them in any case.

This environment is populated by legislators, legislative subcommittees and staff, elected chief executives, fiscal planners and other agents of budgetary control, lawyers and lobbyists for beneficiary groups and for regulated entities, public interest and other advocacy groups, the electronic and print media, and lawyers, courts, and judges. This political environment can provide or withhold resources that are vital to the agency. It can establish constraints, evaluate performance, apply rewards and punishments, and project periodic challenges and opportunities.

How regulation evolves, therefore, depends not only on the statutory framework of regulation and on the attitudes and abilities of regulatory agency officials but also on the ebb and flow of the contending forces in this political landscape.

Predicting how current programs of protective regulation will evolve is therefore not easy. One possibility—which could be called the "path of greater reasonableness"—is that more and more regulatory agencies, recognizing the excesses of legalistic regulation, will institute strategies of flexible enforcement and will try to revise their rules and regulations as well. Such a development might validate a new "life-cycle" theory of regulatory agencies (and their political environment) that would have them learning from experience, acquiring the expertise that enables them to enforce regulations more selectively, and tempering youthful zealotry with greater reasonableness.[1]

Currently, a number of external political forces would seem to impel regulators to take that course. The Reagan administration has interpreted its victory as a mandate not only for more reasonable regulation but also for less regulation. For the past three or four years, industry groups have dramatically increased their investment in political organization, policy-related research, litigation, and lobbying.[2] They now regularly present legislative committees and courts with carefully documented instances of overregulation, selected to make regulatory officials appear rigid and unreasonable or downright ridiculous. More fundamentally, oil shortages, continuing inflation, chronic unemployment, intensified competition from abroad, and accounts of declining productivity gains seem to have convinced political elites and the electorate alike that the United States has entered an era of reduced economic prospects in which the costs of regulation are a legitimate matter of political concern for liberals as well as for conservatives. This concern is reflected in periodic legislative attacks on the powers of certain agencies—most recently the Federal Trade Commission and OSHA. With increasing frequency, agencies have been instructed by law to undertake cost-benefit analyses of proposed regulations, to consider less costly alternatives in preparing rules, and to mitigate adverse impacts on small business.[3]

On the other hand, strong political pressures, in combination with some equally strong bureaucratic tendencies within regulatory agencies, might severely constrain the evolution of more flexible regulation. Switching metaphors, we might liken these forces to a toothed ratchet wheel that allows regulation to turn toward greater stringency from time to time, but then locks it in place, preventing any downward movement except for an occasional notch or two when political antiregulation pressures are intense. Such a ratchet effect is most easily illustrated at the level of regulatory rules.

- Fire codes typically have called first for the installation of fire doors, then sprinkler systems, then one set of fire-retardant construction materials, then another—all without seriously considering whether the addition of each new requirement would justify elimination of some of the old ones under certain circumstances.
- One high official at the California Food and Drug Division told us, "One would think that when new regulations are passed to replace obsolete, ineffective or unreasonable ones, the old ones would be removed—but it doesn't happen." An FDA enforcement official observed, with a touch of pride, that in his 16 years with the agency, "The statutes and regulations are almost never downgraded," except in rare cases of strong public opposition, such as Congress' suspension of the ban on saccharin by the Food and Drug Administration. Enforcement officials themselves, he said, never take the initiative to get rule changes that might "weaken or relax our standards." In fact, although he and other agency officials felt that recent FDA regulations requiring inspections for all infant-formula manufacturing processes represented an overhasty reaction to a highly publicized incident of poor quality control by one manufacturer, he believed, "These rules will never go away now that they are on the books."
- As one nursing home enforcement official observed, "Regulation is always additive. New regulations are added to deal with new problems. But no one examines the effect of new regulations on the old ones. Nobody looks at the second-order effects."

The rachet effect can also be observed at the enforcement level. Adding rules would be more tolerable if enforcement officials informally allowed the manufacturer or nursing home to omit precaution A if it had done B and C (in cases where A would be redundant). Although that kind of flexible enforcement sometimes does occur, the political environment faced by most regulatory officials may make it difficult. Requirement A, after all, is mandated by the law. The inspector might turn out to have been wrong; requirement A may in fact be absolutely necessary to prevent serious harms to innocent people under the circumstances, and it certainly may *appear* to be necessary to outsiders. Hence by omitting requirement A, the inspector, his superiors, and the agency as a whole are vulnerable to criticism by advocacy groups, politicians, judges, news media, or even competitors of the regulated enterprise. Such criticism for undue leniency, or more pervasively, the fear of it, may well be a more potent force, in most agencies most of the time, than all the political pressures for greater flexibility.

Whether and to what extent such pressures against rule-relaxation will withstand pressures to moderate overinclusive and needlessly stringent regulatory rules can only be a matter for speculation. Our judgment, however, is that the ratchet effect is a powerful and persistent effect indeed, and that protective regulation is more likely, over the long run, to follow the path of continued legalism than the path of greater reasonableness. To be sure, as conservative Republicans rush to secure the fruits of their recent electoral triumphs, we are bound to see a great slowdown in the growth of protective regulation. Proposed regulations will be softened or withdrawn. Existing technology-forcing deadlines will be extended. But this is not the same thing as a rollback of regulation from current levels of aspiration or programmatic stringency. It is much harder politically to engineer a rollback than it is simply to slow down or even stop the *growth* of new regulation. The upward movement of the regulatory ratchet can be stalled merely by refraining from action, but downward movement can be had only by applying counterforce to forces already holding the lock mechanism on the ratchet in place.

Of course, sufficiently powerful counterforces can make the ratchet slip a bit, and the most likely areas for a Republican-inspired rollback are certain air pollution controls, automobile safety regulation, and the regulation of small business—fields in which the costs of regulation have been well documented.* In all probability the Reagan administration, given the relatively high Republican intolerance for OSHA and a matching sympathy for small business, will make a determined effort to gain a

---

*In early 1981, Thomas Auchter, appointed head of OSHA by President Reagan, initiated a review of the controversial regulations requiring expensive engineering controls to limit textile workers' exposure to cotton dust. Reagan's appointments to NHTSA and EPA proposed to delay or abolish 34 safety and environmental regulations for new cars and trucks, which they claimed would save consumers $9.3 billion and the hard-pressed automobile industry $1.3 billion in new capital costs. "Reagan's War on Regulation," *Newsweek,* April 20, 1981, p. 77. See also Joann Lublin, "Reagan's Advisers Accuse the EEOC of 'Racism,' Suggest Big Cutback," *The Wall Street Journal,* January 30, 1981.

legislative exemption for this large class of regulatory sites from most federal worker safety rules and enforcement efforts. The extent of the rollback will depend largely on the counterforce applied to the ratchet lock, which in turn depends on whether or not business interests put their political emphasis on regulatory (as opposed to tax and foreign trade) issues. The ability of environmentalist, consumer-oriented, labor, and civil rights constituencies to mobilize a counter-counterforce to preserve regulation will be greatly affected by how thinly their efforts are spread across competing issues, for example, the funding of public employment programs, tax and welfare law changes, and the minimum wage.

While recognizing the central importance of short-run counterforces in the process of pushing the regulatory ratchet back down, it is difficult to predict how strong they will be. We therefore restrict our attention in this chapter to the long-run forces that tend to hold the ratchet lock in position in the first place. These will persist well after the first or even a second Republican administration. They are largely independent of political party control of the policy-making branches of government and even, to a certain extent, independent of the political mood of the general public at any particular moment.

AGENCY RULE ADJUSTMENTS

A rough indication of the infrequency of agency-initiated downward rule revision can be derived from the annual compilation of major federal regulatory initiatives and reform proposals prepared by the American Enterprise Institute (AEI), which monitors regulatory developments at the federal level. While these compilations are far from complete, they are suggestive: in 1978, a year in which the antiregulatory tide had already begun to flow in, the *only* agency-initiated downward revision of regulatory rules noted in the AEI report concerned OSHA's elimination of over 900 safety-related standards (about 10 percent of the total) deemed "unneeded or unrelated to job safety and health." The dozens of other proposed or final regulations listed in that AEI report were to increase the scope or stringency of controls. In the 1979 report, likewise, almost 20 more stringent regulatory rules or proposals were listed, but only one agency-initiated downward revision was noted: the National Highway Traffic Safety Administration announced that, because certain fuel-saving lubricants were not yet available (primarily due to delays in reviews by the Environmental Protection Agency of their pollution potential), industry mileage standards for 1981 model-year light trucks would be relaxed by 0.5 miles per gallon.*

Perhaps even more indicative of the strength of the lock in the ratchet mechanism is the unusual background of the few downward adjustments. In the NHTSA case, the regulation was clearly unenforceable until the lubricants became available. In the case of OSHA's rule-pruning operation, it was widely acknowledged that many of the original OSHA standards were obsolete when they were adopted in 1971, owing to their origins as industry "consensus standards" prior to their promulgation by government. Moreover, OSHA had been by far the most unpopular of all federal regulatory agencies, and business interests, in combination with the president, had pressured the agency to eliminate its many allegedly nitpicking standards. Even so, it took some seven years to get OSHA to initiate the rule reform project.

The AEI compilation, unfortunately, is not complete. It omitted, for example, the highly significant relaxation by the EPA of the ambient air standard for ozone, a primary element in photochemical smog.[4] In 1979, the agency dropped the standard from 0.08 parts per million (ppm) to 0.12 ppm. The background of this revision is unusual as well. First, the EPA was obliged by statutory mandate to review the ambient air quality standards it had promulgated in 1971; the ozone standard was the first to be considered in this process. Second, a particular industry, petrochemicals, had an unusually high stake in lowering the ozone standard—an unusual situation in the general area of protective regulation, where rules often cut across a variety of industries. Finally, the objective case against the 0.08 ppm standard was well documented and very powerful. The change to 0.12 ppm could save from $4 billion to $19 billion between 1979 and 1987, depending on who was making the estimate.[5] White House economic advisers, who were pressing for a standard even lower than 0.12 ppm, argued that, in addition to being exorbitantly costly, the standard was "based on questionable scientific evidence and likely to benefit relatively few persons."[6] For *most* regulations, of course, such elaborate investigations of possible unreasonableness have not been undertaken.

---

*Once again we emphasize that our focus is restricted to protective regulation. Downward revision of *economic* regulation was much in evidence that year. We should also emphasize that we are referring to downward revision of statutes and regulations already on the books. Downward revision of *proposed* regulations during or after the legally prescribed public comment and revision period is quite common.

To be sure, the major regulatory initiatives catalogued by the AEI represent only the tip of the iceberg of regulatory rule changes each year. Most agency initiatives—whether moving regulation upward or downward—adjust the means, rather than the ends, of regulatory programming. They take the undramatic form of changes in the details of regulations or, less formally, of changes in enforcement manuals. Such interpretive modifications redefine terms in statutes and major regulations, redraw jurisdictional boundaries, write in exceptions to reduce overinclusiveness, and respecify criteria for granting variances. Just as huge changes in the effects of the tax code can be wrought by apparently minor changes in regulations concerning methods of calculating depreciation or in the definition of "cost basis," if and when regulatory agencies act autonomously to reduce the stringency of their rules, these reductions might occur principally in this sort of incremental and low-visibility manner.

Some of the most prominent examples of potentially significant revisions made in this mode are the "bubble" and the "offset" policies being developed by the EPA to reduce the regulatory burden of the Clean Air Act.[7] The bubble policy permits firms to meet a pollution standard by reducing the aggregate of discharges (of a particular kind) from a plant while allowing them discretion as to which particular within-plant sources would receive what degree of clean-up. The offset policy applies the "bubble" to a region rather than merely to a single plant and permits one firm, usually a new one, to increase its own discharges on the condition that it obtain reductions in the discharges of another entity.

Like NHTSA's postponement of the 1981 fuel economy standards, the offset policy is remarkable mainly because it was invented under the most extreme duress: without some such mechanism, large new industries would simply not have been allowed to locate in the many urban areas that had not met the national ambient air quality standards established by the EPA.* Whatever one's interpretations of the potential significance of these regulatory adjustments at the EPA, however, the general reliance on interpretive modifications to effect significant downward adjustment

*Moreover, it is not clear whether the offset policy is actually implementable without the EPA making a considerably greater commitment to it than it has, for example, by setting the ratio of old discharges that must be bought up to "offset" new discharges at some reasonable level and providing assurances to industry that the ratio will remain stable over a period of years. The bubble policy also seems to have been unnecessarily limited by certain restrictions on what emissions might be counted as being under the same "bubble."

is probably limited. Interviews with Cal-OSHA officials and with nursing home and food regulatory agencies at both the California and the federal levels suggested that this avenue to reform is relatively little used. The bulk of agency efforts to respecify existing rules are designed not to cure unreasonableness but to close loopholes, making the regulations more rather than less inclusive and stringent.[8]

CONGRESSIONAL RULE ADJUSTMENTS

Most of what the Congress has done in recent years to curb protective regulation has been directed at forestalling prospective regulation rather than cutting back existing regulation—killing the FTC's proposed trade regulation rules concerning funeral homes, for example, and adopting procedural changes like the two-house veto of regulatory rules.[9] And according to the AEI compilations for 1978 and 1979, congressional initiatives creating *more* regulation and more *stringent* regulation far outnumber cutbacks in existing statutes. Still, the few rollbacks Congress did make were in important areas.

- The 1977 Clean Air Act amendments significantly postponed the deadline for achieving the stringent standards for auto pollution emissions and ambient air quality standards (but without relaxing the standards themselves, except for nitrous oxides).* The 1972 Water Pollution Control Act amendments reduced abatement equipment requirements for the early 1980s from "best available technology" to "best conventional . . . control technology."
- In 1977, Congress overrode an FDA ban on the use of saccharin as an artificial sweetener in foods.
- In 1978, Congress relaxed the procedures for registering new pesticides with the EPA. Instead of having to submit complete documentation of safety prior to registration, pesticide manufacturers would be permitted to submit certain data during the post-marketing period. This change was subsequently estimated to have reduced delays by up to three years and to have increased the numbers of new products approved each year.

---

*Other aspects of the 1977 Clean Air Act amendments, however, significantly *increased* regulatory stringency. See, for example, Bruce A. Ackerman and William T. Hassler, *Dirty Air/Clean Coal* (New Haven: Yale University Press, 1981).

• In 1979, the Senate (but not the House) passed a major drug regulatory "reform" bill reducing FDA involvement in certain phases of research planning conducted by drug developers and, given a finding of sufficient urgency, authorizing approval of limited marketing for important new drugs subject to post-marketing surveillance.[10]

What do these congressional actions tell us about the strength of the lock mechanism in the regulatory ratchet? Congress' actions, like the agency actions discussed above, are in one or another respect exceptional and thus attest to the general validity of the proposition that regulation rarely recedes.* These cases entailed unusually high social costs of *not* making some downward adjustment, and powerful action-forcing situations brought this point home to legislators. The saccharin ban would have left Americans without the benefit of any artificial sweeteners (cyclamates had been banned several years earlier). The automobile emission control deadline was extended when it became clear that the only legal alternative would have been to shut down the American automobile industry. In the pesticides case, Congress had received intense and persuasive complaints from farmers about the unavailability of essential pesticides, from small manufacturers that they were being put out of business, and from the pesticides industry concerning the disastrous economic effect of regulations that delayed the marketability of new products for up to three years. In the case of the drug reform bill, the beneficiaries of the relaxation of premarket testing procedures were identifiable victims of diseases who were told, or would be told in the future, that certain potentially therapeutic drugs could not yet be sold in this country (although they might be available in other countries with looser drug regulations). In these cases, Congress was confronting regulatory unreasonableness embodied not merely as higher costs of doing business—costs thus diffused among thousands of customers, factor suppliers, and shareholders—but as pain and suffering experienced by identifiable citizens, business firms, and consumers. But such instances of concentrated costs of excessive regulation are rare.[11] In the usual case,

---

*Our list of five legislatively promoted downward adjustments in protective regulation in 1978 and 1979 may not be complete, reliance on the AEI compilations notwithstanding. It is possible that we have found not only too few items but a distorted sample as well, namely, the items that raised the most dramatic issues of overregulation. We cannot be sure and can only urge further, more systematic research in the matter.

where unreasonableness is diffuse, undocumented, and less politically dramatic, Congress is disinclined to revise the details of regulatory statutes.

WHY REGULATORY RULES RARELY RECEDE

If downward revision of regulatory rules is indeed uncommon, dilatory, and exceptional, there are four possible causes.

Economies of scale in rule writing dictate that major efforts to revise regulations be undertaken in large batches but at infrequent intervals.

When revisions are undertaken, work on the new drives out work on the old.

From the agency point of view the costs of excessive regulation are an externality.

The political environment punishes downward adjustments as selling out.

Economies of Scale. The number of significant rule changes that can be accomplished through low-visibility means, such as revising enforcement manuals, is small. Ordinarily, changes in the regulations are needed, even for such incremental steps as redefining key terms or specifying exceptions. Because proposed changes in regulations must be publicized according to law, such changes turn out to be a high-visibility agency activity and consume enormous amounts of agency resources.* The incremental costs of writing or rewriting any particular rule are small compared to the fixed costs of mobilizing the bureaucratic review-and-clearance procedure and conducting the public notice-and-comment process. Agencies therefore look for ways to "batch" their rule-writing work. One way is to postpone revising existing rules until the agency is

---

*In our analysis of sources of resistance to downward revision of regulatory rules, we refer primarily to the incentives (or disincentives) faced by regulatory agencies. But the same factors and disincentives apply, by and large, to the legislative committees and legislative staffs who would initially be responsible for undertaking statutory revisions designed to make regulation more reasonable.

ready to write new, perhaps unrelated, rules. As a top regulatory official
in the California Food and Drug Division told us:

> [Rule revision] should be done, but there just isn't time. It takes
> resources, and they're scarce. To do it, it means calling in some-
> body from the field, which we really can't afford. . . . We tend to
> take action on regulations only if new ones are needed.

Hence agencies allow a backlog of identified but unattended problems to
build up that will only be dealt with after the backlog has gotten large
enough (or serious enough) to warrant processing the whole batch. In the
meantime, society bears the costs.

It follows then that whatever factors tend to increase the review-and-
clearance costs of regulation writing should also tend to increase the time
lag between regulatory revisions. A program analyst in the federal Health
Care Financing Administration, who was familiar with the regulation-
writing process in that agency, told us:

> In some programs maybe we can do revisions every four years, but
> in others it takes at least that long just for the system to evolve and
> feedback to accumulate from the field. When you do get around to
> making revisions, of course, it takes time to consult with industry
> representatives and consumer groups. In very complex sets of reg-
> ulations like those covering skilled nursing facilities . . . we seem to
> move on about a seven-year cycle, partly because the regulations
> cut across many different regulatory domains, affecting financing
> and eligibility conditions, life safety, medical quality assurance, and
> social services, with different bureaucratic offices responsible for
> each one, all needing to give their clearance. Worst of all, though,
> is the instability in the bureaucracy. Personnel turnover is a prob-
> lem. A new administrator comes in and decides he or she doesn't
> like what revisions were begun by the old administrator. Also, the
> formal bureaucratic procedures change around a lot and set up new
> clearance points just when you thought you'd come close to
> finishing with the old ones. All this is discouraging to the technical
> experts who see the need for changes: they become reluctant to in-
> itiate a move to revise the rules because they expect it will be just
> too frustrating in the end.

Similarly, an official in the California Food and Drug Division told us of the drain on agency energies that occurred in the course of trying to pare down regulations governing low-acid canning processes, some of which had been on the books since 1925.

> First, the experts and bureaucratic factions took a year to hammer out a new set. Then industry had to fight a while to get changes. Then the legal staff got them and changed them all into legal jargon that no one would accept. Then the [citizen] health groups entered, and so on. This all began three years ago and we're hardly further along than when we started. . . . As a result, we almost try to avoid having to change regs and standards.

Thus, technical and bureaucratic difficulties are compounded by the multiplication of hearings, consultations, and legal reviews required both by law and by good politics. In recent years, agency decision-making processes have become more and more formalized in response both to the suspicion of informal contacts between the agency and the regulated industry and to the demand that public interest groups be guaranteed channels of access into hitherto informal regulatory policy-making processes. More procedural formality also facilitates judicial review. Yet as John Dunlop, former secretary of labor, observes, "formal procedures designed to make regulation fair . . . can also make it rigid." He describes, for example, the processing of exemptions under the pension fund regulation law, ERISA:

> If an exemption is proposed, it is then published in the *Federal Register* and comments are solicited; a public hearing can be requested and if, as a result, the exemption is modified, then the procedure may be repeated. The process is often prolonged by different groups taking advantage of procedures to advance their interests; thus, a legitimate exemption may take months to obtain.

Repealing or modifying the rules themselves, Dunlop adds, also is "a lengthy and complicated process and is rarely done."[12]

Revisions as Boring Work. When rule revision is undertaken at all, at whatever lengthy intervals, the task of fashioning downward revisions of various kinds must compete for bureaucratic energy and talent with the more attractive task of making upward revisions. From the point of view of a regulatory agency whose official mission is to prevent social harms, the need for new regulation is always apparent. No matter how stringent the existing rules, bad apple firms find and exploit loopholes, accidents and frauds still occur, and new sources of harm escape the regulations on the books. The consequence is pressure on higher level personnel—from legislative overseers, advocacy groups, and their own staffs—to close these gaps, to study newly discovered hazards, to draft new regulations.[13] In the face of these forward-looking challenges, revising existing rules to avert individual instances of overinclusiveness and excessive stringency is likely to seem not only less important but also relatively boring.

Excessive Regulation an Externality. The central mission of protective regulatory agencies is commonly defined almost exclusively in terms of effectiveness in achieving statutory goals rather than preventing un reasonable costs. Failures of effectiveness, therefore, are commonly regarded by regulatory officials as "their own" problem, something they must worry about, while regulatory unreasonableness, albeit regarded as something of a problem, is not so much *their* problem as it is an unfortunate by-product of the necessary pursuit of effectiveness. For regulatory officials, therefore, unreasonableness, being imposed incidentally on other parties and little felt by themselves, is analogous to what economists call an "externality" of the production process, that is, a cost imposed on society that exceeds the costs borne privately by the firm. Just as producers of steel traditionally were not forced by the market or the liability system to pay fully for discharging their effluents and did not, therefore, regard eliminating pollution as their responsibility, regulatory agencies primarily engaged in producing protection have not been forced by the political environment to pay fully for the costs that stem from excessive regulation and have not regarded the elimination of these costs as their central responsibility.[14]

The analogy between externalized production costs and the externalized costs of excessive regulation is suggestive in other respects as well. Overregulation, like air pollution, often comes in small bits and grows in tiny increments: an overinclusive standard here, a costly order there, the lingering effects of a politically inspired "crackdown," an extra report required to appraise the seriousness of yet another possible problem, and so on. From the agency's point of view, the imposition on any single firm or individual often will not seem very large; it may be that only when one takes the regulatory impact in the aggregate and over time can one be impressed by the level of unreasonableness and the social harm it entails.

To extend the analogy even further, those who suffer from government-engendered unreasonableness can do what citizens do when they suffer from pollution: complain, criticize, and make a general uproar. But since unreasonableness is hard to measure, even for those who endure it and wish to complain about it, the complaints can be discounted somewhat. Indeed, as long as the agency's mission is viewed principally as the prevention of harms, and as long as business complaints are regarded as being tainted by self-interest, the complaints of excess costs or police state harassment can be read by critics suspicious of agency capture and even by regulatory officials themselves as indications that the agency must be doing its job well. After all, the great industrialists of the nineteenth century welcomed belching smokestacks as proof that the ironmaking was going well and that progress was taking place.

As in the case of pollution, the federal government has taken certain steps toward controlling the externalities, that is, holding agencies more responsible for unreasonableness with respect to major new or proposed rules. President Carter, following an initiative by President Ford, ordered executive branch agencies to perform economic impact analyses and to consider less costly alternatives before issuing new regulations. A Regulatory Analysis Review Group likewise was assigned to ferret out proposed major regulations that appear unduly burdensome.[15] Courts have occasionally invalidated regulations not supported by adequate analysis of costs and benefits.[16] There are signs that such interventions have indeed affected the formulation of new regulations.[17] Nevertheless, more careful analysis of proposed rules does not necessarily imply an equivalent effort to undertake detailed analysis and revision of old ones, and indeed, by making the enactment of new regulations more time consuming and intellectually demanding, it may actually further divert busy regulatory staffs from backward-looking rule-revision projects, even if "sunset" reviews are formally mandated. Slowing the upward rate of the regulatory ratchet wheel, as noted earlier, is not the same as turning it back.

The Threatening Political Environment. The political environment surrounding regulatory institutions is highly distrustful. From the business side, regulators who propose tougher rules are met with arguments about technological feasibility and the economic costs of additional requirements, and they always risk being accused of incompetence, ignorance, and overzealousness. These risks are substantial, and in the Republican-dominated political climate of the early 1980s, they are likely to increase greatly. But they are balanced by the risks of seeming too soft and of neglecting the agency's central social mission, risks that are especially salient when downward rule adjustments are at issue. Regulators who propose to trim back existing rules often face charges of moral turpitude: accusations that they are giving in to specific business interests, or are selling out in general, or are illegally diluting the rights and threatening the health and safety of citizens protected by the original laws. The EPA, for example, is said by William Lilley III and James Miller III to have been deterred from readjusting regulations to equalize marginal clean-up costs between steel plants and papermills because this could be characterized as "letting big steel off" while "punishing" the paper industry.[18]

During the 1960s and 1970s, these risks were generally more threatening to regulators than were the risks of criticism from the business side—though of course there were numerous exceptions. While the balance is now shifting, the risk of criticism from the proprotection constituency is likely to continue to be a very powerful deterrent to downward rule adjustments. And because criticism for jeopardizing human life and limb will always occupy a higher moral ground than pleas for cost relief or a reduction in vexatious paperwork, the desire to avoid such criticism will usually be decisive, unless there is a deeper change in the sentiments of the relevant political elite and the public at large.

Nor have agencies just been imagining trouble. The downward adjustments in recent years in certain environmental regulations, for example, were fiercely opposed by environmental groups. Even when they may be prepared to concede some particular point, environmentalists are always concerned (and rightly so) with the precedent-setting effect any concession might have for environmental issues on which they are not so ready to concede. Thus they fought hard to prevent the relaxation of the ambient ozone standard, not only because they strongly desired low-ozone air but also because they feared a domino effect on the standards for new-car emissions, the original achievement of which had been "the toughest and most emotional chapter by far in the long struggle to enact and enforce clean air legislation."[19] Similarly, after OSHA announced its proposal to repeal some 200 nitpicking standards, it turned out that not everyone thought they were nitpicking. Eliminating the rule requiring split-front toilet seats, wrote the director of the National Institute for

Occupational Safety and Health, might mean the "almost complete elimination of the current sanitation standards."[20] A New Mexico safety supervisor said that he objected "violently" to the proposed elimination of certain standards, complaining that "some of my employees could easily be killed." The Bakery and Confectionery Workers International Union objected to the elimination of bakery standards and accused OSHA administrators of "a gross lack of professionalism."[21] When EPA's ban on the pesticide Mirex left farmers and other citizens in southern states defenseless against infestations by fire ants, the agency approved the controlled use of a substitute pesticide, ferriamicide, in Mississippi on a one-year trial basis, but without full prior testing for possible carcinogenic properties. Environmentalists attacked the agency for "violating its own rules," alleging that the decision was a direct result of political pressure by southern congressmen and "special interests."[22] Once Japanese-Americans were included in the lists of those entitled to affirmative action treatment, University of California administrators who proposed to remove them (because Japanese-Americans now achieve college and graduate school degrees and earn incomes at rates far above average) were publicly accused of racism and were criticized by state legislators.

The potential for criticism on the grounds of supposed softness stems not only from private organizations and interest groups; it is also institutionalized in other government units. An environmental affairs director for a major oil company said that on more than one occasion he heard a member of the governing board of the San Francisco Bay Area Air Pollution Control District ask during board meetings what position the South Coast Pollution Control District (centered in Los Angeles) had taken on the issue then before the board, asserting that it would "look bad" for the district to "look softer than L.A." More generally, the federal structure of many regulatory programs ensures that there is always a federal counterpart agency looking over any state agency's shoulder. In the occupational safety and health field, for example, the federal agency even has the right to disapprove of any state standard that is not "at least as effective as" the comparable federal standard. The same basic arrangement also applies in the state-federal joint effort to regulate the quality of care in nursing homes that receive federal Medicare and Medicaid monies.

The courts also are used to attack downward rule revision: agency rules that seek to moderate sweeping regulations in light of experience often are challenged in court by proregulation forces as unauthorized departures from the initial statutory mandate. In 1972, for example, the EPA approved state enforcement plans that authorized temporary variances for pollution sources for whom it would be unexpectedly costly or technically difficult to meet the Clean Air Act's 1975 deadline for attaining primary air quality standards. The Natural Resources Defense Council (NRDC), however, brought a series of lawsuits against EPA; some courts, reading the act literally, ordered EPA to prohibit states from granting variances that would extend beyond the statutory deadline. When the EPA dragged its heels in doing so, the NRDC threatened to bring contempt motions against the EPA, and the agency issued regulations forbidding variances.[23] Even if the agency's position ultimately is upheld in court, as eventually occurred at the Supreme Court level in the *NRDC v. EPA* cases, the prospect of having to expend legal and political resources on such defensive litigation is somewhat of a deterrent to downward rule adjustment.*

The available stock of proregulation political sentiments can also be exploited by business interests seeking competitive advantages. While firms may not always be able to predict how they would fare under the specific terms that might emerge in a new regulatory program, once the regulations are in place the distribution of relative advantages and disadvantages becomes apparent.[24] Proposals to ease regulatory restrictions, at that point, stimulate opposition from the specific interests that foresee losing some advantage. This opposition can conveniently ally itself with more diffusely ideological proprotection interests. For example, according to a *Wall Street Journal* report, major manufacturers of "child-resistant" caps for medicine bottles (an innovation made mandatory by the 1970 Poison Prevention Packaging Act and the Consumer Product Safety Commission) prevailed on the CPSC to reconsider its approval of a smaller company's patented reversible cap that could be used in either a child-proof or an easy-open mode, the latter eliminating arthritic older persons' difficulty with child-proof caps. The large manufacturers, who

---

*Similarly, OSHA often has been taken to court by unions, and it can expect to be sued for violating the Occupational Health and Safety Act should it attempt to moderate existing occupational health standards on the basis of cost-benefit analysis. Lawsuits by advocacy groups can also be expected to challenge attempts to relax existing automobile safety rules, to change regulations that benefit handicapped and non-English-speaking students, to authorize off-shore drilling that would entail exceptions to endangered species laws.

had seen their market share dwindling, apparently persuaded the commission that the reversible cap was contrary to the law's intent: it was only common sense, as a CPSC official put it, to believe that once consumers could get the reversible cap they would favor the easy-open mode and endanger more children.[25]

To take another example, NHTSA safety regulations compel auto manufacturers to use bumpers that will withstand a five mph crash test, which apparently can be done only by producing larger bumpers. But because larger bumpers made of steel (the traditional material) jeopardize automobile makers' ability to comply with federal fuel efficiency laws, the automobile makers planned to switch to lightweight aluminum. To block this change, Senate majority leader Robert Byrd of West Virginia, a steel-producing state, obtained a Department of Transportation study indicating that a less stringent 2.5 mph bumper standard (which could be met with steel bumpers without a significant weight increase) would be much less costly for automobile manufacturers and consumers and would provide almost equivalent protection. Byrd pushed NHTSA to lower the standard but was quickly opposed by Senator Warren G. Magnuson, chairman of the Appropriations Committee. Magnuson is from Washington, a major aluminum-producing state. He attacked the DOT study as flawed and called for retention of the five mph standard until more conclusive studies could be completed.[26]

Finally, initiating the public rulemaking process to consider specific downward revisions exposes the agency to claims for other, more extensive, revisions that agency officials may believe are unjustified, often properly so. There is nothing in the process of seeking comments or holding public hearings on selected revisions that precludes antiregulation forces from trying to effect a larger set of changes and to reopen questions that agency officials had thought settled by arduous negotiations. The agency's formal control over the agenda can be undermined by the publicity that regulated enterprises can obtain through well-orchestrated attacks on overregulation. Indeed, the establishment of regular mechanisms for rule revision might allow regulated enterprises to dominate the agency's agenda, keeping the terms of regulation subject to constant attack and uncertainty. Just as unreasonable regulation is the incidental product of having any sort of beneficial regulation at all, the drive to get rid of unreasonable regulation can produce the side effect (and for some parties, an intended effect) of ridding ourselves of even the beneficial aspects of regulation.

HOW THE REGULATORY RATCHET AFFECTS ENFORCEMENT

If field-level enforcement officials were to modify regulations in particular situations so that costs were kept more nearly in line with benefits, failures to revise excessively stringent and overly inclusive rules would not be quite such a serious problem. A state air pollution law administrator told us that rulemakers in his agency declined to correct a clear technical error they had made in setting maximum SO_2 emissions at 0.04 ppm as a 24-hour average, largely because they did not want to be charged with "retreating"; top enforcement officials, however, responded by quietly advising inspectors to accept emissions of 0.06-0.08 ppm as being "in compliance." Similarly, most of the 900 nitpicking standards abolished by OSHA in 1978 probably never were enforced at all. Most regulations, however, are not based on technical errors and they do deal with significant hazards; in some proportion of cases, it is quite necessary to enforce them strictly. Yet the world is diverse, and in many other situations those same regulations, if strictly enforced, would not produce sensible results. To avoid unreasonableness in those cases would require a much more overt and consistent policy of selective nonenforcement, including the kinds of measures described in chapters 5 and 6.

Some agencies, reacting to the waste and conflict created by legalistic enforcement, have taken conscious steps toward flexibility. But movement in that direction has been and is likely to remain limited, and where instituted it is susceptible to periodic reversions to legalism. For like the locking mechanism on a ratchet wheel, the legal structure and the political environment of most protective regulatory agencies tend to inhibit selective nonenforcement or moderation of the rules. Inspectors are instructed by law and by bureaucratic controls to go by the book. And even if that is not always an inspector's practice with respect to all regulations and all situations, going by the book represents the dominant institutional norm. In 1979, the U.S. Regulatory Council commissioned a study of how regulation affects a particular community. The author, Paul Danaceau, interviewed 75 municipal officials, businessmen, labor union officials, and lawyers in Janesville, Wisconsin. He concluded:

A specific criticism levelled against regulation by supporters and detractors alike is that the people who administer and enforce regulations . . . are too rigid and unyielding in their dealings at the local level. What the people in Janesville say they want is a spirit of accommodation in which the two parties, the regulated and the regulator, try to work out a mutually acceptable solution to a common problem. What they get, they say, is an adversary relationship in which the regulators more often than not try to force something down their throats because it is written in a manual, not because it is supposed to be a better solution.[27]

Why should this be so? First, let us again emphasize that bureaucratic formalism can facilitate supervisory tasks and, by eliminating the need to invest in training or recruitment of persons sufficiently qualified to use greater discretion, can hold down overall enforcement costs. Up to a point, therefore, the norm can serve economic efficiency. Yet commitment to the norm is almost certainly more intense and more widespread than would be warranted by efficiency considerations alone, especially in view of the obvious counterproductive consequences of legalistic enforcement; and it is this quantity of *excessive* formalism that must be accounted for. In general, the factors that hold the regulatory enforcement ratchet in place are similar to those that hold regulatory rules in place. Briefly stated, the incentives for enforcement officials to stick to the rules are strong, while the incentives to be reasonable are, by comparison, weak.

The Hazards of "Being Reasonable." Not everyone is in favor of flexible enforcement. Legislators or agency leaders who attempt to change the law explicitly to authorize more discretion in enforcement can expect vehement attacks from proponents of tougher regulation. In 1979, Senator Richard Schweiker introduced a bill that would exempt firms with good safety records from routine OSHA inspections and would instruct OSHA to respond to most complaints by telephoning employers and simply demanding that they certify the abatement of the hazard. Unions responded not only by lobbying against the bill and accusing Schweiker of heartlessness or worse but also by organizing picketing of his home and office.[28] When EPA officials were debating a draft bill authorizing the agency to suspend enforcement of certain statutory provisions and to implement more incentive-oriented enforcement strategies, intra-agency environmentalists leaked a copy to outside allies. A highly critical article appeared in *The Washington Post,* helping to scotch any possible White House support.[29]

A high enforcement official takes even more substantial political risks if, without first seeking legislative authorization, he or she encourages field inspectors to modify regulatory requirements in the hopes of avoiding unreasonableness and winning cooperation. Flexible enforcement is a tricky business. An inspector's failure to insist on strict compliance can easily come to the attention of complainants (who may be entitled to accompany the inspector on his rounds), or of other enforcement officials (who may revisit the site or review his work), or of representatives of equipment suppliers who visit the factory in question (and can inform competitors of the inspected enterprise). Any of these observers might misinterpret or disagree with the original inspector's assessment of the situation. Not only the inspector but also the agency as a whole can then be accused of "taking the law into their own hands," of favoritism toward the particular enterprise, or of jeopardizing the health and safety of innocent persons. Regulated businesses, fearful that their competitors are getting a break, perhaps by corrupt means, may complain to legislators about excessive regulatory discretion. Even more importantly, if enforcement officials allow inspectors or supervisors to use their own judgment, sooner or later one of them is likely to make an unambiguously weak or stupid decision, one that seriously imperils human health or directly contributes to a fatal accident. In such cases, public accusations of official irresponsibility will be difficult to rebut indeed.

Adhering to the rules, on the other hand, provides regulatory officials a relatively safe harbor from such storms of criticism. Regulators usually realize that going by the book may cause unreasonableness, but they also realize that it is an invaluable symbol of their fidelity to law and dedication to duty. Adhering to the rules also signifies their intention to treat competing enterprises as even-handedly as possible, a norm so potent politically and legally that regulators we interviewed never thought to mention it until we stimulated a discussion of the subject.*

Even when cutting back on enforcement against some targets simply reflects a rational reallocation of resources, lawsuits or criticism by advocacy groups or political superiors may force the agency back into the security of a legalistic full enforcement posture. For example:

- When the FDA announced it would redirect food industry inspections from a primary emphasis on sanitation toward microbiological

---

*The necessity for even-handed treatment of competitors, it might be added, differentiates inspectors from policemen. Disruptive juveniles, for example, unlike businessmen, are not likely to make effective complaints that others were dealt with more leniently by other enforcement officers. For this reason, an inspectorate probably has less leeway for flexibility than police forces do.

and chemical health hazards (on the theory that contamination due to poor sanitation is a relatively minor health hazard in most modern food processing plants), a series of *Consumer Reports* articles attacked the agency for having "casually dismissed" the problem of "filth." The FDA continued to list sanitation at the top of its published list of enforcement priorities.[30]

Civil rights groups, notes Jeremy Rabkin, "protested vehemently on several occasions when the Office of Civil Rights in HEW suggested in 1975 that it would no longer accept responsibility for investigating each individual discrimination complaint it received." To parry the criticism and the threat of a lawsuit that accompanied it, the Secretary of HEW withdrew the plan, pledging the agency would investigate all discrimination complaints. Yet, says Rabkin, Office of Civil Rights officials still believe that "the investigation of individual complaints is a far less productive use of investigative resources" than agency-initiated compliance reviews, and that "fear of antagonizing constituent groups has made headquarters reluctant to clarify for regional offices the appropriate scope of individual investigations or the sorts of issues that are not worth pursuing in practice, whatever their status in official regulations."[31]

San Francisco Bay Area Air Pollution Control District inspectors regularly are assigned to inspect each of the scores of huge gasoline storage tanks at the three major refineries in the area. To do so, they must climb atop the "floating roofs" of the tanks and measure emissions that may be escaping from the seals installed around the edges. The company must provide technicians and safety people to go up with them. A district enforcement official told us that inspectors had never found a violation of the governing standard when a company had told the inspector in advance that the seals were working properly. We then asked why the district persisted in checking each tank, if that were so. Why not get the companies to do it and certify their findings to the agency, and limit inspectors to spot-checks of a random sample of tanks? That is a fine idea, the district official told us, but they could not do it that way. "The state agency [the California Air Resources Board] and the feds [EPA] would say, 'What? You're trusting the industry?' " And because the state board provides much of the funding for the district, "We have little choice but to enforce the regulations they give us the way they say."

If a regulatory agency adopts a policy of discretionary underenforcement for reasons related not to improving enforcement efficiency but to sparing individual firms (or whole industries or society) excessive compliance costs, it is politically even more vulnerable, especially to vague imputations of corruption or co-optation. An obvious strategy for countering such suspicions is to avoid discretion altogether, to stick to the formal requirements as specified in official publications and manuals, and to document the fact that the formalities have indeed been observed. In bureaucratic argot, this general strategy is known as "covering your ass" or "CYA." Indeed CYA emerges as more than a mere strategy; for most lower level officials, at least, it is a master principle that rivals Freud's pleasure principle or Bentham's felicific calculus.

This is not surprising, for the CYA principle speaks to the problem of survival, which is more basic than the experience of mere pleasure and pain. Moreover, the political environment of regulatory officials abounds in dangerous potential predators. Any complainant who is dissatisfied with the results achieved by an enforcement official can call the inspector's superiors or the press and accuse him of laxity or corruption. Under many regulatory statutes, proregulation advocacy groups and public interest law firms can bring well-publicized court actions against the agency for inadequate enforcement, departure from statutory standards and deadlines, or violations of complainants' rights. Even an inspector's own colleagues are not always to be trusted. Ed Martin, as we shall call him, is responsible for issuing air pollution discharge permits for a California pollution control district. A former employee of a major oil company, Martin was charged by another agency employee with favoring his previous employer with respect to the terms of permit application. It took him six months to be exonerated, "but all anyone out there cared about was the charge," he lamented, "not the exoneration." He concluded: "Public agencies exist in a fishbowl, so its safer to stick to the rules that back you up. There's no advantage to discretion, to being reasonable."

Journalists are another important predator species. Any investigative reporter in need of a story can be sure to find one by looking deep enough into a regulatory regime, for at any time the journalist can find bad apple firms or even reasonably good apples with uncorrected and unpunished regulatory violations. In journalese, such subjects are "evergreens" because whenever a story is needed the subject is sure to be alive and ready to go. Of course, some regulatory agencies are consistently greener than others: building code inspection in Chicago, restaurant inspection in New

York, and slum housing inspection almost anywhere. In California, there are periodic exposés of the underside of life in nursing homes and facilities for the mentally ill.

The effect of such news stories, or the prospect of them, is suggested by Bruce Vladeck's analysis of quality-of-care regulation of nursing homes in several states.

> The scandals of the early and mid-1970s changed . . . the political balance, from one in which rigorous inspection was more trouble than it was worth to one where the greatest fear was of revelations by a newspaper or legislative investigator of shocking conditions in a nursing home that had been found adequate by the survey process. Consultants became policemen overnight. Minor problems could no longer be overlooked. Even in the best facilities, every nit had to be picked.[32]

Thus, evidence of direct corruption is not a necessary ingredient for scandal. Scandal arises from the disclosure that bad conditions still exist, together with hints that the owners are reaping unconscionable profits thereby. When that disclosure is combined with revelations that there are uncorrected regulatory violations or that inspectors had not been at the facility for several months, the implication is that the bad conditions are due to lax enforcement and that lax enforcement is due to some undocumented but obvious link between the unconscionable profiteer and the regulatory agency.

The lesson for regulatory agencies is that they are vulnerable to powerful journalistic and political sanctions levied, at unpredictable intervals, against even the appearance of undue leniency. Further, their vulnerability is magnified because these alleged failings typically are described in the news media without the benefit of historical perspective, without a sense of the overall distribution of compliant and noncompliant firms in the regulated population, and without a feeling for what is really possible. The best defense, once again, is to do what state nursing home regulators did, to become rule-following policemen. Additional security is provided by maintaining statistics showing that the agency is conducting regular inspections, imposing high numbers of citations and fines, and mounting prosecutions often—with resulting pressure on inspectors to do what is necessary to keep those statistics at a high level.[33] Thus legalistic enforcement tactics are likely to become and remain entrenched, not because of their useful offensive function of providing more deterrence, but because of their defensive function of showing that the agency has been acting in conformance with law and has been as systematic and as tough as existing manpower and sanctions enable it to be.[34]

To be sure, there are dangers from the other side of the political spectrum as well, and regulatory managers must normally weigh the risks of criticism from proregulation constituencies against the risks of criticism from regulated parties. If a regulatory agency manager insists that enforcement officials go by the book, he can expect more contestation and appeals by regulated enterprises, more pointed criticism when he appears at trade association meetings, periodic telephone calls from legislators on behalf of outraged businessmen, and perhaps (if he is high enough in the agency hierarchy) some sharp questioning at legislative hearings about some particularly absurd instance of legalistic enforcement. In a conservative administration, unhappy businessmen may be able to complain more effectively to top administrators in the legalistic enforcement official's agency. Unquestionably, this sort of criticism takes its toll and produces some efforts to "be reasonable." Whether it can regularly succeed in offsetting the criticism from the other side, however, is doubtful. Though charges of being nitpicking and mindless are hard to take, a defensive regulatory manager, like a field inspector faced with a protesting manager, can respond by occupying a very high moral ground: "We don't make the rules, we enforce them," or "In a democracy, it is not up to us executive branch officials to revise the expressed will of the legislature or to weigh costs of compliance against the health and safety of the public." Furthermore, the manager can also refer to all the good reasons for insisting that inspectors stick to the rules, such as the risks of allowing field officers to make independent (and hence idiosyncratic and potentially erroneous) judgments, the difficulties of training and supervising field officers who are allowed discretion, and the ever-present need to deter corruption. As long as moral attitudes in America remain largely what they have been for a very long time now, most agency managers will probably find it safer to be tough and go by the book than to be flexible and reasonable.

All enforcement agencies are susceptible to at least occasional scandal-mongering, but for some these occasions are almost predictable. They arise from periodic ecological or human catastrophes that are associated with the jurisdictional responsibilities of the agency—fatal accidents, major oil spills, fires or explosions, revelations of toxic contamination, and so on. In the aftermath of such shocking events, investigations by news media and legislatures hasten to seek out the point in the regulatory system that is "at fault," looking especially for signs that unauthorized laxity or corruption in the enforcement process might have been to blame. However sensible the agency's enforcement style and priorities beforehand, one can expect a postcatastrophe crackdown on the industry or process in question, whereby regulations are enforced to the letter and heavy fines are levied and announced to the press.[35]

To be sure, catastrophes are infrequent, and they quickly fade from public and political attention. But postcatastrophe cutbacks in discretion often are written into regulations and are not quickly abandoned by the agency in question. Nor does the experience of "failure" quickly fade in the memory of enforcement officials. Several Cal-OSHA officials we interviewed referred spontaneously to a fatal tunnel explosion almost a decade past that led to legislative investigation and criticism of the agency's consultative enforcement posture. Both industry compliance specialists and FDA officials, interviewed about regulation of the manufacture of intravenous solutions, repeatedly referred to an incident seven or eight years earlier in which a hospital patient had been killed by bacterial contamination in an i.v. bottle. References to these tragedies not only bolster morale for inspectors by reaffirming the importance of their mission but also reaffirm the importance of strict enforcement procedures designed, however crudely and inadequately, to prevent recurrence.

Catastrophes, therefore, are important not only when they happen but also because they might happen in the future. Some kind of serious accident, every top enforcement official senses, can occur at any time. And if discretion is allowed at the field level, however competent the inspectorate is in general, eventually an inspector will be misled or will prove to have been lazy, negligent, or corrupt—perhaps with tragic consequences. Thus the anticipation of catastrophe keeps the lock mechanism on the regulatory ratchet just as firmly in place as if these occasional catastrophes were once-a-week events. In accordance with the CYA principle, agencies that oversee catastrophe-prone activities have a powerful incentive to make sure that, if disaster occurs, it will not appear to be because of some gap in enforcement procedures—such as the exercise of discretion by inspectors.

The Costs of "Being Reasonable." Going by the book usually is not only politically safer, on balance, than selective underenforcement; it is also a lot easier. The benefits of a flexible enforcement policy, after all, would accrue primarily not to regulators but to the regulated entities, while the very considerable costs of the extra efforts involved in trying to be reasonable would be borne by the regulatory officials themselves.

Consider first the costs. Flexible enforcement requires a skilled and dedicated inspectorate, capable of making fine judgments about the degree of risk posed by rule violations and about the adequacy of alternative abatement measures. Inspectors would have to make time for more extended and probing dialogues and negotiations with personnel in regulated entities. Agency officials would have to obtain the resources to recruit and retain more sophisticated inspectors. Supervisors would have to spend more time and effort on training and review. To defend against subsequent criticism for discretionary relaxations of the rules, enforcement officials would be obliged at the very least to undertake more documentation of their reasons for granting an exemption or a variance.

The costs of documentation would be substantial because it is often exceedingly difficult to prove that any given instance of discretionary underenforcement was well motivated and based on sound judgment— rather than the product of laziness, gullibility, or corruption. The actual level of risk presented by a violation or the costs and difficulties of abatement may not be susceptible of precise measurement. Recall the bright fluorescent mold we spoke of in chapter 3 that fails to sprout on containers of contaminated food. The absence of such clear indicators of danger, of course, is what makes governmental regulation seem necessary in the first place. But that ambiguity also presents grave problems for the inspector who thinks, for example, that a piece of production equipment that fails to conform to "good manufacturing practice" regulations nevertheless is producing products safe enough to be sold and who wishes to be able to defend that judgment to his superiors. Research shows that people often disagree about the likelihood of remote but serious risks, and higher regulatory officials are likely to be conservative in this regard. To make an acceptable case to his supervisor, therefore, the inspector might have to explain, in writing, the performance characteristics of the equipment in use, compare them to the prescribed equipment, discuss the adequacy of other safeguards in the factory in question, describe the costs of getting replacement equipment, and so on.

These burdens of justification, it should be emphasized, would be required even if the inspector were invariably correct in his judgments. They do not begin to compare with the immense efforts of self-exculpation and explanation officials would be forced to undertake should they erroneously ignore a violation that is actually serious or that leads to human injury. The mere anticipation of these costs is a powerful incentive for regulators to avoid the necessity for making such judgments or, at a minimum, to require the regulated enterprise to supply extensive documentation and subject them to painstaking bureaucratic reviews before authorizing any departure from the rules. EPA officials, for example, have been conservative and frustratingly slow in evaluating manufacturers' cost-saving proposals under the EPA "bubble policy" because, as an agency enforcement official said, "You only need one or two cases of disasters about how a bubble made the environment worse to blow the whole thing up."[36]

Yet what would regulatory officials receive in exchange for being reasonable and bearing all the costs of further investigation and documentation themselves? Leaving aside the prospect of future employment in the regulated industry, a genuine consideration in some but not most regulated areas, there is not much besides goodwill—and perhaps more cooperation—from the regulated enterprise.* For some officials, of course, the prospect of lower interpersonal tensions would no doubt be very welcome. Indeed, several higher level regulatory officials told us that "burn-out" was a troublesome problem for their field-level enforcers; thus if less conflict led to more constructive problem-solving, inspectors might have a greater sense of accomplishment. But it is not clear that flexible enforcement in fact makes inspectors happier. Recall Steven Kelman's finding that morale was higher and personal tensions were lower among OSHA inspectors, with their policy of uniform toughness, than among their counterparts in Sweden, who were expected to switch from cooperation to coercion and back as the situation required, with all the risks of choosing incorrectly and jeopardizing workers' health

---

*In general, the public-private crossover is most available to persons with a higher degree of technical skill, like industrial hygienists, nuclear safety engineers, or food scientists. Such people are not commonly in lower level enforcement work, however, and many regulatory agencies do not employ many such people at any level. Furthermore, the private sector is not uniformly more attractive than the public sector. We discovered that milk and dairy inspectors, for instance, regarded public agency employment as generally superior in status if not always in salary to employment in the industry. Quality control engineers and lower level technicians told us that the pressures to "cut corners" were too great in industry but that one could escape these in government procurement work. In any case, it is not clear that the desire for future employment in a regulated firm is necessarily well served by a policy of continuing laxity. A firm might be more inclined to try to hire away a tough, combatative inspector than a lax one.

and safety. It would seem easier, therefore, for most inspectors simply to adhere to the rules and to develop defenses against imputations of rigidity. For example, they can assure themselves that while the substance of the rules themselves might be troublesome, the idea of formalistic adherence to the rules is "good" and ought to command assent by most citizens. Furthermore, there is always the fallback: "Maybe you've got a point, but I'm sorry—the evidence here showed a violation. You can always apply for a variance or appeal, you know."

As to possible bureaucratically generated rewards for appropriate underenforcement, there are few of those too. No one keeps an official tally of excessive compliance costs saved by decisions not to enforce the rules as written, and there is no official record of the instances in which inspectors gain improved cooperation in fulfilling the agency's regulatory mission through skillful plea bargaining or the deliberate suspension of threats in favor of persuasive appeals. This situation stands in striking contrast to the usually well-developed systems for recording the number of inspections made and violations cited or the amount of fines levied and collected. Thus it is far more attractive for regulatory officials to make regulated enterprises shoulder the burden of documenting any claims that nonenforcement is justifiable; the regulators can apply the rules as written and allow aggrieved businesses to file applications for formal variances, along with supporting test results, cost figures, and impact analyses.

THE PERSISTENCE OF UNREASONABLENESS

The regulatory ratchet does not prevent all steps toward flexible enforcement, of course. In times of fiscal austerity, budget cuts may compel understaffed agencies to identify the relatively good apples and inspect them less often or to seek compromise in order to avoid drawn-out legal conflict. There are always some points of discretion in the most legalistic enforcement programs; even some OSHA enforcement officials assert, "I can show you case after case where we negotiated procedures to comply that were less strict" than the original abatement order demanded.[37] Individual agency leaders from time to time recognize that flexible enforcement, even with its political risks, can offer dividends in effectiveness as well as in greater reasonableness; they push a reluctant inspectorate and uninterested regulatory rulemakers in that direction, despite the opposition of proregulation interests. The role of such heroes in regulatory affairs is little-chronicled, but we have in mind people like Donald Kennedy, who, as FDA commissioner beginning in 1977, sought to loosen up the so-called identity standards for various processed food and the standards for new drug clearance; or Dennis Dunne, who, as head of a unit overseeing the licensing of nursing homes in California, worked patiently for three years to develop a more flexible enforcement strategy and to train inspectors capable of carrying it out. Individual heroes, however, are always vulnerable to public attack by those who appear more zealous to protect the public and, in any event, are never as permanent a fixture in the regulatory scene as relevant interest groups, career enforcement staffs, and traditional institutional arrangements. Kennedy soon retired to a university presidency, and Dunne was forced out of his position by a legalistically minded superior appointed by Governor Jerry Brown.

More fundamentally, the incentives, conditions, and events that keep the ratchet wheel locked in place are deeply embedded in the structure of "command and control" regulation, to use Thomas Schelling's phrase. They are not likely to be swept away by political tides or personalities that move about closer to the surface. Catastrophes, scandals, and passionate complaints on behalf of victims or potential victims of large-scale organizations and technologies will always be with us, for regulated enterprises (and regulators) will always be fallible. Assessing the extent of risk to life posed by potentially dangerous machines and processes will always be a task bedeviled by uncertainty, and the political risks of erring in the direction of inappropriate leniency (an error that *could* lead to catastrophe) will almost always appear greater than the risks of being needlessly strict (imposing unnecessarily costly burdens on regulated enterprises). The pressures and incentives to avoid relaxing overly ambitious or overly inclusive rules, and to go by the book in enforcing those rules, are powerful indeed and more likely than not ensure that attempts to adjust regulation in a more reasonable direction will be relatively modest and transitory.

PART THREE

INDIRECT REGULATION

CHAPTER EIGHT

PRIVATE REGULATION

•

If the political environment, with all its demands on regulators for the appearance of toughness, fairness, and incorruptibility, is the main cause of regulatory inflexibility, then perhaps the regulators need to be better shielded from that environment. If we could create a legal basis of regulatory authority that would be more independent of public accountability norms, regulators could operate with more discretion, flexibility, and reasonableness.

In fact, such regulators already exist. Most of the regulation that takes place in the United States is already in the hands not of government officials but of the myriad individuals employed in the private sector. An interesting problem for policy design, therefore, is to harness the existing institutions of private regulation more tightly to public purposes.

Consider, for instance, any large-scale manufacturing firm. It employs hundreds of financial auditors, assembly line inspectors, quality control engineers, and legal advisers to police their coworkers' adherence to company standards of quality and performance. Holiday Inns of America, like many other franchising corporations, sends inspectors incognito to check on individual Holiday Inns. Department store buyers inspect their suppliers' products and sometimes their factories. Architects inspect contractors' work at construction sites. The Consumers Union inspects and evaluates hundreds of products. A thousand independent laboratories specialize in product and materials testing, not to mention those that function as subunits in larger manufacturing organizations.

Consider further the numerous rules, regulations, and standards invented and administered by firms in the private sector, ranging from a small firm's informal oral tradition to a large corporation's multivolume looseleaf binders. Product standards, formulated by engineers who serve on a broad array of private committees, cover some 20,000 items, from the width of railroad track to specifications for stainless steel wire used in surgical implants, and the number increases to 55,000 if one includes the specification standards promulgated by large industrial purchasers and government agencies.[1] The American Association of Blood Banks publishes and enforces rules for operating blood banks and handling blood products. Every corporate industrial hygienist we interviewed had at his desk *The Registry of the Toxic Effects of Chemical Substances,* containing "threshold limit values" for safe exposure levels in the workplace for hundreds of chemicals, together with designated measurement techniques; the *Registry* is prepared by conferences of government and private experts and covers many more substances than OSHA has dealt with by regulation.

There is also a multiplicity of institutions wielding sanctions for inadequate performance. For example, although we tend to think of the state board of medical licensure as the ultimate quality enforcer of the medical profession, in fact it is only one of about a dozen quality control institutions that sits atop the medical profession (though not over each practitioner). In hospitals, tissue committees and mortality-morbidity review committees can bar surgeons who repeatedly are found by their peers to have acted unwisely. County medical societies, after reviewing allegations of incompetence or unethical practice, can expel the offending physician, an action that usually has a drastic impact on his income. In product safety, the Underwriters Laboratory can effectively ban an unsafe electrical product from the market simply by refusing or withdrawing its seal of approval. Similarly, private standards-writing bodies, by refusing to amend existing standards, often can preclude the marketing of a new, cheaper substitute that the standard writers find to be unsafe,[2] just as the formulation of a new, higher standard or standard allowing a cheaper substitute may drive older products from the market.

Finally, apart from these more-or-less voluntary private regulatory systems, there has been enormous growth of private inspectorates in direct response to aggressive direct government regulation. Corporations now employ many more industrial safety experts, toxicologists, industrial hygienists, affirmative action specialists, auditors, product safety experts, environmental engineers, and technicians for maintaining pollution control equipment. According to Barry Mitnick, the members of this "response bureaucracy"

> specialize in the regulatory area and center their personal career
> plans on work in this area. They may have put in years of labor to
> gain expertise. . . . Such individuals may support regulation be-

cause it is in their self-interest to do so, as well as because of . . . genuine belief in the purposes of the regulation.[3]

THE QUESTION OF COMPARABLE EFFECTIVENESS

There are many reasons to think that private, internal regulators can be more reasonable than their public counterparts. They are more specialized and more knowledgeable about the risks generated by their company's operation. They are more likely to have the trust of the people they regulate and thus to have access to finer-grained and more relevant information. Unlike government regulators, they sometimes can be seen by their firm's middle-level managers as contributing to the overall goals of the organizations in which they operate. They are freer to use discretion in the application of general standards to particular cases.

There are fewer reasons, however, to think that private regulation would be as effective as public regulation. To be sure, many of the conditions that facilitate reasonableness also facilitate effectiveness. Furthermore, when the private regulatory system is reinforced by the pressures of the marketplace and the liability system and/or originates in a very strong tradition of professional ethics, private self-regulation can accomplish a great deal. Few people would advocate replacing hospital tissue committees with OSHA-like rules and inspectors to prevent unnecessary or incompetent operations, or to substitute government regulation for the private systems that generally ensure that pumps and valves and electrical meters are well made and safe. On the other hand, market conditions and the liability law often do not generate strong pressures for private standard setting and enforcement. Under some circumstances, firms may not be induced to hire professional specialists in quality control or safety or environmental protection, or, if they do, to give them any intracorporate clout. Like the public inspectorate, the private inspectorate also tends to occupy an outsider or even a pariah status in its relevant social niches. It is the formal superego of an organization. It specializes in repressing, blaming, criticizing, admonishing. As one quality control manager put it, "In most industries . . . I feel that quality control is looked upon as a scourge because QC personnel have a tendency to want to act as floodgates, closing down production."[4]

Still, the advantages of private regulation, shielded from excessive demands for political accountability and potentially able, therefore, to provide greater *reasonableness* than public regulation, make it worthwhile to explore ways to improve its *effectiveness* to the point that citizen expectations for ever higher levels of protection can be met. Conceivably, government could help in this regard. It might repair, strengthen, reinforce, improve, modify, and enlarge private regulatory mechanisms—or even help to create them anew.

STIMULATING PRIVATE STANDARDS DEVELOPMENT

Private quality or performance standards, formulated by committees of organizations such as the American National Standards Institute and the American Society for Testing and Materials, exist for a large minority of goods and processes furnished in the marketplace, but not for all the activities for which they theoretically could be designed. Professional and industrial associations have formulated advisory standards for some emissions of chemicals into the environment or the air of factories, but not for most such substances. Product standards apply mostly to products furnished to industrial buyers; relatively few apply to consumer goods.

The substantial gaps stem from the absence of pressure from the marketplace and liability law. Consumers, whether individual or corporate, do not have sufficient knowledge or incentives to boycott the products of polluters. With respect to product standards, large-scale industrial purchasers are relatively few in number, purchase in volume, and want standardized parts and materials they can purchase from any supplier; hence they push suppliers to establish and meet standards of quality and uniformity. Consumers, on the other hand, buy in small volume, base their choices on visual inspection, and usually like the variety of products that the ungoverned marketplace provides. The main areas in which there *is* a good deal of industry regulation of consumer products are wiring, insulation, and standardized connectors for electrical products developed by the Underwriters' Laboratory, and building and plumbing standards developed by a variety of code-writing organizations. In these fields, as in many industrial-level product standards, Adam Smith's "invisible hand" punishes sellers who circumvent the private standards, and the private regulatory scheme is generally effective.

Still, there undoubtedly are many additional cases in which standardization would be beneficial. Why, then, does it not occur? The main answer is that the invisible hand is not skilled at building a consensus among competitors; yet without consensus, no standard can survive.

Typically, firms throughout the industry—and especially the largest firms—send technical representatives to a standards writing committee organized under the auspices of a professional association. Finding agreement on standards, however, is a political as much as an engineering or economic process, and there is nothing in the structure of the marketplace that guarantees that the process will succeed and little in the nature of politics—especially where power is not tightly concentrated—to guarantee consensus. The result is as likely to be anarchy, as various participants differentially emphasize safety, economy, uniformity, or flexibility. Government can play a role in tipping the scales toward consensus, however, by providing either the inducement or the coercive power to stimulate and validate private agreement on common standards.

The mere threat of an outside enemy is sometimes enough to create self-regulating institutions. For example, in order to deflect mounting demands for government regulation, the Association of American Home Appliance Manufacturers was formed in 1967; by 1971 it was pursuing a wide range of self-regulatory activities, including the preparation of safety standards, performance standards, certification, and consumer complaint-handling.[5] Likewise in the case of soft drink bottle manufacturers, safety standards emerged only after considerable political pressure had built up for mandatory regulation. Indeed, once the manufacturers organized to prepare standards, they did succeed in holding the Consumer Product Safety Commission (CPSC) at bay. In early 1977, when the CPSC denied two petitions to promulgate mandatory standards for soft drink bottles, it mentioned the industry's "voluntary" efforts as one of the reasons for its decision.[6]

Regulatory agencies can, and occasionally do, use such industry reactions systematically, employing the threat of direct regulation explicitly to prod trade and professional associations to prepare self-regulatory standards and procedures as an alternative to government prescription, or authorizing them to fill in the details of broadly worded government regulations, subject to some government participation, review, and veto power. In one instance, to reduce the flammability of upholstered furniture the CPSC proposed a regulation that manufacturers thought unduly stringent, complex, and expensive to comply with, given the level of risk involved. The industry responded by developing a voluntary standard that they argued was a reasonable and more practical substitute. The commission agreed to suspend its own proceedings for a year while the voluntary standard was implcmcntcd and cvaluatcd.[7] Thc Food and Drug Administration recently announced that it will review and endorse privately established performance standards for medical devices (such as electrocardiograph machines and glucose testing products), and will set its own mandatory standards only if voluntary standards appear inadequate. One could imagine the Environmental Protection Agency and OSHA similarly using the threat of further regulations to induce private industrial engineers to agree upon standards for emission control technologies—although the Justice Department unfortunately has attacked sharing of technology, in the case of automobile emission standards in particular, as a violation of the antitrust laws. Indeed, proposals for regulatory cooperation with private bodies often are attacked by consumer protection groups.[8]

If government can sometimes stimulate private consensus on standards by the threat of regulation, it can also facilitate or cement consensus when the force of law is needed to ensure joint action and to enforce private standards or ethical codes. The movement to regulate recombinant DNA research, for instance, seems to have evolved out of a highly competitive research environment in which individual researchers were racing to push the scientific frontier forward, creating new and possibly dangerous strains of bacteria. Although it was in the interests of all concerned with such research to slow the pace and agree on methods of controlling the risks, the unwillingness of individual researchers to reveal their analytic strategies in advance of publication prevented a coordinated effort. As a result, some of the leaders in the field managed, between 1973 and 1975, to build a consensus behind the idea of putting certain regulatory responsibilities in the hands of the National Institutes of Health (NIH). They fully expected, however, that the NIH would limit itself to enforcement while allowing the scientific community to prepare the safety standards that the NIH was to enforce.[9]

Occupational and professional licensing laws are traditional models for such government support of self-regulation. Although sometimes poorly staffed and ineffective at the postlicensing enforcement level, and always open to the charge that they reduce competition, professional licensing has often been effective in ridding the field of the most blatantly incompetent and dishonest practitioners.[10] A comparison of the National Association of Securities Dealers (which is authorized by federal law to police member firms for violations of the association's Rules of Fair Practice) with the Securities and Exchange Commission (which inspects nonmember broker-dealers for compliance with comparable standards) indicated that the private association is more diligent in its inspections, swifter in resolving customer complaints, severe in its sanctions (44 members were suspended in 1972), and generally effective in producing compliance.[11]

Nevertheless, there is always suspicion that self-regulating associations will be dominated by larger firms, anticompetitive in thrust, and insensitive to certain consumer interests. In the case of building and construction standards, for example, unions and suppliers of certain materials have been charged with cartelizing their markets and excluding more inexpensive and labor-saving building materials by relying on local governments to enforce building codes embodying standards they themselves develop.[12] Solving the problem of anarchy, it is feared, leads to the problem of tyranny.

Yet the problem of tyranny surely is not insoluble. For the last few years, the Federal Trade Commission, Congress, and the Office of Management and Budget (OMB) have been exploring possible approaches to democratizing the private standards-writing process, considering rules requiring "adequate notice" to all interested parties, allowing an opportunity for them to present their views, and ensuring a balance of membership on the standards-writing committees to include consumers, small businesses, labor representatives, environmentalists, and other concerned parties. A recent OMB proposal would provide government grants to private standard-setting organizations whose procedures meet such guidelines and also provide impartial mechanisms for handling complaints or appeals by dissatisfied participants.[13] The drafters of the Consumer Product Safety Act of 1972 paid careful attention to the same issues. Indeed, the greater danger, as Samuel Florman has argued persuasively, is that government bureaucrats intent on ensuring that no consumer interest goes unsatisfied will encumber a private standard-writing process that has worked remarkably well with a set of time-consuming, conflict-creating formal rules and adversarial procedures that would reduce its essential advantage over government regulation.[14]

MANDATING SELF-REGULATION

A large proportion of socially harmful actions, we have argued, does not stem from amoral attempts to "get away with" fraud or obviously inadequate or illegal safety precautions but rather from gaps or slippages in the private intraorganizational regulatory systems established to prevent major kinds of wrongdoing and harm. Despite internal preventive rules, irresponsibility and dangerous actions continue to occur, stemming from the drift of managerial attention, conflicting goals and pressures, inadequate supervisory and reporting systems, and insufficient powers on the part of internal regulators such as safety and environmental engineers.[15] These weaknesses—which are not always present of course—suggest a set of government strategies to improve internal regulation: the government could enact laws and regulations compelling managers to attend to certain problems, requiring installation of intraorganizational regulators and reporting systems, and strengthening the hand of private regulators within organizations. Thus government regulation would be indirect, not prescribing specific facilities or preventive measures but ensuring the creation of a managerial system that would in turn devise and enforce appropriate standards for each enterprise.

There are already many examples of such indirect regulation. An 1873 California law required every mine to employ a safety supervisor, who was made criminally responsible for accidents due to neglect of duty. The early locomotive safety laws required railroads to establish their own inspection and safety-oriented maintenance programs; the government inspector's primary job was to conduct spot checks of equipment inspected by company maintenance men and to review records documenting the company's adherence to its own rules and inspection schedules. The same pattern was adopted in Federal Aviation Administration regulation of airline safety. California regulations currently require truck operators to have a preventive maintenance program, including systematic inspection of vehicles and maintenance of records showing "the types of inspection, maintenance and lubrication operations to be performed on each vehicle and date or mileage when these operations are due." Motor Carrier Safety Unit inspectors, consequently, are able to concentrate on evaluating the quality of the trucking company's maintenance system and on using that to decide whether detailed and frequent government inspection of the trucks themselves is needed. FDA regulations require manufacturers of intravenous solutions to establish written procedures that prescribe in detail the sanitary and quality control routines to be used in their manufacturing process and to establish a quality control unit with authority to enforce them.

In some cases, the government has required enterprises to set up private regulatory systems to monitor the behavior of persons or businesses outside the enterprise itself. Recent EPA regulations, for example, require producers of hazardous wastes to keep track of each load consigned to a shipper and of its ultimate interment in an authorized disposal site; if the producer does not receive a signed document from the shipper and the disposal-site operator showing that the load has been safely disposed of, it must investigate the fate of the shipment and report any discrepancies to the EPA. The California Public Utilities Commission ordered electric utilities to offer free conservation inspections to any customer who requests them; it would be no surprise if they become mandatory.

Government demands for self-regulatory systems occasionally extend to qualitative problems, which are even more difficult to control by detailed, government-formulated regulations. Universities that receive federal research funds must establish faculty committees and review procedures to examine research proposals, especially those involving biomedical research, that might harm human subjects either physically or psychologically, and if necessary, to work out alternative methods with the researcher. A recent California statute—implicitly recognizing the inability of OSHA rules to cut accidents significantly—requires each employer to establish and maintain its own program of accident prevention, including training of employees in safe work practices and hazards unique to the particular job or workplace. The regulations also mandate scheduled self-inspections and require the company to appoint a responsible management official to run the program. In a very different context, Christopher Stone has described the development of self-regulation by rock music stations under some not-so-gentle prodding by the Federal Communications Commission. In 1971, the commission decided to try to curb the epidemic of popular song lyrics alluding to the pleasures of drug use. It issued a notice to licensees pointing out the problem "and then proceeded to turn responsibility for handling it back onto the broadcasting companies." It invoked the judgment of the licensee to determine the next steps. The broadcasting companies protested, demanding firm rules, but the FCC stood its ground on imposing merely a diffuse call for "responsibility." In another notice a few months later, it wrote:

As to the mechanics of license responsibility . . . disc jockeys could be instructed that where there is a question as to whether a record promotes illegal drug usage, a responsible management official should be notified so that he can exercise his judgment. . . . The Commission is not calling for an extensive investigation of each such record. What is required is simply reasonable and good faith attention to the problem.[16]

Stone reports that his own survey of rock music stations in the Los Angeles area "suggests a thoroughgoing and not at all fractious compliance."

DESIGNATING RESPONSIBLE OFFICERS

Both the California employee safety training requirement and the FCC lyrics-monitoring order compel the enterprise to designate a specific management official to take responsibility for a self-regulatory program. These measures recognize the tendency of large organizations to divide functions so that no single individual seems wholly responsible for a problem (or a mistake), or for ensuring that company rules are followed, or for reminding employees of the long-term consequences of their acts and omissions. With no fully accountable individual, internal control systems can easily break down. When managers can avoid liability by claiming they delegated responsibility for enforcement of programs they set in motion and were not aware of slippage, slippage is more likely to occur.

The designation of an individual to take responsibility for dealing with a problem or a set of risks, on the other hand, increases the organization's constancy of attention to a problem and makes collective evasion of responsibility more difficult. Larger manufacturers with full-time safety specialists have better worker safety records, on the average, than smaller firms in the same industry that generally lack safety specialists. Local labor unions with full-time civil rights officers have better knowledge of antidiscrimination laws and policies and a better record of compliance efforts.[17] The chief of enforcement of California's Food and Drug Division observed that the critical ingredient for compliance with food purity regulations is neither government enforcement nor the ensconcement of "a beautiful sanitation manual . . . in the plant manager's office." Rather, "the key is whether companies give responsibility to certain people to do something about it or to somebody who oversees the whole thing." Progress has come with the development of full-time quality assurance specialists "who sit equally on the organizational chart with production and sales. He goes and tells the president *directly,* 'We need foaming equipment,' and his words are as important as those of the production manager who says, 'We need a new sealer.' He can then argue it out with the president as to the priority of the foamer or the sealer.'' When market and legal pressures have not induced organizations to establish such specialized positions, therefore, it may be useful for government to require such repersonalization of corporate responsibility by law.

Again, such requirements have been established in certain areas. As a condition of receiving federal funds, local school districts must appoint an official—commonly referred to as a compliance coordinator—to specialize in effecting compliance with the requirements of federal civil rights and education-for-the-handicapped laws.[18] A consent decree between American Telephone and Telegraph (AT&T), the Department of Labor, and the Equal Employment Opportunity Commission sets up a detailed system whereby AT&T must continually gather data on applicants by minority groups and sex and record reasons for rejecting applicants. The decree stipulates exactly which officers in the corporation must perform which tasks in the maintenance and monitoring of the system.[19] As noted before, the SEC has required some corporations to establish audit committees, composed of specific members of the board of directors (predominantly "outside" directors, not drawn from the corporation's own management), with specific responsibilities for ensuring compliance with laws preventing diversion of corporate funds and concealment of adverse financial information.[20] Stone has discussed requiring all large corporations to appoint and provide staffs for "public directors," who would be statutorily obligated to oversee programs designed to ensure good faith compliance with regulations, to check the effectiveness of internal compliance systems and in general to serve as a corporate superego.[21] Noting that the food and drug laws require pharmaceutical companies to appoint a qualified investigator to assemble all test data on drugs under development, Stone also suggests that the law might require other critical corporate positions, such as chief safety test engineer for automobile companies or vice-president for environmental affairs in heavily polluting industries, to be filled by individuals meeting legally defined qualifications, whose functions and reporting obligations would be defined by regulation.

How can the public be sure that designated corporate compliance officers will take their responsibilities seriously, or push hard against intraorganizational resistance to the self-regulatory schemes they devise?

It is not possible to be *sure*, of course, but there are a variety of pressures on designated self-regulatory officials, and other pressures might be devised. One is that the sheer fact of designation makes them to blame if their company gets in trouble with government regulatory officials or gets sued in court for failing to maintain adequate precautions against social harms. In addition, if the officer's duties were specified in some detail by law (such as the duty to file compliance reports with the government or tell regulatory officials about known product defects) or even if detailed duties were left to the corporation to prescribe in job descriptions filed with regulatory authorities—then the compliance officer would face personal liability for misrepresentation and for harms caused by his nonfeasance.[22] A related tactic is to require corporate compliance officers personally to sign official reports and records attesting to regular completion of self-regulatory procedures. The importance of the personal signature is brought out in two studies by Stone of egregious corporate misconduct—falsification of test data by a drug company that led to marketing of a dangerous drug, and test falsification by B. F. Goodrich in manufacturing aircraft brakes. "Key actors," Stone observes, "were willing to prepare distortive documents; but they drew the line at putting their names on them." A signature identifies a potential guilty party in the event of a subsequent liability suit; it exposes an individual to charges of perjury, and, as Stone puts it, "people feel a strong psychological connection between their actions and their names."[23] Thus FDA good manufacturing practice regulations for intravenous solutions require companies not only to conduct tests and regularly recalibrate equipment used to detect possible contamination, but also to maintain records showing the signature of each person performing each act of monitoring and calibration. Another method of increasing incentives for designated corporate compliance officers is to insist that they be licensed, for then the regulatory regime acquires an additional and potent deterrent—the threat of disqualification. Even without licensing, Stone points out, legislation could provide that designated public directors, product testing engineers, or pollution control managers found guilty of gross dereliction of duty would be legally disqualified from holding similar managerial positions or directorships in *any* company.[24]

CHANGING THE BALANCE OF POWER

Focusing responsibility for self-regulatory systems on individual officers or directors presumably increases their own motivation and capacity to keep the organization on its toes, attentive to its legal and social obligations and to the risks generated by its operations. But what of their power? A quality control system in a cannery may fall short if the chief quality control engineer, however strongly motivated, cannot get new foaming equipment because the production manager controls the budget and wants a new sealer, or refuses to stop operations for scheduled cleaning during the peak season, or is slow to release maintenance men from established routines to help de-bug new foaming equipment. One way of enhancing the effectiveness of private regulatory systems, therefore, is for the government to try to shift the intraorganizational balance of power, giving the inside regulators more power or influence.

One example of this kind of effort is the National Environmental Policy Act (NEPA), whereby Congress required government bodies with construction or land-management responsibilities to prepare and make public an environmental impact statement analyzing ways in which adverse environmental effects of proposed projects could be mitigated or avoided. Failure to perform this analysis in a timely and serious manner has led to court injunctions stopping planned projects. According to one careful study, NEPA and the threat of lawsuits have led to a major increase in the number, status, and influence of environmental protection specialists in the Corps of Engineers and the Forest Service. Although the impact statement process suffers many drawbacks, the affected agencies have become more concerned with environmental hazards, more knowledgeable about mitigation techniques, and more accessible to the influence of outside environmental groups.[25] Similarly, California law requires builders of substantial housing projects to prepare environmental impact reports for consideration by zoning and planning boards—and by environmental groups—before issuing building permits.

The leverage exerted by intraorganizational watchdogs also can be increased by bolstering their job security. Under a recently enacted Michigan law, for example, employees who are fired or disciplined for reporting alleged regulatory violations to public authorities are entitled to sue their employers for restitution plus attorneys' fees. To prevent abuses of this privilege, Alan Westin has written, "A sound whistle blower's law ought to require an employee, before going public, to use a company's own internal procedures for complaint"; this in turn would create an inducement for firms to establish meaningful internal complaint systems.[26]

A more direct and intrusive method of enhancing the influence of in-house regulators is to change by law the enterprise's authority structure, assigning legally enforceable powers to internal regulatory officials. For example, FDA "good manufacturing practice" regulations for pharmaceuticals require each plant to have a quality assurance unit with responsibility and authority to reject raw materials and to prevent shipment of batches that do not meet quality control standards. The quality control unit in plants manufacturing intravenous solutions, according to FDA regulations, must have those powers plus the duty and authority to "reject the design, engineering, and physical facilities" of the plant and equipment "if, in the opinion of the quality control unit, it is not suitable or adequate" or "not capable of holding the product invulnerable to contamination."[27] Conversations with several officials from one such plant indicate that quality control officials do in fact exercise these powers, even over the objections of production managers. Similar duties and legal power could be given to key officials in other settings, such as officials in chemical plants with responsibility for controlling emissions or disposal of hazardous materials, although it obviously is possible to go too far in this regard.

In some instances, worker safety legislation has conferred on employees the power to override decisions by their superiors. Federal truck safety regulations instruct drivers to check each vehicle themselves for equipment defects or unsafe loading and authorize them to refuse to drive a truck that they feel is unsafe. The Supreme Court recently upheld an OSHA rule that authorizes a worker to refuse to perform a task if the worker "reasonably believes" he or she would risk death or serious injury, and if there is not "sufficient time or opportunity" to call in an OSHA inspector to assess the danger. The regulation also requires the employee first to "have sought from his employer, and been unable to obtain, a correction of the dangerous condition."[28] The resulting "right to refuse work the employee fears is highly dangerous" enhances the power of workers to serve as self-protective regulators on many issues, although the potential for abuse of this power suggests it could lead to considerable labor-management-OSHA conflict. Its real potential lies in stimulating more institutionalized procedures, in which the worker or his representative has some clout, for worker-management consultation over safety issues.

The Swedish experience provides one model for institutionalizing worker power over job safety and health decisions. Pursuant to a 1949 law, each Swedish factory must have a safety steward, elected or appointed by the local labor union, for each 25 to 50 production workers, depending on the size of the plant. The safety stewards—not individual workers—are empowered by law to halt operations on any machine or assignment they consider unsafe.[29] The threat of unreasonableness is substantially moderated, however, by the extensive training provided for safety stewards* and the requirement of regular labor-management consultation on safety issues.

Les Boden and David Wegman of the Harvard Occupational Health Program believe that OSHA's effectiveness would increase greatly if it could follow the Swedish model.[30] They suggest that one or more workers in every medium-sized and large workplace, selected by fellow employees, should take part in a government-run or sponsored training program in occupational safety and health and that workers' representatives should be encouraged to go directly to management with complaints, rather than to OSHA. Their leverage would be enhanced by an OSHA policy of treating as a willful violation employer failure to correct a danger pointed out and documented by a worker's representative. In effect, workers would have the clout of OSHA inspectors without necessarily obliging them to abide by the rules that constrain OSHA inspectors; they could be more reasonable than the rules allow, and also more forceful. Only experimentation, however, would show whether such a proposal could be implemented without risking unwarranted harassment of management by workers. OSHA probably should retain discretion whether or not to punish an employer who fails to follow an employee suggestion, and the sanction should be applied only if the uncorrected danger is unambiguously serious.

In fact, the Boden-Wegman proposal is simply an extension of a process established in many factories and mines by collective bargaining.[31] In one aluminum plant we visited, for example, the bargaining agreement empowers a fearful worker to call in a member of the union safety committee to discuss the matter with his foreman, and if they agree, to have corrective action taken at once; if they cannot agree, a company safety engineer and the full-time union safety officer (whose salary is paid by the company) are summoned. Failing to reach agreement at that level, the union can call OSHA or file a grievance, although this

---

*Both union-designated safety stewards and industrial foremen are paid to attend 20 to 40 hours of basic health and safety training provided by the Swedish government and financed by a tax on employers. Full-time stewards also receive specialized training in chemical hazards, dust control, and the like; the training materials are developed with industry participation.

has not been necessary. Routing complaints through the union safety specialists, moreover, seems to cut down on unreasonable employee complaints because the union specialist quickly develops a certain expertise and a sense of which hazard-abatement measures are most worth fighting for. In an automobile assembly plant with a similar labor-management agreement, a full-time union health and safety representative told us of two hazards—worker exposure to lead dust and fumes from glue that gave workers headaches—that he was able to get abated even though there were no violations of OSHA standards in either case. We interviewed the officers of a local truck-drivers union who had obtained an arrangement whereby supervisors and maintenance workers were obligated to respond in writing to "gripe sheets" filed by drivers, thus creating a written record that would expose any failure to cure safety hazards in each truck. A critical feature of these apparent success stories is not that government regulations (or collective bargaining agreements) give workers uncontrolled power to stop operations they say are dangerous, but that they turn selected workers into additional intraorganizational experts on safety and health and establish systems for communication and dispute resolution.

In several other settings, government has followed a due process strategy to enhance the effectiveness of private regulatory systems. Requiring organizations to set up mechanisms for dealing with complaints with some degree of procedural fairness will, it is hoped, provide adversely affected individuals greater influence over organizational policies. Under the Magnuson-Moss Act, for example, sellers of consumer goods are encouraged to establish fixed procedures to handle consumer complaints concerning warranty coverage. The incentive for sellers to do so is that dissatisfied consumers are obliged to resort to the seller's informal settlement procedure (provided it is written in the warranty and meets FTC standards) before taking civil action in the courts.[32] Under the Education for All Handicapped Children Act, Congress imposed only very general standards on local school districts—mentally and physically handicapped children are entitled to an "appropriate education" in the "least restrictive environment"—but required districts to establish procedures for annual consultation with parents about written educational plans tailored to the child's needs.[33] Adaptation of such models to control risks arising from corporate action is at least worthy of consideration on a case-by-case basis.

INCREASING ORGANIZATIONAL COMPETENCE

To regulatory officials, a major weakness in some intraorganizational control systems is the incompetence of their managers or of the operatives whose actions are the objects of control. Experienced truck safety inspectors, for example, complain that in some companies, people without proper experience are put in charge of maintenance and often have an eye to moving on to other positions in the company as soon as they can. When maintenance management is weak and mechanics do not receive adequate training and pay, it is hard for them to insist on proper safety procedures. Regulations calling for adequate apprenticeship programs for mechanics and requiring an experienced person to be assigned to maintenance management, therefore, may be more important than reams of detailed government regulations prescribing specific maintenance procedures and equipment standards.[34] Many experienced regulatory officials agree that the most important single factor in the quality of nursing homes is not the content of the regulations or enforcement practices, but the quality and professionalism of the chief on-the-scene administrator for each facility. In California, the legislature responded to this belief by enacting a requirement that each home must be run by a licensed administrator who meets certain training or experience requirements.

There is only so much a competent chief can do, however, if the ultimate source of danger is the actions or inactions of incompetent employees whose work is not entirely routinized and checkable by mechanical quality control systems. The effectiveness of self-regulation systems in these cases can sometimes be enhanced, however, by mandatory training for those employees. The idea is by no means a new one. Airline pilots must be trained and retrained, as prescribed by FAA regulations. Drivers for trucking companies must meet special requirements set forth in Department of Transportation regulations. Sometimes the enterprise can be required to do the training, as in the case of Cal-OSHA regulations obligating employers to conduct regular occupational safety-training programs for workers. Sometimes the government can conduct part of the training. After the Three Mile Island accident was attributed to the incompetence of company technicians who misread gauges and were confused by complex warning devices, the Nuclear Regulatory Commission ordered operators of similar plants to attend

NRC training seminars analyzing the Pennsylvania incident. Some observers suggest more stringent regulations to govern the qualifications and training of all nuclear plant operating personnel, so that they might resemble the elite nuclear submarine crews that have served effectively and safely for a good number of years.[35] Requiring special training for operators in other positions of special responsibility, such as drivers of trucks containing hazardous chemical wastes, might be a powerful supplement, or, in some cases, even a substitute, for detailed direct regulation.

Sometimes improving the competence of key personnel presents economic problems. Market conditions may deter employers from paying for training or from paying high enough salaries to motivate them adequately. In California, the frustrations of attempting to mandate elusive nursing home care standards such as "humane treatment" through specific regulations led the state legislature to find that "quality of patient care . . . is dependent upon the competence of the personnel."[36] It also concluded that high turnover (partly due to low pay) and general incompetence of nurses' aides were major causes of poor care. Moreover, it appeared that Medicare and Medicaid fees for patients were not high enough to enable most nursing homes to pay higher salaries. A 1977 law, therefore, established a training and certification program for nurses' aides. As an inducement to participate, the law also provided state funds to help finance the training programs and to pay 20 cents an hour salary increases to aides who were certified. In 1978, the legislature increased the minimum wage law for aides (by an average of 18 cents an hour) and added another increment of 18 cents for those who stayed on the job more than three months. Finally, the legislature provided a subsidy to nursing homes to help pay for those increases.[37]

THE HAZARDS OF OVER-SELF-REGULATION

The California nursing home law, with its mounting wage costs and government subsidies, highlights an important point: the logic of creating and improving self-regulatory systems can easily lead to the same unreasonable results as direct regulation, such as expenditures on specially trained personnel or self-inspection routines that exceed the resulting benefits. Nor is this merely a logical possibility. Despite the impression that delegating ultimate decisions or precautionary measures to private enterprises is an obviously reasonable way of achieving goals, government-mandated self-regulation schemes operate, not infrequently, in an unreasonable and counterproductive manner. For example, a Los Angeles city councilman who proclaimed himself "the first avowed environmentalist elected to public office in Los Angeles" and an indefatigable worker for environmentalist causes wrote in 1978, ". . . with accumulating experience, I am willing to say aloud what I suspect many other environmentalists may believe: *EIRs* [Environmental Impact Reports] *have grown beyond control.* Rather than a procedure to identify and deal with environmental issues, the EIR process has turned into an administrative morass costly to everyone, especially the taxpayers."[38] It is worthwhile, therefore, to examine how and why self-regulation can go awry.

Unreasonableness in direct regulation often occurs because regulatory authorities prescribe specific precautionary devices or abatement methods that, while useful in many settings, are inappropriate or unnecessary in others. Mandatory self-regulation, on the other hand, would seem to avoid this trap by merely ordering enterprises to meet certain *procedural* requirements, such as designating responsible personnel, installing their own control systems, and reporting on their operation. The *substantive* decisions could be left to each enterprise, such as deciding what problems are truly significant in its particular operation and devising appropriate remedies. But procedural requirements can be just as overinclusive as substantive ones, and sometimes just as burdensome. The delays and expense and distortion of modern-day criminal trials[39] are brought about by complex rules of criminal *procedure,* elaborated step-by-step to prevent the recurrence of specific unjust acts, but made applicable to all cases, even those in which the probability of injustice, given all the checks in the system, is very small. That same drive toward uniform treatment and closing procedural loopholes characterizes the elaboration of rules in many mandatory self-regulation programs.

The scenario should be familiar. A serious accident occurs and is traced to a weakness in the internal control system of an enterprise. The legislature or regulatory officials require not just the one enterprise but all those that might cause similar harms to institute certain procedural improvements, such as conducting more frequent self-inspections, appointing a full-time specialist to a key control position, or establishing a committee or a training program. But these steps inevitably will be unnecessary or nearly so in a substantial number of good apple enterprises that for any number of reasons already have effective internal control systems.

Moreover, each time another accident occurs someplace, revealing another weakness, a new round of procedural prescriptions, double-checks, and conformity reports or signatures will be added. The extent to which mandatory self-inspection systems can become overloaded was revealed when the Federal Railroad Administration, responding to the Carter administration's pressure, announced that it was eliminating certain "unnecessary and burdensome maintenance and [self-]inspection requirements" and that this would save the railroad industry over $100 million each year.[40] Similarly, federal regulations requiring universities to establish Human Subjects Committees gradually expanded to require prior clearance not only for medical experiments but for the administration of psychological tests and questionnaires because some queries might be disturbing to some subjects or because the results might be used to perpetuate racist attitudes or practices.[41]

The question then becomes, why haven't enterprises subject to mandated self-regulation simply enforced their self-regulatory programs in a flexible manner, concentrating only on the truly serious risks? After all, the advantage of self-regulation, presumably, is that it can be more flexible than direct government regulation. But that all depends on how the government polices self-regulatory systems. It is rarely easy for government officials to evaluate the quality or effectiveness of such efforts; consequently the regulators may write ever-more-detailed guidelines stipulating the kinds of things a good self-regulation system should contain. Thus government requirements that employers establish safety training programs for employees—a measure that seems to decentralize the task of identifying and preventing hazards—become encumbered with detailed regulations prescribing precisely what must be taught, how often, and how. The self-regulating enterprise, moreover, is instructed to set forth the details of its training, self-inspection, or quality control program in written form.[42] That accomplished, government inspectors evaluate self-regulatory systems by checking the enterprise's written procedures against government guidelines and by making sure the enterprise sticks to its own written procedures and standards. The more regulators or advocacy groups mistrust the motivation of the self-regulating enterprises as a class, or the more regulatory inspectors lack the expertise to evaluate a particular self-regulation system, the more likely they will insist that the enterprise adhere strictly to the written procedures.

The result, of course, is that government "guidelines" come to be treated as binding rules and privately formulated procedures come to be treated with the same legal sanctity as direct government regulations. In the human subjects protection area, for example, the University of California, like many others, felt compelled to write voluntary regulations that directly tracked the all-encompassing "guidelines" promulgated by the Department of Health, Education and Welfare. The university committee, then, justifiably feared that excusing any research projects from review might incur complaints from "true believers" and criticism from HEW for "violating your own rules," a criticism that could lead to a cut-off of all federal research funds to the university. Similarly, OSHA has penalized employers for failure to ensure compliance with the company's own safety rules, even if no OSHA regulation has been violated.[43] A pending Food Safety Act quite sensibly calls upon all manufacturers to identify critical points in their production processes and to write up procedures for controlling and monitoring the hazards that arise at those points. But it also characterizes any food not manufactured in strict compliance with those procedures as illegally "adulterated" and makes it an offense not to report such variation to the FDA. This led a spokesman for the food industry to complain vehemently that the act "commands each processor to write his own criminal code, and never vary from it, unwittingly or otherwise."[44]

It is altogether too easy, moreover, for procedural self-regulation measures to be imposed as an additive obligation, on top of the enterprise's duty to adhere to all substantive government regulations. For example, recently updated FDA "good manufacturing practice" regulations for drugs require each plant to have a designated quality assurance unit, with responsibility and authority to reject new materials and prevent shipment of batches that do not meet quality control standards. But the regulations still insist on regular FDA inspections and strict enforcement of identical federally prescribed quality control and facilities standards for all plants. Occasionally, intraorganizational improvements are traded for the relaxation of direct regulation (e.g., Cal-OSHA's agreement with Bechtel Corporation to suspend enforcement on a large construction site in return for a joint union-management safety program). These trades, however, are rarities. For regulators, it is always politically risky to take any action that could be interpreted as weakening worker or consumer protection, and repealing specific direct regulations (however ineffective or unreasonable or both) in return for the promise of better self-regulation falls in that risky category. Consequently, mandatory self-regulation measures often merely have magnified the unreasonableness that stems from the continuing obligation to comply with direct regulations.

Requiring companies to hire public directors or specially trained safety managers also can tilt over into unreasonableness if imposed in an across-the-board manner on smaller firms as well as large ones, on good apples as well as bad ones. Such measures seem appropriate only if imposed selectively, for example, on specific firms or segments of an industry that have had a demonstrably poor record; we ordinarily do not require probation officers for citizens with a record of law-abidingness. Similarly, there is enough evidence of the artificial rigidities (and high costs) of credentialism that we should not rush into licensing every plant manager, lab technician, food handler, and brakes tester whenever a few have acted irresponsibly.[45] But norms of equal treatment of competitors make *selective* imposition of such requirements difficult, except as a court-imposed penalty for serious violations of direct regulations, and there is always a possibility that legislators will overreact to serious accidents by requiring all enterprises to hire licensed compliance specialists, regardless of the costs and benefits in particular firms.

Mandatory self-regulation also can magnify unreasonable paperwork burdens. When government delegates responsibility for preventing harms to individual enterprises, it invariably requires proof that those delegated responsibilities are met. Enterprises are required to file compliance plans, to reduce all their procedures to written rules and manuals, to document faithful adherence to their self-inspection and quality-control routines, to keep records of all the activities and decisions of designated compliance officers or committees, and to file reports indicating the depth of their consideration of critical problems. These measures for detailed documentation, however, conflict with the goal of making self-regulation more reasonable than direct regulation.

One of the principal aims of relying on self-regulation, after all, is to permit people close to the local situation to identify problems and discover solutions that might not be obvious to outside inspectors. We necessarily want these people (e.g., the quality control engineer in a factory or the principal investigator in a biomedical research project) to have the discretion that permits this aim to be achieved. They cannot be completely programmed without destroying the whole purpose of self-regulation. But the regulatory officials who oversee self-regulation are expected above all to discourage or discover *abuses* of discretion that might cause social harm. Each exercise of discretion by private experts, therefore, must be explained, justified, and supported by data, all arranged in the preprogrammed categories set forth in official reporting forms. Moreover, this paperwork burden falls on precisely those individuals who are sufficiently talented or trained to be given discretionary tasks in the first place; for only they are aware of the subtle nuances that might justify their own discretionary conduct. Only the physician who has studied the case and actually made the decision, for example, can know why he has ordered these lab tests rather than those, or chosen this surgical intervention in order to avoid that form of radiation therapy. And even he may not know precisely his own thought processes, for, after all, "professional judgment" based on experience and hard-to-communicate intuition is bound to play a role in many cases.

If the public regulatory regime were able to distinguish categories of conduct for which less intensified documentation were permitted, or if the documentation could be executed by less valuable personnel, much of the sterile paper-shuffling that increasingly afflicts professionals' work could be avoided. But there are limits to how much seemingly unmonitored self-regulation can be tolerated by public regulators, and there is a natural tendency for the latter to err on the side of requiring more documentation rather than less. As one nursing home inspector told us, "Documentation—that's the name of the game. But nurses are notoriously poor documenters; they do a lot more than they give themselves credit for." The inspector did not ask the next logical question: why nurses had to bother giving themselves credit in the first place. A professional nurse *should* be more concerned with doing creditable deeds than with preparing a creditable record, and systematic efforts to push them toward the latter are bound to be resented when the recording takes a lot of time away from the doing. For similar reasons, special education teachers resent the enormous amount of time they must spend preparing the detailed reports and plans required for every learning-impaired student because they would rather be teaching or analyzing the truly hard-to-diagnose cases.

A second problem that arises from the elaboration of documentation requirements is organizational and personal defensiveness, which actually works against the interests of those the newly reinforced private regulatory system is supposed to protect. Agencies living under the shadow of litigation for alleged inadequacies in their environmental impact statements formalize the internal processes for preparing the documents and write them the way agency lawyers advise to make sure the documents will withstand judicial scrutiny. In the course of this retreat into legalism, the intellectual and analytical objectives of the EIS tend to fall by the wayside. When the environmental analyst is afraid to say that most risks are trivial or moderate, lest his work be attacked as a whitewash in court or in public hearings, it is harder to draw attention to the few risks he believes are really worth worrying about.

When an enterprise seeks to protect itself from lawsuits or regulatory review by emphasizing formal compliance with procedural requirements, the enterprise appears legalistic and all the more untrustworthy to the individuals or groups that the procedural rules are designed to protect. Referring to "mechanically impersonal" compliance by school administrators with the *Goss v. Lopez* requirement of due process hearings for students charged with disciplinary infractions, David Kirp observes, "Defensiveness further erodes the strength of the school's assertion of institutional competence and the credibility of its demands for trust."[46] It can result in a decline into adversarial battle over procedural failings—for under self-regulatory schemes procedural violations provide the main point of legal and political leverage for those who doubt the enterprise's good faith. The communication originally sought by the procedural mechanisms is cut off. According to one environmentalist observer, NEPA probably has had "a negative impact on public involvement," which had been "well established long before NEPA. By tying citizen participation to a process of reviewing and filing documents, NEPA . . . sterilized and stultified the dialogue between agencies and the public that was beginning to develop in the late 1960s."[47] Another manifestation of defensiveness is the sanitizing of written records. In the wake of legislation that gave parents the right to see their children's permanent school files, many records were destroyed or expurgated. As Mark Yudof and David Kirp put it, the legislation "promises to promote among teachers an oral tradition which would rival the Navajo nation."

OVERCOMING UNREASONABLENESS

The preceding examples demonstrate that mandatory self-regulation programs, like direct regulation, can lead to unreasonable costs, displacement of constructive effort, and destructive defensiveness. The critical issues, however, are whether the risks of these adverse effects are lesser or greater under self-regulation, and whether they are less or more subject to correction.

Since key decisionmakers in private regulatory systems, even if subject to detailed procedural rules and legal sanctions for not following them, tend to be less susceptible to the legalistic ethos than are government regulators, self-regulation seems a plus. Employed full-time in the enterprise itself, they are sensitive to the organization's basic mission and aware of how self-regulatory methods, if pushed too far, might have adverse consequences. While concerned with protecting the enterprise in dealings with regulatory authorities, they typically need be much less concerned than the government regulatory official with protecting themselves. Hence they are more likely to resist literal interpretations of the rules, to accept substantial compliance, and to fight for discretion when the requirements are inappropriate or unduly burdensome in particular cases. University professors who complain about requirements imposed by their peers on the human subjects committee or by university affirmative action officers, and production managers who castigate the chief of quality control for insisting too rigidly on adherence to certain testing requirements, undoubtedly would prefer these situations to those in which the human subjects committee and the affirmative action office was staffed by federal bureaucrats, or quality control schedules were established and enforced directly by FDA or National Highway Traffic Safety Administration officials. When the first-line regulators are private professionals, the substantive standards are likely to be more reasonable and more flexibly administered, and procedural rules are more likely to be interpreted in light of their substantive consequences.

In addition, excessive procedural and documentation requirements of the kind that sometimes burden mandatory self-regulatory programs are probably somewhat easier to amend and moderate, on the average, than excessively stringent substantive regulations. One reason is that the cry of "too much paperwork" tends to be politically more acceptable than "too high safety standards." Even environmentalists did not protest when President Carter told Congress in an environmental message that "We do not want impact statements that are measured by the inch or weighed by the pound." Another reason is that it is often quite possible to devise simplified forms or less formal procedures and make a plausible case that they would not substantially reduce the level of protection.[48]

On balance, therefore, government is likely to be more flexible and responsive in dealing with reinforced self-regulation programs than in enforcing direct regulation. As a result, they will be more likely to succeed in eliciting cooperation and in keeping regulatory requirements in touch with the particular needs and costs in different enterprises. Trading direct enforcement of detailed substantive regulations for some kind of strengthened self-regulatory mechanisms represents a fairly promising strategy for controlling social harms and reinforcing social responsibility.

CHAPTER NINE

MANDATORY DISCLOSURE

•

One of the many reasons to look to government inspectors for protection from various social harms is that consumers and workers often lack the information that would enable them to act as their own inspectors. How many among us, after all, can understand the technical characteristics of household products that increase the risks of accidents or decrease product reliability or quality? Surrounded by strange chemicals and complex machinery, how many workers can understand the true hazards to which they are vulnerable or know how to protect themselves from those hazards? Who can determine, standing in the reception room of a nursing home, whether the staff will treat his or her disabled parent humanely? "Hiddenness" need not imply danger or evil, but it does in fact permit the existence of wrongdoing or honest but potentially injurious error.

As we have seen, one solution to the problems caused by hiddenness is to deploy squadrons of government inspectors to penetrate the surface of things and, in effect, to command the correction of the problems beneath that surface. Another approach is to make the citizen his own inspector; the government attempts to ensure that consumers and workers themselves are given the information necessary to uncover and avoid hidden risks or sources of injustice.

The power conferred by information works in two rather different ways: first, with pertinent information the individual consumer or worker can avoid the risky product or situation and, instead, pursue the more secure, more reliable alternative. Second, the aggregate market pressure of informed consumers and workers forces producers to furnish safer and more reliable products and safer and healthier workplaces.

Information that affects the decisions of even a small number of individuals can exert large pressures on producers, since the mechanisms of the marketplace make producers especially sensitive to changes in the marginal demand for their products or for jobs in their workplaces. Even relatively small percentages may be quite large in absolute terms: if only 5 percent of breakfast cereal consumers switch to another brand, after mandatory disclosure of nutritional information, this could mean one million fewer boxes of cereal sold. And if the costs of furnishing the information (plus the governmental costs of seeing that it is done) are not high, such a policy could show rather impressive net benefits in improving nutrition.[1]

In seeking to give information and therefore power to individuals, the government can generate and disseminate the information itself, using its own considerable resources for data-gathering, education, and propaganda. Second, the government can subsidize or otherwise assist private organizations engaged in gathering and providing relevant information to consumers, workers, or citizens at large. For example, OSHA has a limited program of grants for university-based nonprofit organizations that hold workshops and produce written materials designed to educate trade union officials and workers about common workplace hazards. Third, government can require private citizens and organizations, in the course of normally private relations, to furnish information to one another. It is the third approach, covering what are commonly known as mandatory disclosure programs, that we explore in this chapter.

The granddaddies of mandatory disclosure efforts are the Securities and Exchange acts of 1933 and 1934, which required promoters of new stock issues to file extensive registration statements with a new regulatory agency, the Securities and Exchange Commission, and instructed all corporations registered with the agency to furnish periodic reports of certified financial information. Although there is no conclusive evidence that the acts have prevented fraud and price manipulation (over and above more intense market pressures for honesty), they seem to have bolstered the widespread *belief* that the SEC is an effective antifraud enforcer, and this belief has probably contributed to the pool of social trust necessary to maintain a healthy commercial system.[2]

Another example of mandatory disclosure is the informal agreement reached in 1970 by the Federal Trade Commission and the major American cigarette manufacturers, whereby each package of cigarettes would show the number of milligrams of tar and nicotine contained in each cigarette. From data collected by Richard Posner, it appears that, in the years following the implementation of agreement, the market share of the brands in the lower tar and nicotine category increased at a dramatically higher rate than would have been projected from the 1965–70 trend.[3]

Mandatory disclosure also can induce socially responsible behavior on the part of producers by enhancing consumers' bargaining power in face-to-face interactions, even after the time of purchase. Under a 1972 law, used automobile dealers in Wisconsin have been required to inspect each car they sell and to record on a prescribed disclosure form whether designated items (e.g., brakes and lights) are "OK" or "NOT OK." Buyers sign the disclosure statement and are given a copy. The program seems to have had an appreciable impact on used car sales practices. In a study by John Nevin and David Trubek, about 30 percent of dealers surveyed said they now inspect cars more thoroughly.[4] Dealers reported spending between $50 and $75, on the average, to repair safety items on the mandated checklist and about as much for nonsafety items. Interestingly, the study indicates that this has occurred even though many dealers do not show the buyer the disclosure statement until the deal is virtually clinched, and many buyers do not even read the disclosure statement. The main effect of the law probably has been achieved by increasing consumer leverage *after* purchase, in the course of resolving disputes with dealers about alleged defects and the dealers' responsibility to fix them.[5]

Although we have seen no studies concerning the effectiveness of OSHA's and the Environmental Protection Agency's regulations requiring prominent labeling of packages or drums containing hazardous chemicals, interviews in industry provide anecdotal evidence of their impact. The effect is what might be called consciousness raising. In a wire and cable manufacturing company that does not have a trained industrial hygienist on its staff, a young company safety director showed us the warning letters he receives from suppliers of hazardous chemicals, pursuant to government regulation, and claimed these warnings have sensitized him to this important health problem. His company now automatically sends letters to suppliers of chemicals, plastics, and solvents purchased for the first time, asking for identification of hazards and recommended handling information. The safety director of an automobile assembly plant told us that mandated warning labels on drums of solvents used in the plant had stimulated frequent inquiries from workers about the risks they were exposed to.

The mandatory disclosure strategy could also extend to other situations now governed by direct regulation. Nursing homes, for example, might be required to post, in a prominent manner, staffing and care practices of interest to the relatives of patients. Factories might be required to post in the hiring office current and comparative injury rates for most jobs,* or even put up signs, visible to the public, indicating the quantities of major pollutants they discharge into the air and water. A congressional committee has proposed that government inspectors should give "good," "average," or "poor" grades to the managements of nuclear generating plants and make those grades public.[6] Mandated disclosure programs such as these may be undesirable or ineffective. But some may be valuable as supplements to, or even as replacements for, governmental promulgation of substantive standards and enforcement. More important, they might offer a means to accomplish the objectives of direct regulation at a much lower cost in unreasonableness.

MANDATORY DISCLOSURE VERSUS DIRECT REGULATION

Direct regulatory rules based on uniform standards impose all-or-nothing choices on both producers and consumers. Information strategies, on the other hand, permit variety to flourish and allow people to choose what suits them best. Under a strictly enforced regime of direct regulation, substandard or risky offerings are simply not available under the law. Yet some people would be perfectly willing to accept somewhat riskier or lower quality offerings in exchange for certain benefits, such as lower product prices or higher wages; they accept less in quality but incur lower costs. The goal of reasonableness is served by thus having benefits and costs kept in close alignment.

Reasonableness also includes responsiveness, whereby regulated parties under certain conditions have the leverage to bend the regulatory regime in the direction of greater economic reasonableness. The underlying premise is that the regulatory regime should recognize the moral autonomy and at least the potential for moral integrity in the people and institutions being regulated. Thus mandatory disclosure policies are "responsive" in that they enable regulated enterprises to select the appropriate balancing point between risk and cost of risk reduction in its products or facilities, provided that the remaining risks are disclosed (and hence adjustable on the basis of consumer reaction). This idea usually is de-

---

*Under the Occupational Safety and Health Act, employers are now obligated to maintain a log of all workplace injuries and to post the results of OSHA inspections in a place accessible to workers.

fended, however, in terms of liberty for the consumer or worker rather than responsiveness to the producer: if the individual consumer can choose, the individual should choose, and government regulation ought not to constrain his freedom to do so.[7] A good case in point is the problem of saccharin, which appears to be a weak carcinogen in laboratory test animals, and hence may be a weak carcinogen in man as well.[8] Yet saccharin, as the major low-calorie sweetner currently on the market, has benefits as well as risks. (The principal benefit is that dieters can follow their diets without having to forgo entirely the taste of sweetened foods.) Since the individual's choice between saccharin's risks and benefits affects no one but himself and his family, there is no compelling reason for the government to step in and impose a collective choice on the public as a whole. At the same time, though, in order to facilitate intelligent choices, the government should somehow disseminate the information about the risks of the substance.*

Certain technical and political considerations may also argue for relying on an information strategy. For the many industrial chemicals whose effects are not fully understood, for example, it is difficult to formulate mandatory and uniform maximum exposure standards that strike a reasonable balance between risk and expense of control. In such cases, even if direct regulation is ultimately a preferable solution, it may make sense to use mandatory labels, warnings, and other forms of information as an interim protective measure, pending the completion of more detailed scientific and economic analyses.[9] Or it may be politically impossible to impose a "good" standard, and given this problem, a rather imperfect information strategy might be superior to the best of the politically feasible direct regulations. Automobile tires, for instance, probably come in more varieties and subvarieties than a perfectly efficient marketplace would produce. But there is no consensus among either consumers or producers as to what "good" standardization of the product would look like; and politically it is impossible, and perhaps undesirable, to impose standardization of performance, as opposed to

---

*The Food and Drug Administration followed this approach recently when it was petitioned by the Health Research Group, a Washington consumer organization, to ban Darvon, a widely prescribed pain killer, after evidence accumulated that the drug had in numerous cases resulted in death when taken along with alcohol, tranquilizers, and sedatives. Instead, the FDA persuaded the manufacturer to distribute warning leaflets to consumers and physicians, advising the latter to be cautious in prescribing Darvon and to counsel patients on its danger. The FDA itself sent a "drug bulletin" to a million physicians and health professionals, and planned a follow-up. *HEW News,* July 30, 1979.

safety, features on the tire manufacturers. Arguably, then, a third-best alternative is for government to require tire manufacturers to furnish better performance information about their products, for example, expected tread-life, traction, or blowout resistance.

Of course, an information strategy is a priori inappropriate for certain problems and certain objectives. Information is potential power, but if the complementary power resources needed to make information actually work are not available to the citizen, the consumer, or the worker, then information is beside the point. Because current statutes prohibit certain types and degrees of pollution, informing citizens of who is emitting how much of what pollutant might make sense, but in the era before antipollution statutes were passed, such information would have been of relatively little use (except perhaps to aid the building of a coalition to press for passage of the statutes). Information would probably not be as effective a strategy as direct regulation in the worker safety area if the object of regulation is to provide minimum protection even to the worker who is desperate enough to take a job he thinks is too risky for the pay. To take another example, information as to who were the most antiblack employers in Mississippi, during the pre-civil rights era, would not have helped black job seekers as much as effectively enforced antidiscrimination statutes.

These examples raise an interesting, but usually overlooked, issue concerning the relative merits of information and direct regulation strategies. Ideally, the claim that mandatory disclosure might be more reasonable than direct regulation should also stipulate that both strategies can achieve comparable levels of effectiveness in preventing harms, and for some hazards that stipulation cannot be made. But for others it can, even though at first glance it might appear that mere information could not possibly be as effective as direct regulation. Such a presumption, however, fails to recognize that it may be difficult to implement an effective direct regulatory policy because, for example, there are not enough competent inspectors, it is difficult to enact sufficiently specific standards, sanctions are weak and delayed, or legalistic resistance is easily engendered. Under an information strategy, individuals are their own ubiquitous inspectors, tailor their own standards to particular risks, and invoke their own sanctions (such as denying patronage to a firm or demanding certain improvements in working conditions), and in some circumstances, these sanctions are powerful indeed. And even an imperfectly effective mandatory disclosure program might be preferable to a direct regulation program that is underfunded, politically embattled, and badly administered.

Of course, it is also difficult to implement an effective and reasonable information program. The problems of requiring disclosure are surprisingly complicated, and there are substantial tendencies to require "overdisclosure"—the expensive gathering and dissemination of information that benefits few, that may be misleading, and that may unnecessarily inhibit socially useful activities. Of course, these are merely tendencies. While it is sometimes possible to combat them, it is not clear what would be required to produce more consistent successes in ensuring the reasonableness of mandatory disclosure programs. In fact, mandatory disclosure policies are not very numerous and have not been much researched. Our analysis of the problems and prospects of the disclosure strategy, therefore, is necessarily more theoretical than empirical.

THE TENDENCY TOWARD OVERDISCLOSURE

Assumption: The marketplace plus word-of-mouth communication channels probably manage to supply nearly all the information needs and wants of nearly all the citizenry; hence there is not much left of general interest for mandatory disclosures to disclose. Contrary assumption: We are awash in a sea of ignorance and therefore vulnerable to any and every predatory move by producer and employer interests. Although more widely held, the "sea of ignorance" assumption is almost surely further from the truth. Mandatory disclosure requirements could thus end up compelling the disclosure of information that most of the public do not care about very much; such requirements would be both ineffective in controlling misconduct and unreasonably costly.

To see how the marketplace works to supply information to those who want it, consider first the demand side. Although highly precise and highly reliable information about consumer products, to take one example, is quite hard to come by, there are very few important purchasing decisions for which great precision and reliability are really necessary. In most cases, rules of thumb and cognitive shortcuts through the plethora of information that is available are quite sufficient. Consumers rely heavily on their own experience, on brand names or firm names with an established reputation for quality, on any experts they can find in their community, and perhaps most importantly, on the experience of their friends and coworkers.[10]

As for the supply side, producers (and to a lesser extent, perhaps, employers) have an incentive to furnish whatever true information puts their product, service, or job in a better light than the offerings of their competitors. Manufacturers who want to make safety a selling point will go to some lengths to advertise this feature, as Volvo did for its automobiles during the 1960s. Scores of products come with detailed instructions for safe and proper use, including warnings about potential hazards, *without* the spur of government-mandated disclosure rules, partly because of the threat of lawsuits for damages by injured customers, and partly because publicity about illness or injuries caused by a product can have terrible effects on future sales. Although not all foods are equally healthy, since there is consumer demand for healthy foods, a flourishing industry thrives on representing its own food products as being especially nutritious and free of allegedly harmful additives. (Even if most products do not emphasize their unhealthy ingredients on their labels, the ready availability of some products that tout their purity powerfully conveys information about the others by implication.) Since durability is a valued attribute of clothing and of household furniture, consumers often go to high quality retail outlets for such goods, looking, in effect, for insurance against purchasing shoddy goods.[11]

Of course, information supplied by self-interested sellers of goods and services may be truncated or tainted in some way, particularly if buyers have no easy way to police the accuracy or the completeness of the information. This problem applies particularly to goods and services that have complex technical characteristics, so that a buyer cannot inspect them adequately at the time of purchase. The market does solve this problem in part, however, in that it furnishes—for a price—individuals and firms that specialize in inspection and quality control. Title insurance companies are a good example, as they assume, for a fee, the risks of erroneously authenticating the title to real property. Mechanics can be hired to inspect used cars for prospective buyers for whom the area under the hood is a threatening jungle.* Magazines and newspapers readily print articles that disclose the latest scientific findings on the effectiveness

---

*Labor unions presumably could perform similar services, for their members and others, by providing individual job seekers with information about hazards associated with particular jobs in a worksite, or about comparative injury or illnesses for different factories in an industry. Few unions, however, seem to perform that function systematically.

of vitamin supplements or the hazards posed by various foods or chemicals.

Of course, not all consumers take advantage of such intermediaries or canvass their neighbors for information about providers of goods and services; some fail to do so out of ignorance or isolation, others because they feel they cannot afford either the time or the expense. Where such cases are widespread, the market and other private sources might be considered to have produced an incomplete distribution of protective information, and a mandatory disclosure law might be proposed to help provide the poor or ignorant citizen the same level of protection as the sophisticated or the prudent. Under other circumstances, it will be difficult even for the average person to obtain adequate protective information from private sources, perhaps because there is no easy way to distinguish the fly-by-night operator from the reputable one, or because defects associated with products or workplaces do not become apparent for a long while, or because the relevant information is otherwise very costly to produce, extract, or disseminate. Under these conditions, notwithstanding the value of a reputation for honesty and the threat of lawsuits for fraud, some enterprises will find it easy to withhold what might be called "dirty secrets" about risks or defects associated with their operations or products; preventing the cover-up of such dirty secrets is another justification for mandatory disclosure laws. Still another way in which the private market for reliable information can fail might be called the "cloud of confusion" problem: the attributes of certain products and services are so complex that there are no standard shorthand methods of describing their features. For example, we have no standard, recognized metric for the assessment of physicians' services, automobile safety, or the fairness of personnel officers' hiring decisions. Where such clouds of confusion prevail, a government regulation might compel producers to describe their offerings in a more standardized and informative way.

It is not easy to determine when a condition justifying mandatory disclosure—incomplete distribution of protective information, pervasive withholding of dirty secrets, widespread clouds of confusion—actually exists with respect to any given source of harm, and, if it does, how seriously.[12] Moreover, there seems to be a pervasive tendency for consumer advocates, legislators, and regulators to overestimate the seriousness of such conditions and to underestimate the extent to which the market and private sources produce and disseminate generally adequate amounts of protective information. Perhaps this tendency should not be surprising, given the subtle and often indirect ways in which word-of-mouth communication, concern for reputation, liability law, and specialists in evaluation interact to produce information and to counteract misinformation. Nor does it inspire confidence in many observers that information so produced often issues from self-interested parties who, if they do not conceal the truth, might propagate only the truths that happen to serve their interests. It is easy to underestimate most people's abilities to guard against being misled by partial truths and to correct initial errors, especially if one generalizes from one's own occasional, and inevitable, mistakes or imagines, from an excess of paternalism, that certain groups like the poor are thoroughly unlike oneself. Whatever the reason, underestimating the effectiveness of private information-producing sources is common, and it can easily lead to mandatory disclosure programs that are essentially irrelevant and hence wasteful and unreasonable.

Consider, for example, the 1971 Federal Trade Commission rule requiring the posting of minimum octane ratings of gasoline on dispensing pumps. The FTC alleged that car owners—perhaps because they were misled by oil company advertising—were purchasing high-octane premium grade when lower-octane regular would be sufficient to prevent their engines from "knocking" (the only function of the higher octane, according to the FTC).[13] But the FTC's discussion did not clarify exactly how the translation of the words "regular" and "premium" into octane numbers was supposed to curb consumers' propensity to overbuy. The FTC said merely that the current practice "does not afford to the consumer information with any degree of preciseness as to the range of octane ratings available"[14] nor does it "provide the consumer with a criterion to which he can relate the gasoline with engine requirements of his automobile."[15] (Here, the FTC implied, there existed a cloud of confusion—although perhaps combined with the oil companies' dirty secret that regular gas was adequate.) But automobile owners' manuals *did* typically specify "premium" or "regular," words that constituted a criterion by which the consumer could evaluate his car's needs; and if these words were not precise enough for the FTC, they might nevertheless have been precise enough to meet the needs of most buyers and sellers in the marketplace.

To be sure, not all consumers were happy with the availability of only verbal descriptions at the pump. The FTC reported receiving many letters in support of the proposed trade regulation rule from consumers frustrated in their attempts to shop around for octane-rated gasoline. It seems to us, however, that the real source of frustration was more likely to have been the unavailability of actual product variety than the absence of *information* about product variety. That is, technically sophisticated automobile operators might have believed (rightly or wrongly) that their own vehicles could operate efficiently on an octane grade somewhere *between* "regular" and "premium." But the FTC had ample evidence that gasoline refiners and marketers, at the time the rule was being debated, were in fact introducing intermediate grades, labeled with terms like "plus" or "mid-premium," to satisfy just such consumers; and representatives of the Sun Oil and Continental Oil companies testified that, through advertising and other means, they had been attempting (without much success apparently) to educate consumers to appreciate the value of their intermediately graded products.[16]

Sometimes the market and private sources do *not* produce adequate information, and a mandatory disclosure program might indeed be useful either as a substitute for or as a supplement to direct regulation. Unfortunately, however, the very elements that lead to, say, dirty secrets or clouds of confusion often make it technically difficult to devise an effective and reasonably economical mandatory disclosure program. For example, if the problem is ferreting out dirty secrets, mandatory disclosure is feasible when the secrets come in a fairly standard form, as in the case of defective brakes on used cars or other items susceptible to a short checklist of disclosable facts. But undisclosed defects quite often come in an extraordinary variety of forms, so that regulators will have trouble specifying a single item of information that, if revealed, will uncover the secret. It is not easy, for instance, to think of a single disclosable fact about surgeons—apart from the possibility that they had no license to practice—that would clearly indicate the presence or absence of some hidden area of incompetence. Indeed, if one were to search for a simple indicator, the risk is that surgeons would be compelled to disclose facts that in many instances would actually be misleading, such as the number of malpractice suits filed against them within a given period. Similarly, to compel employers to disclose whether discrimination is among their dirty secrets (and thereby to deter discrimination) one could imagine compulsory disclosure of their minority or female "utilization" rates for each department and hierarchical level. But that information may not be probative of a firm's hiring or promotion criteria; a low proportion of female supervisors, for example, might be misinterpreted by a female job applicant as a sign that the firm currently discriminates in promotion, when in fact the imbalance results from a variety of other factors that would not impede promotion of a competent and ambitious woman.[17]

On the other hand, if disclosure regulations seek to capture the full complexity of the potential range of hidden defects and put individual indicators in proper perspective, the result will often be to compel the disclosure of information that is immensely detailed, costly to assemble and disseminate, and well beyond the information-processing capabilities or interests of most citizens. The SEC has steadily elaborated the range of items that offerors of stock must disclose so that the required prospectuses now contain many items of information that have little relationship to the original objective of preventing fraud and are irrelevant to most investors.[18] To meet the requirements of federal disclosure regulations, a Minnesota bank sent to 115,000 customers a 4,500-word booklet setting forth prescribed details about its electronic funds transfer services; in the middle of the booklet, the bank inserted a sentence offering $10 to any customer who would write "Regulation E" on a postcard and send it to the bank. Not one person answered.[19]

Unfortunately, technical problems in finding an appropriately simple (but not misleading) formula and format may not deter government officials from mandating disclosure. The need to defend one's agency, or oneself, against external criticism for sloth or incompetence applies in regard to developing mandatory disclosure regulations as it does in regard to developing more conventional regulations. In 1966, when the National Traffic and Motor Vehicle Safety Act was passed, widely accepted reference standards for motor vehicle tire performance characteristics did not exist. Consumers presumably were adrift in a cloud of confusion concerning characteristics like treadwear, traction, blowout resistance, and price. Among other things, the act stipulated that within two years the Department of Transportation was to promulgate a "uniform quality grading system" for motor vehicle tires. It took the agency until July 1978 to produce its first set of final regulations on the subject, however, and even these were only partial: they did not cover radial tires, which account for over one-third of all replacement tire sales, and they covered only three performance characteristics—treadwear, traction, and heat resistance at high speeds—out of a much larger universe of possibilities. Even this limited grading system was, and still is, extremely controversial. The system was estimated to cost between $150 million and $200 million per year, or some $.75 to $1.00 per tire, and the test results were alleged to be of dubious value to consumers. *Consumers' Research* magazine wrote in October 1976, "If and when the program goes into effect, it may not provide enough clear and usable information to compensate for its costs. . . ."[20] As of early 1981, the result seemed to be more consumer confusion than enlightenment.[21]

How did this unsatisfactory system emerge? Like the administrators of any regulatory program, officials of the National Highway Traffic Safety Administration sought to avoid criticism and blame, whether from the industry or from consumer advocates. The agency progressed from a strategy of delay to a strategy of minimalism. En route it became entangled in a web of technical dilemmas, and the more it attempted to extricate itself, the more insistently did political and legal forces thrust it back into the web, so that in the end the agency was obliged to adopt an expensive and mediocre set of testing procedures simply in order to buy its way out.

Consider the agency's initial dilemma. Administrators had to decide which of literally dozens of performance characteristics should be graded. To their credit, they did realize that tractive capability and treadwear were inversely related, so that if treadwear were to be graded, either a minimum mandatory traction standard should be established (in the interests of safety) or traction should be graded as well (the course it in fact chose).[22] But agency officials initially proposed to omit both treadwear and traction from the list of properties to be graded, probably because these properties were hard to measure and very salient to consumers. Thus if the required grading system were inaccurate or inadvertently biased, it could have unanticipated and unfortunate effects on buying and production patterns. The agency, therefore, initially proposed measures for properties other than traction and treadwear simply because the agency, after some five years of seeming foot-dragging, was under mounting pressures to come out with *something*.[23]

It seems that one reason for the long delay, and the inadequacy of the proposal when it did come, was the relative lack of expertise in the government agencies working on the problem—the National Bureau of Standards and then the NHTSA. This is not to say that the government technicians were incompetent, only that they were not as competent to work up a tire grading scheme as were industry engineers. But technical assistance from industry was deliberately rejected.[24] Likewise, the industry seems at some relatively early point to have decided to refrain from cooperating.[25] A stalemate developed between the industry and the agency, with each criticizing the other's proposals. Litigation begun in 1973 by as associate of Ralph Nader put a stop to whatever minor agency-industry communication remained.

According to a study published by the General Accounting Office in 1975, there was a period, just before the NHTSA's first proposed grading system was published in the fall of 1971, when interest in the system had virtually evaporated in Congress and in the Transportation Department.[26] Between 1965 and 1971, a number of improvements had been made in tire manufacturing and advertising that somewhat reduced the problems that had prompted Congress to mandate the grading system in the first place. In an effort to eliminate the dirty secrets problem, the FTC in 1966 had adopted guidelines for the labeling and advertising of tires. The tire manufacturers trade association had adopted voluntary safety standards in 1965, which became incorporated in 1971 into the NHTSA's compendium of mandatory safety standards.[27] Yet the development of an expensive disclosure program of doubtful effectiveness moved forward with a momentum of its own. According to an analysis by the National Center for Productivity and Quality of Working Life, ". . . regardless of whether the proposed system was workable or useful, there was no incentive to go to Congress or the agency administrator to admit failure, or to say that a regulation does not make sense, or that given current economic and technological realities it is no longer needed."[28]

THE PROBLEMS OF REGULATING INFORMATION

The prospect of unnecessary or ineffective (and hence unreasonable) mandatory disclosure is enhanced by special characteristics of information as an object of regulatory management: it is difficult to determine how much is enough and what is the most effective way of communicating it.

Consider, for instance, the fact that the most convenient vehicle for communicating information about the hazards of foods, drugs, cosmetics, and other household products is the package label. Ordinarily, such labels are small, but the amount of plausibly useful information might be very large. Not only must a label state the general level of risk—which is hard enough, given the inability of most people to understand statistical or actuarial concepts—but it must describe the variety of factors and conditions that might exaggerate the risk. Certain kinds of individuals (e.g., pregnant women, asthmatics, smokers, people who habitually use drug "XYZ," or people who have been exposed to chemical "ABC") might be known to be "hypersusceptible." If this were explained on a label, how able would most people be to locate themselves within (or without) the correct categories of hypersusceptibility? Even more troubling are the conditions of foreseeable misuse and abuse. There is always someone who will pour eau de cologne on a burning candle in order to scent the air, place a steam vaporizer where it can be upset by a child in the dark, or drink excessive quantities of liquor while pregnant. How many such hazards should warning labels attempt to cover? How far should producers be forced to expand the size of labels or reduce other messages in order to accommodate government-mandated information?

Of course, the government need not restrict itself to regulating the label. To overcome the defects of small print, simplistic numbers, or overgeneral warnings, longer leaflets and brochures can be mandated. The Food and Drug Administration, for instance, decided in 1971 to require drug manufacturers to package drugs in boxes on which warnings were to be printed, to enclose an information brochure, and to provide a separate "summarized . . . easy-to-read" leaflet to be distributed by the pharmacist. The FDA has also required manufacturers to supply physicians with brochures to be given to their patients.[29] The package inserts, according to the latest proposed FDA regulations, must include a statement telling the patient to read it; a summary of the information; instructions on how to use the product; activities to avoid when using the drug and circumstances under which it should not be taken; a discussion of side effects, serious adverse reactions, and potential hazards (specifically including possible carcinogenicity, mutagenicity, and effects on pregnant women and nursing infants); and the FDA's reservations about the drug's effectiveness for specific illnesses.

A plausible rationale exists, of course, for each of the disclosures required by the FDA. But the longer and more elaborate the information required in leaflets and brochures, the smaller the print and the greater the possibility citizens will ignore it entirely, as in the case of the Minnesota bank's truth-in-lending booklets. Thus the mode of communication itself becomes the subject of regulation. The FDA regulations on package inserts, for example, prescribe the minimum type size. And if leaflets, even with "type no smaller than ⅟₁₆ of an inch," become too dense and forbidding, should larger ones, better graphics, or poster-sized warnings be required? And if producers can be required to provide posters, why not billboards or periodic television messages? Clearly, limits must be set, but where the line should be drawn is not clear, nor is it clear what principles should be invoked for guidance. Regulators have not called for billboards, of course, but the tendency of many consumer protection advocates to treat disclosure as a goal in itself (and nondisclosure as the moral equivalent of cover-up), as well as their insensitivity to the costs of providing "just a few more words," create powerful pressures on regulators to lean toward more rather than less disclosure, even if the result is information overload for all but the most risk-averse consumers.

A similar tendency toward ever-increasing increments of disclosure stems from the inevitable ambiguity of the communication process. If there is any political conflict at all over the design and execution of the program—as there almost invariably is—then sooner or later the contestants come to arguing over words, type size, display format, and the increments in which percentage differences may, or must, or need not be, stated. Thus the FTC charged a Denver car dealer with violating the Truth in Lending Act, which requires advertisements to state credit terms clearly and conspicuously, for televising advertisements in which a voice or flashing letters in the middle of the screen announced the price and monthly payment terms, while the other credit terms (annual interest rate, total amount to be paid) appeared in a moving line of smaller letters at the bottom of the screen.[30] In 1979, the FTC obliged a bicycle manufacturer to distribute television messages on safe bicycling to offset earlier ads that showed boys riding bicycles like daredevils.[31] Controversies over whether required information is provided clearly and conspicuously can develop the same complexity encountered in the regulation of misleading advertising, in which FTC hearings become bogged down on issues such as whether advertisements may employ the terms "acid indigestion" or "sour stomach."[32]

The difficulty in determining appropriate stopping points in the search for clear methods of communicating the existence of possible hazards has led some advocates of mandatory disclosure to sidestep entirely the issue of effectiveness (and hence of possible unreasonableness). As President John Kennedy put it in announcing a Consumer Bill of Rights in 1962, we have a "right to be informed," pure and simple. Ten years later, a commentator referred to Congress's enactment of the Truth-in-Lending Act as affirming "the right to know rather than relying on any evidence of whether or not the consumer uses the information. . . . The use the consumer makes of the information is peripheral to the main issue of the right to know."[33] Indeed, like all such uses of the term "rights" as a rhetorical or advocacy device, a right to know that seems to admit of no qualification can easily be invoked to demand disclosure that is unrelated to uncovering deception or dispelling confusion at all, but is designed primarily to raise political consciousness or mobilize political pressure with respect to certain issues.[34] In 1971, for example, the Natural Resources Defense Council and the Project and the Center on Corporate Responsibility filed a petition with the SEC requesting that the SEC require registrants to disclose more information about the environmental impact of their activities and about their efforts in the area of providing equal employment opportunities.* Similarly, consumer advocates can defend mandatory disclosure of energy consumption features of household appliances—even when it appears that the costs of testing and providing this information in a manner suitable to diverse use conditions would probably exceed the financial benefits to consumers[35]—on grounds that it will help make consumers energy conscious. Others have suggested that the FTC might order manufacturers of appliances and other energy-consuming goods to "disclose" in their advertising "alternative consumption options."[36]

There is nothing wrong with the political goal of making the citizenry more environmentally and energy conscious, of course. The risk is that mandatory disclosure for such political purposes can become a mechanism whereby the government forces sellers to undertake an uncompensated program of public education—or propaganda, depending on one's viewpoint—thereby turning their packages into minibillboards for messages designed to persuade rather than to prevent deception. There are risks of abuse, of course, in any government program. Yet with respect to disclosure laws, there seems to be a special temptation for government to go further than may be justified because the emphasis on "mere disclo-

---

*The Securities and Exchange Commission complied to the extent of requiring disclosure of environmental litigation and obligations that "may materially affect the earning power of the business." Later, it dropped the materiality test for litigation involving the government. In 1979, it faulted U.S. Steel for failing to disclose (1) internal cost-estimates for complying with *anticipated* control technology not yet mandated and (2) any corporate policy or practice that "is reasonably likely to result" in fines or penalties. Lawyers observed that the SEC's *U.S. Steel* decision will make environmental disclosure for all corporations longer and much more detailed. See Neal S. McCoy and Randy M. Mott, "Filing Changes Seen If SEC Follows Ecology Rules Set in Steel Case," *National Law Journal*, November 26, 1979. However, in June 1981, the SEC proposed revised rules that would restore the materiality test, noting that significant disclosures "have been obscured by lengthy disclosures of relatively inconsequential governmental proceedings."

sure" (as opposed to direct prescription of behavior) and on "only asking them to tell the truth" suggests that such laws are essentially innocent and costless. Demands for disclosure, however, sometimes mask a more cynical struggle for economic and political power and can lead to substantial social and economic costs.

CAPTURE BY INDUSTRY

As noted earlier, a regulatory agency that sets industry-wide standards almost inevitably confers a competitive advantage on the subset of firms in the industry that can most easily achieve compliance; the firms thus favored often become advocates of more stringent regulatory rules and resist efforts to moderate them. The regulation of information is just as susceptible, if not more so, to this form of capture. The tendency is illustrated dramatically by the federal and state "standards-of-identity" regulations governing the marketing of food products. These regulations typically prescribe some mix of permitted, mandatory, and prohibited ingredients, processed according to certain procedures, that qualify a product to be called by a certain name, such as "frozen fried fish sticks" or even "cream cheese."* Thus sellers of products that deviate from the "natural" or original formula—such as "cream cheese" made primarily of nondairy ingredients—are obliged to disclose that fact by prominently labeling their product "imitation cream cheese" or the like. While all this appears to be a legitimate regulatory purpose from every point of view and sometimes is necessary to prevent gradual but hard-to-detect reductions in quality by all producers,[37] it is also inevitable that standards-of-identity regulations present attractive opportunities to engage in various forms of cartel-like behavior, such as discouraging the sale of lower cost alternatives that in fact would satisfy many consumers.

As of 1977, for example, identity standards for ice cream required manufacturers to use a general recipe heavily dependent on nonfat dried milk and required manufacturers who wished to depart from that formula to call their product something other than "ice cream." This standard had

---

*Thus the regulations provide: "Frozen fried fish sticks are clean, wholesome, rectangular-shaped unglazed masses of cohering pieces not ground of fish flesh coated with breading and partially cooked. . . . Frozen fried fish sticks weigh up to and including 1-½ ounces; are at least three-eighths of an inch thick and their largest dimension is at least three times the next largest dimension." *Code of Federal Regulations,* Title 50, 261.1, p. 398.

been guaranteeing dairy farmers a market for about 290 million pounds (or \$183 million worth) of nonfat dried milk they would otherwise not have been able to sell on the open market.[38] The FDA, however, proposed to change the standards to permit the substitution of whey and casein (both of which are fractions of whole milk) for about two-thirds of the milk powder in the standard recipe.[39] The dairy industry bitterly opposed the proposed change, even though in the short run, under the existing price support programs for dried milk, farmers would not lose money but would profit. But in the long (or intermediate) run, dairymen feared the extra \$183 million that the government would have had to pay might undermine political support for the whole price support program. As covered in the mass media, however, opposition to the change was expressed almost wholly in terms of adulterating good old-fashioned ice cream with less natural ingredients. "We want ice cream to stay the real thing," declaimed Congressman Charles Rose of North Carolina in attacking the FDA's proposal.[40] But what, after all, is "the real thing"? If ice cream made from the new recipe has the same taste and texture as ice cream made from the old recipe, as the FDA claimed it would, why is it not "real" ice cream? The constant shadow cast by such a difficult question even when it is unspoken or, worse yet, when it is spoken only by those seeking protection against competition certainly complicates thinking and debate on seemingly practical matters like how much casein should be permitted in ice cream.[41]

Ironically, standards of identity for dairy products, although they originated in part to prevent the displacement of dairy products by nondairy substitutes, also operate to prevent innovation and increase costs within the dairy industry and hence to accelerate loss of market share to those same nondairy substitutes. The development of large-scale dairy product firms is inhibited by a plethora of state regulations (designed in part to protect local producers) that requires a distinctive grading scheme for each state (such as Grade A milk in one state, Grade AA for a similar product in another), thus requiring interstate marketers to prepare and keep track of a large number of different packages for essentially similar products, or to vary the production recipe slightly depending on the product's destination. Consider, too, the effect of identity standards for butter. The dairy industry has a chronic surplus of butterfat. Through physical separation, butterfat can be reduced to two fractions, one relatively hard and one relatively soft. The former is "ideally suited for the baking industry," especially for Danish pastry, according to one prominent dairy technologist, while the latter can be made into a soft spreading butter that is also lower in saturated fats than ordinary butter. But according to existing regulations, if separated in this fashion, neither product could be called "butter."[42]

This example suggests the broader problem of regulatory capture by special interests that has been evident in the context of direct regulation. Under the guise of full disclosure, producer interests are often able to force their competitors, through the regulatory agencies, to describe their products in ways that it is hoped will hurt their sales. Until the last decade or so, much of the FTC's effort in the consumer protection area was expended on cases like those against manufacturers who failed to disclose the foreign origin of Christmas tree bulbs and against the processors of recycled motor oil who were obliged to label their product "reprocessed," even though its performance characteristics were not significantly different from virgin oil.[43]

We have not seen comparable accounts of manipulation of disclosure laws concerning physical hazards presented by products, workplaces, or service establishments, but the same factors would be present and might invite established firms to push for the expansion of disclosure rules under the banner of truth in order to discourage innovative offerings by new competitors.

OTHER COSTS OF MANDATORY DISCLOSURE

Mandatory disclosure entails other social costs as well, some of which are shared with more direct forms of regulation—direct compliance costs (including product testing as well as information gathering, printing, and disseminating), special burdens on small business, and financial outlays by those government units that must regulate and supervise the disclosure process. These costs are not necessarily trivial. For example, the FDA's proposed regulations for package inserts for drugs, which also would require each pharmacy, hospital, clinic, and doctor's office to maintain a filing system to sort information about the medicines they dispense, has been estimated by the FDA to cost $90 million to implement.*[44] Disputes

---

*In February 1981, the FDA stayed the implementation of some of these rules, adopted but not yet in effect, in order to undertake a cost-effectiveness analysis, pursuant to a general Executive Order by President Reagan requiring such studies. In a demonstration of the

over the accuracy of mandatory tar and nicotine ratings for cigarettes and for automobile fuel economy ratings impel the FTC and the EPA, respectively, to maintain their own testing laboratories in order to check up on the ratings provided by the manufacturers' expensive testing programs and to devise ever more sophisticated testing methods.[45]

Of greater interest, perhaps, are the costs to society of inadvertently producing misinformation. For example, the U.S. Department of Agriculture's method for grading meat was based through 1975 on the degree of "marbling." The higher the marbling, the higher the grade. The system was based on a 1936 study that reported a correlation of 0.67 between marbling and beef tenderness.[46] Research in the 1950s, however, reported correlations of only 0.33 and 0.47; and research reported in the 1970s showed an even lower relationship. To make matters worse, the USDA grading was inversely correlated with nutritional value: the higher the grade, the higher the fat and calories and the lower the protein per ounce of meat. Since "choice" beef was priced higher than "good," government grading might have been leading consumers to spend more money for less value.[47]

Imagine also the possibilities of overreaction to labels on products or industrial materials noting that the substance is carcinogenic, even though it probably is not when exposure or use is infrequent or carefully controlled. In such a case, mandatory use of particular "scare words" with deep emotional impact would drive out information derived from experience or common sense and would unnecessarily impede the use of efficient products or the performance of useful jobs. For example, an industrial hygienist we interviewed in an automobile assembly plant told us that dramatically stated blanket warning labels on drums of solvents containing substances such as benzene often get workers upset and reluctant to use them, even though no hazard is posed under the circumstances (such as a low concentration of benzene in the solution, or its use in such a manner as to minimize inhalation of the fumes).

Disclosure requirements also can result in misleading or not particularly valuable information because regulatory agencies, as bodies responsible for effective law enforcement, have an incentive to insist on disclosure formulae, grading methods, and items of information that are

---

forces underlying the ratchet effect, Ralph Nader's Public Citizen Health Research Group and two other public interest groups sued the agency in federal court, challenging its authority to impose the stay.

easy to police. Until recently, for example, the SEC required registrants to use accounting methods that everyone, including the SEC, knew to be misleading. Inventories and capital assets had to be evaluated, for instance, at their historical cost, not at present market value or replacement value,[48] because it was easier to police the integrity of the less relevant but more "objective" historical cost claims. Also the SEC until recently forbade any statement of earnings projections—an item that investors are especially interested in—for this too had the potential for exaggeration if not outright deception. Other disclosure laws, too—such as a franchise marketing law in Wisconsin and the 1975 Federal Real Estate Settlement Procedures Act—seem to have had at least a short-run effect of constricting the flow of information by substituting costly, officially mandated formal disclosure statements for informal, faster and cheaper (if perhaps not quite as systematic and reliable) communication through advertising or telephone inquiries.[49]

The potential for the regulation of information to restrict dissemination of truth together with falsehood is nowhere better illustrated than in the FTC's advertising substantiation program, which requires advertisers to produce, on demand, evidence that product claims have been substantiated prior to making the claims. There is likely to be a large gap between the level of substantiation that will satisfy the advertiser and perhaps even the consumer and the level that will satisfy the FTC. For example, in the *Pfizer* case, in which the FTC initiated the requirement, the company had been marketing Unburn, a lotion that allegedly contained a special ingredient capable of anaesthetizing the nerves in sunburned skin. Pfizer had not scientifically tested the product on human beings, however, as a means of substantiating its claims. Pfizer had merely taken a chemical compound known to have anaesthetic properties in general and relied upon its theoretical ability to retain these properties when mixed with the other ingredients in Unburn. No one in the proceedings actually doubted that claims for Unburn were true or argued that Pfizer's reasoning was faulty. Nevertheless, in the absence of test data, the complaint (which was ultimately dismissed) charged that Pfizer had been engaged in "unfair" methods of competition under Section Five of the Federal Trade Commission Act by making claims without substantiating them by appropriate tests.[50]

The burden of substantiation is indicated by a case in which the FTC ordered Warner Lambert to file a report with respect to a television ad in which one teenager told another that Listerex Acne Scrub "kills germs," has "cleansing grains that scrub away dirt and excess oil," and "fights acne problems." The list of substantiating items of information demanded by the FTC covers two full pages of small print and includes such items as "a full explanation of the meaning of . . . 'acne,' 'pimples,' 'excess oil,' 'cleansing grains' . . . ; a complete explanation of the . . . methodology used" in supporting tests, including "a complete description of the subjects" and "the experience and training of all experimenters; sufficient data to allow one to replicate the study; a full explanation . . . of the degree of effectiveness of Listerex in the treatment of [each of eight forms of acne listed by the FTC staff]"; and "a complete summary of all the documentation . . . in such language as to enable the ordinary consumer to understand it."[51] Not surprisingly, even FTC Commissioner Robert Pitofsky, who created some mandatory disclosure programs while working at the FTC as a lawyer from 1970 to 1973, summarized the difficulties of designing a workable substantiation program with a slight hint of pessimism.

If all or most claims are true, the substantiation process adds little to consumer welfare. Even if a few claims are untrue and the substantiation process helps to disclose them to the seller or to the government, the costs of substantiation may outweigh the combined benefits of disclosure resulting from the avoidance of economic injury and from the greater . . . dissemination of accurate product information. Moreover, vigorous enforcement of the *Pfizer* doctrine might have less of a preclusive effect on false and deceptive advertising, which is already prohibited, than on truthful claims that are too expensive to substantiate. The greater suppression of such claims, or suppression of informational advertising in favor of "puffs" not subject to the substantiation requirement, the more likely it is that the net effect of the requirement will be injurious to consumers.[52]

A NOTE ON ENFORCEMENT

We can only speculate as to what motivated the FTC to devote so much energy, and to require Warner-Lambert to devote even more, to a case in which the consumer could quickly judge whether an inexpensive product in fact performed as claimed. Perhaps it is because the FTC had identified Warner-Lambert as a bad apple—for years it had advertised nonexistent health properties for Listerine mouthwash, until the FTC, after much litigation, forced it to stop.[53] But there are cases in which the FTC has aggressively pursued apparent good apples, with no prior history of deviance, for commiting relatively minor or harmless violations of disclosure-type laws. *Chicago Tribune* columnist Michael Kilian has described a case in which JS&A Group, Inc., a successful Illinois mail-order company specializing in sales of computerized electrical products, violated an FTC regulation requiring mail-order firms to notify customers who pay by check if their orders will not be filled within 30 days and to tell them they have the right to cancel. JS&A violated the rule when a succession of huge snowfalls paralyzed traffic in the Chicago area in January 1979, resulting in a good deal of employee absenteeism and in delays in fixing a computer used to keep track of orders. By Kilian's account, in seven years of operation, JS&A had established a reputation as an honest, reliable company. According to the FTC's investigation, prior to the blizzard there had been only 75 complaints against the company out of 800,000 transactions, and the blizzard produced 225 more, which the company promptly attempted to resolve. Yet despite the absence of evidence of any harm to consumers, the FTC, after hearing JS&A's defense, announced that the company had violated the law and was liable for a $100,000 fine, which it later said it would reduce to $10,000 if the firm would admit wrongdoing.[54]

This, of course, is an extreme case. Nevertheless, it points to an inescapable problem with all disclosure regulations: violations typically pose no immediate threat to anyone. As we have said, even the best and the most justified disclosure policies may directly affect only a small percentage of the consumers and workers whose interests are to be protected. The great majority are therefore wholly unaffected by noncompliance with such policies. Sensing this, regulated enterprises may not take their disclosure obligations very seriously; they may treat noncompliance as a "mere technical" violation. Regulatory officials, in order to counteract this tendency, have to take a tough stand against such violations, and sometimes have to make an example of unfortunate firms like JS&A. The result is that, in agency action against individual violators, the regulation of information is at least as likely to lead to unreasonableness as is direct regulation.

OVERCOMING UNREASONABLENESS

The conceptual difficulties involved in knowing when economic and social conditions might make a mandatory disclosure program worthwhile are compounded by the practical difficulties of implementing a program once it is decided to take the gamble. Clearly, a provisional and experimental approach to policy design in this general area is in order. It is an ideal area for pretesting program concepts and tools through pilot programs. Even post hoc evaluation is likely to prove more feasible here than it has for most programs, since the central problem of constructing adequate control groups is more easily solved. Further, the political costs of admitting previous errors and striking out anew are probably lower, as there are usually smaller financial and symbolic investments in disclosure programs than there are in more direct regulatory programs. That is, the ratchet effect is likely to be less powerful in the case of mandatory disclosure policies. The inability of the NHTSA to back down from its ill-advised tire quality grading system is a contrary example, to be sure. But there have been numerous instances of thoughtful and constructive— albeit sometimes too slow—reform efforts, such as those affecting SEC disclosure rules, FTC regulation of price advertising, and the Employee Retirement Income Security Act, to name just a few.

One solution to the manifold problems of designing and implementing good mandatory disclosure programs is for government to throw the challenge back onto the private sector, at least in those cases involving clouds of confusion. The tire grading system is a good case in point. Consumers Union tested and graded tires for its August 1968 report, and there is every reason to think that private testing organizations could do the job as well as the government and at lower cost. The Department of Transportation effort was seriously impaired by the absence of qualified personnel, by bureaucratic infighting, and by the subordination of the task to higher priority concerns. As an alternative, the government could have simply limited itself to the roles of financial intermediary, contract administrator, and antifraud enforcer. That is, it could have collected taxes from the manufacture or sale of tires, then used the money to hire a private testing firm (in consultation, let us say, with industry interests), and, finally, overseen in a general way the dissemination of the results to the buying public whether at the point of sale or in some other fashion.[55]

The basic strategy of delegating some of the more controversial and/or technical work back to the private sector can take many different forms.

The FDA simply asked competing Florida and California orange growers to sit down and work out an identity standard for "orange drink" that the FDA could then adopt, either with or without further modifications. In some states, the agency regulating nursing homes tries to help groups like the Gray Panthers in their efforts to develop consumers' guides to nursing homes in various localities. The Fair Packaging and Labeling Act of 1966 has been implemented in part through the standards development work of the National Conference on Weights and Measures, which developed a standard model of various package sizes and measures.[56]

Private-public cooperation could perhaps exploit the government's special ability to collect information. The California Bureau of Automotive Repair, for example, has voluminous statistics on consumer complaints concerning all automobile repair shops in the state. It also has data on complaint records for different makes of cars. But political and possibly some legal problems have prevented the agency from analyzing the data and reporting the findings on its own. Linkage to a private research organization, with appropriate safeguards against misleading reporting, conceivably would permit bodies of data like this one to serve a public information function.

To be sure, private-public cooperation in attacking the cloud of confusion is not without its own problems. Consumers Union found the Veterans Administration (VA) very reluctant to part with information the agency had collected over the years about the performance characteristics of various brands and models of hearing aids, of which the VA was a large purchaser. The VA argued, rather reasonably in our view, that the data could be misleading if released in their raw form and, less reasonably, that disclosure might be unfair to manufacturers and a drain on the VA budget.[57] In addition, there is the problem of unreasonableness in the private sector. One of the virtues of the delegation strategy is that it can avoid some of the legalism and nitpicking to which public agencies are susceptible; hence it can get on with the job more expeditiously. But private policing organizations can err on the side of too little caution and too itchy a trigger finger. The July 1978 *Consumer Reports*, for instance, tarred the Chrysler Corporation's Dodge Omni and Plymouth Horizon as "not acceptable," the first such rating given to an American-made car in 11 years. Yet this was the model that six months earlier *Motor Trend* magazine had called "car of the year." The Consumers Union complaint concerned directional instability when the vehicle was driven at expressway speed and its steering wheel given a sharp twitch and then released.[58]

The Omni/Horizon was subsequently defended, however, by the editor of *Motor Trend,* two test drivers employed by *Newsweek*, and the traffic safety unit of the Canadian government.[59] The *Newsweek* test drivers reported: "We concluded that you could induce the instability [Consumers Union] complained about if you really worked at it, and that Chrysler should engineer it out. But we also can't imagine that it would happen in normal use."*

Under some circumstances, producers might be allowed to participate in a rating program voluntarily. Only those who receive good ratings would then choose to participate. But if the nature of the product and/or the industry were such that nonparticipation were a clear signal to consumers of inferior quality, nonparticipation would not injure the program. In 1976, for example, the Department of Commerce initiated a National Voluntary Laboratory Accreditation Program (NVLAP), which tried to induce more competition in the highly concentrated testing and certification industry.[60] Because consumers of testing and certification services find it so difficult to learn about the trustworthiness and reliability of different testing labs, Underwriters Laboratory and a few other such organizations have come to dominate the field. The quite plausible theory behind NVLAP is that U.S. government certification of the certifiers would permit more small laboratories to survive and to compete. The program can be voluntary because normal market incentives would lead laboratories to participate (assuming they could meet the accreditation standards, of course). On the other hand, sometimes a voluntary program would be inadequate: a beer manufacturer may be reluctant voluntarily to disclose the amount of chemical preservatives used in his product (even if he uses less than his competitors) because if his competitors do not follow suit or use different terminology, the innovator risks some loss of sales. Uniform and mandatory disclosure rules would solve this problem. Often a combined policy would be optimal. An interesting example of such a two-tier strategy, combining both voluntarism and coercion, are the regulations concerning nutritional labeling: a food manufacturer need not disclose nutritional information at all, but if he makes nutritional claims for his product then he must do so in a government-prescribed, standardized format.[61]

---

*By way of rebuttal, the October 1978 *Consumer Reports* claimed that a driver might sharply twitch and release the steering wheel in maneuvering to avoid another car.

RECAPITULATION

Mandatory disclosure strategies can help penetrate dirty secrets and dispel clouds of confusion, two problems that beset consumers, workers, and citizens in many situations. Under appropriate conditions, such strategies can furnish the benefits of direct regulation but without as high a price in unreasonable impositions of various kinds. Although mandatory disclosure would not a priori be applicable to perhaps most problems currently addressed by direct regulation, it would be applicable to some, and it is therefore worthwhile to explore the potential benefits of the strategy as an alternative to direct regulation, in whole or in part.

The benefits are only potential in such cases because a great deal depends on how a mandatory disclosure strategy is implemented. Instances abound of poorly conceived and poorly implemented disclosure policies. Even though mandatory disclosure is not direct regulation of the sort examined in earlier chapters, it is after all a form of regulation. As such, it is beset by many of the same tendencies toward unreasonableness and can easily drift into moralism and bureaucratic formalism. One of the great virtues of the mandatory disclosure strategy, however, is that on balance, the errors of overregulation are probably not as costly as those that ensue from direct regulation, and they are probably somewhat easier to correct.

CHAPTER TEN

LIABILITY

•

Socially irresponsible behavior can be deterred by the prospect of private lawsuits as well as by the threat of regulatory inspections and fines. The liability law system, however, is better shielded from the political and bureaucratic pressures that often make direct regulation unreasonably rigid, and it encourages enterprises to tailor protective measures to the specific combination of risks and abatement costs in each particular operation. To some observers, therefore, liability law, as it is or as it might be reformed, is the superior regulatory mechanism. In this chapter, we explore its potential and its limits, as well as a related method of control—government taxation of socially harmful behavior.

THE LIABILITY SYSTEM

Court-ordered damage awards for injuries and illnesses caused by dangerous products or pollutants often extend into the hundreds of thousands of dollars and occasionally into the millions. Even smaller liability judgments usually outweigh the fines typically imposed for most regulatory violations. The mere threat of such lawsuits, therefore, would seem to provide strong incentives for enterprises to control any aspect of their activities that might lead to damage claims, even if the protective measures needed to avoid liability are not mandated by direct regulations.* The prospect of large recoveries, moreover, encourages aggres-

---

*Many people, including regulators, overlook this deterrent effect by seeing the liability law system only as a victim compensation device. They say, "What's the use of compensating the survivors of someone who is killed? It's better to save the victim in the first place by prevention." But liability law can provide *ex ante* protection as well, sometimes even better protection than direct regulation, by posing the threat of very large compensation awards that enterprises anticipate and attempt to forestall by self-selected prevention measures.

sive legal action against violators of liability law. While overworked government enforcement attorneys may be inclined to back off from certain difficult cases, the injured plaintiff's lawyer has a contingent fee arrangement that encourages diligent prosecution of claims. Through pretrial discovery processes, he can compel defendants and their managers to disclose the contents of their files, the technical and economic basis for their decisions, and even their thought processes.[1]

Where the threat of such damage suits is present, enterprises establish their own safety staffs and quality control units to conduct intensive internal inspections, or they submit to inspections by the loss control representatives dispatched by liability insurance companies. These private inspectors are present more often than government inspectors and are more knowledgeable about the specific risks posed by each facility. Yet these private inspectors, largely because they are free of the legal constraints and accountability pressures under which their government counterparts operate, can tailor protective standards more closely to the hazards presented by the particular enterprise and thus minimize unreasonableness.

Similarly, liability standards applied by the courts usually are more generally worded and open ended (and hence more sensitive to the particular context) than the detailed specification standards enforced by regulatory agencies. Courts impose liability only for behavior that actually has caused harm, not behavior that might cause it. The adjudicatory process and the private negotiations that accompany it tend to elicit evidence and focus attention on the risks and the equities present in each specific case. Judges and juries are less susceptible than regulatory officials to charges of capture or selling out, should they decide in favor of a business enterprise, and they are under less pressure to apply the law legalistically so as to shield themselves from blame in the event of some future catastrophe. Similarly, compared to regulatory enforcement officials, plaintiffs in private lawsuits have more freedom to negotiate compromise remedies that depart from the letter of the law without being accused of subverting the public interest.

On the other hand, the liability law system has certain weaknesses that impair its potency as a deterrent to irresponsible behavior. Liability rules place the burden of proof on the injured plaintiff, and proving liability is often difficult, even when the plaintiff's claim is just. Litigation is always very costly and very slow; hence many plaintiffs, especially those with smaller claims, may be discouraged from bringing suit or may be induced to settle quickly for less than their due.[2] Many valid claims never reach court because the victims are poor, uneducated, timid, ignorant of their rights, or fearful of contact with lawyers and courts. Others, who know litigation for the unpleasant experience it is, may decide that the protracted struggle, expense, and animosity associated with lawsuits are not worth the trouble. From the standpoint of the enterprises whose activities might cause harm, the deterrent threat of lawsuits is partially blunted by liability insurance, especially when insurance premiums are not quickly adjusted to penalize less responsible firms to any significant extent. Bad apples can exploit the numerous opportunities for delay afforded by pretrial discovery rules and the complexities of court procedure. For all these reasons, the liability system probably does not in fact force all enterprises to "internalize" all the social costs that result from their negligent or otherwise irresponsible actions.

Programs of direct regulation, in fact, typically have been enacted precisely because the liability system, by itself, seemed to afford inadequate levels of protection. But direct regulatory programs, too, may be somewhat ineffective in practice and are quite likely to lead to a considerable amount of unreasonableness. Hence further questions arise: Can the liability law system be changed or adapted to overcome its weaknesses as a regulatory mechanism? Can it be made to work better than direct regulation, to substitute for it in some areas, or to complement it more fully in others?

Consider, for example, the reforms in liability law represented by the state workers' compensation statutes enacted 50 to 70 years ago—absolute employer liability for all work-related injuries, a fixed statutory schedule of damages, adjudication by specialized administrative tribunals, limited counsel fees, and mandatory insurance for employers. These reforms greatly facilitated claims by injured workers. They impelled employers to make substantial improvements in worker safety, improvements that direct regulatory programs such as OSHA have found it hard to supplement to any significant extent.[3] Moreover, further liability law reforms have been proposed, such as increased workers' compensation benefit levels,[4] sharper merit rating of employers by insurance companies,[5] new standards of liability for occupational illnesses and diseases, and tax penalties for employers with above-average liability experience.[6] Such changes might actually lead to more effective worker protection than OSHA achieves. By pushing liability costs up, they might provide employers with an incentive to do more than OSHA rules require (if doing more would cut liability costs). And they might have that effect without causing nearly as much site-level unreasonableness because they do not depend on strict enforcement of overinclusive specification standards. Law journals today abound with proposals to increase the deterrent effect of liability law with respect to other perils as well, such as dangerous products, consumer deception, and employment discrimination. But can the regulatory potential of liability law be achieved without greatly increasing its propensity for unreasonableness? Or, in comparative terms, can liability law, if made more fearsome and effective, still be made to operate more reasonably than comparable systems of direct regulation?*

AN EXAMPLE: THE PROBLEM OF TOXIC SUBSTANCES

Of the more than 30,000 chemicals in common use, a good many are known to be toxic, a great many more are under varying degrees of suspicion, and still more have effects that are simply unknown. And even chemicals once thought safe have turned out, with disturbing frequency, to be dangerous. Through carelessness, ignorance, or occasional indifference, many of these hazardous substances invade the environment (e.g., transformers containing PCBs deteriorate or seepage occurs from poorly designed industrial waste sites), then find their way, through ground water, the food chain, or direct contact, into man. The results are sometimes horrifying, such as the severe neurological disorders found among employees of a plant producing Kepone in Hopewell, Virginia, and among their families and area residents.[7]

Sometimes such effects are discovered in time to enable victims to sue for relief. Their exposure to the chemical and its responsibility for their illness are reasonably clear, and there is evidence that a particular manufacturer was negligent in not preventing or reducing the hazard. In such cases, which may be occurring with greater frequency, private lawsuits—often class actions involving millions of dollars in liability—would seem to

---

*Unfortunately, as is true in the case of mandatory disclosure policies, good empirical studies of the effects of changes in liability law are scarce, and much of what we have to say about current and past practices is rather speculative. What the future might hold is more speculative still, not only because the future is inherently uncertain but because the institutions of the liability system are exceedingly intricate and susceptible to large perturbations from apparently small changes.

provide a strong incentive for adequate care by chemical companies in the future.[8] But the requisite conditions for such lawsuits do not always apply. The discovery of a hazard may be delayed for years, pinpointing responsibility for its dissemination may be difficult, or it may be impossible to prove, in a legally acceptable manner, that a particular chemical substance (as opposed to heredity, smoking, diet, or other environmental causes) is responsible for certain symptoms. Because toxic substance suits can lead to massive liability awards, manufacturers, along with their insurers and lawyers, can be expected to challenge every scientific and legal weakness in the plaintiff's case, adding months or years of delay and expense to an already slow and costly litigation process.* The liability system alone, therefore, may fail to compensate many fundamentally valid claims of injury from harmful substances, and hence it may fail to provide an adequate financial incentive for manufacturers, users, and disposers of chemicals to invest in expensive scientific studies concerning possible toxicity, or to invest in the controls needed to ensure careful storage, usage, and disposal of known toxic chemicals. Not surprisingly, therefore, in the 1970s direct regulatory controls were demanded.

In 1976, Congress passed the Toxic Substances Control Act (TOSCA) to curb the introduction of toxic chemicals and other substances into the human environment.[9] The regulatory approach taken by TOSCA was adapted from the realm of pharmaceuticals. The burden of proof is on industry to show that a substance is safe before it is put on the market. But the lesson of pharmaceutical regulation—that full testing for all new drugs could result in inordinate delays in introducing new and useful products[10]—was perhaps even more powerful when applied to the entire chemical industry, with its rapid rate of innovation. Thus TOSCA added a new twist: full testing by the manufacturer is not automatically required for each and every new chemical. The manufacturer submits limited information. The Environmental Protection Agency, the enforcing agency, after reviewing this information, must make a demand for full testing of those substances it believes might pose substantial risks, and it must do so within a reasonable period of time. Moreover, with respect to chemicals already on the market, the EPA can demand safety testing, but TOSCA limited such demands to 50 substances per year. All this seems

---

*The same problems of proving causation can also frustrate claims under workers' compensation systems concerning workplace exposures to chemicals whose effects are not well established.

quite reasonable, but effectiveness depends on the EPA's scientific and bureaucratic capacity to judge the substances most in need of testing. Predictably, the EPA has been bogged down in data and scientific controversy, slow to make decisions, and locked in conflict with both the gigantic chemical industry and strident consumer groups. Moreover, manufacturers have been cautious about supplying information for fear that the EPA will not be able to keep valuable trade secrets from their competitors.[11] Direct regulation, clearly, has its problems too.

Stephen Soble has proposed an intriguing scheme that would substitute indirect regulation via a modified liability process for direct regulation via TOSCA.[12] First, Soble's proposed statute, which reflects some provisions of a Japanese law enacted in 1973, would divert claims for compensation for injuries caused by toxic substance pollution from courts of general jurisdiction to a specialized administrative tribunal. Second, it would alter the burden of proof. In the traditional tort or workers' compensation action, the plaintiff must show to a considerable degree of certainty the causal connection between the defendant's conduct (or product) and the claimant's symptoms or injuries, a burden that often cannot be met even by presenting epidemiological studies (assuming they exist) showing a correlation between certain pollutants and a heightened incidence of disease among exposed populations. Soble's proposal, however, would require the claimant to provide only plausible evidence of causality, for example, epidemiological studies indicating statistical correlations. Then, to avoid liability, the *defendant* would have to prove that injuries plausibly linked to exposure to its chemicals in fact stemmed from other causes. Third, the administrative tribunal and its staff explicitly would be assigned responsibility for helping claimants to meet their initial burden of showing a plausible causal link. To that end, the tribunal staff would specialize in gathering and analyzing epidemiological data on the health effects of various classes of chemicals, in looking for patterns among the claims submitted by discrete claimants, and in publicizing those patterns. Fourth, should the tribunal ultimately find the defendant's product the actual cause of a claimant's injury, it would make a certification to that effect, binding in subsequent cases; all "second wave" claimants would be entitled to compensation simply on a showing of similar symptoms and similar exposure to the substance. Fifth, if the causal link is certified, the manufacturer would be strictly liable; that is, having undertaken standard tests and precautions in light of existing scientific knowledge or standard industry practice would not be a defense. Moreover, damages would not be limited to a fixed amount, as under workers' compensation statutes, and therefore might be quite substantial.[13]

Although a number of legal and practical problems would have to be ironed out, Soble's scheme seems to have certain advantages over current practices. Unlike the conventional liability system, a specialized regulatory agency shoulders some of claimants' proof problem and transfers other parts of it to defendant corporations, which are better able to generate the relevant information (on the health effects of exposure to chemicals), or to afford the discovery costs of developing alternative explanations of plaintiffs' injuries. More important, the obligation to disprove possible adverse effects would provide an incentive for chemical companies to track the uses of their more suspect products in society and to gather epidemiological information concerning populations exposed to those substances. And unlike direct regulation under TOSCA, where government officials must ultimately make the key decisions about which chemicals to investigate, how much certainty is enough, and hence how much time and money must be expended on such investigations, the proposed liability scheme places the burden of correct research and judgment on the private firms: unlike EPA officials, they would ultimately pay for their mistakes, either in damage claims arising from too little caution[14] or in foregone profits resulting from too much.* There would be no arbitrary limit on the number of substances that would be subject to intensive investigation; perhaps many more than 50 would be studied. Furthermore, there would not be so many pressures to standard-

*An objection to this system might arise from the fear that chemical firm managers would be tempted to gain sure profits (and credit for them) today by speeding up or cutting down on current testing, while discounting the risk of damage claims 10 or 20 years hence—when they personally might no longer be with the corporation or might have moved up to another job. But that objection may underestimate the impact of the enormous liability threat posed by such a mistake, and hence the motivation of corporations to structure incentives and career lines and pension rights to avert that kind of temptation. Moreover, chemical company officials cannot be sure that a hazardous chemical will not generate certain harms and liability suits soon after it hits the market, as opposed to 20 years later. Insurance firms also would apply pressure: EPA recently issued regulations under the 1976 Resource Conservation and Recovery Act requiring all companies engaged in the manufacture, disposal, and storage of hazardous chemicals to purchase "environmental impairment" insurance policies; insurance firms, it was reported, began demanding that applicants for coverage conduct and submit detailed engineering surveys of chemical storage facilities. Daniel Hertzberg and Georgette Jason, "Insurers Fret Over Covering Pollution Costs," *The Wall Street Journal*, July 17, 1981, p. 29.

ize the approach to investigating any given substance—the usual result of research mandated by government regulations.

Because the Soble approach substitutes an administrative, and rather specialized, tribunal for the regular court system, the result is likely to be a reduction in litigation costs, a greater number of effective claims, more compensation granted to deserving victims, and the accumulation of a body of useful epidemiological data that would contribute to social learning. In these respects, it is superior to the traditional liability system. It gains these advantages, however, while managing to retain the distinctive advantages of the liability system. It is mobilized by the forces of private self-interest and is backed by a penalty structure based on damages actually caused rather than a politically negotiated system of fines. The threat of very substantial damages encourages enterprises to take precautionary measures not limited to those called for by preexisting regulatory rules. Conversely, firms would not be forced, as they often are under direct regulation, to take precautionary measures based on risks that are very remote in the specific instance.

THE LIMITS OF LIABILITY AS A SUBSTITUTE FOR DIRECT REGULATION

If the Soble approach would be both more effective and more reasonable than TOSCA, it does not follow that any similar liability-plus-regulation system would be better than any system of direct regulation or any variant of a simple tort liability system. Any real-life system of social control, which always involves a complex interplay between the controllers and the various parties who might wish to evade control, is quite sensitive to small details in the rules of the game, variations in market structure and incentives, imperfections in technical capabilities, and other basic conditions. We have seen in earlier chapters how this works in the case of direct regulation; the sensitivity of the liability system, in which enforcement is in the hands of thousands of private parties and rule application decentralized to hundreds of semi-autonomous judges and juries, is greater by an order of magnitude. Broad generalizations, therefore, about which sort of system would work better under what conditions would have to be so abstract that they could well be misleading in particular cases.

There are other problems as well in making very general comparisons between liability and direct regulation. For one thing, liability is never absent; all producers are subject to ordinary suits for negligence. We can never choose between direct regulation and liability, but between direct regulation and some reformed version of the current liability system. Yet which particular sort of reform should be held up for comparison? The reform of liability systems can emphasize quite different social values, for example, maximally preventing harm regardless of cost, minimizing the financial costs to producers, facilitating the payment of compensation to injured victims, assuring that all cases are decided justly, minimizing the transaction costs in the system (e.g., lawyers' fees and court costs), and minimizing the sum of transaction costs plus the costs of preventing harms plus the costs of harms that do eventually occur anyhow. This last criterion is preferred by many writers on the subject of liability law considered as social policy.[15] Yet it is certainly not the only defensible criterion, and a number of quite plausible alternative liability reforms could be constructed for the sake of comparison with a direct regulation policy.

Moreover, liability law, by its nature, is constantly reforming itself. "The" law is the array of practices and legal rules in numerous state and federal jurisdictions, in hundreds of separate court districts, and in the minds of thousands of individual judges (not to mention the many more participants like lawyers, jurors, plaintiffs, and defendants who move in and out of the system). It is always evolving, therefore, in a rather decentralized way, with new legal theories popping up here and legal defenses there, looser rules of evidence in this jurisdiction and longer plaintiff-discouraging delays due to crowded dockets in that jurisdiction. To reform such an amorphous social system can be quite difficult. The most available leverage for a state legislature, say, is usually to change the rules defining who is liable to whom for what, although certain procedural changes, like those that facilitate the bringing of class actions, are also possible. Changes in the way particular courts manage their calendars, in the way attorneys charge their clients, or in the business practices of the liability insurance industry, which may be at least as important, are harder to bring about by central direction.

In addition, the scope of social problems for which liability law reforms even arguably would represent an improvement on direct regulation is in fact rather limited. Although a liability approach to regulation should never be ruled out a priori, a good many of the problems with the liability system that led government to undertake direct regulation in the first place are not likely to be solved by any presently conceived reforms. Thus liability law probably is irretrievably inadequate where damages are very remote in time, collective in nature, or impossible to quantify, as in the case of the destruction of dolphins by tuna fishermen, the scarring of beautiful countryside by strip-mining operations, and the gradual depletion of the earth's ozone layer by the release of fluorocarbons from countless sources.

Even when damages are tangible, the transaction costs of the liability system seem insurmountably high in many spheres. Consider air quality regulation, for instance. Usually, a large number of potential plaintiffs (victims of pollution) would have to be joined in a class action suit for the purposes of financing a lawsuit against a pollution source, since the amount of damages suffered by any single individual is generally relatively small and successful litigation is expensive. Class action suits, however, have become more difficult and costly to launch in recent years.[16] The difficulty of aggregating plaintiffs, moreover, is overshadowed by the difficulty of aggregating defendants. If one believes, as many scientists do, that the harm done by certain air pollutants increases disproportionately with their degree of concentration and with their combination with other pollutants, then one cannot assess damages against any single polluter in a crowded air basin without simultaneously proceeding against all other polluters who contribute significantly to the background conditions that make the first polluter's emissions damaging. Yet the difficulty of finding and joining the appropriate defendants in a legally defensible fashion and, in the event of a victory for the plaintiffs, of allocating damage responsibilities among many defendants, pose the same dilemmas for a judge that are now faced by regulators, and the judge would be technically less well equipped to confront them.[17] Direct regulation, emission taxes, or other government-operated schemes* thus seem preferable to direct regulation as the primary strategy for dealing with most air and water pollution problems, although the utility (and the essential justice) of suits for compensation in some cases should not be dismissed.[18]

In other fields, it seems quixotic to expect private citizens consistently to muster the persistence and courage to sue delinquent enterprises. For example, most nursing home residents are far too poor, infirm, and vulnerable to reprisals to instigate a lawsuit against the owners of a facility that mistreats them. Even if the families of a few residents or

*See pp. 292–299 below.

public interest advocates do bring such suits, the problems of proof are forbidding. Courts might be willing to acknowledge a cause of action for breach of contract, much as they have read an "implied warranty of habitability" into the rental transaction, enabling tenants to sue or legitimately to withhold rent from landlords for very poor maintenance. But what would a similar implied warranty to the nursing home resident contain, how would its breach be established, and what would be the measure of damages for incremental additions to the discomfort already suffered by unemployed and infirm old people? Poor housing maintenance leaves tangible evidence, such as broken plaster and door latches and plumbing facilities. Success in nursing home litigation, too, would turn on proving nonperformance only with regard to the most easily documented, and therefore objectively measurable, harms. Although the absence of tender loving care and the consequences that flowed from that condition might be the main source of dissatisfaction, a judge is no more likely to be able to hold a nursing home operator liable for this situation than is a regulator. Moreover, whatever its weaknesses, direct regulation is far easier for patients and their families to activate, and with somewhat less risk of acrimony and reprisal.

Problems of proof are very difficult to overcome in other fields as well, even with the kinds of assistance mentioned in our discussion of Soble's proposal in the toxic substances field. Victims of certain kinds of food poisoning often cannot determine which ingredient caused their illness or which enterprise in the chain of distribution was at fault. Hence government enforcement of *ex ante* regulations concerning additives, sanitation, and storage would seem to be a far more consistent deterrent to irresponsible food processing than the prospect of lawsuits alone—although lawsuits predicated upon proven regulatory violations might add to the deterrent effect of regulation. For the same reasons—difficulty of tracing injuries to their causes with certainty, or lag time between negligent behavior and injury—the threat of private lawsuits cannot fully replace government enforcement of direct regulations for many kinds of water pollution or fire code provisions concerning the adequacy of electrical wiring in buildings.

Finally, even if one could somehow eradicate the problems of cost, delay, plaintiff ignorance, and difficulties of proof, the liability law system, viewed as a deterrent to irresponsible behavior, suffers from a vital theoretical weakness. Like the pure deterrence theory of direct regulation, it rests upon the assumption that business enterprises are perfectly calculating profit maximizers, for whom an adequate threat of liability will induce adequate preventive measures. But many accidents occur not because enterprises deliberately cut corners on safety but because of error. New or marginal companies, short on management expertise and short of capital, may fall far short of accepted industrial practice. Many accidents occur despite a sophisticated enterprise's attempt to install an appropriate quality, safety, or pollution control system; preventive routines occasionally break down from overconfidence, or from unexpected shifts in personnel, or from sudden crises that divert attention. Though one could hardly imagine a greater deterrent to airplane crashes than the resulting multimillion dollar liability claims, crashes sometimes do occur. The same is true for other infrequent but catastrophic harms, such as coal mine explosions, hotel fires, and derailment of trains carrying dangerous chemicals. In such industries, it is neither politically nor morally acceptable to rely entirely on liability law to provide the requisite margin of safety; a fail-safe layer of direct regulation and inspection seems necessary to help prevent slippage in established liability-avoiding routines. A products liability defense counsel specializing in biologics (which are lethal if contaminated) told us that "manufacturers are certainly afraid of lawsuits," but noted that that concern is less pressing than the set of daily hurdles created by FDA good manufacturing practice regulations that help make safety consciousness more immediate and intense.

LIABILITY REFORMS AND UNREASONABLENESS

In recent years, many reforms to strengthen the liability system have been instituted. Legislatures have authorized and facilitated class action suits in some specific fields, such as securities law, antidiscrimination law, and certain consumer protection matters. Lawmakers have subsidized plaintiffs' attorneys' fees, sometimes by direct provision of legal aid, sometimes by rules providing that defendants, including the government, may be ordered to pay the attorneys' fees and other litigation expenses of successful plaintiffs.[19] To provide an incentive to sue even when individual damages are very small, the federal Truth in Lending Act guaranteed individuals who successfully sue violators a minimum recovery from the losing party of $100 as well as attorneys' fees.[20] At the same time, to reduce the court congestion and delay that discourage lawsuits, several jurisdictions have required diversion of certain cases to mediators or arbitrators,[21] or have devised mechanisms for penalizing defendants who unjustifiably refuse early settlement offers.

Changes in substantive law, too, have been designed to reduce plaintiffs' burdens of proof and thus to increase deterrence. Product liability law, for example, has moved in many small increments, and more rapidly in some states than in others, but the most important changes can be summarized as a shift from a negligence standard toward a strict liability standard.[22] In many states, if the injured plaintiff can show his injury stemmed from a defect in the product, he need not prove the manufacturer or seller had been negligent; the defendant can be held responsible even if he took normal or reasonable quality control precautions. "Defect" has been expanded to include "design defects." Manufacturers have been held liable for failing to incorporate in the product known or readily imaginable safety devices or to include warnings that would help prevent foreseeable accidents, even if those accidents arose from misuse of the product or plaintiff's own negligence.[23] From the late 1960s to the 1970s, the number of product liability suits in the courts increased tenfold,[24] and jury awards (based on a sample of cases appealed to higher courts) rose to an average of $221,000 in 1971-76.*[25] Although less frequent in statistical terms, a considerable number of highly publicized multimillion-dollar verdicts and punitive damage awards (the most famous of which was a $125 million verdict against Ford Motor Co. in a case involving an exploding Pinto gas tank) sent shock waves through the business community. One result, the federal Interagency Task Force on Product Liability concluded, was that producers had in fact made noticeably greater efforts to install better quality control systems and to redesign products in order to prevent liability.[26]

Changes in medical malpractice law (as in liability rules applicable to other professions) also have greatly facilitated claims. Many states aban-

---

*A survey of manufacturers of high-risk products by the President's Interagency Task Force on Product Liability revealed that between 1971 and 1976 the average product-liability *claim* rose from $476,000 to $1,711,000. In 1979, according to Jury Verdict Research, Inc., the average verdict in product liability cases was $761,000, although that average was inflated considerably by a relatively small proportion of multimillion-dollar awards. Excluding million-dollar verdicts, the average award was $225,000. Larry Bodine, "7-Figure Verdicts Hit New High," *National Law Journal,* May 4, 1981.

doned the locality rule, which held doctors only to the standard of care common in their locality, rather than to the most up-to-date medical practices in the state or the nation. This has been paralleled by the greater availability of out-of-city physicians or medical school professors willing to serve as expert witnesses for plaintiffs. By 1974, in New York State, a malpractice suit was pending against one in every 10 doctors, in contrast to one in 23 in 1969. In a decade the average value of awards in New York (both litigated and settled out of court) quadrupled. It was not uncommon for a physician to pay $10,000–$12,000 annually in malpractice insurance premiums.*[27]

Even with such changes, of course, the costs and difficulties of litigation undoubtedly leave a great many legitimate plaintiffs out in the cold, and therefore some legal reformers, such as Jeffrey O'Connell, have called for absolute, no-fault liability (but with certain limits on the amount of recoveries) as applied to producers of high-risk products (thus eliminating plaintiffs' burden of proving the existence of a defect) and even as applied to physicians who perform certain medical procedures (such as spinal fusions) that present special risks of harm.[28] Such reforms to lighten plaintiffs' burdens, however, can easily go too far. They can, in effect, impose unreasonable demands on potential defendants, compelling them to invest in costly defensive strategies both before and after the fact of a lawsuit. Like direct regulation, indirect regulation by means of the liability system can also be unreasonable.

Consider, for instance, the area of medical malpractice. Strong evidence indicates that the increase in malpractice litigation has changed the traditional (that is, previously accepted) practice of medicine. Doctors have begun to order more lab tests, more X-rays, more consultations, and more or longer stays in hospitals. An ingenious statistical study by Bruce Greenwald and Marnie Mueller estimated that in 1975 the practice of such "defensive medicine," as it is often called, consumed sufficient resources to account for $2.3 billion in the national medical care bill.[29] This increase in "defensive medicine" undoubtedly produces some benefits. Fear of leaving any stone unturned because of an expensive lawsuit, with all the attendant personal anguish and financial cost, surely leads in some cases to important, even life-saving, diagnoses. Hospitals

---

*In 1979, according to Jury Verdict Research, Inc., the average medical malpractice case verdict, nationwide, was $367,000; excluding million-dollar verdicts, it was $218,000.

have worked harder to institute more rigorous quality control procedures, a field in which some improvements certainly can be made, as
suggested by the success of consultants in hospital risk management.[30] Yet
it has been strongly suggested by many critics that the costs far exceed the
benefits and that the added tests, hospital stays, and expensive procedures mainly prevent lawsuits—or more accurately, successful lawsuits—
rather than actual medical malpractice. One reason, although the point is
certainly debatable, is that most physicians attempt to serve the best
interests of their patients no matter what the liability requirements; the
added malpractice exposure may well have prodded them to undertake
additional tests or procedures, but is unlikely to have added much to their
sense of duty or diagnostic or surgical competence. Another is that
improvements in medical care have come not from deliberate liability
avoidance but from better and continuing medical education and from
the movement toward hospital-centered care, which forces private physicians into regular contact with peers and induces exposure to more
sophisticated practices. Finally, since most of the costs of additional
hospitalization and tests have in recent years been passed on to third-
party reimbursers (Medicare, Medicaid, private health insurance companies), there was not much incentive for doctors or hospitals to econo-
mize on medical tests and consultations even before defensive medicine
became more widespread.

Like the unreasonableness associated with direct regulation, the unanticipated consequences of the liability law's attempt to do good may go
well beyond excess expenditure or precautionary measures. One possible
perverse effect is inducing people to run away from social responsibility
altogether because they fear exposure to excessive liability or entangle-
ment with the aggravations of litigation. The more unpredictable liability
is, the more gun-shy possible defendants may become, and because of the
inherent unpredictability of law applied by scores of judges and juries,
the liability system can be quite threatening to providers of products and
services. For example, in addition to the unnecessary procedures sometimes induced by the threat of malpractice suits—a practice that has been
called "positive defensive medicine"—commentators have perceived an
increase (although it is unclear how pervasive it is) of "negative defensive
medicine," whereby doctors shun certain risky but possibly therapeutic
procedures or, worse yet, turn away certain high risk patients because
they present too great a liability exposure.[31] Negative defensive medicine
would mean, also, hesitating to adopt new medical procedures or to

implement more efficient organizational techniques, such as relying on physicians' assistants or delegating certain functions.*

Withdrawing or limiting activities to lower the likelihood of lawsuits is not restricted to the malpractice field, although systematic data on such effects is not readily available. Landlord-tenant law reforms have diminished a landlord's ability to evict tenants promptly for nonpayment of rent, and have authorized tenants to withhold rent pending an adjudication of their claim that the landlord has breached a judicially implied warranty of habitability. According to Roger Starr, these legal changes have been a significant contributing factor in the disastrous withdrawal of rental housing from the market and the failure to build new units.[32] In a few cases, courts have held insurance companies liable to persons injured as a result of defects in insured buildings or factories that were not detected or remedied by insurance company loss control personnel. The insurers, in short, were held to be liable for negligent inspection. But as Victor P. Goldberg has observed, if these precedents were to become a general rule, the result might well be that some insurance companies would withdraw inspection services entirely.[33]

Untrammeled expansion of liability also can increase the price of certain risky services or products beyond the means of consumers, some of whom, if given the alternative, might prefer a lower cost, albeit riskier, alternative. The rapid rise of medical malpractice liability insurance premiums, it has been estimated, are fully passed on to purchasers of medical care services.[34] Product prices would increase significantly if we adopted absolute "enterprise liability" rules such as those advocated by O'Connell.[35] For example, if sun lamp manufacturers were liable for the thousands of injuries each year that stem from use (or misuse) of their products, they would certainly be induced to install expensive automatic shut-off mechanisms and other devices on every lamp sold, rather than merely offer such mechanisms (estimated to add $14 to the price of each lamp) as an option for more risk-averse consumers willing to pay more.[36]

Finally, the tort-liability system can unreasonably shift to defendants (producers) the responsibility for suppressing risks that can more easily and inexpensively be avoided by the relevant class of plaintiffs (e.g.,

---

*There are arguments, too, that the growing threat of litigation has helped to erode whatever trust between patient and doctor that has survived until now, and hence whatever component of therapeutic care that depends on trust.

consumers and workers). In the products liability field, Richard Epstein observes:

> The expansion of products liability was [deemed] necessary to give producers the proper incentives for developing safe products. Yet . . . in many situations, incentives belong elsewhere in the chain of distribution. A manufacturer of machine tools cannot compel purchasers to keep them in proper maintenance and repair; he cannot prevent the removal of safety guards and warnings; he cannot compel individual workers to observe all the required safety precautions. Yet manufacturers . . . have been held fully liable for damages in precisely these situations. Employers are often in a better position than the original manufacturer to prevent worksite accidents by controlling the work environment or by giving individual employees warnings and instructions about a product's hazards and proper use. General Motors may have billions in assets, but it cannot prevent drunks from speeding or incompetents from rebuilding its car engines . . . the destruction of important defenses, at the very least, may impose perverse incentives. . . . Moreover, it creates the possibility that the good and sensible firm will be dealt with as harshly as the backward and incompetent one, when the very purpose of the law should be to distinguish between them.[37]

Unreasonable effects stemming from court decisions perhaps are more easily reversible than regulatory excesses, as indicated by recent legislative efforts to limit medical malpractice litigation[38] and to make product liability rules more moderate and uniform.[39] Our point is simply that liability law reforms that are designed to overcome very real costs and obstacles to legitimate claims by making the establishment of liability easier, quickly *can* spill over into the same kind of overinclusiveness, unreasonableness, contentiousness, and perverse consequences that characterize legalistic direct regulation.

GETTING THE BEST OF BOTH WORLDS

Can liability law be made into an effective deterrent against irresponsible behavior *without* producing overdeterrence and unreasonably costly precautions? One set of possibilities, suggested by the workers' compensation system and Soble's toxic substances control proposal, would entail a combination of regulatory and litigation strategies, drawing upon the particular strengths of each.

As definers of liability standards, for example, judges operate under certain limitations that may be conducive of unreasonableness.[40] Appellate court judges are generalists, usually untrained either in the technicalities of safety engineering or in economics. They decide on regulatory matters infrequently, and when they do, they see an unrepresentative sample of cases, heavily skewed toward those in which dramatic injuries have occurred. Judges lack an ongoing familiarity with the regulated industry, differences among the firms in it, its economic problems, and whether it has been "improving" over time. Courts cannot systematically monitor the consequences of particular changes in liability law and readjust the standard in light of experience. Some of these weaknesses can be overcome by good lawyers, but many cases are argued by counsel who fail to provide judges with adequate information.

The decentralization of the judicial system also means that each state's standards will be applied by scores of trial judges and juries, each likely to weigh competing values with a somewhat different calculus, often in light of the emotional impact of the injuries sustained by the particular plaintiff. After a jury recently held an automobile manufacturer liable for a driver's severe injuries because of "defects" in the car's design, a federal judge noted that through the accumulation of such suits, "individual juries in the various states are permitted, in effect, to establish national safety standards." But the result, he lamented, is "incoherence in the safety requirements set by disparate juries." In the particular case before him, the judge said, the automobile manufacturer was found liable for not producing a sufficiently rigid frame to protect the passenger from injury; yet, because more flexible "energy absorbing" frames are advocated by some auto safety specialists, the producer of cars with more rigid frames might be found liable by a jury in another case.[41]

Specialized regulatory agencies, on the other hand, enjoy at least a comparative advantage in information gathering and the preparation of standards that reflect an overview of the relevant industry as a whole. The Consumer Product Safety Commission (CPSC), for example, uses a computer-based system for monitoring hospital emergency rooms throughout the country to determine what products are major sources of personal injuries.[42] In considering appropriate safety design standards,

CPSC staff members can assemble data from many manufacturers (not just the defendant) on costs and design alternatives and market trends. The National Highway Traffic Safety Administration gathers data about the accident and injury frequency associated with various models of autos and their components. When an NHTSA official looks at the individual case of an injury from an exploding fuel tank or an erratic carburetor, he knows whether it is a freak event or part of a larger pattern. He also might know something about the performance of comparable components industrywide, about the trade-offs involved among different designs for protecting fuel tanks, and the adequacy of industrywide practices in this regard. Agency officials can consult competent and representative (although of course not disinterested) parties from both large and small firms, independent engineering bodies, and consumer groups, and solicit their views on the most desirable trade-off between safety and other design features.

One approach to making the liability system more predictable and balanced, therefore, might be to facilitate the flow of information from regulatory agencies to lawyers, judges, and juries. Suppose, for example, that *all* attorneys (not just the especially competent ones) had regular and easy access to NHTSA data and analyses concerning the frequency of accidents associated with various components of all car models, and that judges (and juries) therefore were regularly exposed to such data in deciding whether one component has been designed in an unreasonably dangerous way. Specific standards established by regulatory agencies could also be used to impose limits on the impulses of juries. A defendant's compliance with applicable regulatory safety standards might be treated as a presumptively conclusive defense (which it is not under most existing law),[43] rebuttable only by evidence that such regulatory standards are substantially out-of-date and clearly behind the best cost-effective current practices in the industry. Conversely, while juries now often take violation of safety-related standards as conclusive or near-conclusive evidence of negligence,[44] the courts might accord stronger consideration to defenses based on the unreasonableness of regulatory standards as applied to the particular context.

In addition, if the standards and information assembled by regulatory agencies could be incorporated more reliably into the liability process, regulatory agencies might be relieved of the pressure to apply ever tougher preventive requirements on their own. If auto manufacturers faced a more predictable and informed liability system, they would have an incentive to voluntarily recall vehicles that had higher-than-average fatal accident or component failure rates, rather than face enhanced liability exposure.[45] Yet they would be more likely than NHTSA to refrain from recalling vehicles whose repair costs, in the aggregate, would be high but from which relatively few serious accidents and lawsuits were anticipated. NHTSA, on the other hand, might be able to stop recalling so many vehicles for which the costs of recall and repair probably outweigh potential damages.*[46]

Under the Soble proposal for dealing with toxic substances, an administrative agency would assist claimants in overcoming problems of linking their injuries to specific chemicals and responsible sources. In other fields, the mandatory record-keeping and labeling requirements that regulatory agencies have imposed, or might impose, could serve a similar function, and thereby substitute liability claims for direct regulation. For example, recovery by consumers injured by contaminated packaged food, and hence the deterrent effect of the liability system, is facilitated by regulations requiring food-processing firms to maintain detailed production records and to label cans from each batch. Similar labeling and processing regulations for blood plasma products and intravenous solutions make it far more likely today that patients harmed by defective batches of such products could track down the culprit, establish liability, and collect large judgments. We are not certain how adequate such enhanced liability systems are as a deterrent to carelessness, but they suggest an important line of inquiry. To the extent that mandatory labeling and record-keeping makes it unlikely that producers can avoid the massive liability judgments that can stem from sending contaminated products out into the world, it may be possible to relax some of the inflexible direct regulations that prescribe specific facilities, machines, sanitation, or sterlization procedures. Indeed, one could imagine a desirable regulatory life cycle in which regulators mandate detailed safety-oriented technologies or procedures at an early stage in the development of new productive processes, only to deregulate or relax enforcement

---

*Between September 1966 and January 1977, NHTSA compelled auto manufacturers to recall 52.4 million vehicles, or 43 percent of all vehicles sold during this period, for repair of mechanical defects. While we cannot be sure that the benefits of this far-reaching recall policy did not exceed the costs, it is hard to imagine that quite so much could be quite so seriously wrong with America's auto fleet, especially in light of the fact that mechanical failures are a minor cause of all fatal accidents, and that some half of these are maintenance-related rather than production-related.

later as the liability system is made more capable of maintaining pressure for high levels of quality control.

In dealing with the problem of exposure to disease-causing agents in the workplace, too, regulatory record-keeping rules perhaps could help make the liability system both more effective and more reasonable than direct regulation. Workers and their families often have difficulty tracing an illness or disability to exposure in a particular job, for the effects may not be visible for a long period and the worker may have been employed elsewhere in the interim; it is unclear whether or not intervening exposures (or congenital health problems) caused the illness. The effectiveness of the compensation system for such problems (as well as the collective bargaining system) could be improved if employers were obligated to keep and make available to employees records showing the levels of designated chemical exposures associated with specific jobs and specific workers.*[47] This would facilitate epidemiological analyses by regulatory agencies and help claimants' lawyers establish the probability of adverse exposure in particular cases. The costs of such record-keeping might be considerable. But it still might present advantages over direct regulation by OSHA, which, encumbered by judicialized rulemaking, is terribly slow in developing standards for suspected hazards, and rigid and overinclusive in prescribing control technologies when it does act. A government-assisted information system to facilitate valid claims, moreover, would increase incentives for employers and insurance companies to develop early-warning systems and appropriate control technologies.

Where substantial obstacles to private lawsuits against producers remain, government agencies might serve as surrogate defendants, paying compensation directly to injured individuals, while funding such payments by suing responsible private sources themselves or by levying taxes on those sources. In Japan, individuals who live in areas designated by regulatory authorities as special high pollution zones can claim compensation from a government body for administratively validated illnesses or respiratory symptoms that are statistically associated (according to government-sponsored research) with the specific pollutant.[48] The gov-

---

*The failure of employers to disclose known information about job hazards could be treated as grounds for adversely affected employees to circumvent the workers compensation system and bring much larger damage suits and punitive damage claims in the courts. Such a "nondisclosure" theory, in fact, has been employed in lawsuits against employers by workers exposed to asbestos and to cotton dust.

ernment body collects its funds by taxing major pollution sources, including automobile owners, according to their estimated contribution to the level of each pollutant in the designated zone. Similarly, in the state of Maine, a 1970 law established a revolving fund via license fees on all facilities and enterprises involved in the transfer of oil between seagoing vessels and between vessels and shore. Persons claiming property or other injury from oil spills may apply to the fund for compensation, thus sidestepping costly and slow judicial proceedings, assuming they know who might be named as defendant in the first place. If the government body can then establish responsibility for the spill, the polluter must reimburse the fund for all claims that the fund paid out for the spill in question.[49] David Leo Weimer argues that a specialized compensation board consisting of medical practitioners and researchers might effectively be substituted for *both* prior licensing of drugs by the FDA and the normal tort-litigation system. Drug manufacturers would have to deposit funds with the board in an account established for each drug product. This account would be used to indemnify claimants who sustain drug-related injuries for which the manufacturer had failed to warn. Manufacturer payments into the account would continue for twelve years (perhaps even longer would be desirable, in our view) unless the manufacturer were able to demonstrate, in post-marketing studies whose technical quality satisfied the board, that the drug was safe and effective for the conditions for which it was being promoted. In order to increase its own confidence in the results of this postmarketing surveillance, the board would have the authority to pay physicians to send in fully documented adverse reaction reports.[50]

TAXATION, REGULATION, AND LIABILITY

The establishment of government compensation funds, financed by taxes or fees levied proportionately on enterprises according to their potential or actual contribution to the harm in question, underscores a fundamental continuity between liability systems and the taxation of what economists call "externalities" as devices for inducing socially responsible behavior. Taxation is a potentially more flexible and efficient method of achieving regulatory goals than direct regulation.[51] Though it has yet to find much favor among policymakers or among the general public, the basic concept is sound and deserves more respectful attention, at least with respect to pollution control, to which it is better suited than it is to most other objects of protective regulation (which involve more infrequent harmful acts).

If polluters were obliged to pay for the damage they do, they would not pollute as much. Pollution would not be stopped entirely, of course, but under a system in which damages were actually levied on polluters, the only pollution that would remain would be that for which the economic value of the associated production (or consumption) exceeded the amount of damages that the polluter was obliged to pay. From an economic point of view, society would then have found the "efficient" mix of production (or consumption), pollution abatement, and unabated pollution.* As we argued above, however, there are many obstacles to determining and extracting such damage payments through the ordinary mechanisms of the liability system.

Taxation by a government agency, however, would exert the same pressures on polluters as a perfectly functioning liability system. For the incentive effects of the liability system to work, damages need not actually be paid to the victims of some harmful activity so long as the perpetrators of the activity pay *someone*. A taxing authority would be that someone.

In the case of air pollutants that are not highly toxic,† the ideal arrangement would be for polluters to pay a tax on each unit of discharge equivalent to the harm done by the discharge. Compared with the present system of ambient air standards, negotiated emission permits, and mandated abatement technologies, this ideal system would have three advantages: (1) the total amount of social resources invested in pollution abatement would be the efficient amount, neither more nor less; (2) each polluter would be free to seek out the most cost-effective means of reducing his discharges; and (3) the collection of taxes might be considerably smoother than the system of threats and bluffs and noncompliance fines because paying taxes does not entail the same social stigma as conviction for violating direct regulations.

---

*Of course, efficiency might be even more closely approximated if polluters also had the option to "bribe" pollution victims to change their behavior so as to avoid damages, if that were cheaper than abatement. Thus airports might pay noise victims to move away (by purchasing nearby homes), as was done in Los Angeles. See n. 18, above and see generally Ronald Coase's famous article, "The Problem of Social Cost," *Journal of Law and Economics* 3 (1960):1.

†For specific pollutants that are potentially lethal in small quantities, such as dioxin or methyl mercury, direct and specific regulatory controls—assuming an outright ban is not warranted—would be preferable.

Unfortunately, ideal systems exist only in the imagination. Enforcement, for one thing, would not necessarily be smooth. Systems of charges or taxes must still be policed, perhaps more closely and unforgivingly than direct regulation. Abatement machinery easily breaks down or fails to adapt to changes in the manufacturing process. Accurate instrumentation for continuous measurement of emissions is not always available and is usually very expensive. Monitoring emissions—the basis for the tax—thus is a real problem.[52] Generally speaking, this task would require regulations demanding detailed record keeping and reporting by the enterprise, plus a system of government inspection to spot-check reporting and actual performance. Penalties would be prescribed for misreporting, and strong political pressures (by complying firms as well as by environmentalists) would exist for catching and prosecuting cheaters.[53] But due process rules would still make successful prosecution of bad apples difficult. Revelations of misreporting would result in ever more stringent reporting and monitoring systems to prevent cheating, systems that would be unduly burdensome for the good apples. Consequently, a tax or charge system might be subject to many of the same problems of ineffectiveness and unreasonableness as enforcement under direct regulation schemes.

Setting the correct tax also presents a number of problems. The theoretically correct per unit tax is equal to the social damage of the pollution at equilibrium, that is, the point at which further expenditures on abatement would begin to exceed the value of further reductions in pollution in the airshed or watershed. But it is very difficult to calculate the damage done by pollution—and harder yet to obtain agreement on such calculations. What is the social cost of not being able to fish in a given stream? Of losing a beautiful view to smog? Of suffering exaggerated asthma symptoms? Thus the advocates of charges are ready to settle for a tax that aims to produce the same "arbitrary" result as direct regulation, that is, a predetermined ambient standard.[54] If we cannot be assured of the optimal *level* of pollution control, so the argument runs, at least with charges we have a better chance of achieving whatever level is chosen most cost-effectively. Yet, even this concession is insufficient, for there is still the problem of knowing what tax will in fact reduce pollution to the level defined by the ambient standard. The consequences of setting too low a tax would be particularly troublesome when pollutant loadings create threshold effects—imagine the outcry if, after investing huge sums in cleaning up a river so as to restore fishing opportunities, the water contained almost, but not quite, enough oxygen to permit the fish to survive.[55] Indeed, in order to ensure achievement of environmental goals, there may well be strong political pressures to establish tax rates that would be extremely high, resulting in overinvestment (from a social point of view) in pollution abatement.

Of course, there would be no pressure to set taxes excessively high if the regional (or national) charge-setting authority could start low and readily increase the effluent tax to compensate for initial errors. But such tax increases might prove difficult politically, especially if a decision on plant location or investment in expensive capital goods had been predicated on expectations of the lower tax. Tax levels also pose a problem as economic growth occurs in a region. In principle, the effluent tax should rise in order to maintain pollutants at the level set by the ambient standard. However, polluters who were already in place and who would be subject to such growth-induced tax increases would have a powerful incentive to organize to keep out newcomers through politically manipulable devices like zoning regulations or especially high tax rates for new sources.

One way to handle some of the above problems is a system of auctionable pollution rights.[56] Once the ambient standard is set, enough pollution rights could be distributed so as to produce that level of pollution and no more (or less). Enterprises would bid against each other for these rights, with the result that the polluters with the highest clean-up costs would end up paying for and holding the rights, while those with the lowest clean-up costs would clean up. In principle, therefore, the outcome would be identical to that under an effluent charges scheme in which the tax had successfully been set at the optimum level. The auctionable pollution rights system also permits economic growth more readily than a charges arrangement, for as newcomers bid away existing rights from oldtimers (who would then have to clean up further) the value of the rights would appreciate and the oldtimers would profit rather than lose.

The auctionable pollution rights scheme faces some serious political problems, however, that a charges or taxes scheme might avoid. The idea of permitting enterprises to buy and sell a license to pollute is repugnant to many persons who see pollution as a sin rather than as a mere negative by-product of desirable economic and social activity. Moreover, the issue of how to distribute the initial allotment of pollution rights (before the auction begins, as it were) raises vexing questions of equity. To vest all the initial entitlements in the public, that is, in the pollution control agency, which would then sell them for very high prices to industry, would be tantamount to a sudden government expropriation of property that had been enjoyed by private industry with the tacit approval of custom and usage. If, on the other hand, rights are initially vested for free in the polluters themselves, it would be hard to justify virtually any conceivable distributional principle. The most politically sustainable principle would no doubt be proportional to the level of an enterprise's discharges just prior to the initial distribution of entitlements. This rule would turn out to be unfair to enterprises that had already done a great deal to cut back on their discharges, but attempts to modify this simple rule would create an intolerable administrative tangle that might come out even more unfairly.

Perhaps the most serious drawback of a pollution rights auction, however, is that the capital value of the rights is vulnerable to shifts in the political environment. If the pollution control agency were to decide, for whatever reason, that its past policies had been too stringent, the appropriate solution would be for it to issue new rights. But doing so would have the same cheapening effect on the value of the old rights that printing new money has on the money in circulation. On the other hand, if for some reason the demand for existing rights increased—perhaps because new firms badly wanted to locate in the region—the fortunate owners of the rights would enjoy windfall capital gains. Political pressures might come into being to tax these away or, worse yet, to ration the apparently scarce rights among new firms and older polluters. The heavy hand of direct regulation would return and might in some ways be even heavier than it now is, since it would attend to allocating pollution abatement costs among dischargers as well as simply to setting emission and/or ambient standards.

We can conceive of a modification of the pollution rights auction that might avoid the worst of that scheme's potential political and bureaucratic handicaps: an abatement contract strategy, under which, instead of selling licenses to pollute, the pollution control agency should buy contracts to clean up pollution. It would pay polluters, or specialized pollution-control firms, for abatement services, that is, the reduction of their own or someone else's discharges. Abatement service contracts would be allocated by a sealed-bid competitive auction, so that bids would be expected (by conventional economic theory) to approximate the true costs of abatement (including a normal profit). The pollution control agency would choose a certain number of winners—how many would depend on how much pollution it desired to have abated in the relevant planning period—from among the lowest bidders (those who would do the most abatement for the least money), thereby assuring that the overall resource costs of doing the clean-up job would be minimized. (In letting contracts, the agency would not concern itself with exactly who performed the abatement services, at which sources, or by what means. Apart from overall policy planning, the agency's major concern would be to prevent collusion in competitive bidding for abatement service contracts and, once the contracts were let, to monitor contract compliance.) Each subsequent planning period would bring in additional, higher-cost abaters, until finally the airshed reached the desired ambient air standard.[57]

The best method of financing an abatement contracts program should be a matter for further exploration. Although there is no special reason that it should not be financed out of general tax revenues,[58] to do so would relieve the cost burden presently imposed on polluters by the Clean Air Act and state implementation plans. Whether this burden was placed there fairly or not is perhaps debatable, but it seems to us politically unfeasible to shift the burden to taxpayers at this point. Hence, we would suggest that at least partial financing of the portfolio of abatement service contracts be accomplished by means of a tax on polluting (atmospheric) discharges.

As in the case of the two other nonstandard approaches to air pollution control—effluent taxes and pollution rights—implementing the abatement contracts approach requires the pollution control agency to decide on a minimum ambient air quality standard and to compile an inventory of discharges (that is, who is emitting how much). This latter task is necessary so that the amount of clean-up performed can be measured by substracting a current level of discharge from some previously measured level. Although both tasks present many problems and uncertainties, these problems and uncertainties do not seem to differ very much as between the several nonstandard approaches under consideration.

Compared with pollution rights auctions and pure tax schemes, the abatement contracts strategy has several political advantages. First, it substitutes the symbolism of abatement services for that of licenses to pollute, while possibly levying taxes on those who continue to pollute. Second, it collects and distributes revenues in a seemingly rational and equitable manner, that is, in accordance with the costs of clean-up to different enterprises as revealed in a bidding process. Finally, and most importantly, it stabilizes the regulatory environment for affected dischargers. Uncertainty over what future regulatory changes might bring has been one of the most significant, albeit relatively invisible, social costs of the current regulatory policy under the Clean Air Act. Investments are deferred pending clarification of whether the standards and enforcement practices will tighten up, or perhaps loosen up, or at any rate change in such a way as to alter the competitive situation of different firms in an industry. Under an emission taxes approach, uncertainty would still remain in regard to future tax rates. In a system of auctionable pollution rights, the capital value of acquired rights could drop sharply if the pollution control agency decided for some reason to expand its supply. Under the abatement contract strategy, however, the contractual bond between government and those embarked on pollution abatement would stabilize expectations all around, at least for the duration of the contract period.[59]

In an important sense, the abatement contracts strategy is merely an elaborate version of the offset policy that the EPA has been trying to develop since late 1976 with respect to regions of the country that have not attained the primary ambient air standards promulgated under the 1970 Clean Air Act amendments. The essential element of the offset policy is that new firms that generate pollution may move into nonattainment areas provided they obtain emission reductions from existing sources at least equal to the emissions they themselves will create. This policy has developed haltingly for a great many reasons, at least some of which would be removed by the abatement contracts strategy.[60] The offset policy encourages the exchange of something like pollution rights—although for political reasons they are not called that—and thereby creates an allocative process with some of the attendant virtues of the marketplace, that is, responsiveness to social change and tendencies toward greater economic efficiency. It is a marketplace that runs on barter, rather than money, however, and is hampered by awkward regulatory rules. Since the local regulatory authorities have the right to specify a trade-off ratio between emissions to be abated and new emissions of greater than one for one, the advent of new industry can actually work to reduce the total pollution loading in the affected airshed. But there is really no reason for the citizens of the airshed to wait for new firms to come along before attempting to buy out the discharges of an existing firm. Nor is there a reason to limit the financial base for such attempts to that provided by new firms. Offset contracts could be purchased by the local government pollution control agency using as a (partial?) financial base the revenues generated by the effluent tax as applied to the population of existing firms. Moreover, by using a bidding process, the agency would not have to make virtually arbitrary decisions about what trade-off rates to impose on a new firm seeking a discharge permit; in the limited experience to date with offsets, these decisions seem to vary from case to case, thereby raising questions of equity, and creating needless uncertainties on the part of both potential dischargers and pollution agencies.*

The abatement services contracting scheme is most advantageous as a means for stabilizing what would otherwise be a thin and wavering market in pollution rights. There may be other workable means of propping up this market as well. One could imagine, for instance, a government insurance arrangement whereby pollution rights owners could purchase insurance against large (or even small) capital losses in the value of their rights. Or the government might agree to repurchase pollution rights at some discounted price, much in the way that the Federal National Mortgage Association repurchases mortgages from the private sector. Schemes like these would certainly have to be thought through more than we have, of course, especially with regard to solving some of their political problems.

Such plans for stabilizing and financing pollution control, finally, represent a fundamentally different model of regulatory control from that which underlies legalistic direct regulation and even liability law. It implies that government's proper role is not simply to drive productive enterprises toward socially protective behavior by promulgating standards, threatening enforcement, and applying penalties, but also, and perhaps primarily, to devise modes of public-private cooperation in defining, financing, and achieving social goals. This broader social responsibility of government-as-regulator is the subject of our final chapter.

---

*One problem that afflicts offsets also afflicts abatement services contracts: the difficulty of specifying trading regions. This difficulty arises from the intrinsic nature of air pollution, in that it does not stay nicely localized.

CHAPTER ELEVEN

THE SOCIAL RESPONSIBILITY
OF GOVERNMENT

•

In 1981, protective regulation was under sharp attack. A newly elected conservative Republican president and his appointees to major federal agencies promised to roll back the regulatory tide, and few public officials stood up to protest. But the force of regulation is not easily turned aside. Despite growing objections to the many and varied costs of regulation, the public broadly supports the principle of government intervention to protect health and safety, environmental quality, and other humane values. This support is easily transformed into policy by triggering events such as airline crashes and tragic hotel fires that lead to lawsuits, stricter regulations, and tougher enforcement. In a technologically complex and dynamic society, such events are bound to occur sooner or later in virtually every regulatory area. Moreover, as we argued in Chapter 1, even without dramatic triggering events, there is a deductive logic that over a period of years turns even a small hedge of regulatory protections into an ample thicket. Once it is established that regulation should, for example, prevent the dumping of toxic wastes into streams, regulations are in time extended, even by a generally antiregulation legislature, to deal with analogous problems such as waste disposal and oil spills in the oceans and the disposition of uranium mill tailings.[1] If imaginative businesses start using rabbit meat as a substitute for other meats in their products, laws are enacted to extend existing quality control standards and inspection rules to rabbit meatpackers.[2]

Most new regulation may not be unreasonable, of course, but inevitably some of it is, if not in conception, then as applied to many individual cases. As new regulation gradually grows, therefore, so does the agenda for regulatory reform. But reform proposals are not easy to implement. If regulatory officials are urged to be reasonable and enforce regulations flexibly, they may also need greater resources to hire and train more competent inspectors; yet budgets usually will be tight. Officials who attempt to introduce discretion into the enforcement process, moreover, are subject to fierce public criticism for opening the door to official lawlessness, for eroding statutory rights to protection and equal treatment, for being unduly soft vis-à-vis the bad apples, and for appearing corrupt. Thus the safest and by far the easiest course for regulatory officials, all things considered, is to go by the book, to fill loopholes with more specific regulations, to impose more comprehensive recordkeeping and reporting requirements, and to enforce them uniformly.

But the alternative strategies of indirect regulation are not always or easily substituted for command-and-control regulation. Government-reinforced private regulation, mandatory disclosure of risk-related information, private litigation, taxes and charges—if used instead of direct regulation—would decentralize decisionmaking and thereby introduce more flexibility and reasonableness in matching protective measures to regulatory ends. But each would be an adequate substitute for command-and-control regulation for only a limited range of social problems, either because the indirect control strategy would be less effective than direct regulation or because it might neglect egalitarian concerns that direct regulation often is designed to address. On the other hand, efforts to make each indirect strategy more powerful and equal in its effect can lead once again into the mire of unreasonableness.

If, in the long run, the regulatory impulse will persist, and if reform cannot be brought about by simple, global solutions, the challenge for government is the far more complex one of selecting the appropriate regulatory implements more wisely and of developing the competence to regulate more reasonably and responsibly.

ON PLANNING NEW REGULATORY INITIATIVES

Suppose, for the sake of argument, that the federal government were setting out to induce more energy conservation by industry and that some sort of regulatory approach—direct or indirect—were to be used. The following menu of strategies might be reviewed:

- Impose machinery or building design standards. Give enforcement responsibility to OSHA, the Department of Energy, state public utilities regulators, or local building code enforcers.

- Impose performance standards. Give enforcement responsibility to in-house inspectors; require frequent self-audits and submission of reports. License the in-house inspectors.
- Tax wasteful energy consumption. Administer the tax through the private utility rate system.
- Give rebates for reductions below certain average use levels. Finance these out of taxes imposed on wasteful users.
- Require equipment and machinery suppliers (or manufacturers) to develop and disclose energy efficiency ratings of their wares.
- For corporations to which Securities and Exchange Commission regulation is applicable, require disclosure of energy utilization and conservation measures in periodic public reports.
- Require periodic internal energy audits by consulting technicians certified to diagnose wasteful consumption and able to recommend improvements.
- Require the private utilities to supply the results of these energy audits to some or all of their customers or to a public regulatory agency.
- Furnish tax rebates through the general tax system tied to certain types of qualifying investments in machinery or in building remodeling.

And these are only the most plausible strategies. Readers might wish also to concoct examples using modifications of the common law of property, torts, or contracts.*

None of these strategies is a priori without merit. No matter how inappropriate any might seem after sustained analysis, none should be dismissed out of hand before that analysis. In this conclusion lies an important moral: at present, there is no general theory of regulatory design with sufficient power to furnish good guidance on particular questions.† A general theory that would exclude any of the items on our menu of energy conservation strategies would also risk overlooking

---

*Strategies that rely on pure subsidies or pure education and propaganda, for example, are also possible: one does not need to draw on the regulatory domain at all in many cases, except perhaps—but almost always very importantly—for political purposes.

†Although we have, in previous chapters, offered many remarks about the tendencies of certain strategies to fail in some respect, or to be less appropriate for some problems than for others, statements of tendency should not be mistaken for firm laws.

something that might turn out, with appropriate modifications and elaborations, to be a good idea. In addition, perhaps more than one strategy would be worthwhile, or two or more strategies might even be made to complement one another.

Fortunately, the absence of a strong theory about what regulatory strategy works best under what conditions need not impede policy planning and political action. There are few enough major strategic options that a policy designer can check each one in turn in the context of the specific problem being addressed. Our menu of possibilities in the hypothetical case above contained only nine entries. True, each entry could be varied and modified almost infinitely, depending on which criteria in addition to effectiveness were to be emphasized (e.g., reasonableness, accountability, libertarianism, egalitarianism, or paternalism). Indeed, it is precisely the need to account for these additional values in the regulatory design that makes any simple general theory potentially misleading. Yet the *basic* menu of strategic possibilities is sufficiently limited to permit a point-by-point review of each of the items.

Greatly exacerbating the problem of policy choice is the fact that regulatory programs are so susceptible to change over time. They may be propelled into mindless and suffocating legalism or drift into a torpid and ineffective mutualism with the regulated sector—or move in both directions simultaneously. As with all policy, much depends on the implementation process, and implementation in turn depends not only on general institutional and political developments but also on the idiosyncrasies of personalities and turns of events. An idealized version of the future, based on a mixture of weak theory and hopeful assessment of the particulars of the implementation context, will certainly not be the future that actually materializes.[3]

While it may be possible to predict the general direction of departures from the ideal and the process by which they will occur, it is rarely possible to predict the degree. Yet it is on matters of degree that policy design decisions must turn. A somewhat imperfect information strategy might be better for dealing with the above energy-conservation problem than a very imperfect regulatory strategy, for example, whereas if one could hold the imperfections of the regulatory strategy to a moderate rather than a high level, the opposite conclusion might be justified. But how is one to assess these questions of degree? Or other, perhaps equally important matters of degree, like the degree of suspicion that might surround the actions of the public utilities commissioners and their staff?

Or the variability in climate that affects site-specific energy waste? Or the relative importance of behavior as opposed to physical plant in causing such waste? Or the likelihood that the energy auditors sent into the field would actually be competent to do the job?

Policymakers should also note that even the best strategies of direct and indirect regulation might produce results that are worse than doing nothing at all. The constraints on effectiveness are real, as are the incentives toward overregulation and unreasonableness. They cannot simply be wished away. We have shown that the imperatives of the regulatory process force trade-offs: for example, between punishment of the guilty and protection of the innocent, between appropriate consistency and appropriate flexibility, between the rule of law and the rule of reason. Under many conditions, we might simply wish to opt for no regulation at all or, more accurately, for allowing the market, the liability law, and professional norms to develop protective features in the absence of explicit legislative intervention. "Richer is safer," wrote Aaron Wildavsky, and it is true that if we simply encourage plant modernization through economic incentives, many aspects of product and worker safety and environmental protection will continue to improve.[4] In an important sense, indeed, we may already have opted for a "no regulation" policy in certain areas. We have an occupational safety and health administration but not a household safety and health administration, even though many preventable accidents occur in the home. Parents are not licensed for safety and effectiveness despite the fact that thc bad applcs among thcm cause untold social harm. Nurses may bark and snap without fear of government sanction. And university professors, we note with relief, are not liable for the ignorance or folly of their opinions. Not only would regulation of such matters be thought an undue intrusion upon personal freedom, but most people would sense, in strictly cost-benefit terms, that regulation would be unduly expensive, unreasonable, and mischievous. The same may well be true of many proposals for new controls to prevent harms perpetrated by business firms or local government units.

IMPROVING REGULATORY AGENCIES

Nevertheless, government controls do and will continue to make sense in many areas and often with a good deal of urgency. New government offices or agencies will be summoned into being, and most existing agencies will continue to make rules and deploy inspectors. Under the political, legal, and organizational arrangements that currently exist, and under most of those that we can foresee in the future, such agencies will continue as likely sources of regulatory unreasonableness. Are there ways to improve them?

Perhaps the most effective and politically acceptable external controls on regulatory unreasonableness can be imposed through the budget process. When budgets are chronically and predictably constrained, agency ambitions must shrink to fit them. Enforcement officials might then be induced to concentrate primarily on bad apples or on the sources of harm for which direct regulation can provide the most value added. They might be impelled to devise more imaginative ways to work with citizen complainants without using up valuable inspectorial resources and to develop methods of delegating the details of protective measures to regulated enterprises. They might rely more on educational strategies, mandatory disclosure regulations, or assistance to private litigants rather than invest all their resources in more expensive (and probably more unreasonable) direct regulation and enforcement. At the rulemaking level, budgetary pressures, by forcing agency leaders to order their priorities, check the tendency of regulatory officials to lobby for the logical extension of regulatory controls to related (but often more marginal and elusive) problems. Unfortunately, however, there is no guarantee that agencies (or legislatures) will employ the right priorities in cutting back operations, and some agencies have difficulty maintaining an adequate level of effectiveness under existing budgets, much less reduced ones. Some agencies that are unreasonable through lack of competent personnel can be made worse by financial adversity. Thus budgetary restrictions, if employed as an axe rather than as a scalpel, may reduce agencies' ability to accomplish what is desirable.

More selective strategies of controlling regulatory unreasonableness might be discovered if we recall our analogy between regulatory unreasonableness and air pollution: since both are usually by-products of socially constructive activities, eliminating the by-products completely eliminates the constructive benefits as well. Taking the analogy further, if we were to think of unreasonableness as an epidemic sort of injury inflicted on society by careless regulators operating inadequately safeguarded regulatory machinery, or as a form of injustice inflicted by the strong upon the weak, then regulatory agencies might themselves be appropriate objects of regulation. Regulatory unreasonableness would thus be a form of not fully responsible social conduct, and as such, policy approaches toward curbing it can be reviewed by following the same reasoning a policy designer should use in approaching any regulatory objective.

Consider first the possibility of mandated self-regulation. Many recent statutes are relatively explicit in requiring an agency to undertake some form of cost-benefit analysis before promulgating its regulations. In a 1979 article, Robert Reich, the director of policy planning at the Federal Trade Commission, observed that "In recent years, the Congress has passed approximately forty new laws—in health, education, transportation, housing, the environment, and agriculture—that call for evaluation of the economic impact of regulations proposed under them."[5] President Carter's Executive Order 12044 (March 1978), following President Ford's call in 1975 for "inflation impact statements" and echoing the environmental impact analysis requirement of the National Environmental Policy Act, required executive branch agencies to subject major proposed regulations to a form of cost-benefit analysis, including alternative ways of dealing with the problem involved, the economic effects of each alternative, and a justification of the approach selected.

President Reagan's Executive Order 12291 (February 1981) goes a lot further than any of these requirements. It requires that proposed regulations meet the test of economic benefits exceeding costs and also requires that the most cost-effective interventions be selected for whatever level of benefits (or costs) is selected.[6] One may doubt, however, given the technical problems of quantification, that these mandates will be taken too seriously except as rhetoric. This form of mandated self-regulation can be allied with a form of direct regulation. Under the Carter administration, for example, a sort of enforcement agency, the Regulatory Analysis Review Group (RARG), was assigned to oversee the implementation of the Executive Order. The RARG was established as an interagency group chaired by the chairman of the Council of Economic Advisers and staffed by technicians from the Council on Wage and Price Stability (COWPS) and formally administered by the Office of Management and Budget. The OMB was to receive a copy of every "Economic Impact Statement" executed by the agencies, and the RARG was to review those few proposed regulations that it believed most dubious and likely to have a major economic impact. If the RARG was displeased with a proposed rule or regulation, it could publicize its displeasure—or certainly more to the point, threaten to do so. Whether for better or for worse, it was not empowered to do much more. It could not dismiss unreasonable regulators from their posts, and it could not levy fines against unreasonable agencies. The agencies were not obliged to publish a mea culpa, along the lines dictated by the corrective advertising strategy, in the *Federal Register*. The sanctions available to the RARG appear to have been principally adverse publicity, the general hassle involved in having to defend oneself against attack, and the political threat that somehow all these pressures could translate into an eventual diminution of agency authority and perhaps even the following year's annual budget increment.

The two mistakes that can be made in thinking about these essentially political sanctions are to imagine that they are insignificant and, alternatively, to imagine that they are immensely significant. Probably most people tend to underestimate their significance. To agency officials who must survive in a politicized environment in which reputation and publicity are the common currency of social and political interaction, these sanctions are far from trivial. There are reports that, within the regulatory agencies, to have had one's regulation selected for review by the RARG staff had become known as "getting RARGed," even though only eight regulatory proposals actually "got RARGed" between early 1978 and late 1979. RARG could even claim some tangible successes. For example:

An OSHA proposal to regulate worker exposure to the widely used chemical acrylonitril (shown to produce cancer in animals and probably in exposed workers) called for a reduction to three possible ceilings: 2 ppm, 1 ppm, or 0.2 ppm. RARG criticized OSHA for inadequate analysis of the risks actually involved, and noted that, given OSHA's figures, it would cost $4 million in capital investment to prevent a single cancer death under the 2 ppm standard, $29 million under the 1 ppm rule, and $170 million under the 0.2 proposal. RARG argued that the latter figure seemed too high. It also criticized OSHA's refusal (which reflected organized labor's position) to consider the use of less costly personal respiratory equipment as an abatement measure, and its insistence on specifying engineering controls rather than just stipulating the performance limits. Several months later, the OSHA regulations adopted the 2 ppm standard (over an 8 hour period). It insisted on "engineering controls," but gave affected companies two years to comply, and focused only on major producers and users, exempting many consumer-products manufacturers using fibers and plastics containing acrylonitril because the risks seemed small at that point. The Society of the Plastics Industry called the rule "tough but realistic," as did several individual producers.[7]

But like other regulatory agencies, RARG stimulated some forms of resistance.* The quality of the analytic cost-benefit work done by the agencies pursuant to the various statutes and presidential orders calling for such work has been quite varied.[8] Some agencies have not been so willing to take the obligation seriously. Because the cutoff point for susceptibility to being reviewed by RARG was an estimated $100 million in compliance costs, writes Christopher DeMuth, "a suspiciously large number of regulations have been projected to cost $90-95 million."[9] In late 1978, the heads of 35 regulatory agencies countered by forming the Regulatory Council, which proceeded to commission studies to produce better methods of demonstrating regulatory benefits. Environmental groups and labor unions brought lawsuits challenging the right of members of the Council of Economic Advisers to "intervene" on an *ex parte* basis in the rulemaking process.[10] DeMuth summed up the first year and a half of RARG this way:

> While it has clearly brought about improvements in the substance
> of a few regulations, it has also brought about a great deal of con-
> fusion, intrigue, and bad feeling within the executive branch; [and]
> has necessitated occasional (and reluctant) presidential intercession
> to arbitrate disputes over particular regulatory proposals . . . .[11]

That is, the direct regulation of the regulators has produced exactly the mixed results that our analysis of the direct regulation of business would lead one to expect.

Nevertheless, just as the environmental impact statement requirement has compelled major agencies to hire environmental specialists to make their decisions defensible on environmental grounds, the pressures to defend regulations against attack by the RARG forced most agencies to establish internal units to analyze the costs of proposed regulations. Their

---

*At this writing, the counterpart to RARG (and COWPS) established by the Reagan administration is still too young to permit evaluation. It is called the Office of Information and Regulatory Affairs and is housed in the Office of Management and Budget.

influence, sincerity, and competency have varied, but their sheer presence and activity seemed to have an effect on agency consciousness, just as the regulation-induced presence of industrial hygienists and environmental engineers in private corporations seems to affect their consciousness.[12]

The institutionalization of a government review unit external to the regulatory agency is nicely consonant with the Founding Fathers' principle that a properly republican government should be itself governed by an internal system of checks and balances. Regulatory agency zeal—and perhaps self-aggrandizement—is to be balanced by the conservatism of RARG and COWPS. But RARG had no legal sanctions at its disposal, and hence there were proposals to throw in some legal checks as well to superregulate the regulators by increasing the power of Congress, the president, or the courts to veto regulatory decisions.

Congress, of course, has inherent powers to regulate regulatory agencies, either by enacting more specific laws in the first place or by passing laws that selectively repeal or amend existing regulations. More specific statutes would also make judicial review a more potent check. Hence many analysts of regulatory performance call for "clearer statutory standards," for closer legislative oversight, or even for a revival of the moribund constitutional doctrine that forbade excessive delegation of legislative powers.[13] But Congress has rarely been inclined to listen. A busy and politically divided legislature has generally found it difficult to enact specific standards or to engage in detailed supervision or review of specific regulatory agency actions. While new institutional devices have been proposed to make that job easier, such as the one-house legislative veto that would permit either house of Congress to override any agency-promulgated regulation, there is a possibility that a one-house, or even a two-house, legislative veto might ultimately produce a more haphazard and patchwork regulatory fabric than we now have. Some congressional oversight committees would continue to duck petitions to review controversial regulations. Others might use the veto power to terrorize agencies subject to their jurisdiction and deter agency initiatives to modify regulations designed to cut compliance costs. Certain pressing and complex problems, like the management of toxic substances and wastes, are sufficiently tangled up in interagency and federal-state rivalries and in confused communication networks already, without adding a congeries of committees in two separate legislative branches to the mess. Perhaps the prospects would be brighter in other policy areas, but at the very least the legislative veto concept should not be considered an across-the-board remedy.[14]

Direct presidential regulation of regulatory agencies through intervention in specific regulatory decisions has also been sporadic and unpredictable. Moreover, unless expressly authorized by statute, it is of questionable legitimacy.[15] A proposal by Lloyd Cutler and David Johnson, endorsed by the American Bar Association, would give the president formal statutory authority to modify or reverse regulatory actions concerning certain "critical" issues.[16] The small political storm raised by President Carter's direct involvement in the formulation of OSHA's regulation controlling cotton dust, however, suggests that presidents usually would find it unappealing to become directly involved in such highly specific, technically complex, and emotional issues.[17] We would not expect a presidential veto—as opposed to his indirect influence through appointments and through RARG-type analysis by his economic advisers—to be a consistently significant check.

Aggressive judicial review, on the other hand, could be a more pervasive and continuous way of regulating the regulators. In contrast to self-initiated involvement by RARG, Congress, or the president, judicial review can be triggered for virtually every new rule, whether politically controversial or beneath political notice, by aggrieved private parties. In recent years, some courts have been quite activist in demanding more thorough regulatory analysis, overturning proposed regulations founded on questionable scientific research[18] or inadequate analysis of the economic costs posed by regulatory decisions (even when the governing statutes have not clearly required such results).[19] In decisions overturning OSHA's regulation designed to control in-plant benzene fumes, a federal court of appeals insisted that OSHA was obligated to support stringent abatement requirements with better evidence and more careful cost-benefit analysis; the Supreme Court, while stopping short of that question on review, held that OSHA had not demonstrated that the risks would justify reduction of allowable exposures to 1 ppm, as opposed to a somewhat higher (and must less costly to attain) level.*[20]

---

*In a subsequent decision, however, the Supreme Court, disagreeing with the court of appeals position in the benzene case and stating that "the judicial function does not extend to substantive revision of regulatory policy," held that OSHA was *not* compelled by the act to support a stringent cotton-dust control standard by analysis showing that the health benefits of the standard selected exceeded the costs. *American Textile Manufacturers Association v. Donovan,* 49 U.S. Law Week 4720 (June 17, 1981). The court stated that

The benzene decisions point up some weaknesses of aggressive, policy-oriented judicial review of regulatory decisions. As in the case of complaint-triggered inspections of regulated firms, there is a strong likelihood that an activist judicial posture would encourage a large number of appeals. Some proportion of these—perhaps even a substantial proportion—would lack merit and would result in long delays in the promulgation of quite justifiable regulations. Critics of the benzene decisions have put forth a fairly powerful argument that this is what has occurred in this instance.[21] A second weakness of more aggressive judicial review lies in the decentralized and unpredictable character of the judiciary. If judges felt free to review the content of regulatory decisions, for every case in which a reasonable court quashed an unreasonable regulatory decision, there would probably also be at least one other decision in which a proregulation judge, by reading the legislative history willfully or by insisting on better evidence, would block a reasonable agency's attempt to extend an unrealistic statutory deadline, to carve out an exception on cost-benefit grounds, or to roll back a previously established standard. Frequent and aggressive judicial review might lead to overregulation of the regulators and perhaps do more harm than good.[22]

Bureaucratic, political, or judicial oversight is only one way to regulate the regulators. The idea of repersonalizing responsibility within the regulated organization—an idea discussed earlier as a way of improving self-regulation in large business enterprises—might also be applied to the regulators. Personal responsibility tends to become as diluted in government organizations as in private organizations, if not more so. Reports, studies, analyses, citations, and abatement orders are all issued anonymously under the name of the office or organizational unit that produced them. If it were possible for outsiders to pin the blame for sloppy analytical work—or to give credit for good analytical work—on the responsible *individuals,* sloppiness might be somewhat discouraged, as might be the disposition to err in the direction favored by one's immediate boss or peer group. This adjustment in the way government agencies go about their work might not dramatically improve regulation, but it would probably not hurt and, in any case, might be endorsed on the more general grounds of reducing anomie in the bureaucracy.

OSHA must show only that the standard was technically and economically "feasible," that is, capable of being met.

Another institutional change that might improve government self-regulation, analogous to putting general public directors on a corporation's board, is to establish a seat for an economist on regulatory advisory boards. Such boards these days typically have industry, consumer, and technical professional representation; they omit those who have only an indirect stake in holding regulatory costs down, for example, consumers who prefer lower prices to higher quality or citizens who prefer more economic growth or less inflation to cleaner air or water. Professional (or even amateur) economists would not necessarily represent such interests perfectly, but they are trained to be concerned about trade-offs, opportunity costs, the value added of a program or policy, and other concepts that are fundamental to designing reasonable regulatory policies.

The mandatory disclosure approach might also be fruitful. Agencies might be obliged not only to conduct cost-benefit (or risk-benefit) studies, but also to make them public. Under President Reagan's Executive Order 12291, this is in fact required. The obligation to publish cost-benefit analyses might be extended even to minor regulations; instead of the present $100 million cutoff, $5 million might be chosen. (The Reagan order affects only "major" proposed rules.) After all, if such a study were to cost $50,000 to $100,000, this cost would still represent only 1-2 percent of the cost of the regulation, and the study might easily suggest ways to effect more than enough savings to pay for itself. If the news media regularly were enabled to report the estimated aggregate costs of proposed rules, or of a complex of regulations, the electorate might be more sensitized to the inflationary implications of regulatory measures, and agencies might be more concerned with demonstrating that they had selected cost-effective strategies. (This scenario also implies that thought should be given to ways of increasing the economic literacy of journalists.)

Cost-benefit analyses produced by the regulatory agencies themselves are, of course, susceptible to bias; one would expect a tendency to overestimate the benefits of a proposed regulation and to underestimate its costs. In this respect, such studies are no different from some information produced in the private sector under the aegis of mandatory disclosure programs. As we suggested in the latter context, a possible solution might be to contract with an independent group or organization to produce the information. Just as Consumers Union might be engaged to produce tire ratings for the National Highway Traffic Safety Administration, perhaps university or foundation researchers could be engaged to produce the relevant cost-benefit studies for regulatory agencies.

The potential role of private liability law in containing regulatory unreasonableness appears to be rather limited. In principle, of course, regulatory agencies might be induced to maintain more effective internal checks on overzealous and incompetent enforcement officials if the agencies were obligated to pay money damages to enterprises victimized by unreasonable enforcement actions. The federal Equal Access to Justice Bill, in fact, is a gesture in this direction; it makes the government liable for the attorney fees incurred by small businesses that are vindicated in court after challenging or defending themselves against regulatory orders that are not substantially justified.[23] One could imagine extending the Federal Tort Claims Act or amending judicial doctrines of sovereign and official immunity to allow regulated enterprises to recover economic losses due to grossly erroneous adverse publicity generated by regulatory agencies,[24] clearly unfounded summary orders,[25] or other regulatory actions that clearly exceed the agency's legal authority. But most unreasonable regulatory enforcement would not be touched by rules that make the agency liable for patently *ultra vires* actions or grossly negligent fact finding. Site-level unreasonableness occurs when enforcement officials *follow* the law but are indifferent to subtle variations in the seriousness of the violation, the culpability of the violator, and the costs of compliance. Yet it would hardly be feasible to subject an agency to lawsuits for damages based on enforcement orders that are "legal," but whose costs clearly exceed benefits, or some equivalent verbal formula.* Like certain reforms designed to make product manufacturers or physicians act responsibly through easier-to-bring lawsuits, making it easier to sue regulated agencies for "unreasonableness" might result in a vast increase in litigation or, worse, a pattern of defensiveness and excessive timidity on the part of enforcement officials.[26]

If regulatory unreason is an externality like air pollution, then perhaps we should find a way to tax it so as to increase its marginal costs to the offending agency until they equal its marginal costs to society as a whole.

---

*It might be feasible, however, to enable regulated enterprises as defendants to obtain judicial reversal of fines or orders that are technically "legal" but unreasonable under the circumstances, or at least to require agencies to provide substantive (not just legalistic) justifications for arguably unreasonable requirements. This might be thought of as a due process right to nonmechanical (hence reasoned, nonarbitrary) enforcement of legal rules.

An actual unreasonableness tax, of course, would not be feasible, but one current proposal for a "regulatory budget" in the federal government might serve as a fundamental equivalent. The budget would set a maximum amount of regulatory compliance costs that could be imposed on private enterprises by all regulatory agencies within a given period.[27] Each time a regulatory agency promulgated new requirements, therefore, it would reduce other agencies' freedom to impose costly requirements; it presumably would first have to justify the relative importance and reasonableness of its regulation, and draft it so as to minimize the total compliance costs it would "draw down" from the regulatory budget. This inter-agency competitive bargaining process, in effect, would have the same deterrent effect as a heavy tax on excessively costly regulatory proposals. The plan would be very hard to implement, however, because of the problems of obtaining even moderately reliable cost estimates and of making them stick during the political and technical controversy that would surround each major proposed regulation.[28]

A somewhat more workable *retrospective* regulatory budget does, however, seem possible. Instead of trying to control the costs of future regulations, perhaps the focus should be on trimming back the costs of regulations already on the books. Suppose that agencies were obliged periodically to decrease the compliance costs of existing regulations by some percentage, say 5-10 percent every three or four years. Compared with the estimates of future costs, already incurred costs are relatively (though not completely) certain and measurable. Suppose further that agencies were obliged to accept nominations from outside sources, for example, regulated firms and institutions, academics, other government agencies, and legislators, as to which regulations most urgently deserved revision. Any successes at actually cutting down compliance costs could be entered into the political display of performance statistics that agencies now engage in with respect to fines levied or sites inspected.[29]

It might also be desirable to oblige the agency itself to get systematic feedback concerning which of its regulations or enforcement strategies were imposing excessive costs in the field. An agency could attach this function to, say, an ombudsman's office or to a specialized quality control unit that monitored inspectors' decisions for instances of unreasonableness as well as for underenforcement. The monitoring unit could survey regulated enterprises and talk to inspectors to get their views, as well as to study which regulations resulted in the most appeals or highest violation rates.* Just as private self-regulation may be enhanced by requiring enterprises to hire trained experts, regulatory agencies might be required to subject enforcement officials to regular training that sensitizes them to the economic and technical compliance problems of regulated enterprises. Regular public conferences between enforcement officials and representatives of regulated enterprises might be made mandatory.

Unfortunately, it is difficult to devise a means other than adverse publicity to penalize agencies that failed to reexamine existing compliance costs seriously. One possibility, now required by President Reagan's order, is to apply a "sunset" provision to certain regulations so that they would automatically expire after a certain number of years unless they were affirmatively readopted. The basic statutory frameworks of the federal air quality and water quality programs must be reauthorized in 1981 and 1982, respectively; these legislative reviews will certainly be welcome and will very likely lead to modifications in the direction of greater reasonableness. Sunset provisions for most regulations will surely cause many difficulties, however, especially if they applied to so many regulations that the process of "examining" specific regulations is reduced to mere ritual.

Finally, we must point out once again that better self-regulation will not necessarily be free. It surely would be costly to increase reasonableness by, for example, providing more training for inspectors, arranging field visits by office-bound regulation writers to see the real effects of their regulations, gathering good analytic information about costs and benefits, preparing and reviewing analytical reports. Of course, these costs might be repaid many times over by reducing the financial burden of regulation. But the political support for the original investment is likely to be slender. For each agency, the proregulation constituency will object because it will see that resources devoted to increasing reasonableness in effect divert resources from hiring more inspectors and lawyers. The antiregulation constituency will object because it will imagine that the resources will be devoted to *more* regulation no matter what official promises are made about using them to improve regula-

---

*If one wanted to link this self-monitoring function to a mandatory disclosure strategy, periodic reports to the public or to the legislature might be required—although we suspect such a requirement would simply condemn the monitoring unit to permanent isolation in bureaucratic Siberia.

tion—an objective which, in any case, is in some tension with industry hopes for more sweeping deregulation.

The social regulation movement acquired momentum in the late 1960s partly because President Johnson saw it as a way of maintaining the symbolic commitment to government activism on behalf of liberal causes without having to increase the federal budget, which was then straining to finance the Vietnam war. The costs of activism would show up mainly in private ledgers rather than in the government budget.[30] Now it appears that the benefits of a certain type of increased government spending (to increase reasonableness) would show up on private ledgers, while the costs would show up on the public ledger. Ironically, the same budgetary politics that opened the gate of regulatory unreasonableness now stands in the way of narrowing its aperture.

PROFESSIONALISM AND REGULATION

The best-developed social expression of self-regulation is the ethic of professionalism. Can this ethic be applied to regulators? One of the central characteristics of most professions—exemplified best by medicine—is that their practitioners employ tools that can inflict great harm as well as good. In this critical respect, government regulators are very like professional practitioners. Whereas incompetent physicians mount intrusive assaults on the body of the individual person, the incompetent regulator can assault the body politic. Nevertheless, regulators as well as physicians require a fair measure of discretion, and hence trust, in order to be able to carry on their work. As we have seen, when outsiders second-guess decisions made by the front-line practitioners, the outsiders are not much more likely to be right than wrong in their judgments, and fear on the part of the front-line practitioners of being criticized for presumed errors can induce counterproductive conduct on their part.

Like other professionals, regulators as a class possess certain specialized knowledge, not only the technical knowledge required to judge good manufacturing practices in a biologics plant, say, or the degree of conformance of electrical wiring to a building code, but also knowledge of the workings of the regulatory process itself—with its apparatus of rules, inspectors, and sanctions. An understanding of the workings and limits of this triad of elements is an important part of the knowledge base for what might be called the "regulatory profession."*

More particularly, just what is in the fund of specialized knowledge of the professional regulator, or what might it be expected to encompass if fully developed? First, it would include the lore related to effective enforcement—improving the technical means of inspection, bringing pressure against bad apples, training and deploying inspectors, protecting the enforcement agency against corruption and charges of corruption, fending off legislators seeking inappropriate regulatory leniency for their constituents, and designing systems that would both encourage valid complaints and screen out invalid or diversionary complaints. It would also include sensitivity to all the ways in which tough enforcement, if carried out indiscriminately, can limit effectiveness, stimulate legalistic resistance, and cut off cooperation. Professionalism would also entail knowledge of how to make regulation reasonable as well as effective: training field-level enforcement officials in the proper use of discretion, speeding up the process of rule revisions, dampening the impulse of some officials to invoke maximum penalties for unimportant infractions, and encouraging officials to be resourceful in gaining the cooperation of regulated enterprises and in muting unwarranted criticism by the media and advocacy groups. Finally, regulatory professionalism would include knowledge about the grand strategy options in regulatory design, such as mandatory disclosure, self-regulation, charge-based incentives, and combined liability-regulatory systems, as well as command-and-control direct regulation. Today, very few regulators have much knowledge about the limits and possibilities of the strategic approaches other than those embodied in their own programs, but if a regulatory profession were to emerge, its members could educate one another about such matters, thereby creating new knowledge within the profession as a whole that had not existed among its individual members.

Regulators in different agencies, to be sure, do not now think of themselves as part of a regulatory profession. For the most part, they are not fully aware of how many problems they share, and they do not even see themselves as members of a single nominal class. When we gathered a number of them from diverse program areas for a two-day workshop at

---

*Let us again emphasize that we are discussing here only protective, not economic, regulation.

the Graduate School of Public Policy at Berkeley, most were amazed as well as delighted to discover that they had such close kin. As we discussed the generic problems of developing better technical means of inspection and observation, deterring corruption, and bringing pressure on bad apples, many regulators remarked at how surprisingly alike inspection programs were and how surprisingly easy it was for people from such seemingly diverse programs to communicate with one another.

It would not necessarily be a good thing if regulators regarded themselves as a distinct caste. We can easily imagine them reinforcing all their own worst tendencies toward overregulation. On the other hand, we did observe that the regulators at our workshop were even more eager to talk about the problems of reasonableness than about, say, the malefactions of this or that giant corporation. They were concerned, for instance, about the slowness of rule revision, the inflexibility of enforcement, and the relentlessness of the ratchet effect. They fully understood their own fallibility and were, after a fashion, prepared to recognize the greater realism of the civilian perspective compared with their own official perspective.

We found that regulators rarely get to share the frustrations of working out a reasonable regulatory system with people outside their immediate work environment, and it might be a very good thing indeed if they could see themselves as part of a larger community of public functionaries (and perhaps private ones too) that understands and respects efforts to make regulation more reasonable. As we have noted, the political and bureaucratic environment of recent years has rewarded appropriate stringency a good deal more than it has rewarded appropriate leniency, and punishes inappropriate leniency a good deal more harshly than it punishes inappropriate stringency. It is certainly possible that a professional association of regulatory officials might fill a useful niche in the regulator's personal environment, providing peer approval for appropriate reasonableness and peer criticism for inappropriate stringency. The talk could just as easily turn to how to fend off demagogic legislative or interest group attacks for supposedly inappropriate leniency as it could to how better to badger businessmen and corporate managers.

THE PUBLIC PHILOSOPHY OF REGULATORY PROFESSIONALISM

Whatever the accoutrements of regulatory professionalism, and whatever its most desirable institutional expression (if any), its ethics and principles must merge with the ethics and principles of some larger political theory or "public philosophy." The central tenet of an acceptable public philosophy of regulation must, in our view, be the affirmation that norms of social responsibility originate in society or in public opinion, and not in the state. Rules and regulations promulgated by legislators and regulatory officials merely express or intensify underlying social norms and values; they do not create them. An instrument is required to articulate and enforce social norms of responsible action, of course, and government agencies are frequently the chosen instrument. But the *distinctive* competence of such agencies is the deployment of enforcement officials and the imposition of sanctions rather than the specification of how the diffuse body of community sentiment and norms should apply to a particular case. That latter task is undertaken constantly—indeed primarily—by citizens rather than government officials. Our legal system, indeed, is pervaded by practices, such as the use of lay juries and reliance on informal negotiations, to ensure that civilian notions of justice and responsibility will infiltrate and influence the behavior of official norm-enforcers.[31]

The distinction between the society and the state as originators of norms of social responsibility is important because the formalized statements of general normative beliefs incorporated in legal regulations by the institutions of the state may not correspond closely to the norms of social responsibility found in society, especially as applied to particular cases. Society's version of responsible behavior typically is inchoate and complex, reflecting a mixture of values and concerns. Commonly, sentiments simultaneously favor safety and risk, freedom and control, equality and efficiency, uniformity and diversity, and different segments of the population differ in their weighting of these values. The actual working (or desired) norms of social responsibility emerge through a process of balancing conflicting values, not only in the marketplace and in the courtroom but in countless discussions in living rooms and barrooms and factory lunchrooms as well. Most importantly, these working assessments are almost always conditional, fluid, and subject to adjustment on the basis of slight shifts in many factors, ranging from the prior relationship of the specific persons affected by a dispute to specific economic and human consequences of alternative dispositions. That is why, for example, we rely upon a dialogue among jurors rather than a fixed legal formula to determine culpability in criminal cases and liability in cases of alleged negligence.

By contrast, regulatory agencies are typically devoted to a single mission. Their efforts to distill particular versions of social responsibility from their general statutory mandates are constrained by their focus on a particular set of objectives that are given unconditional legal primacy, or at least a presumption of primacy. Of all the values at stake in the welter of real life situations, they are expected to emphasize one. Norms of due process and equal protection compel them to embody their policy decisions in fixed legal rules and to apply them uniformly. Moreover, they operate in a public arena in which they are particularly susceptible to pressures from protection-minded constituencies and interest groups and legislators to elaborate and enforce protective rules, a susceptibility much aggravated by the political climate created (largely inadvertently) by the media. But strict enforcement and the prevention of harms are not always the socially responsible courses. If the costs—and not just the financial ones—of prevention are very much in excess of benefits, and if there are no overriding egalitarian or paternalistic considerations to offset this imbalance, then one might reasonably say that more mandated prevention was socially irresponsible. It almost certainly would conflict with the more conditional and flexible normative approach of the civilian perspective.

In addition, without an awareness of the social sources of the idea of social responsibility, we may inadvertently diminish or damage those sources. Like any other idea, "social responsibility" can be faded and tired or rich and vital. A lot depends on how it is expressed in concrete social settings, how people talk about it, how people give it meaning in their day-to-day conduct. That the government has "taken more responsibility" for the prevention of social harms through regulation has led to "more responsibility," in some sense, in the firms and institutions being regulated. Today, largely because of government regulation, more people think about social concerns such as equal opportunity, environmental protection, chemical hazards, and accident prevention; a great many people now are specialists in these matters. Yet, we are concerned lest quantity come at the expense of quality. To the degree that the regulatory reach of the government quickens the conscience and stimulates the thinking of people working in regulated enterprises, extending that reach serves to enliven and enrich the cultural idea of social responsibility. Unfortunately, the outstretched hand of government regulation is often covered with horns and scales. What it touches, it bureaucratizes. It commands the keeping of records, the learning of rules and regulations, the installation of standardized procedures. It sets in motion a correspondence (and often a litigation) between the regulated enterprise and the regulatory agency over misunderstandings, suspicions, and merely technical derelictions; internally, it sets in motion an analogous succession of memoranda and committee meetings on the same topics. The hand of government regulation creates not only responsibility itself, therefore, but also an apparatus for guaranteeing what the government defines as responsibility. The apparatus is anything but inspiring. It says that the idea of responsibility is tedious, procedural, and impersonal. It has always been hard to act responsibly. Now one is likely to get a headache on top of it.

What government creates in large part is not responsibility but accountability, and these two ideas are not identical nor even entirely compatible. We can define responsibility as doing what one judges to be right in a problematic situation involving someone else's welfare, and accepting the moral blame for any harms that flow from one's judgment. Accountability, on the other hand, implies doing what an outside reviewing party, not immediately present in the situation, will subsequently judge not to have been wrong. In the abstract, therefore, one can imagine a set of all the responsible courses of action open to an individual in a situation and compare it with the set of all actions that would meet the relevant accountability requirements. These two sets might overlap. If they do not, and if a course of action from the second set is chosen, one can say that *accountability displaces responsibility*.

To give up on a course of conduct that one thinks is right in favor of another course simply because the latter reflects the will of those to whom one is accountable is to act irresponsibly in an important sense. One common concern of professionals in bureaucracies, for instance, is that they will be obliged to act against their consciences in order to satisfy bureaucratic imperatives fashioned by their hierarchical superiors. The company physician may be forced to withhold data on workers' health conditions from the workers themselves because management does not want to be liable for workers' compensation payments; or a design engineer may be forced to substitute shoddy components in order to hold costs down; or a nursing home administrator may be forced by the owner to change the bed linen less frequently in the interests of higher profits. From the point of view of the professionals obliged to carry them out, these are irresponsible courses of action. Up to a point, the professional can rationalize such apparent irresponsibility by reflecting on his or her occasional triumphs on behalf of virtue. But persistent failure cannot be blinked away so easily, and once recognized it leads to demoralization and cynicism. In consequence, the will to succeed diminishes and so too does the possibility that one will draw sustinence from the limited successes of weeks, months, or years past.

The erosion of responsibility in this fashion does occur, perhaps extensively. Yet precisely because the scenario is so well understood and is so much the object of earnest social discourse, this sort of blatant irresponsibility can be combatted and its scope somewhat contained. But the erosion of responsibility by government-imposed accountability may occur more insidiously because it is harder to recognize. It occurs when one is obliged to act by one's overseers in a way that nominally serves socially responsible goals but is in fact ineffective either in an absolute sense or in light of the social costs imposed. This happens, for example, when a safety engineer is forced by OSHA to spend his limited budget on remodeling or on new equipment when he believes he should spend it mainly on training new workers in safety procedures; or when a university administrator is obliged to spend $100,000, say, to hire five affirmative action minority coordinators when the same money could be better used to furnish scholarships to 40 minority undergraduates; or when a marine biologist spends six months documenting, for an "Environmental Impact Statement," the obvious fact that sea lions could be harmed by nearby oil production activities when he believes it would make more sense to focus on methods to avoid having these activities disturb the habitat during the breeding season. Whereas the road to demoralization in the previous scenario led through cynicism, this one leads through futility. The road is paved only with good intentions, but the stones are planned and ordered by people who do not understand the diversity of the local terrain or the needs of the ever-changing groups of laborers who will build it. Although the stones conform to standards and regulations, they are not what the foreman on the site needs to make a proper road.

The foreman in this metaphor can stand for an entire stratum of individuals who occupy positions of trust and responsibility in the society: teachers, doctors, hospital administrators, factory food inspectors, plant managers, fire chiefs, auditors, journalists, public school principals, city planners, nurses, presidents of large corporations, nuclear safety engineers, lawyers, and so on. As we noted earlier, these are the people who bear the brunt of accountability requirements imposed by official regulators. They are also the cultural carriers of the idea of responsibility.

What they think and say about their work, and about themselves, gives shape and substance to the idea. If they and their work become enmeshed in the toils of proceduralism, red tape, and other expressions of bureaucratic formalism, the idea of responsibility is in trouble—if not now or in the very near future, then perhaps in ten or twenty years; and if not with respect to social harms already known and charted then with respect to harms the character of which we cannot even begin to define at the moment.

Of course, we do not know whether this trusteeship stratum *is* becoming progressively demoralized or, if so, how rapidly. The quality of the problem, however, if not its extent, is well captured in these comments addressed by a retiring workplace safety engineer in a large steel mill to his counterpart in another company. Retirement would not be so bad, he said, because

> I no longer can be considered a progressive saver of people; I respond only to OSHA compliance officers and grievance committeemen. . . . It just ain't the same ballgame. No longer room for imagination, dedication, loyalty to a cause, pride of accomplishment and desire to serve. . . . The brother's keeper philosophy on which our old group lived . . . is no more. It has given way to a posture which asks, "Is it required by OSHA?" . . . I suppose the best tipoff is that our [new] Safety Director is a lawyer . . . .

Regulators, remember, like physicians, can do harm as they seek to do good. If physicians sometimes destroy our tissues instead of mending them, so do regulators sometimes diminish our capacity for social responsibility instead of enhancing it. The risk of having the state push accountability requirements into the farther reaches and deeper recesses of social life is that, in the long run, everyone will be accountable for everything, but no one will take responsibility for anything. Thus the social responsibility of regulators, in the end, must be not simply to impose controls, but to activate and draw upon the conscience and the talents of those they seek to regulate.

NOTES

●

CHAPTER ONE

1. See Preface for an explanation of methodology and data sources.
2. See pp. 26–28 in manuscript.
3. Jonathan R. Hughes, *Social Control in the Colonial Economy* (Charlottesville: University of Virginia Press, 1975), p. 133. See also Wallace Johnson, "America's First Food and Drug Laws," *Food, Drug, and Cosmetic Law Journal* 30 (1975).
4. See *Seaman v. Patten*, 2 Caines N.Y. Term Rep. 312 (1805), finding the inspector-general not liable to the owner for "mistake or want of skill" in confiscating beef.
5. Ernst Freund, *Standards of American Legislation*, 1965 ed. (Chicago: University of Chicago Press, 1917), p. 77.
6. The quoted language is from a California state law of 1889. See Lucille Eaves, *A History of California Labor Laws* (Berkeley: University of California Press, 1910), p. 322. See also Lawrence M. Friedman, *A History of American Law* (New York: Simon and Schuster, 1973), p. 402, describing a similarly worded Massachusetts statute. For the English precedents, see Bernice Martin, "Leonard Horner: A Portrait of an Inspector of Factories," *International Review of Social History* 14 (1969): 412; and Adelaide M. Anderson, *Women in the Factory* (London: John Murray, 1922).
7. Friedman, *History of American Law*, p. 402.
8. In addition, the Safety Appliance Act of 1893 (amended in 1903) required installation of standardized automatic couplers and the most advanced brake systems; the Block Signal Act (1906) and the Signal Inspection Act (1920) mandated the use of automatic signaling systems. See Irving Scharfman, *The Interstate Commerce Commission*, Bernard Margolius, "The Interstate Commerce Commission and the Development of Safety Legislation," *George Washington Law Review* 1 (1937): 712, 743–745. These railroad regulations reflected federal safety-oriented inspection programs that went back to 1838 for seagoing vessels. See U.S., Attorney General's Committee on Administrative Procedure, *Monograph No. 10, Department of Commerce, Bureau of Marine Inspection and Navigation* (Washington, D.C.: U.S. Government Printing Office, 1940).
9. See Spencer L. Kimball, *Insurance and Public Policy: A Study in the Legal Implementation of Social and Economic Public Policy, Based on Wisconsin Records, 1835–1959* (Madison: University of Wisconsin Press, 1960), pp. 292–295.
10. Lawrence M. Friedman, *Government and Slum Housing: A Century of Frustration* (New York: Rand McNally, 1968), pp. 27 and 38–39.
11. Robert H. Wiebe, *The Search for Order: 1877–1920* (New York: Hill and Wang, 1968), p. 191. See also James Weinstein, *The Corporate Ideal in the Liberal State: 1910–1918* (Boston: Beacon Press, 1968).

12. Gerald Nash, *State Government and Economic Development: A History of Administrative Policies in California, 1849–1933* (Berkeley, Calif.: Institute of Governmental Studies, 1964), pp. 153 and 236.

13. See ibid., pp. 148 and 238.

14. See E. Patrick McGuire, *The Product-Safety Function: Organization and Operations* (New York: The Conference Board, 1979).

15. Cited in J. Willard Hurst, *Law and the Conditions of Freedom in the Nineteenth Century United States* (Madison: University of Wisconsin Press, 1956), p. 73.

16. Not infrequently, the perception of higher levels of risk may have been erroneous, as in the case of food purity and safety. See U.S., Congress, Senate, Committee on Governmental Affairs, *Study on Federal Regulation*, Appendix to Vol. VI, *Framework for Regulation* (95th Cong., 2d sess., December 1974), p. 395. The increase in workplace accident rates was probably due to the tight labor market that began in the mid-1960s and to the demographic changes that brought a higher proportion of young workers into industry. Younger workers, with less experience and higher turnover rates, generally experience higher injury rates. See Robert S. Smith, *The Occupational Safety and Health Act: Its Goals and Its Achievements* (Washington, D.C.: American Enterprise Institute, 1976).

17. See James Q. Wilson, "The Politics of Regulation," in *Corporate Responsibility and the Business Predicament*, ed. James McKie (Washington, D.C.: The Brookings Institution, 1974), pp. 135–168, and Mark V. Nadel, *The Politics of Consumer Protection* (Indianapolis: Bobbs-Merrill, 1971), pp. 34–40.

18. See Kenneth W. Clarkson, Charles W. Kadlec, and Arthur B. Laffer, "Regulating Chrysler Out of Business?" *Regulation*, September/October 1979, pp. 44–49.

19. See Rich Jaroslavsky, "Douglas Costle's Balancing Act," *The Wall Street Journal*, April 11, 1980.

20. See American Enterprise Institute, *Major Regulatory Initiatives During 1979* (Washington, D.C.: American Enterprise Institute, 1980).

21. Frederic B. Siskind and Glenn M. Shor, *The New York Times*, a report on the results from a national poll of 1,000 individuals over 18 conducted for the Union Carbide Corporation; see also U.S., Council on Environmental Quality, *Public Opinion in Environmental Issues, Results of a National Opinion Survey* (Washington, D.C.: Council on Environmental Quality, 1980).

22. It seems, for instance, that in the United States the only demographic factor that appears as a consistent correlate of good health is education. See Victor R. Fuchs, "The Economics of Health in a Post-Industrial Society," *The Public Interest*, Summer 1979, pp. 3–20. Survey evidence concerning the distribution of support for environmental regulation, however, shows only a very modest correlation with educational level. See Everett Carl Ladd, Jr., "Pursuing the New Class: Social Theory and Survey Data," in *The New Class?* ed. B. Bruce-Briggs (New Brunswick, N.J.: Transaction Books, 1978), p. 109, Table 8-5.

23. Irving Kristol, *Two Cheers for Capitalism* (New York: Basic Books, 1978), p. 26. See also Paul H. Weaver, "Regulation, Social Policy, and Class Conflict," *The Public Interest*, Winter 1978, pp. 58–59.

24. Weaver, "Regulation, Social Policy, and Class Conflict," p. 59.

25. Reported to us by the environmental affairs director of a major aluminum manufacturing corporation.

26. Letter to the Editor, *Regulation*, March/April 1979, p. 4.

27. John E. Jackson and Robert A. Leone, "The Political Economy of Federal Regulatory Activity: A Case Study of Water Pollution Controls in the Pulp and Paper Industry" (Paper presented at the National Bureau of Economic Research Conference on Public

Regulation, Washington, D.C., December 1977). See also Clarkson, Kadlec, and Laffer, "Regulating Chrysler Out of Business?"; and U.S., Small Business Administration, *The Impact on Small Business Concerns of Government Regulations that Force Technological Change* (Washington, D.C.: Small Business Administration, 1975).

28. Small Business Administration, *The Impact on Small Business Concerns.*

29. Peter Navarro, "The Politics of Air Pollution," *The Public Interest*, Spring 1980, pp. 36 and 38; and Bruce A. Ackerman and William T. Hassler, "Beyond the New Deal: Coal and the Clean Air Act," *Yale Law Journal* 89 (1980): 1466. See also Jaroslavsky, "Douglas Costle's Balancing Act," p. 16.

30. See Douglas D. Anderson, "Who Owns the Regulators?" *The Wharton Magazine*, Summer 1980, p. 14; and Douglas D. Anderson, *Regulatory Politics and Electric Utilities* (Boston: Auburn House Publishing, 1981). See also Suzanne Weaver, *Decision to Prosecute: Organization and Public Policy in the Anti-Trust Division* (Cambridge: MIT Press, 1977), on incentives to government attorneys for aggressive prosecution.

31. *Martin Luther King Jr. Elementary School Children v. Michigan Board of Education*, 473 F. Supp. 1372 (E.D. Mich. 1979); and N. Epstein, *Language, Ethnicity and the Schools: Policy Alternatives for Bilingual-Bicultural Education* (Washington, D.C.: Institute for Educational Leadership, George Washington University, 1977).

32. See Neal S. McCoy and Randy M. Mott, "Filing Changes Seen If SEC Follows Ecology Rules Set in Steel Case," *National Law Journal*, November 26, 1979, pp. 26–27.

33. See Derek Bok, "The Federal Government and the University," *The Public Interest*, Winter 1980, pp. 80–101.

34. See Paul Quirk, "Food and Drug Administration," in *The Politics of Regulation*, ed. James Q. Wilson (New York: Basic Books, 1980). Also see Jerry Mashaw, "Regulation, Logic and Ideology," *Regulation*, November/December 1979.

35. There is little systematic research on television coverage of regulation. One exception is *Television News Covers Nuclear Energy: A Ten Year Perspective*, a detailed content-analysis of videotapes done in 1980 by the Media Institute, Washington, D.C., a research organization funded primarily by business. The study found that only after the Three Mile Island accident in March 1979 did the evening news shows of the three major networks give substantial attention to nuclear power safety.

36. James L. Payne, Letter to the Editor, *Regulation*, July/August 1980, pp. 1–2.

37. Michael Harris, "BART Tube Fire Drills Urged for Passengers," *San Francisco Chronicle*, January 26, 1979.

38. The Media Institute, *Television News Covers Nuclear Energy*, found that television news stories on the subject consisted primarily of charges and countercharges, with the balance tilted toward critics of nuclear energy. Similar findings emerge from analyses of television documentaries on pesticides and herbicides by the Council for Agricultural Science and Technology, Ames, Iowa, an association of agricultural scientists.

39. "New Revelations in DC-10 Jet Probe," *San Francisco Chronicle*, June 20, 1979.

40. Jerome Doolittle, assistant administrator, Federal Aviation Authority, letter to the authors, August 29, 1979.

41. See Richard Posner, "A Theory of Negligence," *Journal of Legal Studies* 1 (1972): 29.

42. Council on Environmental Quality, *Tenth Annual Report* (Washington, D.C.: U.S. Government Printing Office, December 1979), p. 666, Table 12-4.

43. Murray L. Weidenbaum and Robert DeFina, *The Cost of Federal Regulation of Economic Activity* (Washington, D.C.: American Enterprise Institute, 1978), pp. 13–15. The $500 estimate of compliance costs for new automobiles may be somewhat inflated due to inappropriate inclusions and to counting some items twice. An analyst for the National Highway Traffic Safety Administration estimated the comparable figure at $250, as reported in Mark Green and Norman Waitzman, *Business War on the*

Law: An Analysis of the Benefits of Federal Health/Safety Enforcement (Washington, D.C.: Corporate Accountability Research Group, 1979), pp. 30 and 102–104. We are inclined to believe that Weidenbaum and DeFina are closer to the truth than are their critics, however, mainly because the Green and Waitzman volume is so evidently plagued by conceptual mistakes and confused rhetoric. The impact on individual firms can be staggering. The financially beleaguered Chrysler Corporation recently estimated that complying with mandated safety and pollution control regulations in the 1978–85 period would involve $280 million in fixed costs alone (e.g., research and development and retooling). See Clarkson, Kadlec, and Laffer, "Regulating Chrysler Out of Business?"

44. See Jack Miske, "Capital Formation and 10-5-1," *Foundry Management and Technology*, April 1979.

45. Lawrence S. Bacow, *Bargaining for Job Safety and Health* (Cambridge: MIT Press, 1980).

46. "Copper Firms: Cost of Regulation to '87 Put at $3.5 billion," *The Wall Street Journal*, April 26, 1979, p. 31; Raymond S. Hartman et al., "The Economic Impacts of Environmental Regulations on the U.S. Copper Industry," *Bell Journal of Economics* 10, no. 2 (Autumn 1979): 589–618. The high ratio of operating costs to initial capital expenditures for pollution control and OSHA regulations is confirmed by a detailed study of compliance costs in 48 major corporations, conducted by the accounting firm of Arthur Anderson and Co. See Michael E. Simon, "The Business Round Table Study: What We Did," *Regulation*, July/August 1979, pp. 20–21.

47. See, for example, Green and Waitzman, *Business War on the Law*. The evidence of inflated cost projections is often drawn from exaggerated estimates of the consequences of OSHA's vinyl chloride regulation. See David Doniger, *The Law and Policy of Toxic Substances Control: A Case Study of Vinyl Chloride* (Baltimore: Johns Hopkins Press, 1978); John Mendeloff, *Regulating Safety: A Political and Economic Analysis of the Federal Occupational Safety and Health Program* (Cambridge: MIT Press, 1979), chap. 4. But see Herbert Northrup, Richard Rowan, and Charles Perry, *The Impact of OSHA* (Philadelphia: The Wharton School, 1978), noting that vinyl chloride monamer manufacturers spent $9 million to comply, or $6,187 per worker, and polyvinyl chloride producers spent $119 million, or $23,751 per worker. Operating costs for both industries increased annually.

48. See, for example, Marvin Kosters, "Counting the Costs," *Regulation,* July/August 1979; and Green and Waitzman, *Business War on the Law*. With respect to calculating benefits, see A. Myrick Freeman III, "The Benefits of Air and Water Pollution Control: A Review and Synthesis of Recent Estimates" (Report prepared for the U.S. Council on Environmental Quality, 1979).

49. See Stephen Rhoads, "How Much Should We Spend to Save a Life?" *The Public Interest*, Spring 1978.

50. Albert L. Nichols and Richard Zeckhauser, "Government Comes to the Workplace: An Assessment of OSHA," *The Public Interest*, Fall 1977, pp. 36–39. See also Mendeloff, *Regulating Safety*, and Bacow, *Bargaining for Job Safety and Health*.

51. Council on Environmental Quality, *Tenth Annual Report*, pp. 655 and 666, Table 12-4. We have interpolated the cost estimate from figures for 1978 and 1987 in Table 12-4. Concerning the political propensity to choose water pollution goals for which economic costs exceed benefits, see Bruce Ackerman et al., *The Uncertain Search for Environmental Quality* (New York: The Free Press, 1974).

52. See G. Christian Hill, "Los Angeles's Setback in Smog Battle Raises Doubts in Other Cities," *The Wall Street Journal*, November 20, 1979, pp. 1 and 39. Also Eugene P.

Seskin, "Automobile Air Pollution," in *Current Issues in U.S. Environmental Policy*, ed. Paul R. Portney (Baltimore: Johns Hopkins Press, 1978).

53. See also the analysis of noise abatement regulations in Smith, *The Occupational Safety and Health Act*, chap. 3. With respect to the issue of personal protective equipment versus engineering solutions to workplace problems, it should be noted that wearing the equipment imposes a real, if intangible, cost on the worker. A proper cost-benefit analysis would take this into account, although in practice this is not often done. See James C. Miller III and Bruce Yandle, eds., *Benefit-Cost Analyses of Social Regulation: Case Studies From the Council on Wage and Price Stability* (Washington, D.C.: American Enterprise Institute, 1979).

54. See, for example, Edward Koch, "The Mandate Millstone," *The Public Interest*, Fall 1980; Paul Danaceau, *Regulation: The View from Janesville, Wisconsin, and A Regulator's Perspective* (Washington, D.C.: U.S. Regulatory Council, March 1980); and Bok, "The Federal Government and the University."

CHAPTER TWO

1. The Fourth Amendment bars only "unreasonable" searches and seizures and thus has not been thought to bar inspections. The Supreme Court has held that the inspector, in some programs at least, must apply to a judge or magistrate for a search warrant when the "inspectee" does not voluntarily consent to the inspection. See *Marshall v. Barlow's Inc.*, 436 U.S. 307 (1978) (warrant needed for OSHA inspection). But, the court added, a warrant could be issued on evidence less than "probable cause" to suspect a violation. OSHA need only show that a business has been chosen for inspection "on the basis of a general administrative plan for enforcement . . . derived from neutral sources."

2. FDA officials have on occasion condemned entire lots or crops on the basis of unrepresentative samples. See James O. Freedman, "Summary Action by Administrative Agencies," *University of Chicago Law Review* 40 (1972): 33; *U.S. v. 43½ Gross Rubber Prophylactics*, 65 F. Supp. 534 (D. Minn. 1946); and *Anderson & Co. v. U.S.*, 284 Fed. 542 (9th Cir. 1922).

3. See generally Jerry L. Mashaw, "Civil Liability of Government Officers: Property Rights and Official Accountability," *Law and Contemporary Problems* 42 (1978): 8. Official immunity may not apply if the inspector has obviously and willfully exceeded his legal authority or has undertaken an unreasonable and unconstitutional search, but such extreme arbitrariness is rare. Even if liability can be established, courts ordinarily will not order compensation for losses resulting from the adverse publicity that often accompanies government action. See *Mizokami v. U.S.*, 414 F.2d 1375 (Ct. Cl. 1969); and Ernest Gellhorn, "Adverse Publicity by Administrative Agencies," *Harvard Law Review* 86 (1973): 1380.

4. Freedman, "Summary Action by Administrative Agencies," pp. 20 and 61.

5. See, for example, the Occupational Safety and Health Act, Sec. 6(b)(5); and the Safe Drinking Water Act, Sec. 1412(a)(2).

6. See Toxic Substances Control Act, Sec. 6(a).

7. Peter Schuck, "The Curious Case of the Indicted Meat Inspectors," *Harper's*, September 1972, p. 81.

8. Ibid., p. 82.

9. Robert Rabin, "Agency Criminal Referrals in the Federal System: An Empirical Study of Prosecutorial Discretion," *Stanford Law Review* 24 (1972): 1036; and James Q.

Wilson, *The Investigators: Managing the FBI and Narcotics Agents* (New York: Basic Books, 1978).

10. Report of the Industrial Accident Commission of the State of California, 1914, p. 35.

11. Paul B. Downing and James Kimball, "Enforcing Administrative Rules: The Case of Water Pollution Control" (Paper presented at the National Bureau of Economic Research Conference on Public Regulation, Washington, D.C., December 15–17, 1977). The same pattern appears to be common in England for worker safety and water pollution control regulation. See W. G. Carson, "White Collar Crime and the Enforcement of Factory Legislation," *British Journal of Criminology,* October 1970, pp. 383–398; and Keith Hawkins, *Environment and Enforcement* (London: MacMillan Press, forthcoming).

12. See, for example, Rabin, "Agency Criminal Referrals."

13. For a vivid description of this process, see Philip Schrag, "On Her Majesty's Secret Service: Protecting the Consumer in New York City," *Yale Law Journal* 80 (1971): 1529.

14. For an account of these incentives to compromise among investigators in a consumer fraud office, see Susan Silbey, "Consumer Justice: The Massachusetts Attorney General's Office of Consumer Protection" (Ph.D. diss., University of Chicago, 1978), p. 318.

15. See, for example, Pietro Nivola, "Municipal Agency: A Study of the Housing Inspectorial Service in Boston" (Ph.D. diss., Harvard University, 1976); and U.S., Senate, Subcommittee for Consumers, Committee on Commerce, Hearings on the Food Amendments of 1974, p. 97. On the conflict between agency and Justice Department lawyers generally, see Donald L. Horowitz, *The Jurocracy: Government Lawyers, Agency Programs and Judicial Decisions* (Lexington, Mass.: Lexington Books, 1977).

16. Hawkins, *Environment and Enforcement.*

17. James S. Turner, *The Chemical Feast* (New York: Grossman Publishers, 1970), p. 120.

18. For an excellent discussion of this issue, see Christopher D. Stone, *Where the Law Ends: Social Control of Corporate Behavior* (New York: Harper and Row, 1975).

19. Frances Zemans, "Civil or Criminal Litigation of Disputes: A Rose by Any Other Name . . ." (Paper prepared for the Midwest Political Science Association, Chicago, 1977).

20. See Nivola, "Municipal Agency," chap. 5; Maureen Mileski, "Policing Slum Landlords" (Ph.D. diss., Yale University, 1973). For the same tendency in other agencies, see Bruce C. Vladeck, *Unloving Care: The Nursing Home Tragedy* (New York: Basic Books, 1980); and Stan Crock, "The Troubling Consent Decrees," *The Wall Street Journal*, May 18, 1978. (The SEC settles 90 percent of civil complaints by consent order to avoid uncertainty of court outcomes).

21. See Richard Posner, "The Federal Trade Commission," *University of Chicago Law Review* 37 (1969): 47; and Richard Posner, "The Behavior of Regulatory Agencies," *Journal of Legal Studies* 1 (1972): 305. An enforcement agency can, however, concentrate its resources on the big case that pushes the law to its limits. See, for example, Weaver, *Decision to Prosecute*; see n. 20, p. 327.

22. See Hearings of the Special Subcommittee on the Sylmar Tunnel Disaster, California State Assembly General Research Committee, September 2, 1973.

23. Office of Technology Assessment, *An Evaluation of Railroad Safety* (Washington, D.C.: U.S. Government Printing Office, 1978).

24. For example, botulism, although a constant threat in the production of canned goods, has been almost completely eliminated. And regulators of milk and dairy products in California today have difficulty remembering any outbreaks of the bacterial diseases that led to regulation early in the century.

25. See Mileski, "Policing Slum Landlords," and Hawkins, *Environment and Enforcement,* chap. 7.

26. See *Environmental Defense Fund v. Ruckelshaus,* 439 F.2d 584 (D.C. Cir. 1971); and *Environmental Defense Fund v. Hardin,* 428 F.2d 1093 (D.C. Cir. 1970).

27. See Ken Hechler, "The Development of the Federal Coal Mine Safety Act of 1969," *West Virginia Law Review* 77 (1975): 612 and U.S., Congress, Subcommittee on Government Operations, Enforcement of Federal Mine Health and Safety Laws (93d Cong., 1st Sess., October 31, 1973).

28. See, for example, Nicholas A. Ashford, *Crisis in the Workplace: Occupational Disease and Injury* (Cambridge: MIT Press, 1976).

29. See Claire Townsend, *Old Age: The Last Segregation,* Ralph Nader's Study Group Report on Nursing Homes (New York: Grossman Publishers, 1971); and Mary Adelaide Mendelson, *Tender Loving Greed* (New York: Knopf, 1974).

30. See, for example, Mark Green, *The Closed Enterprise System* (New York: Grossman Publishers, 1972), p. 162; David P. Riley, "Taming GM . . . and Ford, Union Carbide, U.S. Steel, Dow Chemical," in *With Justice for Some,* eds. Bruce Wasserstein and Mark Green (Boston: Beacon Press, 1971); and Michael K. Glenn, "The Crime of 'Pollution': The Role of Federal Water Pollution Criminal Sanctions," *American Criminal Law Review* 11 (1973): 835; and Kenneth A. Manaster, "Early Thoughts on Prosecuting Polluters," *Ecology Law Quarterly* 2 (1972): 471.

31. See, for example, E. Pendleton Herring, *Public Administration and the Public Interest* (New York: McGraw Hill, 1936); Avery Leiserson, *Administrative Regulation: A Study in Representation of Interests* (Chicago: University of Chicago Press, 1942); Marver H. Bernstein, *Regulating Business by Independent Commission* (Princeton, N.J.: Princeton University Press, 1955); and Grant McConnell, *Private Power and American Democracy* (New York: Knopf, 1966).

   For critiques of the capture theory, see Louis Jaffe, "The Effective Limits of the Administrative Process," *Harvard Law Review* 67 (1954): 1105, 1109, and Weaver, "Regulation, Social Policy, and Class Conflict."

32. See, for example, Turner, *The Chemical Feast*; Robert C. Fellmeth, *The Interstate Commerce Omission: The Public Interest and the ICC* (New York: Grossman Publishers, 1970); Joseph A. Page and Mary-Win O'Brien, *Bitter Wages: The Report on Disease and Injury on the Job,* Ralph Nader Study Group Reports (New York: Grossman Publishers, 1973); Edward Cox et al., *The Nader Report on the Federal Trade Commission* (New York: R. W. Baron, 1969); and John S. Esposito and Larry Silverman, *Vanishing Air: Ralph Nader Study Group in Air Pollution* (New York: Grossman Publishers, 1970).

33. Turner, *The Chemical Feast,* p. 121.

34. *Sierra Club v. Morton,* 405 U.S. 727, 945–947 (1972). (Justice Douglas dissenting.) Also George Stigler, "The Process of Economic Regulation," *Antitrust Bulletin* 17 (1972): 207.

35. Statement at a University of California, Berkeley, seminar in 1979 by a federal regulatory commissioner who had also been a congressional staff member shaping important consumer protection legislation in the late 1960s and early 1970s.

36. See, for example, Alfred Marcus, "Environmental Protection Agency," in *The Politics of Regulation,* ed. Wilson, for an account of legislative concern about criticism concerning "capture" in drafting the 1970 Clean Air Act amendments.

37. Harry Meyer, Jr., "Does Government Regulation Work?" in *Blood Policy: Issues and Alternatives,* ed. David B. Johnson (Washington, D.C.: American Enterprise Institute, 1976).

38. See Richard B. Stewart and James E. Krier, *Environmental Law and Policy*, 2d ed. (Indianapolis: Bobbs-Merrill, 1978), p. 351; also see William Lilley III and James C. Miller III, "The New 'Social Regulation,' " *The Public Interest*, Spring 1977.

39. See *Portland Cement Association v. Ruckelshaus*, 486 F.2d 375 (D.C. Cir. 1973), *cert. denied*, 417 U.S. 921 (1974).

40. See *Union Electric Co. v. Environmental Protection Agency*, 427 U.S. 246 (1976).

41. See David Currie, "OSHA," *1976 American Bar Foundation Research Journal* (1976): 1107, 1134.

42. See, for example, Dianne R. Levine, "Exposure to Inorganic Arsenic in the Workplace," in *Benefit-Cost Analyses of Social Regulation*, eds. Miller and Yandle; *American Iron and Steel Institute v. OSHA*, F.2d (3d cir. 1978) (discussing OSHA's coke oven emission standards); and *American Petroleum Institute v. OSHA*, 581 F. 2d 493 (5th cir., 1978). OSHA's argument that it is not compelled by the Act to undertake cost-benefit analysis of alternative health standards was upheld by the U.S. Supreme Court in *American Textile Manufacturers Association v. Donovan*, 149 U.S. Law Week 4720 (June 17, 1981).

43. For an intelligent discussion of the issues, see William Havender, "Ruminations on a Rat: Saccharin and Human Risk," *Regulation*, March/April 1979.

44. 21 U.S.C. 348(c)(3)(A). See also Daryl Freedman, "Reasonable Certainty of No Harm: Reviving the Safety Standard for Food Additives, Color Additives, and Animal Drugs," *Ecology of Law Journal* 7 (1978–79): 245–284.

45. "Dilemma for U.S. Drug Watchdogs," *San Francisco Chronicle*, December 24, 1977. By stating the trade-off in terms of "health conditions against dollars," of course, Kennedy, like some other regulators, makes the decision seem easier than it actually is by glossing over the fact that increased "dollars" spent on precautions can result in higher prices (perhaps prohibitively higher for some consumers) or delay in the introduction of useful new products.

46. *TVA v. Hill*, 437 U.S. 153 (1978). A subsequent 1978 amendment to the Endangered Species Act established a review board with more discretion to grant exemptions and to consider economic as well as environmental factors.

47. Automobile manufacturers must gather information from dealers and tell the NHTSA of reported defects. Under OSHA and corresponding state programs, employers must report serious accidents to the agency and keep a log of all injuries that result in lost days of work. Manufacturers must report to the Consumer Product Safety Commission accidents involving their products that come to their attention.

48. See James Moorman, "Toxic Waste Control: Jail Sentences Possible," *National Law Journal*, January 1, 1979, p. 17.

49. See generally, "Note: Beyond the Prima Facie Case in Employment Discrimination Law: Statistical Proof and Rebuttal," *Harvard Law Review* 89 (1975): 387.

50. See Earl Leiken, "Preferential Treatment in the Skilled Building Trades," *Cornell Law Review* 56 (1970): 84. For a critical account of the evolution of affirmative action regulations in employment, see Nathan Glazer, *Affirmative Discrimination: Ethnic Inequality and Public Policy* (New York: Basic Books, 1975), chap. 2.

51. For a review of these laws, see Paul R. Portney, "Toxic Substance Policy and the Protection of Human Health," in *Current Issues in U.S. Environmental Policy*, ed. Portney.

52. Clean Air Act amendments of 1970, Sec. 207, 211. For an example of the use of such powers, see "EPA Denies Request of Tenneco Unit to Sell New Gasoline Additive," *The Wall Street Journal*, December 18, 1978, p. 15.

53. A list of 27 federal health- or safety-related statutes incorporating criminal penalties for

corporate executives is reported in Daniel O'Keefe and Marc Shapiro, "Personal Criminal Liability Under the Federal Food, Drug and Cosmetic Act: The Dotterweich Doctrine," *Food, Drug, and Cosmetic Law Journal* 30 (1975): 50–56.

54. The leading recent case is *U.S. v. Park*, 421 U.S. 658 (1975). See also Prakash Sethi and Robert W. Katz, "The Expanding Scope of Personal Criminal Liability for Corporate Executives," *Food, Drug, and Cosmetic Law Journal* 32 (1977): 544.

55. See "EPA Orders Changes in Pollution Controls of Certain Chevettes," *The Wall Street Journal*, April 19, 1979, p. 37.

56. See, for example, "Ford Ads Attempt to Save Pinto from Bad Publicity," *The Wall Street Journal*, August 17, 1978, indicating that the recall of 1971–76 model Pintos for fuel tank modifications (at an estimated cost of up to $40 million) led buyers to shy away from 1978 model cars, for which no problem was involved, with the loss of millions of dollars in sales.

57. See, for example, "U.S. Recalls Compressors for Noise Rule Violation," *The Wall Street Journal*, May 2, 1979, p. 24.

58. See *Nor-Am Agricultural Products v. Hardin*, 435 F. 2d 1151 (1970).

59. "EPA Cuts Off Aid for Colorado Roads and Sewage Plants," *The Wall Street Journal*, March 3, 1980, p. 14.

60. Anne Somers, "Regulation of Hospitals," *The Annals of the American Academy of Political and Social Sciences* (March 1972): 69. Health and Human Services officials inspect nursing homes for adherence to quality-of-care regulations, and the secretary of HHS has summary power to suspend payments for noncompliance, which can quickly force most homes out of business. See *Aquavella v. Richardson*, 437 F.2d 397 (2d Cir., 1971).

61. See generally Richard Stewart, "The Reformation of American Administrative Law," *Harvard Law Review* 88 (1975): 1669; Robert B. Reich, "Warring Critiques of Regulation," *Regulation*, January/February 1979; and David Vogel, "Promoting Pluralism: The Public Interest Movement in the American Reform Tradition," *Political Science Quarterly* 95 (Winter 1980–81).

62. See "Note: Judicial Control of Systemic Inadequacies in Federal Administrative Enforcement," *Yale Law Journal* 88 (1978): 407. In *American Public Health Association v. Veneman*, 349 F. Supp. 1311 (D.D.C. 1972), the FDA was ordered to speed up "efficacy reviews" for already marketed drugs. The FDA apparently was forced to increase manpower allocated to that program tenfold.

63. See *Coffey v. City of Milwaukee*, 74 Wis. 2d 526, 247 N.W. 2d 132 (1970); and *Winmar v. City of Marysville*, California Superior Court, Sutter County, No. 20653 (1978).

64. OSHA regulations also state that an employer's failure to pay employees for time spent on the walkaround is discriminatory treatment within the meaning of the section of the act forbidding discrimination against complaints.

65. *Green v. Superior Court*, 10 Cal. 3d 616, 517 P.2d 1168 (1974). See also Alan Heskin, "The Warranty of Habitability Debate: A California Case Study," *California Law Review* 66 (1978): 37.

66. See *Continental Steel Corp.*, 3 OSHRC 1410 (1975).

67. See, for example, Federal Mine Health and Safety Act of 1969, Sec. 103 (30 U.S.C. Sec. 801 ff.).

68. William K. Muir, Jr., *Legislature: California's School of Political Capacity* (Chicago: University of Chicago Press, forthcoming).

69. See Kathleen Kemp, "Social Responsibility and Coercive Sanctions in Economic Regulation" (Paper presented at the Symposium on Regulatory Policy, Houston Conference, Houston, Texas, November 18–19, 1979).

CHAPTER THREE

1. Bacow, *Bargaining for Job Safety and Health*, p. 6; see n. 45, p. 328.
2. Manuel Gomez, Richard Duffy, and Vince Trivelli, *At Work in Copper: Occupational Health and Safety in Copper Smelting* (New York: Project Inform, 1979). For an account of how the variability of punch presses complicates OSHA's attempt to mandate safety devices, see Mendeloff, *Regulating Safety*; see n. 47, p. 328.
3. See, for example, Ben Stein, *The View from Sunset Boulevard* (New York: Basic Books, 1979); Daniel Henninger, "The Advocates: TV Films Beat Up Mr. Whiplash," *The Wall Street Journal*, March 14, 1980, p. 19; the Media Institute, "Crooks, Conmen and Clowns: Businessmen in TV Entertainment," New York, 1981 (more than half the characters identified as heads of big business are portrayed as engaging in criminal activities).
4. See Philip Schrag, "On Her Majesty's Secret Service: Protecting the Consumer in New York City," *Yale Law Journal* 80 (1971): 80.
5. Steve Frazier and Steve Weiner, "Many Cattlemen Ignored the Federal Ban on Use of DES to Speed Animals' Growth," *The Wall Street Journal*, July 15, 1980, p. 48.
6. See Silbey, "Consumer Justice," p. 226; see n. 14, p. 330.
7. Melvin J. Hinich and Richard Staelin, after analyzing FDA data, found that the frequency of inspection and reinspection of food-processing firms bore no systematic relationship to the number of violations found or the firms' cleanliness levels. This finding is inconsistent, they point out, with the hypothesis that such firms adjust compliance to the likelihood of being caught and fined, while it is "consistent with the hypothesis that a firm sets a particular contamination level based on the market (and possibly on the more important FDA standards) and keeps this level." "Regulation of the U.S. Food Industry," in U.S., Congress, Senate, Committee on Governmental Affairs, *Study on Federal Regulation*, Appendix to Vol. VI, *Framework for Regulation*, 95th Cong., 2d sess., December 1978, pp. 437–438.

   For the effect of market pressures on compliance with antifraud standards, see Robert Nelson, "The Economics of Honest Trade Practices," *Journal of Industrial Economics* 24 (1976): 281–293. Also see H. Laurence Ross and Neil Littlefield, "Complaints as a Problem-Solving Mechanism," *Law and Society Review* 12 (1978): 199, 211–212.
8. The Ford Motor Company sustained a $125 million jury award (primarily for punitive damages) for deaths caused by an inadequately designed gas tank in its Pinto automobile (the award was reduced to $3.5 million by the judge). See Richard A. Epstein, "Is Pinto a Criminal?" *Regulation*, March/April 1980.

   Johns Mansville, other asbestos manufacturers, and their insurers have paid an estimated $50 million in over 4,000 damage suits on behalf of workers who suffered or died from exposure to asbestos fibers, and can be expected to pay hundreds of millions more. See Kenneth Schept, "Asbestos Suits Catching Fire," *National Law Journal*, August 18, 1980, p. 1.

   Pittston Corporation, whose inadequately contained strip-mining slag heap destroyed the village of Buffalo Creek, West Virginia, after heavy rains washed it loose, was forced by a lawsuit to pay $13.5 million in damages to residents and survivors. See Kai T. Erikson, *Everything in Its Path: Destruction of Community in the Buffalo Creek Flood* (New York: Simon and Schuster, 1977), p. 230.

   Velsicol Chemical Corp., a cattle-feed mixing firm, and its insurers were sued by 200 Michigan farmers whose cattle had to be destroyed after discovering that the defendants had negligently mixed a toxic chemical with the feed; the defendants paid over

$40 million in damages. "Velsicol Settles 70 Tainted Feed Cases," *The Wall Street Journal*, October 24, 1979, p. 16.

9. See Bacow, *Bargaining for Job Safety and Health*, p. 94.

10. Experienced water pollution control enforcement officials state that "the fear of adverse publicity is a key factor in gaining compliance." Charles Maus, Virginia State Water Control Board, quoted in Downing and Kimball, "Enforcing Administrative Rules"; see n. 11, p. 330. See also Lyman Ostlund, "Attitudes of Managers Toward Corporate Social Responsibility," *California Management Review* 19 (Summer 1977): 38.

11. Downing and Kimball studied enforcement of water pollution regulations and found "frequency of inspections clearly increases when control agency personnel perceive a firm as 'problem.' " They also note that if a firm has been found in violation the regulatory agency "may be more reluctant to compromise on future compliance dates and levels of control. This implies that the expected penalty for the first violation included the additional cost of raising the frequency of inspections and the probable future standards and penalties." See Downing and Kimball, "Enforcing Administrative Rules," p. 26.

12. The president of a financially hard-pressed aluminum company told us he decided not to fight regulatory requirements to supplement existing air pollution control equipment with a $15 million filter system—despite his engineers' belief that the additional improvements in ambient air quality would be insignificant. He explained, "We have tried to build a reputation as a progressive company. We have to be clean." But why should a manufacturing company that does not deal with the general public care about its image in that way, we asked. "Some of our [industrial] customers might be concerned, and the banks might be too."

Note, too, that corporations charged with serious regulatory violations frequently take out large ads in *The Wall Street Journal* or in the financial section of *The New York Times* that outline the company's record of social responsibility or plans for the future.

13. Steven Kelman, "Regulating Job Safety and Health: A Comparison of the U.S. Occupational Safety and Health Administration and the Swedish Worker Protection Board" (Ph.D. diss., Harvard University, 1978), pp. 519–520, revised version, Kelman, *Regulating America, Regulating Sweden: A Comparative Study of Occupational Safety and Health Regulations* (Cambridge: MIT Press, 1981). See also Les Boden and David Wegman, "Increasing OSHA's Clout: Sixty Million New Inspectors," *Working Papers for a New Society*, May/June 1978, pp. 43 and 45. Boden and Wegman describe the gradual deterioration of a model program for controlling worker exposure to beryllium; the deterioration was due to poor front-line supervision.

14. In addition, many regulatory violations stem from willful sabotage by low-level employees. See, for example, John Emshwiller, "Atomic Showdown: Many Nuclear Plants Are Found to Contain Flaws in Construction," *The Wall Street Journal*, October 24, 1979, p. 1.

See generally, Anthony Downs, *Inside Bureaucracy* (Boston: Little, Brown, 1967), pp. 143–145; Thomas Schelling, "Command and Control," in *Corporate Responsibility*, ed. McKie; and Martin Landau and Russell Stout, "To Command Is Not to Control," *Public Administration Review* (1979).

15. Stone, *Where the Law Ends*, provides a number of examples; see n. 18, p. 330. See also George Getschow, "Overdriven Execs: Some Middle Managers Cut Corners to Achieve High Corporate Goals," *The Wall Street Journal*, November 8, 1979, p. 1.

16. Michael Teitz and Stephen Rosenthal, *Housing Code Enforcement in New York City* (New York: The Rand Institute, 1971), p. 34.

17. Fred Delmore and Kermit Sloane, "FDA's Voluntary Compliance Program," quoted in Turner, *The Chemical Feast*, p. 123.
18. Chester Bowles, *Promises To Keep: My Years in Public Life 1941-1969* (New York: Harper & Row, 1971), p. 25. See also Louis Kriesberg, "National Security and Conduct in the Steel Gray Market," *Social Forces* 34 (1956): 286.
19. Kelman, "Regulating Job Safety and Health," p. 531.
20. For an excellent discussion of this phenomenon, see Jerry Mashaw, "Regulation, Logic and Ideology," *Regulation*, November/December 1979.
21. Vladeck, *Unloving Care*, pp. 161–162; see n. 20, p. 330.
22. Jeremy Rabkin, "Office for Civil Rights," in *The Politics of Regulation*, ed. Wilson, pp. 325, 332.
23. John T. Dunlop, "The Limits of Legal Compulsion," *The Conference Board Record*, March 1976, p. 26.
24. Hinich and Staelin, "Regulation of the U.S. Food Industry," p. 416.
25. Peter Hutt, "How Safe Is Safe?" in *The Design of Policy on Drugs and Food Additives*, National Academy of Science (1974).
26. James Q. Wilson, "The Politics of Regulation," in *Corporate Responsibility and the Business Predicament*, ed. James McKie (Washington, D.C.: The Brookings Institution, 1974), pp. 151–152.
27. Michael Levin, "Politics and Polarity: The Limits of OSHA Reform," *Regulation*, November/December 1979, pp. 33, 36. See also Bacow, *Bargaining for Job Safety and Health*, p. 8.
28. A revealing illustration and analysis of this tendency is provided by Ackerman et al., *The Uncertain Search for Environmental Quality*; see n. 51, p. 328.
29. See Dunlop, "The Limits of Legal Compulsion"; and Steven Kelman, *Regulating America, Regulating Sweden*.
30. The relevant research is summarized in Bacow, *Bargaining for Job Safety and Health*, pp. 39–40.
31. Vladeck, *Unloving Care*, p. 169.
32. Kelman, "Regulating Job Safety and Health," p. 556.
33. Vladeck, *Unloving Care*, p. 158. Since 1974, Vladeck says, Medicare, Medicaid, and state surveys have been consolidated to a greater extent. Still, between surveys by state, local, and federal officials to enforce fire, sanitation and building codes, quality-of-care regulations, and medical "utilization review" regulations, Vladeck observes, "It is . . . quite possible for a single nursing home to be inspected literally several dozen times a year, by a dozen different agencies. . . ."
34. Referring to variance procedures for exceptions to air pollution regulations or citations, a petroleum company environmental affairs official told us, "Filing a variance is filing a legal document. It takes lots of preparation, and then it goes before a hearing board that has lots of other business. By the time they hear it, the violation notice and the problem that led to it are three months old. It's ancient history."
35. The EPA, for example, was sued repeatedly by the National Resource-Defense Council and other environmental groups for granting or permitting state agencies to grant variances under the Clean Air Act, and its authority to do so was severely restricted by the courts, which apparently felt that the variance procedure provided too great an opening for industry and unreliable administrators to undermine statutory objectives. See R. Shep Melnick, "Into the Regulatory Thicket: The Impact of Court Decisions on Federal Regulation of Air Pollution" (Ph.D. diss., Harvard University, 1979).
36. Christine Hassell, "A Look at a Federal Enforcement Agency" (Unpublished paper, on file with the authors, 1979).

37. The term "morality of cooperation" is taken from Philip Selznick, *Law, Society and Industrial Justice* (New York: Russell Sage Foundation, 1969), chap. 1. Its converse is the "morality of obligation," which is the morality of legalistic law enforcement.

38. OSHA's strategy can be defended, of course, on the grounds that by focusing responsibility at the plant manager's level rather than at that of individual foremen it will induce more intense supervision and eliminate foot-dragging by less responsible foremen. But to corporate officials, a degree of decentralized responsibility is regarded as essential to economic efficiency, motivation, and responsible management. For OSHA to disregard that reality, to treat as one that which is intentionally and, it is thought, justifiably kept asunder, is seen as unreasonable.

39. Plasmapherisis centers are generally storefront operations where blood is taken from donors (usually paid), then centrifuged to separate out the plasma, and the rest is put back into the donor. Under state and federal regulations, donors must be carefully screened and retested to ensure that they are healthy, and regulations limit how often they can give (sell) their blood. Regulations also are concerned with maintaining the highest standards of sterility and with proper labeling, freezing, and storage of the plasma. The frozen plasma is then sent to manufacturers (such as Maxwell) for fractioning into subproducts, such as hemoglobin and gamma globulin.

40. Maxwell had suffered severe losses in the early 1970s due to a single accident. A hospital patient died as a result of a bacterial growth in an intravenous solution; it probably got there, a Maxwell engineer told us, via a hairline crack in the bottle that went undetected by Maxwell's supplier and by Maxwell. Maxwell had to recall *all* of its intravenous products until the cause was found, and sales were severely affected. Ultimately, the company was taken over by a larger corporation with financial depth to make up Maxwell's losses resulting from the incident. Maxwell officials seemed to believe that one more incident "would blow us out of the water."

41. Hinich and Staelin, "Regulation of the U.S. Food Industry," p. 425. They note that in 1973–75, FDA officials removed 47 million pounds of food from human consumption for violations of sanitation rules, although approximately 70 percent of its total resulted from violations that admittedly "did not represent a significant or substantial health risk," p. 401.

42. See, for example, Small Business Administration, *The Impact on Small Business Concerns*, p. 204.

43. Ibid., p. 71. See also Marcus, "Environmental Protection Agency," in Wilson, *The Politics of Regulation*, p. 283; see n. 36, p. 331.

44. Janice Simpson, "Antipollution Costs Drive Copper Firms Into Debt," *The Wall Street Journal*, December 28, 1978. See also Gomez et al., *At Work in Copper*. The 1977 Clean Air Act amendments, in response, gave the agency authority to grant additional five-year grace periods to finance and install SO_2 technologies.

45. See *PACCAR v. NHTSA*, 573 F.2d 632 (1978). See also "White Motor Says Simpler Technology Helps in Truck Part," *The Wall Street Journal*, September 18, 1979, p. 5.

46. See Northrup et al., *The Impact of OSHA*; see n. 47, p. 328.

47. U.S., Commission on Federal Paperwork, *Final Summary Report* (Washington, D.C.: U.S. Government Printing Office, 1977), p. 5.

48. "The Regulation Mess," *Newsweek*, June 12, 1978, p. 86.

49. Herbert Kaufman, *Red Tape: Its Origins, Uses and Abuses* (Washington, D.C.: The Brookings Institution, 1977), pp. 7–8.

50. Della Peretti, "Implementation Problems in the Standardized Testing Program" (Unpublished paper, on file with the authors, March 1980).

CHAPTER FOUR

1. For summaries of studies of the benefits of recent protective regulation, see *Benefits of Environmental, Health and Safety Regulation*, prepared by the Center for Policy Alternatives, Massachusetts Institute of Technology, for U.S., Congress, Senate, Committee on Governmental Affairs (96th Cong., 2d sess., March 25, 1980), and Green and Waitzman, *Business War on the Law*; see n. 43, p. 327.

2. The extent of positive effects on quality of care, as opposed to physical facilities, is less certain. See generally, Vladeck, *Unloving Care*; see n. 20, p. 330.

3. Gomez et al., *At Work in Copper*; see n. 2, p. 334.

4. Marcus, "Environmental Protection Agency," p. 300; see n. 36, p. 331. A. Myrick Freeman III, "Air and Water Pollution Policy," and Seskin, "Automobile Air Pollution Policy," in *Current Issues in U.S. Environmental Policy*, ed. Portney. There have been major decreases (about 67 percent) in pollutants emitted by new cars as well, but not enough to *reduce* the total level of pollution produced by old vehicles and the rising numbers of new ones. See G. Christian Hill, "Los Angeles's Setback in Smog Battle Raises Doubts in Other Cities," *The Wall Street Journal*, November 20, 1979, pp. 1 and 39.

5. See Michael S. Lewis-Beck and John R. Alford, "Can Government Regulate Safety? The Coal Mine Example," *American Political Science Review* 74 (1980): 745–755.

6. U.S. Department of Health, Education and Welfare, *HEW News*, June 19, 1979.

7. See "J. Walter Thompson Settles U.S. Charges That It Prepared Deceptive Ads for Sears," *The Wall Street Journal*, April 16, 1979, p. 10.

8. See Arnold Weber, "Manager's Journal," *The Wall Street Journal*, March 5, 1979, p. 18; "Labor Letter," *The Wall Street Journal*, January 22, 1980, p. 1; and Ronald Alsop, "The Poison Brigade: Need for Toxicologists Soars as Firms Widen Product Safety Tests," *The Wall Street Journal*, September 4, 1980, p. 1. See also Liz Gallese, "Analytical-Instruments Industry Booms as Government Regulations Proliferate," *The Wall Street Journal*, March 2, 1979, p. 24.

9. See Robert Ullmann, "General Motors and the Auto Workers: OSHA Reshuffles the Deck," *Working Papers for a New Society* (May/June 1978): 50 and 52.

10. See Bacow, *Bargaining for Job Safety and Health*, pp. 61–67.

11. See, for example, Leonard Lund, *Corporate Organization for Environmental Policymaking* (New York: The Conference Board, 1974); E. Patrick McGuire, *Managing Product Recalls* (New York: The Conference Board, 1974); and McGuire, *The Product-Safety Function*.

12. U.S., Environmental Protection Agency, Office of Toxic Substances, *Voluntary Environmental Activities of Large Chemical Companies to Assess and Control Industrial Chemicals* (Springfield, Va.: National Technical Information Service, 1976). But see Ashford, *Crisis in the Workplace*, noting that industrial occupational health specialists tend to concentrate on proven hazards, rather than on emergent or potential problems.

13. *Making Prevention Pay*, Draft Final Report of the Interagency Task Force on Workplace and Health, December 1978, chap. 1, p. 1.

14. See legal philosopher Lon Fuller's insightful discussion of this point in "Two Principles of Human Association," *Nomos* 2 (1969), and *The Morality of Law* (New Haven: Yale University Press, 1964), chap. 1.

15. Nivola, "Municipal Agency," p. 134; see n. 15, p. 330.

16. See also Bacow, *Bargaining for Job Safety and Health*, p. 49.

17. John Mendeloff, "Costs and Consequences: A Political and Economic Analysis of the Federal Occupational Safety and Health Program" (Ph.D. diss., University of Califor-

nia, Berkeley, 1977), p. 555. See also Mendeloff, *Regulating Safety* (see n. 14, p. 326) and Bacow, *Bargaining for Job Safety and Health*, chap. 3.

18. Some of the details, to quote a newspaper summary of the FAA report, are as follows: "McDonnell Douglas has always recommended that the pylon and engine be removed separately. But in 1977, an American Airlines supervisor . . . thought of removing the engine and pylon as a single unit [with a forklift truck]. That would halve the time required. After checking with McDonnell Douglas and United Airlines . . . the supervisor went ahead with the technique . . . [and] thought that the procedure 'went beautifully.' American then moved its DC-10 maintenance to Tulsa. . . . [T]he company did set up a course covering [the forklift technique], but if a mechanic finished only 20 hours of the 40-hour course, he was credited with having completed all of it . . . American's . . . technique called for removing bolts and the forward part of the pylon first and from the aft part last. But in Tulsa, American mechanics were doing it backwards . . . perhaps allowing the aft bulkhead to move enough during the procedure to be cracked. . . ." See "Behind the Crash: FAA Inquiry Charges Many Errors in Manufacturing and Maintenance of DC-10 Airliners," *The Wall Street Journal*, July 17, 1979, pp. 1 and 25.

19. Mitchell Rogovin, *Three Mile Island: A Report to the Commission and to the Public* (Washington, D.C.: U.S. Regulatory Commission, 1980), vol. 1, p. 89. See also David L. Sills, C. P. Wolfe, and Vivien B. Shelanski, *The Accident At Three Mile Island: The Human Dimension* (Boulder, Colo.: Westview Press, 1981).

20. Vladeck, *Unloving Care*, p. 153.

21. See Kelman, "Regulating Job Safety and Health," p. 533; see n. 13, p. 335. After criticism by Congress, OSHA directors instructed inspectors to concentrate on "serious" violations to a greater extent. The number of citations for serious violations did increase. The safety director of a multiplant manufacturing corporation told us that his company in fact began to receive many more "serious" citations (and hence higher fines) in 1977. But in his view, it seemed to be primarily a bookkeeping change; the citations received, he believed, did not in fact involve higher risk situations.

22. *Making Prevention Pay*, p. III-2.

23. Northrup et al., "The Impact of OSHA," p. 218; see n. 47, p. 328.

24. A study by the California Division of Labor Statistics and Research found that in the 450 iron and steel foundries in the state, there were 16.2 lost workdays due to injuries per 100 full-time workers each year, compared with 5.1 for manufacturing companies as a whole. *CAL/OSHA Administrative Research Bulletin No. 1: Iron and Steel Foundries*, San Francisco, 1977.

25. The tendency of enforcement officials to be extremely sensitive to lack of deference or to other challenges to their authority has been noted in a variety of contexts. See, for example, Irving Piliavin and Scott Briar, "Police Encounters with Juveniles," *American Journal of Sociology* 70 (1964): 206; Albert J. Reiss, Jr., *The Police and the Public* (New Haven: Yale University Press, 1971); and Silbey, "Consumer Justice," p. 221.

26. See, for example, *Dow Chemical Co. v. Costle*, U.S. District Court, E.D. Mich., 1978; "Chemical Plants Want EPA to Halt Flights Over Plants," *National Law Journal*, July 9, 1979, p. 7; and "Business Backlash: More Companies Bar Regulatory Agencies from Factories, Files," *The Wall Street Journal*, January 22, 1979, p. 1.

27. It is difficult to know for sure whether the environmental engineer's posture was more representative of his company's general policies and actual practices than the safety engineer's. It is also possible that the safety engineer, rather than being a disaffected good apple, as we inferred, was really an unprincipled, calculating bad apple and always was. Only very deep study of an organization's behavior can hope to achieve certainty.

Our objectives, however, are more analytical than empirical. Hence any errors in interpreting a firm's real motives are not damaging to our argument, as long as responses of the kind we describe are plausible responses to legalistic enforcement and occur in the world with at least some frequency.

28. Kelman, "Regulating Job Safety and Health," p. 595; see n. 13, p. 335.
29. See Larry Bodine, "Car Wars: Ford Strikes Back," *National Law Journal*, September 8, 1980, pp. 1, 12.
30. Mari Malvey, Memorandum, on file with authors, 1978.
31. *Marshall v. Barlow's Inc.* See also *Salwasser Mfg. Co. v. Municipal* Court, 94 Cal App. 3d 223 (1979), holding not only that employers can insist that Cal-OSHA inspectors obtain a warrant for routine inspections but also that the agency must show probable cause to believe violations exist in a plant in order to obtain such a warrant.
32. Robert D. Moran, "Employer Protection Against OSHA Inspections," *Foundry Management and Technology*, April 1979, pp. 108–110.
33. See Nolan Hancock, "Employer Retaliation Can Chill Workers' Support for OSHA," *AFL-CIO Federationist*, July 1980, pp. 13–14. Hancock emphasizes that the employer's obligation to comply with an abatement order is legally suspended pending resolution of legal appeals.
34. See Steven Kelman, "Occupational Safety and Health," in *The Politics of Regulation*, ed. Wilson.
35. See David Vogel, "How Business Responds to Opposition: Corporate Strategies During the 1970s" (Paper presented at the American Political Science Association Annual Meeting, Washington, D.C., September 2, 1979).
36. For a powerful example, see Michael Kilian, "Snowed Under by the FTC," *Inquiry*, May 26, 1980, pp. 5–8.
37. See Ernest Gellhorn, "The Wages of Zealotry: The FTC Under Siege," *Regulation*, January/February 1980, p. 33.
38. Moran, "Employer Protection Against OSHA Inspections," p. 105.
39. Gomez et al., *At Work in Copper*, vol. 3, p. 44.

CHAPTER FIVE

1. See James Q. Wilson, *Varieties of Police Behavior: The Management of Law and Order in Eight Communities* (Cambridge: Harvard University Press, 1968); Donald Black, "The Social Organization of Arrest," *Stanford Law Review* 23 (1971): 1087; Donald Black and Albert J. Reiss, Jr., "Police Control of Juveniles," *American Sociological Review* 35 (1970): 63; Piliavin and Briar, "Police Encounters with Juveniles"; and Egon Bittner, "Police on Skid Row: A Study of Peacekeeping," *American Sociological Review* 32 (1967): 699.
2. See, for example, William L. F. Felstiner and Lynne A. Williams, "Mediation as an Alternative to Criminal Prosecution," *Law and Human Behavior* 2 (1978): 223; and Melvin Eisenberg, "Private Ordering Through Negotiation," *Harvard Law Review* 89 (1976): 637.
3. See David Bayley, "Learning About Crime—The Japanese Experiment," *The Public Interest*, Summer 1976.
4. William K. Muir, Jr., *Police: Streetcorner Politicians* (Chicago: University of Chicago Press).
5. Ibid., pp. 213–214.
6. Richard McCleary, "How Structural Variables Constrain the Parole Officer's Use of Discretionary Powers," *Social Problems* 23 (1975): 209.

7. Kelman, "Regulating Job Safety and Health," p. 608; see n. 13, p. 335.
8. Silbey, "Consumer Justice," p. 334; see n. 14, p. 330.
9. *Making Prevention Pay*, Draft Final Report of the Interagency Task Force on Workplace Safety and Health, December 1978, pp. VII-3, VII-4.
10. Kemp, "Social Responsibility and Coercive Sanctions in Economic Regulation"; see n. 69, p. 333.
11. Nivola, "Municipal Agency," p. 130; see n. 15, p. 330.
12. Ibid.
13. Hawkins, *Environment and Enforcement*, chap. 7.
14. This discussion draws upon the notion of "responsive law" elaborated by Philippe Nonet and Philip Selznick, *Law and Society in Transition: Toward Responsive Law* (New York: Harper & Row, 1978).
15. See Robert Lane, *The Regulation of Businessmen—Social Conditions of Governmental Economic Control* (New Haven: Yale University Press, 1954).
16. Hawkins, *Environment and Enforcement*, ch. 7; see n. 11, p. 330.
17. Inspector of Factories, *Annual Report for 1969*.
18. Peter Blau, *The Dynamics of Bureaucracy* (Chicago: University of Chicago Press, 1955), p. 170.
19. Silbey, "Consumer Justice," p. 220.
20. Ibid., p. 328. On the countervailing businessmen's conception that consumers are out to cheat the merchant, see Martin Bronfenbrenner, "The Consumer," in *Social Responsibility and the Corporate Predicament*, ed. McKie.
21. Silbey, "Consumer Justice," p. 330.
22. California Assembly Bill 2441 (1978).
23. Kelman, "Regulating Job Safety and Health," p. 534.
24. Hawkins, *Environment and Enforcement*, ch. 7.
25. Small Business Administration, *The Impact on Small Business Concerns*, p. 93; see n. 27, p. 326.
26. Ibid., p. 94.
27. Mendeloff, *Regulating Safety*, pp. 43–46; see n. 47, p. 320. Noise problems, it should be noted, are often quite difficult to engineer out. Managers of a small aluminum foundry told us that, after being cited and fined by OSHA for noise violations, they hired acoustic consultants and spent an additional $5,000 on specially designed baffles, placed between machines, to reduce noise generated by metal-grinding equipment. The baffles, however, were largely ineffective, and noise regulations could be met only by giving the employees industrial earmuffs. The money spent on the much more expensive engineering-out effort, they felt, was mostly wasted.
28. *Making Prevention Pay*, pp. III-24–25.
29. See also Virginia B. Ermer, "Street-Level Bureaucrats in Baltimore: The Case of Housing Code Enforcement" (Ph.D. diss., Johns Hopkins University, 1972), p. 73.
30. Nivola, "Municipal Agency," p. 168.
31. The Age Discrimination in Employment Act, for example, requires the enforcement agency to try to settle complaints by negotiation or by seeking voluntary compliance before undertaking prosecution. See *Brennan v. Ace Hardware Co.*, 496 F.2d 368 (8th Cir., 1974). The Consumer Product Safety Act provides that before an order giving public notice of defects or ordering refunds on repairs, the agency must provide an opportunity for a hearing. 15 U.S.C.A. Sec. 2064. See also Silbey, "Consumer Justice," pp. 162 and 454.
32. See Lewis Solomon, "Restructuring the Corporate Board of Directors: Fond Hope or Faint Promise?" *Michigan Law Review* 76 (1978): 581.
33. See, e.g., Silbey, "Consumer Justice," p. 383.

34. For an intelligent effort to devise such criteria in the context of criminal case plea bargaining, see Conrad Brunk, "The Problem of Voluntariness and Coercion in the Negotiated Plea," *Law and Society Review* 13 (1979): 527.
35. Gomez et al., *At Work in Copper*; see n. 2, p. 334.
36. Richard Wade, "CAL/OSHA Emphasizes Occupational Health," *CAL/OSHA News*, September 1979.
37. Daniel Machalaba, "On the Track: To U.S. Rail Inspector, Drive for Safety Means Long Days in the Sun," *The Wall Street Journal*, August 24, 1978, p. 19.
38. See Robert Angelotti, "Enforcement Policy Objectives in the Changing Food Environment," *Food, Drug and Cosmetic Law Journal* 30 (December 1975); Joseph Hile, "Food and Drug Administration Inspections—A New Approach," *Food, Drug and Cosmetic Law Journal* 29 (February 1974): 101.

CHAPTER SIX

1. See Leslie Maitland, "Inspection Laxities Found in Fire Department," *The New York Times*, July 13, 1980, p. 1. Among a sample of merchants whose premises had been officially listed as inspected, 95 percent said that they had *not* been inspected, according to interviews by New York City Fire Department investigators. Inspectors followed by undercover investigators often were found to engage in noninspection activities; a few even held other jobs. Officials of the Firefighters Association attacked the legitimacy of undercover surveillance of inspectors.
2. Kenneth Culp Davis, *Discretionary Justice: A Preliminary Inquiry* (Urbana: University of Illinois Press, 1971).
3. See Nonet and Selznick, *Law and Society in Transition*; see n. 14, p. 341.
4. Herbert Kaufman, *The Forest Ranger: A Study in Administrative Behavior* (Baltimore: Johns Hopkins University Press, 1960).
5. See Blau, *The Dynamics of Bureaucracy*, p. 171; see n. 18, p. 341.
6. Kelman, "Regulating Job Safety and Health"; see n. 13, p. 335.
7. One air pollution control district official illustrated the difficulties he has encountered in firing incompetent inspectors by referring to one inspector who could not drive when he got the job—even after his fourth accident within a year, the district still could not fire him. The same official complained that because of affirmative action goals, educational standards for the job had been lowered, and officials were required to undergo extensive searches for "promotable" minorities before hiring from outside the agency. "When I was asked by a bright environmental resources student how a qualified person like him could get a job with the district," the official related, "I asked him, 'Can you type?' We have so many requirements to hire from within and promote the clerical personnel that he would stand a better chance of getting the job by starting as a clerical worker! That's why it's so difficult to get qualified people."

    A senior FDA enforcement official complained that to facilitate affirmative action goals, "Civil Service has allowed substitution of even unrelated experience for relevant education. Our inspectors need to know the scientific method and they need to know how to write. Many now know neither. We used to give a written exam but the Civil Service Commission forced us to give it up."
8. See, for example, Steven Kelman's account of the ethos of the safety engineers and industrial hygienists who dominate OSHA and their resultant resistance to White House criticism for failure to take economic analysis more seriously. Kelman, "Occupational Safety and Health Administration," in Wilson, *The Politics of Regulation*, pp. 250–253, 261, and 263; see n. 13, p. 335. See also Richard Neustadt, *The Swine Flu*

Affair: Decision Making on a Slippery Disease (Washington, D.C.: U.S. Government Printing Office, 1978).

9. See, for example, Daniel Machalaba, "On the Track: To U.S. Rail Inspector, Drive for Safety Means Long Days in the Sun," *The Wall Street Journal*, August 24, 1978, p. 19.

10. Hawkins, *Environment and Enforcement*, chap. 3.

11. To attract and retain experienced mechanics as inspectors, the California Motor Carrier Safety Unit offered (as of 1978) a starting annual salary of $18,168 and a top salary of $26,436. FAA safety inspectors started at $15,920; the highest grade (GS-12) paid $23,087, plus in-grade step increases. Federal Railroad Administration inspectors, many of whom have been track supervisors for railroad companies, were paid $20,000 to $28,000. Trainees in the California Food and Drug Division inspection program started at $13,584, but once made an inspector (Food and Drug Specialist), the salary started at $17,388; the highest grade was $24,060. OSHA's starting salary for inexperienced inspectors, by contrast, was only $10,507; those with at least a year of graduate training or experience started at $13,014; the highest grade safety specialist—three years of graduate training or experience—got $19,263.

12. See Muir, *Police: Streetcorner Politicians*, pp. 253–256 and 264; see n. 68, p. 333.

13. Ibid., p. 183.

14. Lord Robens, Chairman, *Report of the Committee on Safety and Health at Work* (London: HMSO, 1972) (Robens Report), p. 67.

15. Kelman, "Regulating Job Safety and Health," p. 534.

16. Hawkins, *Environment and Enforcement*, chap. 8.

17. Teitz and Rosenthal, *Housing Code Enforcement in New York City*, p. 55; see n. 16, p. 335.

18. This approach has been used by worker safety agencies in Canada. See Robens Report, pp. 68 and 173.

19. Robert A. Kagan, *Regulatory Justice: Implementing a Wage-Price Freeze* (New York: Russell Sage Foundation, 1978); and Blau, *The Dynamics of Bureaucracy*.

20. See Kagan, *Regulatory Justice*, pp. 111–117, 150–152.

21. Ibid., pp. 117–121.

22. Northrup et al., *Impact of OSHA*, p. 220; see n. 47, p. 328.

23. See Murray Edelman, *The Symbolic Uses of Politics* (Urbana: University of Illinois Press, 1964).

24. *Making Prevention Pay*, p. VII-6; see n. 13, p. 335.

25. Malcolm M. Feeley, *The Process Is the Punishment: Handling Cases in a Lower Criminal Court* (New York: Russell Sage Foundation, 1979).

26. Paul T. Hill, *Enforcement and Informal Pressure in the Management of Federal Categorical Progams in Education* (Santa Monica, Calif.: The Rand Corporation, 1979).

27. Hawkins, *Environment and Enforcement*, chap. 7.

28. Mendeloff, *Regulating Safety*, chap. 7; see. 47, p. 328.

29. Hill, *Enforcement and Informal Pressure*.

30. Philip Schrag, "On Her Majesty's Secret Service: Protecting the Consumer in New York City," *Yale Law Journal* 80 (1971).

31. The MCSU gives out ratings derived from its inspections only if the inspected firm consents. But insurers apparently have enough leverage to get their insureds or potential insureds to obtain such consent.

32. See Ernest Gellhorn, "Adverse Publicity by Administrative Agencies," *Harvard Law Review* 86 (1973): 1380; which discusses possible safeguards against inappropriate use of adverse publicity.

33. Leon Mayhew, *Law and Equal Opportunity* (Cambridge: Harvard University Press, 1968). See also Alfred Blumrosen and Leonard Zeiss, "Anti-Discrimination Laws in Action in New Jersey," *Rutgers Law Review* 19 (1963): 84.

34. Vladeck, *Unloving Care*, p. 160; see n. 20, p. 330.
35. A study of regulation of the hamburger industry found that "consumer reports of suspected violations are usually found to be groundless" or to relate to relatively minor problems. Irwin Feller et al., *Economic and Legal Aspects of the Benefit-Cost Relationships of Federal, State and Local Regulations Concerning the Production and Sale of Ground Beef* (Pennsylvania State University, Center for the Study of Science Policy, 1977) vol. III, pp. 13 (2)-52, 55. The President's Interagency Task Force on Workplace Safety and Health reported that OSHA inspections in response to employee complaints accounted for 40 percent of all inspections in 1978, and 80 percent in industrialized regions, "virtually eliminating other inspections there." Yet most complaints come from large unionized workplaces, where there are likely to be relatively comprehensive safety programs and union safety advocates (p. III-12). Moreover, only about 20 percent of inspections in response to complaints about occupational *health* problems discover citable violations (p. V-30, fn. 56). Silbey, "Consumer Justice," asserts, at p. 217, "Most estimates put the percentage of complaints [to consumer fraud prosecutors] that contain no apparent grounds for legal action at 90–95 percent"; see n. 14, p. 330. That does not mean that all those complaints were unjustified. Many did not result in legal action because the seller immediately agreed to a refund. In other cases, the consumer, in common parlance, had been "ripped off," but no legally actionable fraud or deception had been involved; the citizen had made a bad deal. Teitz and Rosenthal, *Housing Code Enforcement in New York City*, note that complaining tenants have an incentive to exaggerate the seriousness of their complaint (p. 30) and that telephone operators in the agency "tend to record a complaint as an emergency rather than risk criticism for neglecting true emergencies." As a result, inspectors sent out to investigate reported emergencies in 1968 found "valid emergencies" in only 23 percent of cases and no violations at all in 33 percent, sometimes because repairs had been made by the time the inspector arrived (p. 31).
36. See *Making Prevention Pay*, pp. III-11–III-15.
37. Labor unions object to letter responses to complaints because this technique "completely undermines the principle of no advance notice of OSHA inspections" and because it increases the risk of subtle or not-so-subtle employer retaliation against employee-complainants. See Margaret Seminario, "OSHA's Future: Fighting Perennial Battles," *AFL-CIO Federationist*, July 1980, p. 20.

    OSHA recently adopted such a plan for certain informal complaints after a Senate bill threatened to require it. The plan is strongly opposed by unions.
38. Teitz and Rosenthal, *Housing Code Enforcement in New York City*, pp. 38-40.
39. See Robert Klonoff, "The Problems of Nursing Homes: Connecticut's Nonresponse," *Administrative Law Review* 31 (1979): 1.
40. See Mileski, "Policing Slum Landlords"; see n. 20, p. 330. See also Gomez et al., *At Work in Copper*, Vol. 2, p. 202, noting that before OSHA, occupational safety inspections in Texas were keyed to above-average worker compensation claim rates; see n. 2, p. 334.
41. See generally Nina Cornell, Roger Noll, and Barry Weingast, "Safety Regulation," in *Setting National Priorities: The Next Ten Years*, eds. Henry Owen and Charles L. Schultze (Washington, D.C.: The Brookings Institution, 1976), p. 487, arguing that the agency should concentrate on discovering problems in fields (or firms, we would add) where there is a low level of information or a high degree of uncertainty about potential hazards.
42. Hawkins, *Environment and Enforcement*, chap. 4.
43. Kelman, "Regulating Job Safety and Health," pp. 537 and 608.

44. See *U.S. v. Simon*, 425 F.2d 796, 806–807 (3d Cir. 1969).
45. See Simon Lorne, "The Corporate and Securities Adviser, the Public Interest, and Professional Ethics," *Michigan Law Review* 76 (1978): 425, 446–462. See also "Facing Up to the Facts: SEC is Suing Lawyers for Failing to Uncover Municipal Bond Frauds," *The Wall Street Journal*, July 26, 1977.
46. "SEC Act of 1933 Release No. 5868 (September 26, 1977), *Federal Securities Law Reporter* (CCH), Par. 81, 305. See also "SEC Plan Would Require Firms to Report on Adequacy of Internal Audit Systems," *The Wall Street Journal*, April 20, 1979, p. 9.
47. Paul Verkuil, "A Study of Informal Adjudication Procedures," *University of Chicago Law Review* 43 (1976): 739, 763–764, n. 97.
48. M. T. Maloney and Bruce Yandle, "Bubbles and Efficiency: Cleaner Air at Lower Cost," *Regulation*, May/June 1980, pp. 49–52. See also Margaret Yao, "Clean Air Fight: Plain Dust is the Key to Pollution 'Bubble' at Armco Steelworks," *The Wall Street Journal*, October 1, 1980, p. 1, detailing one firm's use of the bubble concept.
49. See Timothy Clark, "New Approaches to Regulatory Reform—Letting the Market Do the Job," *National Law Journal*, August 11, 1979, p. 1316.
50. *Making Prevention Pay*, p. VII-7.
51. Bechtel, according to state officials, had a below average injury rate in the past and a good record in prior OSHA inspections. Under the arrangement, Cal-OSHA will not perform any routine inspections of the complex construction site and will answer complaints only if serious safety or health hazards appear to be involved. *CAL/OSHA News* 3, no. 2 (May 1979).
52. See, for example, Dunlop, "The Limits of Legal Compulsion" (see n. 23, p. 336) and Peter Schuck, "Litigation, Bargaining and Regulation," *Regulation*, July/August 1979.
53. Dunlop, "The Limits of Legal Compulsion."
54. Schuck, "Litigation, Bargaining and Regulation."
55. Kelman, *Regulating America, Regulating Sweden*; see n. 13, p. 335.
56. See Schuck, "Litigation, Bargaining and Regulation," pp. 32–33.
57. The source for this story is a staff member at the EPA. It would be easy to recoil in horror from such highly bureaucratic conduct and reasoning and to proclaim that top managers should not let such standards through. But often the real choice is between a bureaucratically oriented decision with only moderately bad consequences and one with very bad consequences.
58. Serge Taylor, "Environmentalists in the Bureaucracy" (Ph.D. diss., University of California, Berkeley, 1979), to be published as *Environmental Analysts in the Bureaucracy: The Impact Statement Strategy of Regulatory Reform* (Stanford University Press).
59. Richard Elmore, "Complexity and Control: What Legislators and Administrators Can Do About Implementation" (Monograph, Institute of Governmental Research, University of Washington, Seattle, April 1979).

CHAPTER SEVEN

1. The traditional life-cycle theory, as put forward most prominently by Bernstein, *Regulating Business by Independent Commission*, viewed the supposed cycle pejoratively as a decline from admirable youthful zeal to dishonorable capture and inaction; see n. 31, p. 331. Bernstein's life-cycle theory has been criticized by Roger Noll, *Reforming Regulation* (New York: The Brookings Institution, 1971); Jaffe, "The Effective Limits of the Administrative Process," p. 1105 (see n. 31, p. 331); and

Weaver, "Regulation, Social Policy, and Class Conflict" (see n. 23, p. 326). See also Barry Mitnick, *The Political Economy of Regulation* (New York: Columbia University Press, 1980).

2. See, for example, Richard E. Cohen, "The Business Lobby Gets Its Act Together," *The National Journal*, June 28, 1980, p. 1050.

3. Robert Reich has counted approximately 40 new federal laws with such provisions. See Reich, "Warring Critiques of Regulation," *Regulation*, January/February 1979.

4. Another useful compilation is U.S., Regulatory Council, "An Inventory of Innovative Techniques, 1978–1980." It lists by our count four reforms for 1979 involving formal "reductions" in regulations. The FAA moved from a one- to a three-year cycle in the safety recertification of amateur-built aircraft; the FTC rescinded 145 outdated trade practice rules; the Coast Guard permitted manufacturer self-certification of minor lifesaving equipment like flares; the SEC exempted small securities issues from the full range of disclosure requirements. This compilation also omitted the ozone standard revision, however. See also "White House Reports Progress in Reform of U.S. Bureaucracy," *The Wall Street Journal*, September 1, 1979, p. 25 (80 "unnecessary" mine safety standards rescinded); "EPA Plans to Waive Some Pollution Rules for Rubber Industry," *The Wall Street Journal*, December 14, 1979, p. 16.

5. Dick Kirschen, "EPA's Ozone Standard Faces a Hazy Future," *National Journal*, December 16, 1978, pp. 2015–2019.

6. Ibid., p. 2015. See also James E. Krier and Edmund Ursin, *Pollution and Policy: A Case Essay on California and Federal Experience With Motor Vehicle Air Pollution, 1940–1975* (Berkeley: University of California Press, 1977), p. 208.

7. Clark, "New Approaches to Regulatory Reform" (see n. 49, p. 345); Bruce Yandle, "The Emerging Market in Air Pollution Rights," *Regulation*, July/August 1978, pp. 21–29; and Maloney and Yandle, "Bubbles and Efficiency" (see n. 48, p. 345).

8. Regulatory Council, "An Inventory of Innovative Techniques" reports two instances of what appear to be "downward" interpretive modifications for 1979. The Department of Housing and Urban Development allowed certain qualifying local governments to administer its environmental impact and construction standards reviews for residential subdivisions, and the EPA exempted small businesses from certain regulations (pp. 38 and 44).

9. "Congressional Control," *Regulation*, May/June 1980, p. 12; Ernest Gellhorn, "The Wages of Zealotry: The FTC Under Siege," *Regulation*, January/February 1980, p. 33.

10. Quirk, "Food and Drug Administration," in Wilson, *The Politics of Regulation*, p. 233 (see n. 34, p. 327); American Enterprise Institute, *Major Regulatory Initiatives*, pp. 41–42 (see n. 20, p. 326).

11. The air and water pollution standard rules, too, involved such massive expenditures that they clearly cut into investment capital in some industries, such as steel production, and hence involved visible and relatively concentrated costs for some communities. Even so, the relief provided by the Water Pollution Control Act, for example, was no more than modest, and the best estimate of benefits and costs under the relaxed rules showed the latter in excess of the former by some $6–7 million in 1985. Benefits are estimated at $12 billion, costs at $18–19 billion. We have interpolated the cost estimate from figures for 1978 and 1987 in Table 12-4 of the 1979 Report of the Council on Environmental Quality. The benefit estimate appears on p. 655.

12. Dunlop, "The Limits of Legal Compulsion"; see n. 23, p. 336.

13. See Wilson, *The Politics of Regulation*, p. 377 (see n. 34, p. 327); and Jerry Mashaw, "Regulation, Logic, and Ideology," *Regulation*, November/December 1979.

14. For further development of the analogy between market and nonmarket failures, see Charles Wolf, Jr., "A Theory of Nonmarket Failure: Framework for Implementation Analysis," *Journal of Law and Economics*, April 1979.

15. See Susan Tolchin, "Presidential Power and the Politics of RARG," *Regulation*, July/August 1979; and Timothy B. Clark, "Carter's Assault on the Cost of Regulation," *National Journal*, August 12, 1978.

16. See, for example, *Marshall v. American Petroleum Institute*, 581 F2d 493 (5th Cir. 1978) (OSHA benzene standard), recently affirmed on other grounds by the U.S. Supreme Court. However, the Supreme Court later disapproved of the 5th Circuit Court's decision, holding that cost-benefit analysis was not required where not clearly required by statute. *American Textile Manufacturers Institute v. Donovan*, 49 U.S. Law Week 4720 (June 17, 1981). See also David Doniger, "Defeat in Benzene Exposure Case No Death Knoll for OSHA Standards," *Natural Resources Law Journal*, September 15, 1980.

17. In general, see Christopher C. DeMuth, "Regulatory Costs and the 'Regulatory Budget' " (Faculty project on regulation, Discussion Paper R-79-03, Kennedy School of Government, Harvard University, December 1979). and DeMuth, "Constraining Regulatory Costs—The White House Programs," *Regulation*, January/February 1980, Part I, pp. 13–26.

18. Lilley and Miller, "The New Social Regulation," p. 59; see n. 38, p. 332.

19. Kirschen, "EPA's Ozone Standard Faces a Hazy Future."

20. Timothy B. Clark, "What's All the Uproar Over OSHA's 'Nit-picking' Rules?" *National Journal*, October 7, 1978, p. 1596.

21. Ibid.

22. See "Pesticide Gets Limited EPA Approval Despite Beliefs That It May Cause Cancer," *The Wall Street Journal*, March 10, 1978. The EPA had received 20,000 letters about the resurgence of fire ants, which interfere with farming and sting people and livestock. The EPA approval of ferriamicide was confined to one state and precluded spraying by airplane and application by tractors on farm lands.

23. See R. Shep Melnick, "Into the Regulatory Thicket: The Impact of Court Decisions on Federal Regulation of Air Pollution" (Ph.D. diss.; Harvard University, 1979).

24. John E. Jackson and Robert E. Leone, "The Political Economy of Federal Regulatory Activity: A Case Study of Water Pollution Controls in the Pulp and Paper Industry" (Paper presented at the National Bureau of Economic Research Conference on Public Regulation, Washington, D.C., December 1977).

25. Paul Goldberg, "Glenn Morris's Reversible Medicine Cap Leads to a Federal Flip-Flop on Safety," *The Wall Street Journal*, August 20, 1980, p. 25.

26. See "Two Senators Clash on Kind of Bumpers to be Used on Autos," *The Wall Street Journal*, March 27, 1979, and "Battle of the Bumpers," *The Wall Street Journal*, May 5, 1979.

27. Paul Danaceau, *Regulation: The View From Janesville, Wisconsin and a Regulator's Perspective* (Washington, D.C.: Regulatory Council, March 1980), p. 10.

28. See, generally, Michael Levin, "Politics and Polarity: The Limits of OSHA Reform," *Regulation*, November/December 1979.

29. See Alfred A. Marcus, "Converting Thought to Action: "The Use of Economic Incentives to Reduce Pollution" (Paper presented at the Annual Meeting of the American Political Science Association, Washington, D.C., September 4, 1979).

30. Hinich and Staelin, "Regulation of the U.S. Food Industry," pp. 415 and 433; see n. 7, p. 334.

31. Rabkin, "Office for Civil Rights," in Wilson, *The Politics of Regulation*, pp. 347 and 445, notes 112–117.

32. Vladeck, *Unloving Care*, pp. 161–162.

33. Moreover, changing the "stats" to demonstrate tough-looking "reforms" is a common way to parry criticism. When OSHA under heavy pressure for citing too many nonserious violations that entailed only annoying "mosquito bite" fines, agency leaders

announced a change in policy. Sure enough, OSHA's published statistics soon showed a dramatic doubling (from 1977 to 1979) of "serious violations," carrying higher fines. According to the safety director of a large multiplant manufacturing company whom we interviewed, while his firm received a far higher number of "serious" violations and fines, as far as he could tell the violations were not in fact more serious. In fact, his company experienced an improved safety record over those years. A possible corroborative bit of evidence is that the percentage of "serious" violations contested by employers doubled from 1977 to 1979. See Nolan Hancock, "Employer Retaliation Can Chill Workers' Support for OSHA," *AFL-CIO Federationist*, July 1980.

34. For other analyses of legalistic regulatory behavior in terms of minimizing political risks, see Wilson, *The Politics of Regulation*, pp. 376–377; Hinich and Staelin, "Regulation of the U.S. Food Industry," p. 415. See also Muir, *Police: Streetcorner Politicians*, whose treatment of the imbalance of risks faced by policemen stimulated our parallel analysis of regulatory officials.

35. See, for example, the FAA's crackdown on compliance with aircraft maintenance regulations following the 1979 crash of a DC-10 that killed 250 people. "FAA Seeks $1.5 Million Fine on Braniff for Alleged Maintenance Rule Violations," *The Wall Street Journal*, November 7, 1979, p. 8.

36. Yao, "Clean Air Fight"; see n. 48, p. 345.

37. The OSHA director for Kansas, quoted in Sanford L. Jacobs, "Rather Than Dicker With OSHA, 'Model' Foundry Closes Up Shop," *The Wall Street Journal*, September 15, 1980, p. 31.

CHAPTER EIGHT

1. U.S., Federal Trade Commission, "Self-Regulation—Product Standardization, Certification and Seals of Approval" (Preliminary Staff Study, Precis, 1971); Samuel C. Florman, "Standards of Value," *Harper's*, February 1980, pp. 62–70.

2. See Florman, "Standards of Value," p. 68.

3. Barry Mitnick, "An Incentive System Model of Organization and Regulatory Design" (Paper presented at the 1979 Annual Meeting of the American Political Science Association, also issued as Working Paper 359, Graduate School of Business, University of Pittsburgh, p. 24).

4. J. B. Van Cronkhite, "Please Don't Eat The Instructions," *Quality Progress*, December 1969, p. 12.

5. Michael S. Hunt, "Trade Associations and Self-Regulation: Major Home Appliances," in *Regulating the Product: Quality and Variety*, eds. Richard E. Caves and Marc J. Roberts (Cambridge: Ballinger, 1975), pp. 39–55. See also Albert B. Stridsberg, *Effective Advertising Self-Regulation* (New York: International Advertising Association, 1974).

6. Carol Chapman, "Industry Self-Regulation Through Voluntary Standards: A Case Study of Bottle Safety," August 25, 1978, p. 10.

7. See Stan Crock, "Safety Commission Has Avoided War on Regulation," *The Wall Street Journal*, February 6, 1980.

8. See ibid.; "Agencies Are Advised to Use Standards Set by Industry to Cut Cost to Government," *The Wall Street Journal*, January 18, 1980, p. 18; "U.S.-Private Coordination on Rule-Making is Urged," *National Law Journal*, January 1, 1979, p. 10; and Philip J. Harter, *Regulatory Use of Standards: The Implications for Standards Writers* (Washington, D.C.: National Bureau of Standards, NBS GCR 79-171, November 1979).

9. Haim Erder, "The Emergence of the Recombinant DNA Controversy: An Organization Analysis and Public Policy Implications" (Fels Discussion Paper no. 116, School of Public and Urban Policy, University of Pennsylvania, November 1977). See also, Susan Wright, "Recombinant DNA Policy: From Prevention to Crisis Intervention," *Environment*, November 1979, pp. 34–37 and sources cited therein.

10. In recent years, many licensing boards have stepped up post-licensing enforcement efforts in response to pressures from consumer groups, leading some lawyers to complain that the effort to appear tough sometimes leads agencies to deprive accused professionals of even the rudiments of due process. See Jonathan Winer and R. Foster Winans, "Licensing Boards Under Fire," *National Law Journal*, February 18, 1980.

11. This is not to imply any evaluation, pro or con, of the adequacy of the NASD rules themselves. See Securities and Exchange Commission, *Report of Special Study of Securities Markets*, 4 R Doc. no. 95, 88th Cong., 1st sess., 1963; and Robert N. Katz, "Industry Self-Regulation: A Visible Alternative to Government Regulation," in *Protecting Consumer Interest: Private Initiative and Public Response*, ed. Robert N. Katz (Cambridge: Ballinger, 1976).

12. Garrett A. Vaughan, "The Business of Supplying Information: Does It Tend to Monopoly? The Case of Voluntary Industrial Standards" (photostat, n.d.)

13. See "Agencies Are Advised to Use Standards Set by Industry to Cut Cost to Government," *The Wall Street Journal*. January 18, 1980, p. 18.

14. See Florman, "Standards of Value," p. 62.

15. For example, an inquiry into construction of nuclear reactors showed that while utilities had established extensive quality assurance systems and safety inspections, supervisors sometimes ordered workers to do cosmetic patching jobs on flaws in newly poured cement structures in hopes of getting them past the company's inspectors, and construction personnel sometimes threatened inspectors who pointed out defects in their work. See Emshwiller, "Atomic Showdown"; see n. 14, p. 335.

16. Stone, *Where the Law Ends*, pp. 218–219; see n. 18, p. 330.

17. See Michelle Hoyman, "Coercive and Noncoercive Mechanisms for Compliance with the Civil Rights Act of 1964" (Paper delivered at Midwest Political Science Association meeting, 1974).

18. See Paul T. Hill et al., *A Study of Local Education Agency Response to Civil Rights Guarantees* (Santa Monica, Calif.: Rand Corporation, 1979).

19. "AT&T Discrimination Settlement," *Labor Relations Reporter* 8 *(BNA)*: 73, 87–96, cited in Christopher Stone, "The Place of Enterprise Liability in the Control of Corporate Conduct," *Yale Law Journal* 90 (1980): 1, 37.

20. See Bayless Manning, "Thinking Straight about Corporate Law Reform," *Law and Contemporary Problems* 41 (1977): 3, 28. Even without specific regulatory requirements to do so, many corporations have "voluntarily" established audit committees, and at least 35 major corporations have established "public responsibility committees" of the board to deal with issues such as affirmative action, community relations, pollution, product quality and safety, and occupational safety and health. Michael Lovdal, Raymond Bauer, and Nancy Treverton, "Public Responsibility Committees of the Board," *Harvard Business Review* 55 (1977): 40, 60.

21. Stone, *Were the Law Ends*, chap. 15.

22. Stone writes, "Were the office of, say, chief test engineer [for an automobile company] established . . . in such a way that it was his legal duty to keep a record of tests, and to report adverse experiences at once to the Department of Transportation, we would be far better off. A superior who asked the chief test engineer to 'forget that little mishap' would not only be asking him to risk some unknowable person's life and limb . . . he would be asking him to violate the law. . . ." See ibid., p. 191. See generally, Note,

"Structural Crime and Institutional Rehabilitation: A New Approach to Corporate Sentencing," *Yale Law Journal* 89 (1979): 353.

23. Stone, "Where the Law Ends," p. 195.
24. Ibid.
25. Taylor, "Environmentalists in the Bureaucracy"; see n. 58, p. 345.
26. Alan F. Westin, "Manager's Journal: Michigan's Law to Protect the Whistle Blowers," *The Wall Street Journal*, April 13, 1981. See also Alan Westin, *Whistle-Blowing: Loyalty and Dissent in the Corporation* (New York: McGraw-Hill, 1981).
27. *Federal Register*, "Current Good Manufacturing Practice in the Manufacture Processing, Packing or Holding of Large Volume Parenterals for Human Use," June 1, 1976, Sec. 212–222.
28. *Whirlpool Corp. v. Marshall*, 444 U.S. 823 (1979).
29. Boden and Wegman, "Increasing OSHA's Clout," pp. 43 and 47 (see n. 13, p. 335); Andrea Hricko, "Health and Safety Training in Sweden," *The Monitor* (Labor Occupational Health Program, University of California, Berkeley, March 1977); Kelman, *Regulating America, Regulating Sweden*, pp. 199–203.
30. Boden and Wegman, "Increasing OSHA's Clout."
31. For descriptions of several major labor-management safety plans, see Bacow, *Bargaining for Job Safety and Health*; see n. 45, p. 328.
32. See Laurence P. Feldman, "New Legislation and the Prospects for Warranty," *Journal of Marketing* 40 (1976): 41, 44.
33. See *Lora v. Board of Education*, 456 *F. Supp.* 1211 (E.D. N.Y. 1978) for a discussion of the provisions and rationale of the Education for All Handicapped Children Act.
34. Since 1976, Michigan has licensed automotive repair facilities, and automobile mechanics as well. A licensed facility is required to provide a certified master mechanic in every category of repair service the facility offers, and beginning in 1978, "any work concerning major service or repair performed by a non-certified mechanic" was to be "inspected and approved by one who is certified in the pertinent specialty." See Ruth W. Woodling, "Auto Repair Regulations: An Analysis" (Institute of Government, University of Georgia, February 1976), pp. 14–15. The Michigan approach of permitting noncertified mechanics to remain in the market neatly avoids many of the cartelization problems implicit in the usual "licensing" approach, wherein nonlicensed personnel are prohibited from furnishing services altogether. On improving the quality of automobile repair generally, without detailed direct regulation, see Eugene Bardach, "Where to Get a Good Fix," *Policy Analysis*, Spring 1977.
35. See Adam Walinsky, "Nuclear (T)error," *Newsweek*, May 7, 1979. See also John Emshwiller, "Utilities Scramble to Find Workers Qualified to Operate Nuclear Plants," *The Wall Street Journal*, November 11, 1980, p. 31., noting some consequences of tougher NRC personnel standards.
36. Assembly Bill 3619 [Duffy Bill] (1977).
37. Assembly Bill 1426 (1978). There are conflicting reports on whether turnover has in fact decreased.
38. Dick Kirschen, "Paperwork is Having a Big Impact on Environmental Statements," *National Journal*, July 16, 1977, p. 1119. See also Bernard Frieden, *The Environmental Protection Hustle* (Cambridge: MIT Press, 1979).
39. See, for example, Macklin Fleming, *The Price of Perfect Justice* (New York: Basic Books, 1974); and John Langbein, "Understanding the Short History of Plea Bargaining," *Law and Society Review* 13 (1979): 261.
40. Burt Schorr et al., "Relaxing Rules: Federal Agencies Ease, Lift Some Regulations That Burden Business," *The Wall Street Journal*, September 4, 1979, p. 1.

41. The University of California, Berkeley, for example, filed an "Assurance of Compliance with DHEW Regulations," asserting it will require review of all faculty research projects involving human subjects, including those in which "information is sought from them directly (as through interview, questionnaire) or indirectly (as through observation)." The "risks" it promises to protect them from, the university regulations continue, include not only "physical risks" but also "psychological risks" ("the possibility that a subject will undergo a significant degree of psychological damage or discomfort directly or indirectly") and "social risks" ("possibility that the research may cause the subject to suffer a loss of personal reputation . . . or suffer personal degradation in the eyes of other persons"). See generally, Thomas Killin Dalglish, "Protecting Human Subjects in Social and Behavioral Research: Ethics, Law, and the DHEW Rules: A Critique" (Ph.D. diss., Center for Research in Management Science, University of California, Berkeley, May 1976); Mark S. Frankel, "The Development of Policy Guidelines Governing Human Experimentation in the United States: A Case Study of Public Policy-Making for Science and Technology," *Science and Medicine* 2 (1975); and Paul Seabury, ed., *Bureaucrats and Brainpower: Government Regulation of Universities* (San Francisco: Institute for Contemporary Studies, 1979).

42. For example, OSHA regulations insist that a minimally acceptable respiratory protection program must include (1) written statements of all operating procedures, (2) proper scientific procedures for selection of the proper respirators, (3) detailed fitting procedures and training on proper use, (4) assigning respirators to individual workers on an exclusive basis, (5) provision for cleaning after each day's use, (6) proper storage procedures, (7) a systematic inspection and maintenance program, (8) a work area surveillance program, (9) periodic program evaluation, and (10) periodic medical examinations. Of course, each of those requirements in itself seems desirable and logically necessary, but may be overinclusive or needlessly detailed in many settings. For another example, see Urban Lehner, "Just Who Regulates Kitty Litter Factory?" *The Wall Street Journal*, November 14, 1978, p. 1.

43. See *Cape and Vineyard Division of New Bedford Gas Co. v. OSHRC*, 512 F2d 1148, 1154 (1st Cir. 1975); and Robert Moran, "Employer Protection Against OSHA Inspections," *Foundry Management and Technology*, April 1979, p. 112.

44. Eugene Lambert, "Dancing With the Gorilla," *Food, Drug and Cosmetics Law Journal* 30 (July 1975): 410.

45. See the Robens Report, p. 87, deploring the tendency for overlicensing in Great Britain, where, for example, the Mines and Quarries Act specifies qualifications for managers, undermanagers, surveyors, and other mining jobs, and requires them to obtain government certificates issued under the supervision of a Mining Qualifications Board.

46. David L. Kirp, "Proceduralism and Bureaucracy: Due Process in the School Setting," *Stanford Law Review* 28 (1976): 864.

47. Sally K. Fairfax, "A Disaster in the Environmental Movement," *Science*, February 17, 1978, p. 746.

48. Eugene Bardach and Lucian Pugliaresi, "The Environmental-Impact Statement vs. the Real World," *The Public Interest*, Fall 1977, pp. 22–38.

CHAPTER NINE

1. See generally George S. Day, "Assessing the Effects of Information Disclosure Requirements," *Journal of Marketing* 40 (1976): 42; David A. Aaker and George S. Day,

eds., *Consumerism: Search for the Consumer Interest*, 2d ed. (New York: The Free Press, 1974); and Hans B. Thorelli, Helmut Becker, and Jack Engledow, *The Information Seekers: An International Study of Consumer Information and Advertising Image* (Cambridge: Ballinger, 1975).

2. The controversy over the effects of SEC disclosure rules on stock prices was initiated by George Stigler, "Public Regulation of the Securities Markets," *Journal of Business* 37 (April 1964): 117–142, and continued in Irwin Friend and Edward S. Herman, "The SEC Through a Glass Darkly," *Journal of Business* 37 (October 1964): 382; George Stigler, "Comment," *Journal of Business* 37 (October 1964): 421; and Irwin Friend and Edward S. Herman, "Professor Stigler on Securities Regulation: A Further Comment," *Journal of Business* 38 (January 1965): 1. See also Henry G. Manne, "Economic Aspects of Required Disclosure Under Federal Securities Laws," in *Wall Street in Transition*, Henry G. Manne and Ezra Solomon (New York: New York University Press, 1974).

   The argument as to the effects of SEC disclosure on investor confidence is made by A. A. Sommer, Jr., in *Regulating Transactions in Securities: The Expanding Impact on Corporate Managers, Investors and the Financial Community*, ed. Jeremy L. Wiesen (St. Paul, Minn.: West Publishing Co., 1975), pp. 311–319.

3. Richard A. Posner, "The Federal Trade Commission's Mandated-Disclosure Program: A Critical Analysis," in *Business Disclosure: Government's Need to Know*, ed. Harvey J. Goldschmid (New York: McGraw-Hill, 1979), pp. 331–359. Posner sets against this result the *decline* in market share of the brands in the *second-lowest* category of tar and nicotine content. However, this trend could easily have resulted from smokers, switching out of this category into the lowest category.

   Other evidence concerning the effectiveness of mandatory disclosure programs comes from market researchers concerned with testing the effects of potential (rather than actual) and voluntary (rather than mandatory) programs. Newly provided label information affected consumer purchasing decisions with regard to phosphate detergents (believed to be environmentally harmful) and foods with varying degrees of nutritional content. See John A. Miller, "Labeling—The State of the Art" (Cambridge: Marketing Science Institute, March 1, 1978), p. 50; and Karl E. Henion, "The Effect of Ecologically Relevant Information on Detergent Sales," *Journal of Marketing Research* 9 (February 1972): 10–14. Also see R. J. Lenahan et al., "Consumer Reaction to Nutritional Labels on Food Products," *The Journal of Consumer Affairs* 7 (Summer 1973): 1–12. Similar findings have been made with respect to consumer reaction to mandatory "unit pricing" labels on supermarket shelves. See Day, "Assessing the Effects of Information Disclosure Requirements"; and Kent B. Monroe and Peter J. LaPlaca, "What are the Benefits of Unit Pricing?" in *Consumerism*, ed. Aaker and Day, pp. 193–204.

4. John Nevin and David Trubek, "An Investigation of the Retail Used Motor Vehicle Market: An Evaluation of Disclosure and Regulation" (Study prepared by the Center for Public Representation, Madison, Wisconsin, 1979).

5. Ibid., Table V-10, p. 48. On the reasons for the general unreliability of the private used car market, see George A. Akerlof, "The Market for Lemons: Quality Uncertainty and the Market Mechanism," *Quarterly Journal of Economics* 84 (August 1970): 488–500.

6. Arlen L. Large, "Public Grading of Nuclear Plant Owners by the NRC is Proposed by House Panel," *The Wall Street Journal*, October 2, 1980, p. 17.

7. Under the "least restrictive alternative" principle employed by some state courts, a product may not be banned by direct regulation if the harms associated with it can be mitigated by a strategy of mandatory disclosure. See Guy Miller Strouve, "The Less

Restrictive Alternative Principle and Economic Due Process," *Harvard Law Review* 80 (1967): 1463.

8. On the uncertainties in estimating the potency of carcinogens, see William Havender, "Ruminations on a Rat: Saccharin and Human Risk," *Regulation*, March/April 1979.

9. Andrew S. Krulwich, general counsel of the Consumer Product Safety Commission, has recommended this alternative for his agency. See Krulwich, "The Negative Practical Effects of Regulatory Reform Legislation," *National Law Journal*, June 30, 1980, p. 31.

10. See Posner, "The Federal Trade Commission" (see n. 21, p. 330); Everett Rogers and F. Floyd Shoemaker, *Communication of Innovations* (New York: The Free Press, 1975); and James S. Coleman et al., *Medical Innovation: A Diffusion Study* (New York: Bobbs-Merrill, 1966).

11. See Robert Nelson, "The Economics of Honest Trade Practices," *Journal of Industrial Economics* 24 (1976): 281–293.

12. One further justification for mandatory disclosure might be noted. Many consumers in some contexts want to have the government relieve them of the responsibility of learning and of choice by banning risky products, imposing mandatory and self-operating safety devices, and the like. See Paul Kleindorfer and Howard Kunreuther, "Descriptive and Prescriptive Aspects of Health and Safety Regulation," (International Institute of Management, Berlin, 1978) and Howard Kunreuther et al., *Disaster Insurance Protection: Public Policy Lessons* (New York: John Wiley & Sons, 1978).

13. *Federal Register* 36, no. 242, December 16, 1971, p. 23872.

14. Ibid., p. 23875.

15. Ibid., p. 23872.

16. Ibid., p. 23873.

17. See Carl Hoffman and John Shelton Reed, "Sex Discrimination? The XYZ Affair," *The Public Interest*, Winter 1981, pp. 21–39.

18. George J. Benston, "The Effectiveness and Effects of the SEC's Accounting Disclosure Requirements," in *Economic Policy and the Regulation of Corporate Securities*, ed. Henry G. Manne (Washington, D.C.: American Enterprise Institute for Public Policy Research, 1969), pp. 23–79.

19. See Malcolm E. Wheeler, "The Public's Costly Mistrust of Cost-Benefit Safety Analysis," *National Law Journal*, October 13, 1980, p. 27, citing the *Los Angeles Times*, July 23, 1980, Part IV, p. 1.

20. See the excellent analysis of the controversy by the National Center for Productivity and Quality of Working Life, "The Uniform Tire Grading System: A Case Study of the Government Regulatory Process," Spring 1980, pp. ix–x (hereinafter referred to as the Center Report).

21. See Ralph E. Winter, "Requirement for Tire Grading Has Makers Feuding, Buyers Confused," *The Wall Street Journal*, April 7, 1981, p. 25.

22. Center Report, pp. 48–49. See also Ralph E. Winter, "Tire Makers Plan to Emphasize Radials That Last Longer and Aid Fuel Economy," *The Wall Street Journal*," September 6, 1977, p. 36.

23. The proposal was published in the *Federal Register*, September 21, 1971.

24. Center Report, p. 32.

25. From the chronology published in Appendix B to the Center Report, industry's position appears to have hardened in 1968.

26. Center Report, p. 35.

27. Ibid., pp. 14–15.

28. Ibid., p. 54.

29. *HEW News*, January 24, 1978, pp. 78–85.
30. See "FTC Won't Buy Selective Emphasis in TV Credit Ads," *The Wall Street Journal*, March 16, 1979, p. 2.
31. *The Wall Street Journal*, July 9, 1979, p. 6.
32. *The Wall Street Journal*, February 13, 1978.
33. G. Bymers, "Seller-Buyer Communications: Point of View of a Family Economist," *Journal of Home Economics* 64, no. 2 (1972): 59–63. Quoted in William L. Wilkie, "Consumer Information Processing: Issues for Public Policy Makers," in *Research for Consumer Policy*, ed. William Michael Denney and Robert T. Lund (Cambridge: MIT Center for Policy Alternatives, Report no. CPA-78-7 to the National Science Foundation, March 1978), pp. 185–200.

    We do not know how powerful or widespread the "truth for its own sake" ideology is in policy-making strata or in the general public, but there are pockets of seeming irrationality that may reflect the presence of the doctrine, like the recent ruling by an FTC official that claims made on behalf of foods stressing their low cholesterol or saturated fat must warn that "the relationship of diet to the risk of heart or artery disease is the subject of controversy among scientific experts but the prevailing view in the scientific community is that the relationship exists and prudence in the diet is indicated although not established." *The Wall Street Journal*, March 20, 1978, p. 21. That consumers should receive such warnings is certainly desirable, but it is questionable to impose such high standards of scientific discourse on food advertising or labels.
34. See Russell B. Stevenson, Jr., "The SEC and the New Disclosure," *Cornell Law Review* 62 (1976): 50.
35. Robert T. Lund, "Life-Cycle Costing as a Societal Instrument," in *Research for Consumer Policy*, ed. Denney and Lund, pp. 185–200.
36. George R. Heaton, Jr., and Judith I. Katz, "Consumer Energy Conservation and Advertising: An Examination of the Relevant Sources of Law," (MIT Center for Policy Alternatives, January 27, 1978), pp. 17–18.
37. Thus Irwin Feller and his associates have defended mandatory content legislation for ground beef (e.g., stipulating maximum fat content):

    Without restrictions in the composition . . . firms will be unable to determine if rival firms are offering ground beef at lower prices because of lower costs (quality remaining unchanged) or because of . . . lower quality. . . . Higher priced stores are confronted with a situation of either lowering prices (and thus profit margins) or lowering quality (leading to a possible . . . industry-wide decline in standards. . . .).

    Feller, *Ground Beef Study*, vol. III, pp. B(2) 119–120; see n. 35, p. 344.
38. "Ice Cream: Dairymen Imperiled by FDA's Recipe," *Science* 197 (August 26, 1977): 844–845.
39. According to estimates by the U.S. Department of Agriculture, savings to the consumer would have amounted to about 2.5 percent. Ibid., p. 844. And according to FDA Commissioner Donald Kennedy, "The new standards will produce ice cream equivalent in taste and texture of what we are used to." *San Francisco Chronicle*, August 3, 1977. Kennedy was quoted testifying before a House committee.
40. "Ice Cream," *Science*, pp. 844–845.
41. See generally Laurence Tribe, "Ways Not to Think about Plastic Trees: New Foundations for Environmental Law," *Yale Law Journal* 83 (1974): 205.
42. Ernest Glaser, president of Avoset Foods (Speech to the International Association of Milk, Food, and Environmental Sanitarians, August 1970), p. 3. Of course, standards-related excess costs and rigidities are only some of the many reasons for the problems of the dairy industry.

43. See Posner, "The Federal Trade Commission," p. 71 et seq. See also the FTC's involvement in standards for "orange drink" as part of a trade war between Florida and California orange growers, as recounted in Turner, *The Chemical Feast*, p. 61.

44. See "Patient Package Inserts Inflate Medical Cost," *Consumer Alert Comments*, January 1980. The high costs of complying with and enforcing SEC disclosure rules have been well documented. See, for example, George J. Benston, *Corporate Financial Disclosure in the UK and the USA* (Lexington, Mass.: D.C. Heath, 1976); and Daniel S. Berman, *Going Public: A Practical Handbook of Procedures and Forms* (Englewood Cliffs, N.J.: Prentice-Hall, 1974).

45. See Anthoney Ramirez, "Smokers Being Misled by FTC's Tests on Low-Tar Cigarets, Researchers Say," *The Wall Street Journal*, October 9, 1980, p. 13 (describing criticism of the smoking "technique" of FTC's "smoking machines" used for test purposes); "EPA May Revise Fuel-Use Rating System to Better Reflect On-the-Road Experience," *The Wall Street Journal*, September 30, 1980, p. 10.

46. David L. MacKintosh and Jay L. Hall, "Fat as a Factor in the Palatability of Beef," *Kansas Academy of Science* 39 (October 1936): 53–56.

47. John A. Miller, David G. Topel, and Robert E. Rust, "USDA Beef Grading: A Failure in Consumer Information?" *Journal of Marketing* 40 (January 1976): 25–31.

48. See Benston, "The Effectiveness and Effects of the SEC's Accounting Disclosure Requirements," p. 28.

49. On truth-in-lending, see William C. Whitford, "The Functions of Disclosure Regulation in Consumer Transactions," *Wisconsin Law Review* (1973): 400–470. On franchise marketing, see Shelby D. Hunt and John Nevin, "Full Disclosure Laws in Franchising: An Empirical Investigation," *Journal of Marketing* 40 (1976): 53.

> Full disclosure laws impose substantial costs on franchisors, in the form of filing fees, amendment fees, legal costs, accounting costs, printing expenses, and executive time. Registering in Wisconsin typically consumes two to three months and approximately $3,000. Although these costs may be nominal for large corporations, they can be devastating to small franchisors . . . [page 62]

They conclude that one effect was that the growth rate of smaller franchisors in Wisconsin was reduced to about one-fourth the national growth rate.

50. *Pfizer, Inc.*, 81 FTC 23 (1972).

51. The terms of the FTC substantiation order are set forth in Stephen G. Breyer and Richard B. Stewart, *Administrative Law and Regulatory Policy* (Boston: Little, Brown & Co., 1979), pp. 834–837.

52. Robert Pitofsky, "Beyond Nader: Consumer Protection and the Regulation of Advertising," *Harvard Law Review* 90 (1977): 683.

53. On the Listerine case, see ibid., pp. 692–700.

54. Michael Kilian, "Snowed Under by the FTC," *Inquiry*, May 26, 1980, pp. 6–8.

55. It is, of course, conceivable that a private testing laboratory obliged to work out a program acceptable to all the varied interests in the area would have ducked the issues just as the NHTSA did. But in that case, the government would have been in a position to put financial pressure on the contractor and to act as an "honest broker" among the other interests.

56. Brian Davidson, "Federal Packaging and Labeling Act" (Seminar paper, Graduate School of Public Policy, University of California, Berkeley, May 3, 1978). These have been adopted on a state-by-state basis.

57. Marylee McCune, "The VA Seal of Approval" (Seminar paper, Graduate School of Public Policy, University of California, Berkeley, May 3, 1978).

58. *Newsweek*, June 26, 1978, p. 55.

59. *The Wall Street Journal*, June 29, 1978.

60. For a description of the program, see *Federal Register*, March 10, 1977, pp. 13326–13329.

61. *Federal Register*, January 19, 1973, p. 2125. For a discussion of how a two-tier strategy might work in the automobile repair industry, see Bardach, "Where to Get a Good Fix," pp. 273–275.

CHAPTER TEN

1. See Stuart M. Speiser, "How the Entrepreneur-Lawyer Changed the Rules of the Game," *National Law Journal*, December 1, 1980, p. 48. Speiser notes, for example: Even though other nations have government regulations and manufacturing experts who are equally knowledgeable and dedicated to aviation safety, they are not pushed to the limits of their safety performance as American manufacturers are by the litigation system. The knowledge that [if an accident occurs] they will have to face intensive questioning for weeks at a time, covering every piece of paper that they handled in connection with the design of an airplane, has a sobering effect on the personnel of manufacturers, airlines and government agencies.

2. See generally Marc Galanter, "Why the 'Haves' Come Out Ahead," *Law and Society Review* 9 (1974): 95; and Jeffrey O'Connell, "Expanding No-Fault Beyond Auto Insurance: Some Proposals," *Virginia Law Review* 39 (1973): 749.

3. See James R. Chelius, "Liability for Industrial Accidents: A Comparison of Negligence and Strict Liability Systems," *Journal of Legal Studies* 5 (1976): 293.

   In California, injured workers receive 66 percent of their normal paycheck during temporary disability; with no income tax, Social Security, or other deductions, this approaches normal take-home pay. Compensation premiums are enormous in dangerous occupations such as logging ($18–$20 for each $100 in wages), certain steel foundry jobs ($10 or more for each $100), and stevedoring ($50 per $100). See *Making Prevention Pay*, p. IV-5; see n. 13, p. 335. A smallish steel foundry in California with 120 employees and annual sales of $5 million (generating, as an estimate, $250,000 in after-tax profit at the very best) would pay over $100,000 in workers' compensation premiums a year. An annual savings of 25 percent for a good safety record would yield a savings of $25,000. This would seem to provide considerable incentive to cut accident rates and severity.

4. See *Report of the National Commission on State Workmens' Compensation Laws* (Washington, D.C., 1973). In recent years, in fact, benefit scales have increased more rapidly than inflation.

5. See *Making Prevention Pay*, pp. IV-5, IV-9, noting that 15 percent of employees in the nation, working in 85 percent of all firms, were covered by workmen's compensation policies that were not experience-rated by firm (p. IV-9). The president's task force concluded that it was not feasible to require insurance carriers by law to apply experience-rating to those small firms, because of the inordinate difficulty and cost of doing so with any degree of reliability and fairness.

6. *Making Prevention Pay* proposed amending the federal tax code to allow employers to deduct the *average* cost of workers' compensation premiums for their industry and firm size, thus rewarding lower-injury rate employers, penalizing those with higher rates, and inducing both to try to perform better. See ibid., p. IV-11.

7. See Christopher Stone, "A Slap on the Wrist for the Kepone Mob," *Business and Society Review* 22 (1977); and Stephen Soble, "A Proposal for the Administrative Compensation of Victims of Toxic Substance Pollution." *Harvard Journal of Legislation* 14 (1977): 694–696.

8. See, for example, *Borel v. Fibreboard Paper Products*, 493 F.2d 1076 (5th Cir. 1973), opening the way for lawsuits by thousands of exposed workers who inhaled asbestos fibers over the years and, apparently as a result, contracted asbestosis (an emphysema-like disease) and mesothelioma (a lung cancer). In one such case, a jury awarded $450,000 to an insulation installer who suffered from asbestosis; in another, a widow won $3 million. See Kenneth Schept, "New Liability Theory Tested: Asbestos Suits Catching Fire," *The National Law Journal*, August 18, 1980, p. 1; and Andrew Kreig, "Billions Hinge on Asbestos Appeal: Insurers Fight Over Who Pays Claims," *National Law Journal*, October 15, 1979, pp. 3 and 6.

9. See, generally, Paul R. Portney, "Toxic Substance Policy and the Protection of Human Health," in *Current Issues in U.S. Environmental Policy*, ed. Portney.

10. See, for example, David Seidman, "The Politics and Economics of Pharmaceutical Regulation," in *Public Law and Public Policy*, ed. John Gardiner (New York: Praeger, 1977).

11. See Douglas Martin, "Search for Toxic Chemicals in Environment Gets a Slow Start, Is Proving Difficult and Expensive," *The Wall Street Journal*, May 9, 1978, p. 40; Dick Kirschen, "The New War on Cancer—Carter Team Seeks Causes, Not Cures," *National Journal*, August 6, 1977, pp. 1220–1224.

12. Soble, "A Proposal for the Administrative Compensation of Victims of Toxic Substance Pollution," pp. 729–753.

13. In Soble's proposed statute, compensation for "pain and suffering" would be authorized, unlike workers' compensation, but would be limited to one-half the total award.

14. What of the smaller company that might be out of business by the time liability claims come in? To ensure financial responsibility for claims, and hence incentive to take adequate current precautions, the government might require mandatory insurance structured to "survive" the insured, if necessary, or posting of 30-year liability bonds for firms that market certain classes of chemicals. There is a precedent for liability bonds in the regulations requiring strip mining firms to post bonds covering the cost of restoring strip-mined lands.

15. See, for example, Guido Calabresi, *The Costs of Accidents: Legal and Economic Analysis* (New Haven: Yale University Press, 1970); Richard Posner, "A Theory of Negligence," *Journal of Legal Studies* 1 (1972): 29.

16. See *Eisen v. Carlisle and Jacquelin*, 417 U.S. 156 (1974) (notice must be sent by plaintiff to all members of the class); *Sosna v. Iowa*, 419 U.S. 393 (1975); and "Developments in the Law: Class Actions," *Harvard Law Review* 89 (1976): 1319. The Supreme Court has also limited the aggregation of very small claims under state law in the federal courts by holding that the $15,000 jurisdictional minimum for such "diversity of jurisdiction" actions must be met by each member of the class. *Zahn v. International Paper Co.*, 414 U.S. 291 (1973). A plaintiff's lawyer in a sex discrimination class action against a large manufacturing company told us that her law firm's investment in prosecuting the action would be a minimum of $200,000, including attorney's time, fees for computer specialists and data processing, fees for other expert witnesses, and costs of identifying members of the plaintiff class.

17. *Diamond v. General Motors Corp. et al.*, 20 Cal. App. 3d 374 (1972). For a thorough analysis and review of the literature concerning limitations of the liability system's capabilities to control air pollution, see Stewart and Krier, *Environmental Law and Policy*, chap. 4.

18. For example, scores of private lawsuits by homeowners near airports, claiming both property damage and personal injury, have provided a primary impetus for control of "noise pollution" in the vicinity of airports. See Edward J. Burke, "Legal Roar over Jet Noise," *National Law Journal*, December 1, 1980.

19. Payment of counsel fees and litigation expenses for successful plaintiffs is authorized, for example, by the Clean Air Act (1970), the Federal Water Pollution Control Act (1972), the Noise Pollution Act (1972), the Safe Drinking Water Act (1974), the Marine Mammals Protection Act (1972), the Toxic Substances Control Act (1976), and a number of civil rights and employment discrimination laws.

20. This Truth-in-lending Act provision, combined with the class action mechanism, was very threatening to banks, department stores, and other suppliers of credit. See, for example, Jonathan M. Landers, "Of Legalized Blackmail and Legalized Theft: Consumer Class Actions and the Substance-Procedure Dilemma," *Southern California Law Review* 47 (1974): 842. The contention was that the huge potential liability of thousands of $100 claims forced defendants to settle rather than to run the risk of losing, even if legal liability was highly debatable. Congress later amended the act to omit the $100 minimum recovery provision from class actions and to limit recovery in class actions to "the lesser of $100,000 or 1 percent of the net worth of the creditor." 15 U.S.C. Sec. 1640.

21. See, for example, Clement Work, "California Adopts Arbitration Plan," *National Law Journal*, July 9, 1979, p. 3 (all civil cases where amount in controversy is less than $15,000). Arbitration also has increasingly been used in the medical malpractice area.

22. This section draws upon the summary account of doctrinal changes set forth in Richard Epstein, "Products Liability: The Gathering Storm," *Regulation*, September/October 1977, p. 15; and Gary T. Schwartz, "Understanding Products Liability," *California Law Review* 67 (1979): 435. See also Richard Higgins, "Producers' Liability and Product-Related Accidents," *Journal of Legal Studies* 7 (1978): 299, charting the rapidity of the rise of manufacturers' strict liability in the 1960s and 1970s.

23. To take one dramatic example, in a Washington case cited by Epstein, "Products Liability," the plaintiff lost a leg in a machine built by the defendant company. Plaintiff's fellow employees had forcibly removed a metal panel atop the machine to repair it and then replaced the panel with a piece of cardboard upon which plaintiff stepped while the machine was running. His lawyers argued that the machine was defectively designed because it did not have readily removable and replaceable panels and was not equipped with an automatic interlock device that prevents operation when the panels are not securely in place. The jury awarded plaintiff $750,000.

24. O'Connell, "Expanding No-Fault Beyond Auto Insurance," pp. 749 and 755.

25. U.S., Department of Commerce, Interagency Task Force on Product Liability, *Final Report* (Springfield, Va.: National Technical Information Testing Service, 1970), pp. II-56 and III-3.

26. Ibid., pp. IV-2, IV-5–IV-8, and VI-47. A 1978 Conference Board survey of 300 large manufacturing companies indicated that two-thirds had established new or augmented product safety units within the preceeding six years. McGuire, *The Product Safety Function*, Table 1, p. 5.

27. See *Newsweek*, June 9, 1975, pp. 58–60.

28. O'Connell's model "enterprise liability" statute would read, "Any enterprise is subject to enterprise liability for bodily injury to any human being resulting from the operation of typical risks associated with the activity of the enterprise." O'Connell, "Expanding No-Fault Beyond Auto Insurance," pp. 773 and 792. See also his book, *Ending Insult to Injury: No Fault Insurance for Products and Services* (Urbana: University of Illinois Press, 1975). A similar plan has been advocated by Clark Havighurst and Laurence Tancredi, "Medical Adversity Insurance—A No-Fault Approach to Medical Malpractice and Quality Assurance," *Milbank Memorial Fund Quarterly* 51 (Spring 1973), reprinted in *Insurance Law Journal*, no. 613 (February 1974): 69–77. See also Clark

Havighurst, "Medical Adversity Insurance—Has Its Time Come?" *Duke Law Journal*, 1975, p. 1233.

29. Bruce C. N. Greenwald and Marnie W. Mueller, "Medical Malpractice and Medical Costs," in *The Economics of Medical Malpractice*, ed. Simon Rottenberg (Washington, D.C.: American Enterprise Institute, 1978), p. 83.

30. For example, Henry C. Damm, a Ph.D. in endocrinology and biostatistics, heads a growing firm that conducts detailed inspections of client hospitals, looking for deficiencies in characteristic danger spots, such as improperly functioning temperature controls in laboratory refrigerators, lax personal hygiene practices among emergency room personnel, failure to conduct routine blood analyses in the obstetrics ward (to detect possible Rh problems), improperly functioning monitors and alarms in the coronary care unit, and inadequate recording of adverse drug reactions. See "Doctor Fail-Safe," *Newsweek*, July 26, 1979, p. 79.

31. A law review project in defensive medicine, "The Medical Malpractice Threat: A Study of Defensive Medicine," *Duke Law Review* (1975): 939, concluded that there was *not* a significant level of defensive medicine. Its measures, however, were quite imperfect, and the results came from 1969–70, which antedated the explosion in malpractice litigation.

32. Roger Starr, "The End of Rental Housing," *The Public Interest*, Fall 1979.

33. Victor P. Goldberg, "Tort Liability for Negligent Inspection by Insurers" (Working paper no. 90, Department of Economics, University of California, Davis, 1977). If insurance companies were also held to have a legal duty to inspect as well as to inspect carefully, Goldberg points out, insurers would surely charge for their added exposure, perhaps inducing more firms to self-insure and thus reducing the incidence and effectiveness of "outside" safety inspections.

34. See Greenwald and Mueller, "Medical Malpractice and Medical Costs."

35. See note 28, supra, and accompanying text.

36. See "Safeguards for Sunlamps Ordered," *San Francisco Chronicle*, November 9, 1979, p. 22.

37. Epstein, "Products Liability," p. 19.

38. See, for example, R. Scott Jenkins and William Schweinfurth, "California's Medical Injury Reform Act: An Equal Protection Challenge," *University of Southern California Law Review* 52 (1979): 829, 838, and 839.

39. See, for example, Sheila L. Birnbaum, "Wholesale Changes Are in Store if the Model Act Becomes Law," *National Law Journal*, March 17, 1980, p. 19, on the Model Uniform Product Liability Act, developed by the U.S. Department of Commerce; and Larry Bodine, "Product Liability Bill Gaining Support," *National Law Journal*, September 22, 1980, on preemptive congressional product liability act.

40. The leading work pointing out the limitations of courts as policymakers is Donald L. Horowitz, *The Courts and Social Policy* (Washington, D.C.: The Brookings Institution, 1977), although his case studies do not involve "regulatory" policymaking. Nor does the leading defender of judicial capacity, Abram Chayes, "The Role of the Judge in Public Law Litigation," *Harvard Law Review* 89 (1976): 1281, concentrate on such matters. But see R. Shep Melnick, "Into the Regulatory Thicket: The Impact of Court Decisions on Federal Regulation of Air Pollution" (Ph.D. diss., Harvard University, Cambridge, 1979).

41. *Dawson v. Chrysler* 630 F.2d 950 (3rd Cir. 1980).

42. See Robert Verchalen, "Keying Product-Related Accidents," *Trial*, January-February 1972; Robert Frye, "NEISS, Medical Records as an Important Contribution to Consumer Product Safety," *Medical Record News* 1 (April 1975): 23. For an example in

which the CPSC monitoring system produced a regulatory success story, see Steven Kelman, "Regulating by the Numbers—The Consumer Product Safety Commission," *The Public Interest,* Summer 1974, p. 83.

43. See, for example, *Hubbard-Hall Chemical Co. v. Silverman,* 340 F.2d 402 (1st Cir. 1965); Andy Pasztor, "Pinto Criminal Trial of Ford Motor Co. Opens Up Broad Issues," *The Wall Street Journal,* January 4, 1980.

44. Traditionally, courts have held that violation of regulatory standards is only prima facie proof of negligence. See cases collected in William Prosser, *Torts,* 4th ed. (St. Paul: West Publishing Co., 1971). p. 196; and Jerry Mashaw and Richard Merrill, *The American Public Law* System (St. Paul, Minn.: West Publishing, 1975), chap. 12, pt. 5. But some more recent cases have held that regulatory violations impose absolute liability. See *Van Gaasebeck v. Webatuck Central School District,* 21 N.Y. 21 234 (1967) (school bus regulations); *Koenig v. Patrick Construction Corp.,* 298 N.Y. 313 (1948) (workplace safety regulation); and *Javins v. First National Realty Corp.,* 428 F.2d (D.C. Cir. 1970) (housing code violations breach warranty of habitability and bar landlord's suit for possession).

45. An indication of the interaction of liability law and "voluntary" recalls was provided in late 1978 when Remington Rand recalled more than 200,000 rifles as a result of disclosures of design defects in a single lawsuit brought by a Texas lawyer who had been horribly wounded by the accidental discharge of a Remington rifle. See Speiser, "How the Entrepreneur-Lawyer Changed the Rules of the Game," p. 48. The effectiveness of the liability-recall connection can be blunted, however, if manufacturers hesitate to announce a product recall for fear that it will be taken as evidence of negligent product design in pending or subsequent lawsuits; automobile companies reportedly have resisted recalls contemplated by NHTSA for that reason. See Bodine, "Car Wars"; and Albert Karr, "Troubled Ford Faces Biggest-Ever Recall Order," *The Wall Street Journal,* July 18, 1980, p. 21. To counteract this tendency, the courts could rule that evidence of subsequent recalls is inadmissible in product liability suits, just as some courts have ruled (for the same reason) that evidence of subsequent repair to machinery or product redesign is inadmissible in suits based on injuries from a particular machine or product. See Sheila L. Birnbaum, "Growing Trend to Deny Admission of Post-Accident Remedial Measures," *National Law Journal,* July 23, 1979, p. 18.

46. See Alan Altshuler, with James P. Womack and John R. Pucher, *The Urban Transportation System: Politics and Policy Innovation* (Cambridge: MIT Press, 1979), pp. 228–229.

47. Schept, "New Liability Theory Tested"; and Wendell Rawls, Jr., "Class Action Planned on Lung Illness in Textile Mills," *The New York Times,* October 19, 1979.

The Toxic Substances Control Act now requires manufacturers to keep certain records and to report to the EPA (not to workers) any evidence of adverse health effects. OSHA regulations require employers to monitor worker exposures to certain chemicals, such as lead.

48. For the details of the Japanese plan, see Julian Gresser, "The 1973 Japanese Law for the Compensation of Pollution-Related Health Damage: An Introductory Assessment," *Law in Japan* 8 (1975): 92.

49. See Thomas R. Post, "A Solution to the Problem of Private Compensation in Oil Discharge Situations," *University of Miami Law Review* 28 (1974); 524, 538–541; Stewart and Krier, *Environmental Law and Policy,* pp. 612–615 (see n. 38, p. 332). A number of similar funds, supported by contributions from potential sources, are proposed in William F. Baxter, "The SST: From Watts to Harlem in Two Hours," *Stanford*

Law Review 21 (1968): 1, 53-57. See also "Senate Approves Clean-Up Bill for Toxic Wastes," *The Wall Street Journal*, November 25, 1980.

50. David Leo Weimer, "The Regulation of Therapeutic Drugs by the FDA: History, Criticism and Alternatives" (Discussion paper no. 8007, Public Policy Analysis Program, University of Rochester, New York, May 1980).

51. See generally Charles L. Schultze, *The Public Use of Private Interest* (Washington, D.C.: The Brookings Institution, 1977).

52. See Harold Wolozin, "The Economics of Air Pollution: Central Problems," *Law and Contemporary Problems* 33 (1968): 227, 234–237; Alfred A. Marcus, "Converting Thought to Action: The Use of Economic Incentives to Reduce Pollution" (Paper presented at the Annual Meeting of the American Political Science Association, Washington, D.C., September 4, 1979). Marcus reports that an EPA analysis of a charges scheme for controlling solid waste disposal concluded that it would be difficult to implement: "State agencies did not have the capability to collect good data on emissions. Under a [charges] system, an accurate reading of the emissions of every source was necessary, because all sources were liable to charges depending on how many pounds of pollution they emitted. Under direct regulation, the only purpose of monitoring was to determine if a source exceeded a fixed standard. As long as it was in compliance, an accurate measure of emissions was not necessary."

53. One would imagine even more severe pressures for "full enforcement," and higher expenditures for inspectors under tax or charge systems than under direct regulation; in tax systems, each undetected unit of pollution would not only be a violation of the law and dangerous to the environment, but also would be costing the government money and cheating law-abiding competitors.

54. Frederick R. Anderson et al., *Environmental Improvement Through Economic Incentives* (Baltimore: Johns Hopkins University Press for Resources for the Future, 1977), p. 7.

55. Susan Rose-Ackerman, "Market Models for Water Pollution Control: Their Strengths and Weaknesses," *Public Policy* 24, no. 3 (Summer 1977): 3383–3406; and Ackerman et al., *The Uncertain Search for Environmental Quality*, pp. 262–269.

56. See J. H. Dales, *Pollution, Property, and Prices* (Toronto: University of Toronto Press, 1968).

57. In its original conception, the abatement services strategy was called "the buyback strategy," and was intended as a substitute for mandatory deposits, imposed by statute, on beer and soft-drink containers. See Eugene Bardach, Curtis Gibbs, and Elliott Marseille, "The Buyback Strategy: An Alternative to Container Deposit Legislation," *Resource Recovery and Conservation* 3 (1978): 151–164.

58. Justification for financing of pollution abatement out of general tax revenues can be found both in principle and in practical considerations. See R. H. Coase, "The Problem of Social Cost," *Journal of Law and Economics* 3 (1960): 1.

    The principle of indirect subsidy has been reflected in certain provisions of the U.S. tax code, such as allowing tax-exempt financing of abatement equipment through municipal pollution control bonds. See George Peterson and Harvey Galper, "Tax Exempt Financing of Private Industry's Pollution Control Investment," *Public Policy* 23, no. 1 (Winter 1975): 81, and five-year amortization of "certified pollution control equipment," subject to a number of restrictions and limitations. See Daniel Givelber and Daniel Schaffer, "Section 169 of the Internal Revenue Code: An Income Tax Subsidy for the Control of Pollution," *Arizona Law Review* 14 (1972): 65.

59. The importance of stabilizing the regulatory environment probably argues against tying

the financing of the program too closely to a tax on emissions. As abatement proceeded and emissions were reduced, the shrinking tax base would require a steady increase in the tax rate in order to hold revenues contant or increase them. Just how rapidly—and politically sustainable—this increase would occur would be unpredictable, however, and it seems to us very desirable to avoid such unpredictability.

60. Most of our discussion of the EPA offset policy comes from Craig Breedlove, "Economic Development with Clean Air: An Evaluation of the Offset Policy" (Master's essay, Graduate School of Public Policy, University of California, Berkeley, June 1978). See also Yandle, "The Emerging Market in Air Pollution Rights," *Regulation*, July/Aug. 1978, pp. 21–29.

CHAPTER ELEVEN

1. See American Enterprise Institute, *Regulation and Regulatory Reform: A Survey of Proposals of the 95th Congress* (Washington, D.C.: American Enterprise Institute for Public Policy Research, 1980), pp. 3–24.

2. Ibid.

3. On the problems of policy implementation generally, see Eugene Bardach, *The Implementation Game: What Happens After a Bill Becomes a Law* (Cambridge: MIT Press, 1977).

4. Aaron Wildavsky, "Richer Is Safer," *The Public Interest*, no. 60, Summer 1980, pp. 23–29.

5. Robert Reich, "Warring Critiques of Regulation," *Regulation*, January/February 1979, pp. 37 and 39.

6. See George Eads, "Harnessing Regulation: The Evolving Role of White House Oversight," *Regulation*, May/June 1981.

7. See "Labor Unit Issues Final Regulation on Acrylonitrile," *The Wall Street Journal*, October 2, 1978, p. 4.

8. Once again, we must remind the reader of what we said in chapter 1: a great many cost-benefit analyses are incompetent or deliberately misleading and therefore not to be trusted. Even good ones are normally incomplete because they do not and can not measure or quantify certain benefits or costs; in any case, the methodology is, in principle, not applicable to important political questions of *who* pays and *who* benefits. Good cost-benefit analysis settles few questions of policy, but it does help to improve the dialogue.

9. Christopher C. DeMuth, "Regulatory Costs and the 'Regulatory Budget' " (Faculty project on regulation, Discussion Paper R-79-03, Kennedy School of Government, Harvard University, December 1979), p. 29. See also DeMuth, "Constraining Regulatory Costs—The White House Programs," *Regulation*, January/February 1980, Part I, p. 13.

10. See cases in Paul R. Verkuil, "Jawboning Administrative Agencies: Ex Parte Contacts by the White House," *Columbia Law Review* 80 (1980): 943, 945–946.

11. DeMuth, "Regulatory Costs," p. 17.

12. David Harris, staff economist at the Council on Wage and Price Stability (Lecture, University of California, Berkeley, February 26, 1980).

13. See, for example, Lowi, *The End of Liberalism*; and Antonin Scalia, "A Note on the Benzene Case," *Regulation*, July/August 1980.

14. See Antonin Scalia, "The Legislative Veto: A False Remedy for System Overload," *Regulation*, November–December 1979, pp. 19–26.

15. See Verkuil, "Jawboning Administrative Agencies," p. 943.
16. Lloyd N. Cutler and David R. Johnson, "Regulation and the Political Process," *Yale Law Journal* 84 (1975): 1395; and ABA Commission on Law and the Economy, *Federal Regulation: Roads to Reform* (1979).
17. See Tolchin, "Presidential Power and the Politics of RARG," pp. 44–49 (see n. 15, p. 347); and Verkuil, "Jawboning Administrative Agencies."
18. See, for example, *Portland Cement Association v. Ruckelshaus*, 486 F2d 375 (D.C. Cir. 1973).
19. See, for example, *International Harvester Co. v. Ruckelshaus*, 478 F.2d 615 (D.C. Cir. 1973).
20. *American Petroleum Association v. OSHA*, 581 F.2d 493 (5th Cir. 1978), affirmed on other grounds; and *Industrial Union Department, AFL-CIO v. American Petroleum Institute*, 448 U.S. 607, 65 L.Ed. 2d 1010 (1980). See also cases in James C. Miller III and Thomas F. Walton, "Protecting Workers' Hearing: An Economic Test for OSHA Initiatives," *Regulation*, September/October 1980.
21. See Doniger, "Defeat in Benzene Exposure Case No Death Knell for OSHA Standards," pp. 26–27; see n. 16, p. 347.
22. For indications that this may have occurred in judicial review of EPA's air pollution regulation, see Melnick, "Into the Regulatory Thicket" (see n. 40, p. 359), and his shorter paper, "Judicial Capacity and Environmental Litigation" (Paper presented at the American Political Science Association Annual Meeting, Washington, D.C., 1980).
23. See David Danford, "Bill Would Pay Attorney Fees for Besting U.S.," *National Law Journal*, August 20, 1979, p. 5. For public interest groups' counterarguments, see Ruth Marcus, "Fee Bill Upsets Public Groups," *National Law Journal*, July 14, 1980, p. 7.
24. See Ernest Gellhorn, "Adverse Publicity by Administrative Agencies," *Harvard Law Review* 86 (1973): 1437–1440.
25. See James O. Freedman, "Summary Action by Administrative Agencies," *University of Chicago Law Review* 40 (1972): 1.
26. See Jerry L. Mashaw, "Civil Liability of Government Officers: Property Rights and Official Accountability," *Law and Contemporary Problems* 42 (1978): 8.
27. The idea was first proposed by Robert W. Crandall, "Federal Government Initiatives to Reduce the Price Level," in *Curing Chronic Inflation*, ed. Arthur M. Okun and George L. Perry (Washington, D.C.: The Brookings Institution, 1978), p. 2.
28. For a pessimistic but slightly less dismissive view of the regulatory budget concept, see Christopher DeMuth, "The Regulatory Budget," *Regulation*, March/April 1980, p. 24.
29. Admittedly, the numbers might not be very meaningful, and the pressure to produce them would give agencies some incentive to overregulate in the first place so as to gain credit for subsequent reductions.
30. Mark V. Nadel, *The Politics of Consumer Protection* (Indianapolis: Bobbs-Merrill, 1971), pp. 39–40.
31. See, for example, Miriam Damaska, "Structures of Authority and Comparative Criminal Procedure," *Yale Law Journal* 84 (1975): 480; Mortimer R. Kadish and Sanford H. Kadish, *Discretion to Disobey: A Study of Lawful Departures from Legal Rules* (Stanford, Calif.: Stanford University Press, 1973); and Melvin Eisenberg, "Private Ordering Through Negotiation Dispute Settlement and Rulemaking," *Harvard Law Review* 84 (1976): 637.

INDEX

———————————————— ● ————————————————

Accidents, 23, 208–209, 235–236, 238, 282, 288. *See also* Airplanes, accidents; Coal mining, accidents; Highway accidents; Nuclear power plants, accidents; Workplace accidents
Advertising, 14, 250; regulation, 21, 95, 116, 256, 258–259, 264–266, 267
AEI. *See* American Enterprise Institute
Affirmative action, 21, 50, 71, 199, 241, 322. *See also* Bilingual education
Agriculture, 11, 32, 60. *See also* Department of Agriculture; Food industry
Airplanes: accidents, 24, 101, 282, 300; regulation, 32, 51, 228, 233. *See also* Federal Aviation Administration
Air pollution, 59, 280, 299n. *See also* Emissions
Air pollution control, 30, 128, 139, 187, 189, 196, 293–294; regulations, 20, 28, 63, 85–86, 87–89, 175, 187, 189, 190, 198, 202, 211, 222. *See also* California, air pollution control; Clean Air Act (1963)
Aluminum industry, 96, 201; regulation, 17, 118, 138; worker safety and health, 4–5, 87, 96–98, 108–109, 111, 143–144, 231–232
American Enterprise Institute (AEI), 188–189, 190, 191, 192n
Atomic Energy Commission. *See* Nuclear Regulatory Commission
Attitudes. *See* Environmental engineers, attitudes; Nursing home inspectors, attitudes; Safety engineers, attitudes
Auchter, Thomas, 187n
Automobile accidents. *See* Highway accidents

Automobile dealers, 245, 258
Automobile industry, 10, 15, 60, 250, 288, 289–290; worker safety and health, 81, 95–96, 113, 147, 168, 177, 232, 263
Automobile regulation, 26, 51, 52–53, 113, 174, 187; for safety, 14, 200n, 201, 227, 289–290; of exhaust emissions, 28, 47, 191, 192, 222; of tires, 247–248, 254–256, 267, 312
Automobiles, 252–253
Automobile safety, 13, 27, 250, 251, 268–269, 283, 288. *See also* Automobile regulation, for safety

Bacow, Lawrence, 58
Bakery and Confectionery Workers International Union, 199
Bay Area Air Pollution Control District. *See* San Francisco Bay Area Air Pollution Control District
Bechtel Corporation, 176, 237
Benefits. *See* Cost-benefit analysis; Social benefits
Bilingual education, 21, 53, 67, 68
Biologics industry regulation, 18, 60, 70–71, 83–84, 89, 209, 224, 228–229, 282, 290. *See also* Food and Drug Administration, Bureau of Biologics
Blau, Peter, 133
Blood bank regulation, 56, 94, 143, 146, 149–150, 218
Blood plasma industry regulation. *See* Biologics industry regulation
Boden, Les, 231
Boston, Mass., 141; housing codes, 100, 129